THE OVERLOOK

# MARTIAL ARTS READER

# MARTIAL ARTS READER

## AN ANTHOLOGY OF HISTORICAL AND PHILOSOPHICAL WRITINGS

### EDITED BY RANDY F. NELSON

**THE OVERLOOK PRESS**
WOODSTOCK, NEW YORK

First published in 1989 by
The Overlook Press
Lewis Hollow Road
Woodstock, New York 12498

Library of Congress Cataloging-in-Publication Data

The Overlook martial arts reader / edited by Randy F. Nelson.
    p.  cm.
  Bibliography: p.
  1. Martial arts—East Asia.  I. Nelson, Randy F, 1948–
II. Title: Martial arts reader.
GV1100.81.E18095  1989
796.8′095—dc19                            88-22558
ISBN: 0-87951-459-0

Sixth Printing

# CONTENTS

# PREFACE

The martial arts of East Asia have a history and philosophy curiously dissociated from the art of war. Indeed they have no exact counterparts in the West at all. The very phrase *martial art* seems to us a contradiction in terms. That one might achieve virtue, and not only virtue but also enlightenment, while studying violent techniques of personal combat seems at best a mockery of religious and ethical principles. With what justification have both ancient and modern martial artists spoken of peace, harmony, and reconciliation as representing the very highest levels of their arts?

To answer such a question one would, ideally, be familiar with some fourteen hundred years of Chinese, Korean, Japanese, and Okinawan history while having at the same time a specialist's understanding of Taoism, Confucianism, and Buddhism. Added to this should be an awareness of the folklore of East Asia and an appreciation for changing military tactics over a millennium and more. Even then Westerners would be further handicapped by a scarcity of accurate information on the martial arts themselves and a superfluity of what Gichin Funakoshi called "nonsense" about the aims and methods of the martial arts. For more than a hundred years after the opening of Japan in 1854 there was not even in English a reliable bibliography on this subject.

Nevertheless, there has been, especially in the last century, a gradual accumulation of authoritative writing on the martial arts, enough to refute many of the popular stereotypes and to address some of the more substantive questions having to do with the history and philosophy of the martial arts. It is toward this end that *The Overlook Martial Arts Reader* is offered. It is a book presenting some of the authoritative texts from the disparate martial arts, rather than an artificially "unified" story. Readers are thus encouraged to compare the views of some of the great masters and to test the claim of this preface that there is a recognizable philosophy, if not a common history, linking discipline to discipline.

A caution. By and large the literary tradition of the martial arts is a modern one (an exception being the *T'ai Chi Ch'uan Ching* attributed to the Taoist Monk Chang San-feng [1279–1386]). Although most of the arts discussed in this text have their origins in ancient unarmed fighting systems, the evolution into martial *art* is in fact comparatively recent. Even judo, that quintessentially Japanese martial art, was not codified as *jiudo* until 1882 when Jigoro Kano founded the Kodokan; and Professor Kano himself was touring the United States with speeches and demonstrations as late as the 1930s. It is also daunting to realize that the art eventually known in the West as karate-do remained largely unknown in Japan itself before 1917. And the founder of the art of aikido, Master Morihei Uyeshiba, did not die until 1969.

Although an anthology by definition suggests multiple points of view and a certain latitude in subject matter, this present volume does in one sense present a unified story: it is the story of a journey. There is, on one hand, the journey of the semimythical Bodhidharma from India to the Shaolin monastery in south China, arguably in the third decade of the sixth century A.D. (see Haines). It is more by tradition than established fact that the Shaolin monks are regarded as the first martial artists in East Asia. Indeed, the influence of Bodhidharma seems to have represented more of a renaissance than a naissance. Still, it is probably true that another, more vaguely defined "journey" began at this monastery, namely the gradual spread of certain stylized fighting techniques in a northeasterly direction into Okinawa, Korea, and Japan.

The original eighteen "hands" of Bodhidharma's Lo-Han system (initially a system of physical exercises rather than a fighting art) evolved into many more techniques, and the Lo-Han was adapted in many different ways to suit local terrain, weather, folkways, weapons, and even body types. By A.D. 750 there had arisen in China perhaps half a dozen distinguishable "arts." What is surprising, though, is the rise since that time of a fairly coherent philosophy unifying martial artists of different disciplines over great distances and many eras. So while it does make sense to talk about a physical and even cultural "distance" from the Shaolin monastery of the sixth century, it also makes sense to acknowledge a kind of unity of purpose among serious martial artists of different times and places. Basically this philosophy, perhaps better denominated an attitude, is influenced by and yoked to the three great religions of East Asia: Taoism, Confucianism, and Buddhism. With Taoism the martial arts share a concern with the "way," an intuitive, often mystical process of learning and living. From Confucianism comes an emphasis on hierarchy, respect for seniors, duty, and loyalty. In Buddhism, and in many of the martial arts, is the concern with right perception, meditation, and enlightenment. These traits are of course not unique to the religions just named nor to any one of the martial arts in particular, but precisely because there has always been a certain degree of "mixing" and a simultaneous evolution in both the religions and the martial arts it makes some sense to talk about common ground in all of these systems.

To be sure, the idea of a "journey" of the martial arts is only convenient shorthand for describing an evolution, and one should be careful in making statements about *the* history of the martial arts. Complications inevitably arise. There are, for instance, tomb paintings from Koguryo (an ancient kingdom of Korea) in recognizable tae kwon do postures dating from before A.D. 427, a century prior to the advent of Bodhidharma or the influence of Buddhism. The metaphor of the journey can also be immeasurably complicated by geography (China alone is large enough to justify a martial history of several volumes), by politics (the degree to which Korea and Okinawa were dominated by Japan at various times directly influenced which arts were practiced in the subject countries), and by social station (bladed weapons were sometimes forbidden to conquered peoples and commoners). Also, practicing one style of ch'uan fa in China, as opposed to some other, meant usually that one was born in such and such a geographical region ("northern" versus "southern" systems are still distinguishable today). In Japan, on the other hand, selecting one particular martial art or even one particular school (ryu) was, and often still is, to make a deliberate and self-conscious choice of a "philosophy." There are, in addition, some important national differences relating to the various martial arts. In Japan the "rules" of martial behavior were codified and idealized to a degree not done in the other countries of the region. In China the great size of the country contributed to a multiplicity of schools: the present government recognizes some 382 named systems of wushu, or military art. In Korea the various kwons (schools) were eventually unified in the name of nationalism into one art (tae kwon do) which put an emphasis on tenacious fighting for a right cause against overwhelming odds, a holdover perhaps from years of domination by Japan.

Nevertheless, all of these differences are more differences of degree than of kind. More instructive than differences, I believe, are what the martial arts have held in common for more than a thousand years: the overwhelming emphasis on the development of moral character (see Levine), the defensive rather than offensive nature of the arts (see Funakoshi), the respect for order and harmony (see Lerner), the reverence for the teacher (see Funakoshi again), and, above all, the notion of transcendence—that the right practice of certain forms, postures, breathing techniques and the mastery of certain attitudes allows one to put off the temporal and enter a profound meditative state (see Leonard and Herrigel).

As Dave Lowry points out in his *Autumn Lightning*, studying the martial arts is not something one "adapts" to his life, but rather one adapts the life to the art. It means changing one's values, attitudes, and behavior. It does not mean taking up a hobby. One does not "do" kendo or aikido, for instance, with the same expectations that one "does" tennis. And it is partly through this realization that one puts his life in tune with countless masters and students who have come before him.

In compiling this anthology I have consciously sought out works representing a wide variety of martial arts, written by masters and students from many backgrounds and times. Nevertheless, I have not attempted to make the contents representative of all martial arts; nor have I tried to present any sort of geographical, political, racial, or sexual balance—on grounds that the best writing does not reflect such organization. So while the present volume does not pretend to set forth a complete history or an absolutely unified philosophy, it does set forth examples from which can be inferred certain right principles. In this book are authors who are themselves founders and originators of particular schools and arts (Kano, Miyamoto, Funakoshi), authors in a direct line of descent from grandmaster to student (Liang), and Western scholars who are first-hand observers and students themselves of the traditional arts (Herrigel, Nicol, Miller, Leonard, Levine, Harrison). In short, *The Overlook Martial Arts Reader* presents as a sort of "primary text" the most authoritative writings on the martial arts ever assembled in English.

In organizing the material I have made Part I of this reader a historical section, serving, I hope, as a kind of introduction to the rest of the book. Part II contains philosophical writings having to do primarily with the intimate relationship among teacher, student, and goal. In Part III I have arranged works having to do with training and discipline, hoping to suggest that physical doing cannot be separated from "abstract" philosophy. Part IV is entitled "Other Aspects" and treats subjects as diverse as the education of samurai women and the connection between the liberal arts and the martial arts. Part V is a bibliography, abridged from my own *The Martial Arts: An Annotated Bibliography* (New York: Garland, 1988), the most comprehensive bibliography available in English. Certainly I do not want to suggest discrete divisions by organizing this present volume as I have: indeed there is a great overlap of theme among all these categories, and I would be more pleased than not to have a reader suggest that an article from the "Training and Discipline" section belongs more properly in "The Philosophy." There is, I believe, a point after which training and discipline *are* philosophy, and vice versa. It is the hidden message of this book.

*Randy F. Nelson*
*Davidson, 1988*

# ACKNOWLEDGMENTS

This book benefits from the ideas of many people, all of whom deserve more than the brief mention I can give them here. Kate Whitaker, Valerie Eads, Don Miller, and Donald L. Levine suggested ways to organize a martial arts anthology and brought specific articles and excerpts to my attention. I acknowledge their expertise and appreciate their help.

Had my friends Hansford Epes and John Savarese not untangled my computer errors, I would still be sitting, puzzled, in front of a blinking monitor. Deidre M.S. Frontczak of Werner Erhard Associates; Patricia James of Macdonald Publishers, London; and staff members of the Rosalyn Targ Literary Agency helped track down copyrighted material and advised me on obtaining permission to reprint several pieces. Assisting with proofreading were my valued colleagues Caroline Buxton, Chris Clarke, Maria Douglas, John Engel, John Freeman, Daniel Grau, Taylor Mayo, Leslie Morris, Greta Ratliff, and Rob Sitton. Thank you.

Mary Beatty and Hazel Goodman of the Davidson College Library aided with bibliographical research at every stage of preparation. Also I am indebted to the librarians at the Firestone Library of Princeton University, the Charlotte-Mecklenburg Public Library, the Library of Congress, the Davidson College Library, and the New York Public Library for their professionalism in helping me to locate materials.

Deborah Baker and Tom Funk of Overlook Press gave valuable advice and answered innumerable questions; I am greatly in their debt. And I acknowledge the support and understanding of my family, Susan, Miles, Ian, and Matthew, without whom the entire enterprise would have been meaningless. I am very grateful for what you all have contributed to this book.

*Randy F. Nelson*
*Davidson, 1988*

## PART I

# CULTURE AND CONFLICT: THE HISTORIES

**BRUCE A. HAINES**

# CHINA

China, like India, has been the nurturing spot for numerous martial art forms. While some of these arts were actually initiated in China, many were brought in from other countries and so Sinicized after centuries of practice in China that today they appear to be of Chinese inspiration.

It is difficult, even with access to reams of statistical data, to determine bases or patterns for behavior, and the task is enormously amplified when the behavioral patterns were established hundreds of years in the past. For this reason, it cannot be authoritatively determined why the earliest ch'uan fa schools were so secretive that it was considered a capital offense to display the techniques to the uninitiated. This particular behavior pattern has made extremely difficult the task of the historian studying Chinese weaponless martial arts.

In the field of weaponless combat, China undoubtedly was the catalyst introducing the techniques that have eventually come to be called karate. While the major Chinese precursor of karate is ch'uan fa in Mandarin Chinese, it is more popularly known as kung-fu (pronounced "gung-foo"). Although we call ch'uan fa a Chinese martial art, it is doubtful that it is wholly a product of Chinese genius. We know, for

---

*Bruce A. Haines (b. 1934) began studying karate in 1954 under the tutelage of Japanese masters who had settled in Hawaii. His 1962 master's thesis for the University of Hawaii was one of the first histories of karate in English. Since that time Haines has campaigned against what he has called the public's "monumental ignorance" of karate and against the Westernization of the martial arts.*

example, that from India's influence on China there arose at least one form of bare-handed fighting, the pioneer of which was the Indian monk Bodhidharma.

Bodhidharma is an obscure figure in history. The most reliable sources for our knowledge of the man are generally considered to be *Biographies of the High Priests* by Priest Tao-hsuan, written in A.D. 654, and the *Records of the Transmission of the Lamp*, by Priest Tao-yuan, written in 1004. But the earliest written source concerning Bodhidharma is found in a work entitled *Records of the Lo-yang Temple*, by Yang Hsuan-chih in A.D. 547. These seemingly authentic sources notwithstanding, however, modern scholarship has been reluctant to accept any single version of Bodhidharma's existence, or it asserts that all accounts of the Indian monk are legendary (see Paul Pelliot in *T'oung Pao*, 1923). On the other hand, eminent Buddhist-historians such as D.T. Suzuki, Kenneth Ch'en and Heinrich Dumoulin feel that Bodhidharma was an actual person despite the many admitted sprinklings and spicings of myth that have been added to his biography.

Bodhidharma was the third child of King Sugandha in Southern India, was a member of the Kshatriya, or warrior caste, and had his childhood in Conjeeveram (also, Kanchipuram, Kancheepuram), the small but dynamic Buddhist province of Madras. He is said to have received his religious training from the dhyana master Prajnatara, who was responsible for changing the young disciple's name from Bodhitara. An apt pupil, Bodhidharma soon exceeded his contemporaries so that by the time of his middle age, he was considered to be very wise in the ways of dhyana, or Zen practices. When Prajnatara died, Bodhidharma set sail for China, possibly because of a death-bed wish from his old master, according to the *Records of Lo-yang Temple*. On the other hand, Tao-yuan's *Records of the Transmission of the Lamp* indicate that the decision to go to China was made by Bodhidharma alone, because he was saddened by the decline of Buddhism in the areas outside of India proper.

Accounts of Bodhidharma's activities in China vary considerably with the reference cited. Tao-hsuan's *Biographies of the High Priests* states that Bodhidharma first arrived in China during the Sung dynasty (420–479) of the Southern Dynasties (420–589), and later traveled north to the Kingdom of Wei. But the traditional date of Bodhidharma's entry into China has been 520 (*vars.* 526, 527). This appears to be rather late if Tao-hsuan's *Biographies* is accurate in placing him at the Yung-ning Temple at Lo-Yang in 520. *Biographies* further states that a Buddhist "novice" called Seng-fu joined Bodhidharma's following, was ordained by Bodhidharma after an undisclosed period of study, and then left to journey to south China where he passed away in 524 at the age of sixty-one. Basic mathematics tells us that if Seng-fu were, indeed, sixty-one in 524, and had been the minimum acceptable age for ordination (20 years old at the time) when so honored by Bodhidharma, he would have been twenty in *ca.* 483, putting the Indian monk in China considerably earlier than the traditional date of 520.

A variation of the above theory, found in the *Records of the Transmission of the Lamp* (1004), places Bodhidharma in Canton in 527. After some time there, he traveled northward, meeting the Emperor Wu of the Liang dynasty (502–557) at Chin-ling (now Nanjing). It was at this time that the now famous question-and-answer dialogue took place between the learned monk and the Emperor Wu. Realizing that this form of dhyana "questioning" was of little avail with the pious but worldly monarch, Bodhidharma left the court for the Shaolin Monastery, where significant events then took place.

Bodhidharma's meeting with Liang Wu-ti appears neither in the *Records of the Lo-yang Temple* nor in the *Biographies*, written in 547 and 654 respectively. Since the *Records of the Transmission of the Lamp* was compiled 350 years after the *Biographies*, when Zen practices had already been well established in China, it is possible that the Bodhidharma-Emperor Wu debate was invented as a reverent allegory for explaining specific Zen tenets. Again, there are insufficient historical correlations to enable us to draw a firmly based conclusion.

After the famous but historically questionable encounter between Bodhidharma and the Emperor Wu, Bodhidharma's life is centered around the Shaolin Temple and Monastery located in Honan Province. Tradition states that upon seeing the emaciated condition of the monks of this temple, Bodhidharma instructed them in physical exercises to condition their bodies as well as their minds.

In several works dealing with ch'uan fa and its Okinawan counterpart, karate, reference is made to the close tie between Bodhidharma's Shaolin exercises and the above-named fighting arts. The factual basis for these hypotheses is the series of drills Bodhidharma introduced to the Shaolin monks, called shih pa lo han sho, or in English, "Eighteen Hands of the Lo-Han."

At the present time Lo-Han is used to designate all famous disciples of the historic Buddha, but more generally the term refers to those five hundred arhats (Sanskrit term for those who achieved Nirvana) who are supposed to reappear on earth as Buddhas, according to Buddhist mythology in some sects of the religion.

The precise meaning of Lo-Han in Bodhidharma's time, however, is lost, and we are forced to rely on the educated assumption that they were some form of temple guardians of Hindu origin. It also appears that their original Hindu number was sixteen, and that the Chinese added two to bring the number to eighteen.

According to E.T.C. Werner in his monumental *Dictionary of Chinese Mythology*, there does not appear to be any historical account of the first introduction of the Lo-Han into the halls of the Buddhist temples. Werner goes on to state that the eighteen Lo-Han did not exist before the time of a Buddhist poet and artist named Kuan-hsiu (832–912). However, we have already seen that martial arts tradition states that the shih pa lo han sho were introduced at the Shaolin Monastery sometime before 520, thus designating Bodhidharma as the initiator of the term "Lo-Han" in Chinese culture.

For our purposes, however, the main significance of the shih pa lo han sho, via Bodhidharma, is that it is reputed to be the basis for the famous Shaolin ch'uan fa.

This theory, on the other hand, raises a number of questions. For example, Bodhidharma's chief concern was apparently to cultivate the minds of his followers so that enlightenment could be achieved. Why would a Zen patriarch conceive a form of ch'uan fa, which, at least in its present stage of evolution, is a brutally effective weapon of combat? The answer, most probably, is that Bodhidharma never intended his shih pa lo han sho to be a violent martial art. There is certainly nothing to be found in the Bodhidharma image, as portrayed by the existing references, that would connect him with the later slapping, striking, punching, grunting, and generally violent masters of Zen Buddhism.

Here is an interesting hypothesis that has been overlooked by historians to date. The term originally applied to Bodhidharma—"wall gazing Brahmin"—is a misnomer. Reliable accounts (e.g., Chou, *A History of Chinese Buddhism*; Werner, *Dictionary of Chinese Mythology*) show that Bodhidharma was a member of the Kshatriya or warrior caste in India. As such, he was exposed to all existing forms of weaponless fighting from boyhood. The Kshatriya's most notable bare-handed fighting technique was called vajramushti, which is translated as: "one whose fist is...adamant; of a Kshatriya, or warrior; the clenched fist as a weapon." Mendicant Buddhist monks as well as the Kshatriya are said to have utilized vajramushti techniques, and there is little doubt that as a Kshatriya in India and later a peripatetic monk in China, Bodhidharma learned this technique of fighting. Whether the shih pa lo han sho is specifically an extension of vajramushti forms will probably never be known, since little has been written about the development of vajramushti per se, and references linking Bodhidharma with "self-defense" techniques are scarce. Toa-hsuan's *Biographies of the High Priests* (654) fails to mention Bodhidharma in a connection with anything that could be linked to martial arts. Of course, this omission does not mean that Bodhidharma did not introduce the Shaolin monks to some unique physical and perhaps martial art, especially since few academicians have taken an active interest in the mundane martial arts associated with historical events, and several of the most careful historians who hold strong reputations in defining "things Oriental" have "missed the boat," so to speak, when classifying all Asian combat forms as simply "boxing" or "pugilism."

The development of the Shaolin style of unarmed self-defense, though popularly associated with Bodhidharma, has a varied history, again depending on the source. The most plausible version indicates that after Bodhidharma left the monastery, many of the other monks of the Shaolin set out to disseminate his teachings. Contrary to the belief of D.T. Suzuki and others, the martial arts tradition which surrounds Bodhidharma attributed two books to his genius which were found a short while after his demise, secreted in the walls of the temple.

The first work, entitled *Hsi Sui Chin* was said to have been transcribed by Bodhidharma's disciple Hui K'o and has since been lost to the world. The second work, *I-Chin-ching*, has been translated several times and clouding this work is the possibility that it is a forgery from a period well after Bodhidharma's death. Tradition has it that these writings are not only filled with the spirit of Zen Buddhism, but that they also reveal Bodhidharma's position on physical activity as a means of body hygienics. The dubious nature of these writings, however, makes them unacceptable as conclusive historical documents.

Several decades after the death of Bodhidharma a certain ch'uan fa master named Ch'ueh Yuan Shang-jen verified the existence of Bodhidharma's "Eighteen Hands of the Lo Han" exercise and combined these movements with numerous forms of his own style. The obscurity surrounding the life of Ch'ueh Yuan Shang-jen is no less than that which is present in every work dealing with ch'uan fa. The existing biographical data on him tells us little more than that he came from either Honan or Shantung Province. But our interest in him is not in his biography but in the fact that he is credited with increasing Bodhidharma's original eighteen hand-and-foot positions to seventy-two.

After Ch'ueh had spent some time popularizing his expanded version of the Shaolin ch'uan fa, he traveled to Shensi Province where he met with another martial arts master named Li. Ch'ueh and Li are said to have enlarged the seventy-two strokes to one hundred and seventy, and to have given the best of these movements such names as dragon, tiger, snake, and crane.

The authoritarian French source *La Médecine Chinoise Au Cours Des Siècles* refers to the previously mentioned Ch'ueh Yuan Shang-jen as Kiao Yuan, claiming that it was he who initiated the additional movements to the shih pa lo han sho (up to 173 movements) and gave to it a decalog of moral precepts. Whether Ch'ueh Yuan and Kiao Yuan are one and the same is not known, as the Romanization of the two surnames gives nearly the same pronunciation. At any rate, it was Ch'ueh Yuan (or Kiao Yuan) who was responsible for the rise and fame of the Shaolin ch'uan fa, and therein is where our interest lies.

Most ch'uan fa forms practiced in the twentieth century are descendents of the one hundred seventy (*var.* 173) hand-and-foot positions of Ch'ueh Yuan, and though they have undergone a steady evolution they can still be traced ultimately to Bodhidharma's embryonic eighteen positions. Yet one more historical episode exists that clouds even this well-authenticated conclusion. During the Sui period (589–618), brigands attacked the Shaolin Monastery. Various futile attempts were made by the resident monks to protect themselves until at last one priest called the "begging monk" drove off the outlaws with a virtuosity of kicking and punching styles. This performance so impressed the other monks that they asked the "begging monk" to instruct them in this fighting form, which later developed into the famous Shaolin ch'uan fa.

Since the popular version in Japan and most of Asia persists that it was Bodhidharma who founded the Shaolin ch'uan fa, some readers may mistakenly associate the "begging monk" with Bodhidharma. This assumption is immediately ruled out, however, when we see that the "begging monk" lived during the Sui period which began in A.D. 589, and well after Bodhidharma's death (*ca.* 534). Hence, the account of the so-called "begging monk" seems to represent a conflicting version of the founding of the Shaolin ch'uan fa.

Regardless of one's motives in favoring one account over the other, there are too many references in favor of the Bodhidharma legend to make other narratives truly convincing. In all probability, this spiritual pioneer of Zen in China can be creditied with the founding of at least one form of the Shaolin style of ch'uan fa. But, as the major task of revising Bodhidharma's original eighteen-stroke exercise to one hundred seventy offensive and defensive movements belongs to the previously cited ch'uan fa master Ch'ueh Yuan Shang-jen, we deduce that ch'uan fa, as a truly lethal military art, developed with this man.

The Shaolin ch'uan fa is the first school of bare-handed fighting listed under the general heading of "External School" or Wai Chia. The "External School" is the major classification under which eight other styles are grouped. The exact date of origin for this terminology is not known. It was probably used at first to categorize various types of ch'uan fa under one heading after the Shaolin style came into existence.

The other eight forms listed under the "External School" are: Hung Ch'uan and T'au T'ei Yu T'an T'ui both from the Sung period (A.D. 1127–1279); the Hon Ch'uan, Erh-lang Men, Fan Ch'uan, and Ch'a Ch'uan styles dated from the Ming dynasty (A.D. 1368–1644)—the latter form used exclusively by Chinese Moslems; and two styles attributed to the Ch'ing period (A.D. 1644–1911), called Mi Tsung Yi and Pa Ch'uan.

In nearly every instance, the founders of these eight ch'uan fa styles were said to have been Taoist deities or demigods. The real creators of these various forms appear to be lost to the world and, as the so-called godlike inventors are timeless entities in the mythology of China, many Chinese believe that ch'uan fa has always existed. Historically dating the first public display of the above named styles of ch'uan fa has thus far been impossible. The importance of the ch'uan fa Taoist association will be discussed later.

The same obscurity found in the history of the "External School" is likewise seen in the background of the "Internal School" of ch'uan fa, called Nei Chia. These forms are all from Sung or post-Sung dynasty dates and are called: Wu Tang P'ai, T'ai Ch'i Ch'uan, Pa Kua Ch'uan, Hsin Yi Ch'uan, Tzu Jan Men, and Liu He Pa Fa.

Bodhidharma's final days are shrouded in the mystery of marvelous and supernatural events. After transmitting the "dharma" to his disciple Hui K'o at the Shaolin Temple, one version has it that he died and was neatly and properly buried on Hsiung-erh Shan (Bear's Ear Hill), in Honan Province. Those who ascribe to this "neat and proper" theory vary in his death date between 529 and 535. However, we then encounter a work entitled *Shen-hsien t'ung-chien*, wherein a Wei official en route to Central Asia for a good-will mission reported a cordial meeting at Ch'ung-lin (Onion Range) in the Belaturgh Mountains of Turkestan. Carrying a single sandal, Bodhidharma was asked by the official where he was going, to which the monk replied: "I am going back to the Western Heaven [India]."

This tale was later reported to the Wei Emperor who accordingly exhumed Bodhidharma's tomb, wherein he found...one sandal. The emperor, awed by this "resurrection," attempted to preserve the surviving foot garment in the Shaolin Monastery, but even it disappeared (reportedly stolen) before the passage of two centuries.

Bodhidharma's final exit in Chinese history under such strange circumstance is certainly in character with the general mode of sixth-century Chinese thought. Mysticism, magic, and supernatural entities were the "stuff" of which early Chinese folklore, and post first-century Buddhist religious thought, were made.

There is every possibility that some type of weaponless combat developed in China long before the advent of Bodhidharma. According to one authority, a certain form of ch'uan fa evolved in China approximately five thousand years ago during the reign of the semimythical Yellow Emperor, Huang-ti.

There is further reference to the birth of this art in the dynastic history known as the Han Shu (Han Dynasty 209 B.C.–A.D. 24), but the date ascribed to it is much too remote in antiquity to be convincing. Thus, other than saying that something akin to ch'uan fa-karate developed very early in China, we can make no definitive statements about its beginning.

Secret societies have played an important role in Chinese history from earliest times; however, the first outspokenly antigovernment group existed near the end of the Han dynasty, called the "Carnation Eyebrow Rebels." Because of the effectiveness of this society in accomplishing its aims, the list of such organizations grew until eventually wherever political oppression became intolerable, or a foreign power came to rule (such as the Mongols of Marco Polo's time), these secret societies led the fight in restoring desirable government.

Since 1644 a foreign Manchu dynasty had controlled China's destiny, subjecting the multitudes of Chinese to the role of second-class citizens. Agitation for reform and overthrow of the Manchu autocracy brought swift reprisals to participants therein. So, to end this government oppression, Chinese secret societies went "underground" and became the leading protagonists for anti-Manchu activity.

The Ch'ing dynasty (1644–1911) of the Manchus thus became a leading target for revolutionary activities of various groups, with the famous and powerful "White Lotus Society" heading the attempted coup, which included such secret anti-Manchu groups as the "Three Incense Sticks," "The Rationalist Society," and the "Eight Diagrams."

Then, in the middle of the nineteenth century, Western powers began their long-anticipated economic and military assault on the

"Middle Kingdom." A beleaguered China, proud of her ancient civilization and scornful of the Occidental "barbarians," was unsuccessful in forestalling European aggression and final victory. England led the way in opening China's sealed doors, forcing her to war in 1839 and 1856, with the French joining the British in the latter encounter. These involvements cost China the island of Hong Kong which was ceded to the British for war reparations, as well as numerous "treaty ports" on the Chinese mainland, not to mention various other "rights" and advantages.

Western imperialism was at first only a minor irritation to the general mass of Chinese people for whom foreign invasion was an expected part of life. In the past millennia of Chinese history the transgressors had eventually left China of their own accord or, being Mongoloid peoples, they were assimilated into the Chinese culture and not thought of as invaders. The foreign Manchus, though in control of China for nearly three hundred years, had been oppressive rulers and Chinese hatred was centered on the Manchu dynasty. However, after the Opium War of 1839, England and all other foreign "barbarians" slowly became the objects of Chinese animosity. After a time the United States joined additional European nations in obtaining similar guarantees in China. By the beginning of the twentieth century Chinese sovereignty had virtually ceased to exist.

Hatred of Western domination reached a breaking point in 1900 when the Boxers staged their famous rebellion. The significance of this revolt for our purposes lies in the fact that the Boxers represent a type of ch'uan fa activity.

The term "Boxers" was first applied to ch'uan fa cultists by Westerners in China when they saw a similarity between ch'uan fa and their own brands of pugilistic encounter. And, although very few ch'uan fa schools seem to have participated in the Boxer Rebellion, they became lumped together under the term "Boxers" which was eventually used by the invading Westerners to indicate any Chinese secret society or group that demonstrated hatred of the West. One large group of Boxers, and it seems that this society was more responsible for the term "Boxers" than any other, was called the I-Ho-Ch'uan or "Righteous and Harmonious Fists," of which only a small portion were ch'uan fa practitioners. The I-Ho-Ch'uan was a branch of an older secret organization, the aforementioned "Eight Diagrams," founded near the close of the Ming Dynasty. This "Eight Diagrams" was probably not a ch'uan fa association either, but affiliated with it were certain ch'uan fa groups such as the I-Ho-Ch'uan. The "Eight Diagrams" society became a leading anti-Western clique before and during the short Boxer war of 1900.

Two other Boxer groups which may have had strong ch'uan fa membership were the K'an and Ch'ien Boxers. These two groups were active in northern China during the 1900 rebellion and were associated with both the I-Ho-Ch'uan and the "Eight Diagrams." Besides the more clandestine activities of the various secret societies, the 1900 war also attracted multitudes of Chinese men, both young and old, who formed into bands of "gymnasts" and who practiced numerous forms of ch'uan fa.

In retrospect, the Boxer Rebellion was an unorganized mass revolt against foreign controls in China. The amount of actual ch'uan fa activity was slight, although the ruling Manchu aristocracy and the peasantry seemed to have been mesmerized by ch'uan fa performers into believing that they could outdo the mighty Western military science with their weaponless art. It is interesting to note that the appeal of ch'uan fa was sufficient to enlist the masses in this revolt against the foreign elements, in spite of the knowledge that their opponents would be retaliating with every type of firearm in their possession. As it turned out, most of the actual combat during the rebellion was conducted with weapons. The empty-handed or true ch'uan fa styles seem to have been employed primarily for propaganda purposes.

> For two months, from June 20 to August 14, (1900), the Kansu Army of Tung Fu-hsing and hundreds of "righteous" people flourished all sorts of magic weapons such as soul-absorbing banners, sky-covering flags, thunderbolt fans, and flying swords. They succeeded in killing only one important person, the German Minister Von Ketteler.

In every true art form, whether aesthetic or practical, some part of the artist's technique is kept secret. This is especially true of Chinese ch'uan fa. Even at the present time, ancient ch'uan fa is kept in relative secrecy among the physical culture clubs that practice this art. In the past five years in the United States, ch'uan fa secrecy and selectivity have appeared to diminish somewhat, so that whereas before only those of pure Chinese ancestry were accepted as students, now all racial groups can be found studying the art. However, upon closer scrutiny it can be seen that many techniques normally included in ch'uan fa are excluded from the open teachings, and are taught to those of Chinese ancestry at a different time or in a separate location.

The twentieth century, far from witnessing the demise of ch'uan fa, has seen a great rise in its popularity. In Communist China, Mao Tse-tung [has] utilized the appeal of ch'uan fa to enlist participants in his gymnastic program, as well as for a pragmatic form of self-defense that everyone is urged to learn. Numerous Chinese "boxing" magazines are printed in [Red] China and Hong Kong, with thousands of readers throughout the Chinese communities of the world.

From the foregoing it can be seen why the recent opening of ch'uan fa doors to Westerners has met with much opposition from certain ch'uan fa societies. Of course, those who have taken the step usually claim that they teach non-Chinese participants only a watered-down version of the true art, and that the "secrets" have never been divulged to the Western world. So, though it appears that kung-fu (the common term for ch'uan fa in the West) is becoming a universal art along with the other karate-like styles of self-defense, it is possible that we will never see it practiced as it once was in the fabled temples of Shaolin.

KURT SINGER

# THE SAMURAI: LEGEND AND REALITY

### THE DISCOVERY OF BUSHIDO

For almost half a century after Japan had been reopened to foreign intercourse, she remained to the West a closed, recondite being, half veiled in legend, difficult of access, and inviting but a small number of lovers of exotic art, archaic custom, and mercantile profit. It was only after her decisive victory over Tsarist Russia in 1904–05 that she came to be regarded as a political force of the first order, able to influence the fate of Western nations and therefore inviting intellectual efforts to appraise her true character. Thus she justified the thought of those philosophers who derive the sense of reality, of objective existence, from feelings of resistance, of hardness experienced.

"We recognise," wrote a war-correspondent of that epoch, "almost grudgingly and in spite of ourselves, the existence of a moral force that appears able to govern and sway the whole conduct of a whole people, inspiring not a caste but a nation, from highest to lowest, to deeds that are worthy to rank among the most famous in history and legend. We want to know what this force is, whence it comes, and what it means;

---

As a professor of sociology and economics at the Tokyo Imperial University in the 1930s, Kurt Singer felt himself to be a "translator" for both Japanese and European cultures. He explained differences between East and West in terms of geometry, the West being obsessed with symmetry and control, the East content with asymmetry and flow. His essay on the samurai is meant to contrast the code of bushido with the Christian concept of knighthood.

■ 15

the sense of its existence makes us jealous, uncomfortable, almost annoyed." To this question an answer had been given by a Japanese scholar of great literary parts who possessed an intimate knowledge of the cultures of the East and of the West. This was Dr. Inazo Nitobe, a samurai by birth, a Quaker by faith, and, later, one of the leading officials of the League of Nations. In a number of books and essays, the first of which was published in 1899, he drew the attention of foreign readers to the existence of the Japanese warrior's moral code, bushido, in which Nitobe saw not only the "commanding moral force of his country," but also the "totality of the moral instincts of the Japanese race . . . in its elements coeval with our blood and therefore also with our religion of Shintoism." The hyperbolic formula was so catching, and Dr. Nitobe's persuasive talent was so impressive, that many Western writers felt authorized to regard bushido as the common denominator of all they admired (or scorned) in Japanese life or politics.

In the years of the Anglo-Japanese alliance the admirable aspects of bushido seemed uppermost in Western minds. After the First World War, when Japan's claims to hegemony in the Far East began to delineate themselves rather clearly, the word *bushido* came to be uttered only with diffidence, and not seldom with a sneer. Dr. Nitobe's account of the virtues of Samurai-Japan was discarded as romantic; yet his theory of bushido as the explanation of all Japan's national endowments and aspirations was retained, and henceforth everything Japan did and said was labelled bushido—including the Emperor cult and the expansionist foreign policy, Shinto and the "spirit of Japan" (Yamato damashii), and many things intensely disliked and courageously opposed by Dr. Nitobe, an ardent pacifist and unflinching liberal, whose conflicts with the nationalist groups of army officers are well known. It is true that certain Japanese nationalist writers and societies made some use of the bushido theory—a fact that recalls the fate of Georges Sorel's theory of violence: which was, in his view, a weapon in the fight of the proletariat for emancipation; but it was applied eventually in Italy and Germany in the interests of the professed enemies of Bolshevism. Dr. Nitobe was not responsible for the turgid statements of hyperpatriots. His only fault was to treat in a transport of unbridled enthusiasm a theme that demanded precise definition and historical sense.

### ORIGINS OF THE WARRIOR CLASS

It is untrue, except in a narrow lexicographical sense, that the term *bushido* does not occur before the beginning of the twentieth century.

Authoritative writings on the Way of the Warrior appeared two centuries earlier, in the Genroku period, some generations after the establishment of the Tokugawa Shogunate. Yamaga Soko was the head of an eminently influential military school, whose teachings are said to have kindled the spirit in which the Forty-Seven Ronin sacrificed their lives in avenging their lord's death, and whose spiritual descendant was Yoshida Shoin, the inspirer of those who led the Meiji Revolution. Yamaga Soko left a record of his lectures, a book called *Shido*—*shi* denoting the feudal retainer or gentleman, *do* meaning "the way," the norm, obligation, law (cognate with the Chinese *tao* and recalling the origins of the Greek *dike*). A smaller treatise by the same author is entitled *Bukyo-shogaku*—the Lesser (*sho*) School (*gaku*) of the Teachings (*kyo*) of the Samurai (*bu*). Evidently the idea of bushido remained unchanged, whether its verbal equivalent was *shido*, *bukyo*, or *budo* (as with Daidoji Yuzan, Yamaga Soko's pupil, author of the authoritative and sober *Budo Shoshinshu*, "A Primer of the Warrior's Ways").

Sir George Sansom observes that bushido is "a difficult subject leading into fruitless controversies." I venture to think that it is not more difficult than any other major chapter in the history of moral and political thought; that most perplexities have arisen from careless use of terms and from emotional undertones or arguments; and that it is neither fruitless nor impossible to distinguish here between realities and words, historical facts and propagandist figments.

Unfortunately Professor Hall Chamberlain, the founder of Japanology, by an unguarded statement, so seldom seen in his careful writings, appears to have misled later commentators. In an essay entitled *The Invention of a New Religion*, first published in 1912 and, from 1927, appearing as an Appendix in *Things Japanese* (in the last edition not prepared by himself) he affirms:

> Bushido, as an institution or a code of rules, has never existed. The accounts given of it have been fabricated out of whole cloth, chiefly for foreign consumption.... The very word appears in no dictionary, native or foreign, before the year 1900.... Neither Kaempfer, Siebold, Satow, nor Rein—all men knowing their Japan by heart——ever once alludes to it in their voluminous writings. The cause of their silence is not far to seek. Bushido was unknown until a decade or so ago.

This statement, however, proves too little and too much. If bushido (the Way of the Warrior) is a term and thing unknown before 1900 it follows that it cannot have been a myth invented or used in order to support the Meiji monarchy, which at that late date needed no such artificial underpinning. As for Dr. Nitobe—his liberal convictions and affiliations are so well known that the emergence of the title theory of bushido under his name cannot be construed as a machination of governmental or hyperpatriotic origin. It can be shown, moreover, that for good reasons the patriotic literature of the Meiji period, and well beyond that period, preferred to appeal to other ethical doctrines rather than to the Way of the Warrior, the moral heritage of the unruly samurai. It was only later that references to the samurai virtues appeared in the programs of nationalist associations with greater, although (except in propaganda for foreign consumption) not conspicuous, frequency—a paradoxical but not uncommon reflex of foreign styles of thinking observable in the ideas of Japanese nationalists.

Japanese scholars innocent of propagandist leanings, such as Professor Massaharu Anesaki, have traced the origin of such teachings to the Kamakura period and the subsequent "times of trouble" under the Hojo regents and Ashikaga shoguns; when a new class of warriors rose to power and, in a long laborious process, made the military fief the administrative and economic foundation of a unified feudal government, with its seat first at Kamakura and later in Muromachi, Kyoto. This new class was in a typically Japanese fashion at the same time archaic and revolutionary, loyalist and anarchic. It was led by great families, claiming Imperial decent, that had built up for themselves an imposing house-power far from the capital in semi-autonomous country districts, based on a kind of manorial economy.

The new class of warriors originated when the conscription system of the bureaucratic monarchy introduced from China fell into decay, and when the rise of the slo-en (immunities of quasi-manorial character) led to a demand for courageous and determined men willing to protect manorial estates in times of widespread unrest and uncertain allegiances. The warriors were recruited from the peasant class, from families of former provincial notables, and from the dissatisfied and adventurous residuum existing in the crevices of every society.

To weld these heterogeneous elements together under the guidance of the local branches of the great metropolitan houses was no mean achievement; and it is much to the credit of the Kamakura rulers that a spiritual foundation for the solution of the problem was sought in the new school of Zen meditation introduced into Japanese Buddhism from China, with its ideals of serenity and simplicity, calm resignation, rock-like determination undismayed by death, and mystic realization of the unity of all beings.

The first written testimonies of the new spirit were the yuikai ("teachings left," or spiritual legacies) and kakun (family laws). These moral instructions, addressed by clan heads to their descendants, were held in reverent regard by their families and their retainers. Their faith was Buddhist: it was impregnated by the belief in the interdependence of all cosmic life, thought, and action: but they continued to invoke the help and protection of Shinto deities and ancestral spirits. Of the yuikai and kakun Professor Anesaki observes that in these documents "the practice of loyalty to the sovereign and fidelity to family traditions" was strongly underlined, and "the virtues of charity, justice, honesty, modesty, valour were also included." Anesaki goes on:

> Advice was given to the heirs of military leaders as to administration of feudal territories, treatment of soldiers, care of provisions, and as to codes of honor in peace and war. In short, religious beliefs and worldly wisdom, spiritual training, military discipline, moral ideals and practical counsels were fused into the one principle of the warrior's honor. The principle and practice of bushido, the Way of the Warrior, found here definite formulation, and these teachings were destined to sway the ruling classes throughout coming centuries. Some of these documents exercised an influence beyond the limits of the clans and families and became in some respects a national heritage.

The house-laws of military clans, including those of the ruling family of the Tokugawa clan, are the linear descendants of these early spiritual legacies. To withhold from them the name of code or institution is only possible if the use of these terms is unduly restricted to rigid systems resembling the *Deuteronomium*, the *Institution* of Justinian, or the *Code Napoléon*. The contents of the Samurai laws retained a certain fluidity and plasticity; this kept them alive and able to survive in periods of violent change and revolutionary ferment. To deny that they had a decisive influence on the formation of the Japanese character and of Japanese thought and society is to allow oneself to be blinded by one's own scepticism. Neither Hall, Chamberlain, nor Sansom, although ready to discount much that is contained in hyperbolical eulogies, has carried his disbelief in any superior congenital moral quality of the Japanese so far as to declare the ethics of the samurai to be mere legend, artificially constructed in the Meiji period for political purposes. It was a pattern of ideas and ideals clothed with the authority first of the clan head or the ruler, later of the military scholar and patriotic leader. Instead of denouncing it as a fiction, one ought to dwell on the abyss that separates the genuine ethics of the samurai from recent ideologies patterned upon the pseudomyths of contemporary European totalitarianism. Far from being a creed demanding the expansion of the Japanese Empire, the rule of the sword, and the subjugation of foreign people by the descendants and retainers of the Children of the Sun, the ethics of the samurai belonged essentially to a *static* world molded by Buddhist feeling and Confucian thought. The Christian knight sought "adventure" in order to prove his prowess; to fight against uncouth villains, giants, and devilish monsters, in defense of women and the poor; to serve the Church and to further the triumph of Christianity. A straight line leads from the Paladins of Charlemagne and the Knights of Arthur's Round Table to the Crusades and to the Conquistadores. They are all attracted by unconquered spaces and the lure of the *mission* with all its possibilities of adventure. The samurai does not experience such urges; which lead the knight on and on into the vast darkness of the unknown, riding like the *miles Christianus* of Dürer's engraving through perilous forests infested by Death and the Devil.

Zen meditation has taught the true samurai the way inward. His is a will to enter the sphere where there is no fear of dying nor hope of afterlife, because the borderline between life and death has been experienced as illusory. This inward sphere does not demand meritorious deeds, because good and evil have lost their childlike simplicity. To be moved by transports of enthusiasm and fighting ardor, carried as it were on the surge of a great wave crashing against the cliffs of fate, is not his ambition: rather it is to become like a rock on which the waves of life rush in vain. He who attains enlightenment has left far behind him churches, holy books, sacred images, and theological dogma. He has regained that pristine state in which the soul becomes one with the Absolute, and in which a new power of determination springs up from depths that are unfathomable.

Buddhist ethics appear, at least to Western eyes, negative and preparatory rather than normative and creative. In Zen the main concerns are to be freed from impediments of salvation, to be subject no longer to "hunger" in all its various forms, to eliminate the distinction between I and You, Good and Evil, Man and the Whole, Life and Death—and not to shape this life of ours according to some divine image. The ethics of the samurai center on the teachings of how to die, how to be undismayed, unmoved, unshakeable, free from all-too-human interests and entanglements. From this height of an amoral (not necessarily immoral) mysticism a steep, short path leads to the regions of nihilism and quietism. But it would not be quite fair to make Zen meditation responsible for what it sometimes became in dull and in dissolute souls. Similiar dangers mark the way of every religion and first attract the attention of critics alien to that creed.

I am not trying to maintain that the average samurai did partake of ultimate enlightenment. But his thought was moving in a spiritual magnetic field, the pole of which was not action in the outer world, but annihilation of externals, readiness for sacrifice and for complete self-abnegation. The treatises on bushido written in the first half of the Tokugawa era contain, it is true, many exhortations not to neglect training in arms and not to think war a remote possibility, and with good reason; for this was a period in which the warrior had become a kind of official, exposed to the lures of a luxuriant growth of urban pleasures in an age of systematic seclusion, thorough pacification and political stagnation.

Here too, however, the dominant note remained the insistence on a mental discipline able to subdue the desire to personal enjoyment and gain, laziness and license, and to keep awake the readiness for service. The style of every activity the samurai might indulge in, the performance of the tea ceremony, the singing of utai, the practice of archery as well as of the ceremonial for committing suicide—all bear the imprint of such discipline; the monkish color of garments echo its spirit. To achieve complete mastery of one's natural inclinations, to attain unruffled serenity in utter adversity, not to exult in triumph nor to yield to sorrow, are the main objects of this code of behavior. The Noh-play preserves the ascetic style of this life more faithfully than any treatise or anecdote. It shows that we are confronted here not with doctrinaire demands and vain transports, but with a form of life that has been lived, certainly in various degrees of purity and vigor, but a life unquestionably real, of great dignity and austere beauty.

## IDEALS AND REALITIES

Form everywhere easily degenerates into mere formalism, courage into brawling, loyalty into servility, calmness into insensitivity. Later writers, in extolling the samurai spirit, have often dwelt on the virtues of martial bravery and one-sided loyalty as if they had been the pillars of samurai ethics. Commonplace courage, however, cannot be termed the inspiring force of bushido. The warriors who, from the end of the

Heian age, flocked to the banners of the new feudal leaders of Japan needed no exhortation to physical bravery; they delighted in fighting and were not much afraid of losing their poor lives. What the heads of clans on their deathbeds, the chiefs of feudal governments in their codes and injunctions, felt urged to infuse into the sturdy and crude minds of their retainers was a spiritual conception of their duties, a discipline molding the whole life of the warrior, an image of the Right Life that if sincerely lived could justify the warrior's claim to dominion over the other classes. The samurai was not to be a man of more rights, but of more duties.

These duties were not one-sided. In a typical oath and pledge exchanged by lord and retainer in southern Kyushi late in the fifteenth century, the retainer swears that he will serve the lord "with single devotion and without a second thought," while the lord, acknowledging the promise of loyalty, replies: I will regard your important affairs as my own, and we will mutually rely and be relied upon; if despite this understanding a calumny or an evil report should arise, we would mutually explain ourselves, with complete frankness." The lord's pledge is put under the sanction of the most dreaded deities of medieval Japan, including the sun goddess of Ise, Hachiman (the war god), and the deities of Kumano and Suwa. An obligation protected by such deities cannot at that period be considered as a mere formality.

As in every relation between men unequal in power, wealth, and rank, it is reasonable to expect that in practice the strict balance between the rights of the lord and of the retainer would not always have remained untilted. In the East, where patriarchal structures dominated all social and political thought, it was almost unavoidable that the retainer's duties should be assimilated by those of filial piety; this occurred in classical Chinese thought and survived in the bushido teachings of such Japanese as Yamaga Soko and Yuzan; the more the lord assumed the authority of a father the more it tended to become absolute, for according to Oriental notions the son had no rights against his sire. But in Japan, as in China and in the European Middle Ages, the retainer had not only the right but also the duty to remonstrate whenever he deemed the lord's action unjust or inappropriate. A samurai who blindly fulfilled the will of his lord against the voice of his own conscience was called a neishin (cringeling, fawning parasite) or choshin ("a favorite who steals his master's affections by means of servile compliance"—Nitobe). If all efforts at persuasion failed, the retainer's protest had to take the form of suicide (seppuku).

Instances of disloyalty, and of samurai changing sides, during the centuries of internal troubles and civil wars are frequently reported in the Japanese chronicles; but only a biased mind could undertake to estimate the proportion these cases bore to normal loyal behavior. Questions of honor are singularly ill-suited for statistical treatment. We have no means of knowing whether the majority of the samurai—or, for that matter, any class in any country—did or did not remain below the standard set by codes and treatises. The very existence of literary admonitions shows that the virtues the samurai was asked to cultivate were not expected to spring up spontaneously. Yuzan, the greatest authority on Tokugawa bushido, says clearly that many samurai had only inferior grades of qualities. To take bushido as a natural quality inherent in the Japanese race is a mistake reserved for later writers seduced by easy biologisms. Until the end of the nineteenth century there was no attempt to deny that, for Japanese too, bushido was difficult to achieve. But it was not thought impossible. In fact, it is a gratuitous assumption to state that the higher bushido teachings remained mainly on paper, without becoming a living force in the life of real men, stronger and weaker men alike.

At all times, and with all groups, the demands of higher systems of ethics have been fulfilled only by a moral elite in a position to impose their standards on populations unable to live up to them, yet unable at the same time to deny the righteousness of such standards. There was, however, a better chance of a samurai fulfilling the norms of bushido than a Christian living according to the teachings of the Sermon on the Mount, with its paradoxical if not hyperbolical demands. To be generous, dutiful, circumspect, obeying father and authorities, frugal, sober, diligent, and composed in the face of death or misery; all this is not according to everybody's nature; but it imposes less strain on the psychic structure of natural man than the demand to love one's enemies and to tender the right cheek after the left cheek has been struck.

It was the historic mission of the Tokugawa age to inject the spirit of the samurai into ever-widening circles of Japanese society, in attenuated vigor and purity, but not necessarily in a debased form. It was a movement resulting in one of the most complete democratizations of an aristocratic set of ideals of which history has left us a trace. Even the attitudes of the housewife and the student, the shop apprentice and the courtesan, mirrored, in suitable diminution, the attitude of the feudal retainer to his lord.

The tremendous wave of enthusiasm aroused in the quarters of the ordinary town dweller by the herioc vendetta of the Forty-Seven Ronin demonstrates that the spirit of the samurai has ceased to be a class-morality at the beginning of the eighteenth century. The merchant and artisan townsman recognized the values for which the samurai lived and died to be at the center of national ethics: and this popular wave of emotional adherence must have been no less effective than the revival of the Ancient Learning and of primeval Shinto in preparing the way for the final welding together, five generations later, of all classes into the modern nation. While the West bade farewell to the spirit of the feudal age in the historical plays of Shakespeare and Cervantes' *Don Quixote*, in Japan this spirit expanded, duly diluted, into the minds of the rice dealers and luggage carriers of the greatest metropolis of those times, Yedo, later Tokyo: and the typical "Yedokko," the common man of its streets and shops, was proud to live his life in a manner that would have pleased Don Quixote rather than Sancho Panza.

There is, of necessity, a danger inseparable from all such vulgarizations of highstrung moral ideas. The citizen of the great towns, his wife and his courtesan lovers, were attracted to bushido mainly by the forces of sentiment, and often by a desire for what was strange, colorful, and exciting: to such demands one answer was the drama of the Tokugawa era, the Kabuki, an inexhaustible source of strong emotion, unheard-of action, intense color, and expression carried to the limit of the grotesque. All this was alien to the true samurai spirit, whose canon can be gauged from the style of the Noh-play, austere, calm, subdued, and chaste. Thus it occurred that the life of the samurai was presented to the commoner in its extreme cases, verging on crime and madness, and placing strains on the sensibility and humanity of the theatregoers that made, and continue to make, the parterre often swin in tears and the gallery explode in raucous cries of ecstatic acclamation.

The foreigner, finding access to the Noh difficult for both internal and external reasons, was easily fascinated by the Kabuki and by the tales written for Western readers in the early days, which were both readable and crudely illustrated: his impressions must have been reinforced by the hyperdramatic actor-woodcuts of the ukiyoe school of popular artists. He was thus misled into taking these variations on samurai themes for the essence of bushido. Hence came the apparently ineradicable Western tendency to think of the samurai as a grotesquely gesticulating half savage habitually murdering his own children for the benefit of his Lord, sending his wife to a brothel in order to buy a good steed, and finally committing suicide in skillfully prolonged agonies. These are famous themes of Japanese literature, but it would be as wrong to regard them as typical of the Way of the Warrior as to consider eating from a leper's bowl or living on the top of a column to be characteristic of ordinary Christian life. All these enter the class of "flagrant cases," not to be explained away, but to be relegated to the border region to which they belong.

The great Tokugawa treatises on bushido, by Yamaga Soko and Yuzan, do not even mention such extremes. Their tone is moderate, their teaching sensible; they never exaggerate the demands of a single virtue, and their scale of values bears no trace of a soldier caste bent upon self-glorification. Their teaching breathes an atmosphere jejune and colorless and is inspired either by the late Confucianist Sung philosophy of Chu-hsi (first introduced by Zen monks and some centuries later adopted as State orthodoxy), or by more intrepid thinkers eager to discard the Sun commentators and their static ethics of conformity, so convenient to authoritarian rule. These bolder spirits groped their way back to the pure springs of early Confucianism. Compared with the Zen warriors of earlier ages there is certainly a loss of spiritual tension, but until the end the attainment of spiritual freedom remains the central virtue.

To determine to what extent the behavior of modern Japanese is still shaped by the teachings of bushido is an undertaking as difficult as to assess the degree to which Christian ethics still mold the actions and bearing of contemporary Europeans. The Meiji Restoration was the work of the samurai, mainly of lower rank, with strong economic grievances and fierce patriotic passions, but it led to the abolition of the samurai class by the new state. The loss of powerful privileges; the continuation and, as often as not, the aggravation of their financial difficulties, above all for those samurai who did not find a suitable place in the new social framework as officers, officials or entrepreneurs, policemen or farmers; the unfulfilled hopes of glorious military enterprises discarded by the prudent Meiji Emperor and his chief adviser: all this led to much discontent among the former samurai, who sought redress by rebellious undertakings, unceasing agitation and occasional assassinations. To one familiar with these well-known facts it must appear quite unlikely that the authorities could have made any attempt to establish bushido—the spirit of the most troublesome class in the land—as the foundation of the new state ethics.

What happened in the Meiji era was not that bushido was made the basis of state ethics, but that loyalty was redefined and given a new content and orientation. For a least five hundred years bushido itself had been, in terms of practical politics, dissociated from service to the Imperial House. The loyalty of the samurai was mainly due to his feudal lord, the daimyo; and some of the most celebrated deeds of the samurai had been performed in assisting their daimyo against Imperial armies. But the "loyal men" who died in the Ueno battle and at Wakamatsu were, in the eyes of the Emperor, rebels against Imperial Rule. The idea that true loyalty was due to the Emperor only became the official guiding principle of political conduct during the Meiji era. No bushido myth was invented; but feelings and attitudes, based on a mythical tradition that had remained for seven centuries overshadowed by the rule of the samurai class, were reestablished in order to annihilate the wrong work and confused loyalties of the feudal age—a process recalling the rehabilitation of Roman myths and cults by the Emperor Augustus.

If the past state and future possibilities of Japan are to be gauged correctly, it is of paramount importance to distinguish these processes from the political and propagandist fictions produced at the beginning of the twentieth century. The Emperor-myth and the samurai tradition are genuine; but in recent decades they have been exploited as tools of nationalist and imperialist propoaganda and thereby discredited. Yet it would be not only against historical truth, but also detrimental to sound political judgment, to mistake them for phenomena of the same order of flimsiness as such purposive paper myths as "The White Man's Burden," "The General Strike," or "The Nordic Race."

Survival of the samurai tradition is far from being a literary phenomenon. When the samurai class as such was abolished, its ideals remained in force, unquestioned. Even now it is often possible to distinguish by their bearing and action Japanese of samurai stock from those of commoner's origin (heimin). It was only during the China Incident that the distinction between samurai and heimin was removed from a man's registration papers.

The prewar curriculum of the state schools, at least until not long before the Second World War, was not responsible for any artificial stimulation of martial interests. The school system of the Meiji era was liberal in outlook, and the examples illustrating ethical teaching were drawn from a wide range of facts in which the samurai tradition occupied no greater space than any country would devote to the meritorious deeds of her own past. It would be a serious mistake to believe that it was governmental propaganda that made the modern Japanese ready to fling their lives away and suffer what appears intolerable.

Not all the disregard for life and happiness, verging on a passionate desire to sacrifice oneself for the good of the national whole, can be ascribed to the samurai tradition. There lives in the Japanese both the mind of the tribe, compelling the individual to surrender before the needs of the human beehive, and the soul of the mystic, finding supreme fulfillment in abandoning a self conceived to be one with the Soul of the Universe, or Buddha. Between these two extremes, limiting cases of human morals, the Way of the Samurai, like every ethic of a chivalrous type, holds an intermediate position, drawing strength from both sources.

To the Japanese the true character of the samurai is expressed in the cherry blossoms; which suddenly open under the morning sun and as suddenly fall to the ground when shaken by the winds of spring. If the foreign reader experiences a certain difficulty in reconciling this image with what he has seen of, and read about, the callous insensitivity and unbridled violence of Japanese warriors, let him follow the course of history upstream, and he can find in the story of Taira Atsumori an indication of what the symbol meant before it became a conventional formula. When after the fatal defeat at Ichi-no-tani by the hands of Yoritomo the Taira clan sailed from the main island, Atsumori, a nephew of the great Kiyomori, was the last to leave the shore. Challenged by one of the strongest of the enemy warriors, he turned his horse back, fought against the greatest odds and was killed. When his adversary looked beneath the helmet of the slain, he discovered the smiling face of a boy of fifteen, and in the folds of his armor a piece of precious brocade containing a famous flute made out of Chinese bamboo. On the eve of the fight, the Taira had held a festival in the shadow of impending disaster, with music filling the last hours before defeat and death overcame them.

The world is not rich enough in dreams of knighthood to make light of such images of heroic serenity and refined ardor, virile intrepidity and spiritual aloofness. The fighting instincts and the aesthetic sense of the Japanese race have here been tempered by Indian mystical thought and Chinese cosmic ceremonial. It is in this spirit penetrating every detail of life in peace and war, poetry and archery, ritual and leisure that we may find the true measure of the Japanese mind. For it is not to be discovered in an abstract idea, or system, or work of art, or institution. The image and the spirit do not attain the beauty of the Greek Miracle or the transcendent Grace descending on the Christian's Passion. But they have given an example of daring blended with delicacy, firmness allied to lightness, transport to taste; an exquisite achievement the memory of which should not be allowed to be tainted by the all too common misuses to which the figure of the samuraid has often been subjected in an epoch of universal disorder and growing confusion.

If a nation has strayed far from the center of her true greatness, the task is not to make her forget her past, but to remind her of the true meaning of her deepest inspirations and her highest dreams. Thus, after a general and total expiation, the ravaged earth may be prepared for a new beginning; which an Asian nation may conceive as a return to the Way of which Lao-tse has spoken:

> In it all sharpness is blunted
> All tangles untied
> All glare tempered
> All dust smoothed.

## NOEL PERRIN
### *from*
# GIVING UP THE GUN

In early January 1855, the *U.S.S. Vincennes,* an eighteen-gun sloop
of war under Commander John Rodgers, USN, dropped anchor in the
Southern bay of Tanegashima Island, twenty miles below Kyushu, at the
southern tip of Japan. The *Vincennes* was the flagship of the newly
created United States Surveying Expedition to the North Pacific Ocean;
she had come to begin a six-month survey of Japanese coastal waters.
The Japanese were not at all eager to have foreigners prowling around
their islands, but they were powerless to prevent it. Not only did they
lack a navy, but just the year before, under the sixty-four-pound guns of
Commodore Perry's fleet, they had reluctantly signed the Treaty of
Kanagawa, the celebrated "opening of Japan." The treaty specifically
authorized this survey.

Sometime on January 9TH, Commander Rodgers led an armed
party ashore on Tanegashima to buy stores. He was poorly equipped for
business transactions, having no knowledge of Japanese and no
interpreter—having nothing, in fact, but an English-Chinese dictionary. Nevertheless, he did get his wood and water, bargaining for them
in sign language. He also got a good look at native life. The thing that
impressed him most about the islanders was their almost complete
ignorance of ordinary nineteenth-century weapons.

---

*Born in New York City in 1927 and educated at Williams, Duke, and
Cambridge, Noel Perrin early distinguished himself as a teacher and
scholar. He is currently professor of English at Dartmouth.*

"These people seemed scarcely to know the use of firearms," he noted in his report to the Secretary of the Navy. One of [my] officers caught the Japanese word for gun with which a very learned man was displaying his knowledge to his companions. It strikes an American, who from his childhood has seen children shoot, that ignorance of arms is an anomaly indicative of primitive innocence and Arcadian simplicity. We were unwilling to disturb it."

In writing his report, Commander Rodgers showed himself to be almost as Arcadianly simple as the Tanegashimans themselves. They were innocent about guns, all right, but it was an acquired innocence, not a primitive one. The ancestors of those islanders had not only used guns but had been the first in Japan to do so, and during the mid-sixteenth century guns were known all over Japan as tanegashima. Later the standard name became teppo, and this is presumably the word the American officer overheard in 1855. By then the Japanese had moved from swords to guns, and back to swords again. They had learned to cast cannon of respectable size, and had nearly—but not quite—unlearned the art again. They had fought battles in the late sixteenth century using more guns than any European army possessed.

But of all this Commander Rodgers knew nothing. He didn't even know that his very survey was repeating one done by the Spanish in 1612. Nor is his ignorance surprising. In 1855 no American knew much about Japan. The country had been closed to foreigners for nine generations. The oldest institution in Commander Rodgers's America was Harvard University, founded in 1636—and Sakoku, the Closed Country Policy, was three months older than Harvard. There was little he could have learned from books. The *Encyclopedia Americana*, if Commander Rodgers had happened to study it before sailing, would have given him four pages of of rather garbled information about Japan. The *Britannica* could have told him more, but not much. That learned work would have informed him that the country was ruled by the descendants of "Jejessama," by whom they unquestionably meant Tokugawa Ieyasu. "Jejes" is an anglicization of "Ieyasu," and "sama" is an honorific. It would be roughly comparable if a Japanese encyclopedia had said that the first president of the United States was a person named "Honorable George"—or, better yet, Honorable Joji," since this is how "george" would appear in Japanese.

As to weapons the *Britannica* would have told Rodgers that in the Japan of 1855 swords were the "principal and best weapon.... They were far superior to the Spanish blades so celebrated in Europe. A tolerably thick nail is easily cut in two without any damage to the edge."

In the matter of cutting nails, the *Britannica* was correct.

Of guns, past or present, he would have learned virtually nothing. The whole story of the Japanese adventure with guns, to the extent that it was ever known in the West, had been pretty well lost over the centuries. Even now it has not been fully recovered.

But one fact is certain. The Japanese were keen users of firearms for nearly a hundred years. They then turned back to swords and spears. Few scholars agree completely on what made them do it, or on how, having gone so far with guns, they were able to retrace their steps. Contemporary accounts are scarce.

The story begins clearly enough, however. It starts within a mile or two of where the *Vincennes* anchored in 1855, a little over three centuries earlier. The year was 1543, and a Chinese cargo ship—maybe half the size of the *Vincennes*—had come into that same small harbor. The ship's name, if it ever had one, has been lost. Concerning the one hundred men on board, though, much survives. Most of them were Chinese trader-pirates of a type common at the time. One, however, was an educated Chinese sailor whose name appears in Japanese as Goho, and three were Portuguese adventurers, also of a type common at the time. Portugal had had a colony in India since 1510, and Portuguese men and ships were beginning to appear all over the Far East. The three Portuguese rovers aboard this ship are the first Europeans known to have reached Japan.

Two of them had arquebuses and ammunition with them; and at the moment when Lord Tokitaka, the feudal master of Tamegashima, saw one of them take aim and shoot a duck, the gun enters Japanese history. Using Goho as an interpreter, Lord Tokitaka immediately made arrangements to take shooting lessons. Within a month he had bought both Portuguese guns. He is supposed to have paid a thousand taels in gold for each of them—a sum difficult to translate accurately into modern terms. But it was a lot of money. Seventy years later you could buy a good arquebus in Japan for two taels. It's somewhat as if Winchester rifles had originally sold for $10,000 each, and gradually dropped to $20. Sixty years later still, six taels a month was regarded as fair wages for a workingman.

The same day that Tokitaka bought the guns, he ordered his chief swordsmith, a man named Yatsuita Kinbei, to start making copies of them. There is a sad story that Yatsuita, unable to get the spring mechanism in the breech quite right, gave his seventeen-year-old daughter to the captain of a Portuguese ship that arrived some months later, in return for lessons in gunsmithing from the ship's armorer. Whether that is true or not, it is certain that within a year Yatsuita had made his first ten guns and that within a decade gunsmiths all over Japan were making the weapon in quantity. An order for five hundred tanegahima put in by Lord Oda Nobunaga in 1549 is still on record. So is an account of the skill with which Japanese samurai quickly learned to use guns. The book called *Teppo-ki* or *History of Guns* describes Lord Tokitaka's drill procedures in the middle 1540s. "All his vassals from far and near trained with the new weapon," says *Teppo-ki*; "and soon, out of every hundred shots they fired, many of them could hit the target a hundred times."

By 1560, the use of firearms in large battles had begun (a general in full armor died of a bullet wound that year), and fifteen years after that they were the decisive weapon in one of the great battles of Japanese history.

All this represents what would now be called a technological breakthrough. As present-day Japanese writers like to point out, the Arabs, the Indians, and the Chinese all gave firearms a try well ahead of the Japanese, but only the Japanese mastered the manufacturing process on a large scale, and really made the weapon their own.

There were good reasons for Japan's special success. The country was a soldierly one to begin with. As St. Francis Xavier wrote in 1552, after a two-year stay in Japan, "They prize and honor all that has to do with war, and there is nothing of which they are so proud as of weapons adorned with gold and silver. They always wear swords and daggers, both in and out of the house, and when they go to sleep they hang them at the bed's head. In short they value arms more than any people I have ever seen." St. Francis had seen a good many, beginning with his own warlike relatives in Spain. It is probably fair to say that military glory was the goal of every well-bred male in sixteenth-century Japan, except a handful of court nobles in Kyoto. Their goal was literary glory.

Furthermore, at the moment when firearms arrived, Japan happened to be in the middle of a century-long power struggle. The Japanese name for the period from 1490 to 1600 is Sengoku Jidai, or Age of the Country at War. Several dozen major feudal lords were vying to get military control of the country, make a puppet of the shogun (the emperor was already the shogun's puppet), and rule. Naturally, such men were interested in new weapons and in anything else that would give them an advantage.

Equally important, Japan had already reached a high level of technology. Her copper and steel were probably better, and were certainly cheaper, than any being produced in Europe at the time. Her copper, indeed was so cheap that in the seventeenth century it had begun to be exported all over the world, just as Japanese electronic equipment is now. Despite the enormously high shipping costs in that age of sailing ships, the Dutch, for example, found it profitable to send Japanese copper ten thousand miles to Amsterdam. In Japan it cost them thirty-three florins per hundred pounds, delivered to their docks in Nagasaki. In Amsterdam they sold it at fifty-nine florins—still a shade under the price of Swedish copper at sixty florins. Most Dutch founders preferred it for casting bronze cannon.

In iron and steel, Japan could undersell England. England was the recognized leader among European producers. So much was this the case that in the years just before the Spanish Armada, the Spaniards made frantic attempts to import iron cannon from England to arm the Armada with. And despite the English embargo, they did get twenty-three black-market cannon in 1583, for a total weight of 13.5 tons of iron.

But when the British East India Company opened a trade center in Japan in 1613 and tried shipping in some ingots, they got nowhere. Here is a mournful excerpt from the company's year-end trade summary for 1615: "Coromandel Steel was in no esteem; some which came in on the *Hoseander* being considered inferior to Japan iron. English iron would sell still worse, the best Japan iron being but 20 mace the picul." That is, ten shillings for 125 pounds.

Nor was Japan any mere producer of raw materials. She was a great manufacturing country, then as now. She led the world in paper products, for example. One of the Jesuit missionaries estimated that there were ten times as many kinds of paper produced in Japan as in Europe. This list extended to an Oriental version of Kleenex, a product the Japanese were making in bulk at least three centuries before Americans suppose themselves to have invented this useful item. They even exported it. An Englishman named Peter Mundy, happened to be in Macao, on the China coast, in 1637, and was much impressed when he saw some Osaka merchants' representatives using it.

"Some few Japoneses wee saw in this Citty," Mundy later wrote. "They blow their Noses with a certaine sofft and tough kind of paper which they carry aboutt them in small peeces, which having used, the Fling away as a Fillthy thing, keeping handkerchiefes of lynnen to wype their Faces." Naturally Mundy was impressed. In England, at the time, most people used their sleeves.

But the thing Japan manufactured most of was weapons. For two hundred years she had been the world's leading exporter of arms. The whole Far East used Japanese equipment. In 1493, admittedly an exceptional year, 67,000 swords were shipped to China alone. A hundred and fourteen years later, a visiting Italian merchant named Francesco Carletti noted a brisk export trade in "weapons of all kinds, both offensive and defensive, of which this country has, I suppose, a more abundant supply than any other country in the world." Even as late as 1614, when things were about to change, a single trading vessel from the small port of Hirado sailed to Siam with the following principal items of cargo: fifteen suits of export armor at four and a half taels the suit, eighteen short swords at half a tael each, twenty-eight short swords at a fifth of a tael, ten guns for four taels, ten guns at three taels, and fifteen guns at two and a half taels.

These were top quality weapons, too. Especially the swords. A Japanese sword blade is about the sharpest thing there is. It is designed to cut through tempered steel, and it can. Tolerably thick nails don't even make an interesting challenge. In the 1560s one of the Jesuit fathers visited a particularly militant Buddhist temple—the Monastery of the Original Vow, at Ishiyama. He had expected to find the monks all wearing swords, but he had not expected to find the swords quite so formidable. They could cut through armor, he reported, "as easily as a sharp knife cuts a tender rump." Another observer, the Dutchman Arnold Montanus, wrote that "Their Faulchions or Scimeters were so well wrought, and excellently temper'd, that they will cut our *European* blades asunder, like Flags or Rushes. . . ."

Stories of wonder weapons and superhuman feats abound in sixteenth-century literature, and most of them now seem merely to show what good liars (or how credulous) our ancestors were. They believed in mermaids and the philosopher's stone, too. But Montanus's story can be checked, and has been. The distinguished twentieth-century arms collector George Cameron Stone once took part in a test in which a sixteenth-century Japanese sword was used to cut a modern European sword in two. And there exists in Japan right now a film showing a machine-gun barrel being sliced in half by a sword from the forge of the great fifteenth-century maker, Kanemoto II. If this seems improbable, one must remember that smiths like Kanemoto hammered and folded and rehammered, day after day, until a sword blade contained something like four million layers of finely forged steel. (Or, rather, until the *edge* of the blade did. The rest was of much softer steel. A whole blade made like the edge would be as brittle as glass, and shatter at the first blow. This technique of varying the hardness was one that European smiths never perfected, which is why European swords were never as sharp.) People who could make weapons of this quality were not going to have much trouble adapting their technology to firearms.

Finally. Age of the Country at War or not, Japan was in booming good health. During the sixteenth century it had a larger population than any European country: twenty-five million people, compared to sixteen million in France, seven million in Spain, and four and a half million in England, and maybe a million in what is now the United States. Agriculture was flourishing. So was the building industry. A Jesuit named Luis Frois saw Lord Oda Nobunaga's newly built castle at Gifu in 1569, and reacted the way his colleague Gaspar Vileda did to the monks' swords. "I wish I was a good architect, or had the gift of being able to describe places well," Father Frois wrote his superior, "because I assure you emphatically, that among all the palaces and houses which I have seen in Portugal, India, and Japan, I never yet saw anything comparable to this in freshness, elegance, sumptuousness, and cleanliness."

As for education, the Buddhist monks maintained five "universities," the smallest of them larger than Oxford or Cambridge at the time. And while no exact statistics are available, there is every reason to believe that the general literacy rate was higher in Japan in 1543 than in any European country whatsoever.

Interest in the arts ran high, too. Career military officers—that is to say, members of the bushi class—were expected to read and quote the classics between battles, while in 1588 the senior military commander in the whole country gave a series of poem parties. A timely poem could sometimes even save a man's life. During a suspected rebellion, for example, a court noble named Lord Tameakira was being held for questioning by the military governor of Suruga, a tough samurai. It was believed that Lord Tameakira knew the whole plot, and that a little judicious torture would make him reveal it. While they were building the fire, Lord Tameakira requested an inkstone and paper. Everybody supposed that he was going to write out a confession, and the paper was promptly brought. Instead he composed a poem.

> It is beyond belief!
> I am questioned not on the art of poetry
> But on the things of this transient world!

The military governor and his staff were so impressed by the elegance of this response that they released Lord Tameakira unharmed.

That incident occurred well before the arival of guns. But interest in literature had, if anything, increased during the interval. Indeed, Father Organtino Gnecchi, still another missionary stationed in Japan in the late sixteenth century, thought that the general level of culture (religion excepted) was higher than back home in Italy. Italy was, of course, at the height of the Renaissance. Don Rodrigo Vivero y Velasco, the retiring Spanish governor of the Philippines, came to much the same conclusion after a visit in 1610. This was not the conclusion that Spaniards came to, for example, in Peru.

## FRANCIS L. HAWKS
*from*
# NARRATIVE OF THE EXPEDITION OF AN AMERICAN SQUADRON TO THE CHINA SEAS AND JAPAN

While contemplating these substantial evidences of Japanese generosity, the attention of all was suddenly riveted upon a body of monstrous fellows, who tramped down the beach like so many huge elephants. They were professional wrestlers and formed part of the retinue of the princes, who kept them for their private amusement and for public entertainment. They were some twenty-five in number, and were men enormously tall, and immense in weight. Their scant costume, which was merely a colored cloth about the loins, adorned with fringes and emblazoned with the armorial bearings of the prince to whom each belonged, revealed their gigantic proportions in all the bloated fullness of fat and breadth of muscle. Their proprietors seemed proud of them, and were careful to show their points to the greatest advantage before our astonished countrymen. Some two or three of these monsters were the most famous wrestlers in Japan, and ranked as the champion Tom Cribs and Hyers of the land. Koyanagi, the reputed bully of the capital, was one of them, and paraded himself with the

---

*When Commodore Perry steamed into Japanese waters, he took with him an official historian for the expedition, Francis L. Hawks, D.D., LL.D. (1798–1866). The Treaty of Kanagawa (1854) opened Japan to the West; and Hawks' Narrative, concerned largely with the diplomatic formalities, became by default the first limited account of Japanese manners widely available in America. The following excerpt, remarkable more for its condescension than for its accuracy, is no doubt the first description of Sumo ever recorded in English.*

■ 37

conscious pride of superior immensity and strength. He was especially brought to the Commodore, that he might examine his massive form. The commissioners insisted that the monstrous fellow should be minutely inspected, that the hardness of his well-rounded muscles should be felt, and that the fatness of his cushioned frame should be tested by the touch. The Commodore accordingly attempted to grasp his immense arm, which he found as solid as it was huge, and then passed his hand over the monstrous neck, which fell in folds of massive flesh, like the dewlap of a prize ox. As some surprise was naturally expressed at this wondrous exhibition of animal development, the monster himself gave a grunt expressive of his flattered vanity.

They were all so immense in flesh that they appeared to have lost their distinctive features, and seemed to be only twenty-five masses of fat. Their eyes were barely visible through a long perspective of socket. The prominence of their noses was lost in the puffiness of their bloated cheeks. Their heads were almost set directly on their bodies, with merely folds of flesh where the neck and chin were usually found. Their great size, however, was due more to the development of muscle than to the deposition of fat, for, although they were evidently well fed, they were not less well exercised and capable of great feats of strength. As a preliminary exhibition of the power of these men, the princes set them to removing the sacks of rice to a convenient place on the shore for shipping. Each of the sacks weighed not less than one hundred twenty-five pounds, and there were only a couple of the wrestlers who did not carry each two sacks at a time. They bore the sacks on their right shoulder, lifting the first from the ground and adjusting it without help, but obtaining aid for raising of the second. One man carried a sack suspended from his teeth. Another, taking one in his arms, turned repeated somersaults as he held it, apparently with as much ease as if his tons of flesh had been only so much gossamer, and his load a feather.

After this preliminary display, the commissioners proposed that the Commodore and his party retire to the treaty house, where they would have an opportunity of seeing the wrestlers exhibit their professional feats. The wrestlers themselves were most carefully provided for, having constantly about them a number of attendants, who were always at hand to supply them with fans, which they often required, and to assist them in dressing and undressing. While at rest they were ordinarily clothed in richly adorned robes of the usual Japanese fashion, but when exercising, they were stripped naked, with the exception of the cloth about the loins. After their performance with the sacks of rice, their servitors spread upon the huge frames of the wrestlers their rich garments and led them up to the treaty house.

A circular space of some twelve feet in diameter had been enclosed within a ring, and the ground carefully broken up and smoothed in front of the building. In the portico, divans covered with red cloth were arranged for the Japanese commissioners, the Commodore, his officers, and their various attendants. The bands from the ships were also present, and enlivened the intervals during the performance with occasional lively strains. As soon as the spectators had taken their seats, the naked wrestlers were brought out into the ring. The whole group, being divided into two opposing parties, tramped heavily backward and forward, looking defiance at each other, but not engaging in any contest. Their object was merely to parade their points, to give the beholders, as it were, an opportunity to form an estimate of their comparative powers, and to make up their betting books. They soon retired behind some screens placed for the purpose, where all, with the exception of two, were again clothed in full dress and took their position on seats in front of the spectators.

The two who had been reserved out of the band, on the signal being given by the heralds who were seated on opposite sides, presented themselves. They came in, one after the other, from behind the screen, and walked with slow and deliberate steps, as became such huge animals, into the center of the ring. Then they ranged themselves, one against the other, at a distance of a few yards. They crouched for a while, eyeing each other with a wary look, as if each were watching for a chance to catch his antagonist off his guard. As the spectator looked on these overfed monsters, whose animal natures had been so carefully and successfully developed, and as he watched them glaring with brutal ferocity at each other, ready to exhibit the cruel instincts of a savage nature, it was easy for him to lose all sense of their being human creatures, and to persuade himself that he was beholding a couple of brute beasts thirsting for one another's blood. They were, in fact, like a pair of fierce bulls, whose nature they had not only acquired, but even their look and movements. As they continued to eye each other they stamped the ground heavily, pawing as it were with impatience, and then stooping their huge bodies, they grasped handfuls of dirt and flung it with an angry toss over their backs, or rubbed it impatiently between their giant palms, or under their stout shoulders. They now crouched low, still keeping their eyes fixed upon each other and watching every movement, until, in an instant, they had both simultaneously heaved their massive forms in opposing force, body to body, with a shock that might have stunned an ox. The equilibrium of their monstrous frames was hardly disturbed by the concussion, the effect of which was but barely visible in the quiver of the hanging flesh of their bodies. As they came together, they had thrown their brawny arms about each other, and were now entwined in a desperate struggle, each striving with all his enormous strength to throw his adversary. Their great muscles rose with the distinct outline of the sculptured form of a colossal Hercules. Their bloated countenances swelled up with gushes of blood which seemed ready to burst through the skin of their reddened faces. Their huge bodies palpitated with emotion as the struggle continued. At last, one of the antagonists fell, with his immense weight, heavily upon the ground, and being declared vanquished, was assisted to his feet and conducted from the ring.

The scene was now somewhat varied by a change in the kind of contest between two succeeding wrestlers. The heralds, as before, summoned the antagonists. One, having taken his place in the ring, assumed an attitude of defense with one leg in advance as if to steady himself. His bent body, with his head lowered, was placed in position, as if to receive an attack. Immediately after, in rushed the other, bellowing as loud as a bull. Making at once for the man in the ring, he dashed, with his head lowered and thrust forward, against the head of his opponent, who bore the shock with the steadiness of a rock, although the blood streamed down his face from his bruised forehead, which had been struck in the encounter. This maneuver was repeated again and again, the same one acting always as the opposing, and the other as the resisting, force. Thus they kept up their brutal contest until their foreheads were besmeared with blood, and the flesh on their chests rose in great swollen tumors, from the repeated blows. This disgusting exhibition did not terminate until the whole twenty-five had, successively, in pairs, displayed their immense powers and savage qualities.

From the brutal performance of these wrestlers, the Americans turned with pride to the exhibition—to which the Japanese commissioners were now in their turn invited—of the telegraph and the railroad. It was a happy contrast, with a higher civilization presented, to the disgusting display on the part of the Japanese officials. In place of a show of brute animal force, there was a triumphant revelation of the success of science and enterprise, to a partially enlightened people. The Japanese took great delight in again seeing the rapid movement of the Lilliputian locomotive. One of the scribes of the commissioners took his seat upon the car, while the engineer stood upon the tender, feeding the furnace with one hand, and directing the diminutive engine with the other. Crowds of Japanese gathered around, and looked upon the repeated circlings of the train with unabated pleasure and surprise, unable to repress a shout of delight at each blast of the steam whistle. The telegraph, with its wonders, though witnessed before, still created renewed interest, and all the beholders were unceasing in their expressions of curiosity and astonishment. The agricultural instruments having been explained to the commissioners by Dr. Morrow, a formal delivery of the telegraph, the railway, and other articles, which made up the list of American presents, ensued. The Prince of Mema-saki had been delegated by his coadjutors ceremoniously to accept, and Captain Adams appointed by the Commodore to deliver, the gifts. Each performed his separate functions by an interchange of suitable compliments and some half dozen stately bows. After this, a detachment of marines from the squadron were put through their various evolutions, drills, etc., while the bands furnished martial music. The Japanese commissioners seemed to take a very great interest in this military display, and expressed themselves much gratified at the soldierly air and excellent discipline of the men. This closed performances of the day. The commissioners having accepted an invitation from the Commodore to dine with him on the twenty-seventh, the Japanese retired to the treaty house, and the Americans returned to the ships. The Japanese presents were all boxed and sent, together with the rice and charcoal, on board the storeship *Supply*. After being duly addressed to the proper department of the government, they were stored away for future shipment.

## E.J. HARRISON
### *from*
# THE CULT OF COLD STEEL

The Japanese sword has been called "the living soul of the samu-rai," and the etiquette connected with its handling was of the most minute description. A very trustworthy outline of the more important rules occurs in *Fu-so Mimi Bukuro: A Budget of Japanese Notes*, by the late C. Pfoundes, a Japanese scholar and investigator whose work is too little known, on the principle, no doubt, that a prophet is without honor in his own country. The volume mentioned comprises a series of articles contributed to the *Japan Mail* of Yokohama and republished in book form in 1875. From a copy in my possession I extract the following:

> To touch another's weapon, or to come into collision with the sheath, was a dire offense, and to enter a friend's house without leaving the sword outside was a breach of friendship. Those whose position justified the accompaniment of an attendant invariably left the sword in his charge at the entrance or, if alone, it was usually laid down at the entrance. If removed inside, it was invariably done by the host's servants, and then not touched with the bare hand, but with a silk napkin kept for the purpose, and the sword was placed upon a sword-rack in the place of honor near the guest

*The first Caucasian to become third dan black belt in judo, E.J. Harrison (1883–1971) spent many years in the Orient as a British diplomat and journalist. His books on the martial arts published between 1912 and 1959 were pioneering works, and he remained an active judoka at the London Budokwai until his death at 88.*

and treated with all the politeness due to an honored visitor who would resent a discourtesy. The long sword, if two were worn, was withdrawn, sheathed, from the girdle with the right hand—an indication of friendship, as it could not be drawn and used thus—never by the left hand, or placed on the left side, except when in immediate danger of attack. To exhibit a naked weapon was a gross insult, unless a gentleman wished to show his friends his collection. To express a wish to see a sword was not usual, unless a blade of great value was in question, when a request to be shown it would be a compliment the happy possessor appreciated. The sword would then be handled with the back toward the guest, the edge turned towards the owner and the hilt to the left, the guest wrapping the hilt either in the little silk napkin always carried by gentlemen in their pocketbooks or in a sheet of clean paper. The weapon was drawn from the scabbard and admired inch by inch, but not to the full length, unless the owner pressed his guest to do so, when, with much apology, the sword was entirely drawn and held away from the other persons present. After being admired it would, if apparently necessary, be carefully wiped with a special cloth, shealthed and returned to the owner as before.

Considering the exaggerated veneration in which the native katana has been held from the earliest times it is not surprising that the occupation of a swordsmith should in feudal days have been regarded as an honorable profession the members of which were men of gentle blood. In this context the following comment taken from Lord Redesdale's *Tales of Old Japan* may interest my readers:

In a country where trade is looked down upon as degrading, it is strange to find this single exception to the general rule. The traditions of the craft are many and curious. During the most critical moment of forging of the sword, when the steel edge is being welded into the body of the iron blade, it is a custom which still obtains among old-fashioned armorers to put on the cap and robes worn by Kuge, or nobles of the Mikado's court, and, closing the doors of the workshop, to labor in secrecy and freedom from interruption, the half gloom adding to the mystery of the operation. Sometimes the occasion is even invested with a certain sanctity, a tasselled cord of straw, such is hung before the shrines of the Kami, or native gods of Japan, being suspended between two bamboo poles in the forge, which for the nonce is converted into a holy altar.

In the hands of an expert swordsman the best blades will cut through the dead bodies of three men, laid one upon the other, at a blow. "The swords of the Shogun used to be tried upon the corpses of executed criminals; the public headsman was entrusted with the duty, and for a 'nose medicine,' or bribe of two bus (about three shillings), would substitute the weapon of the private individual for that of his lord."

It is equally characteristic that the technical skill and imagination of many of the country's leading artists and craftsmen should have been lavished upon the adornment of this deadly weapon. Thus its various accessories were often cunningly wrought in metals and alloys. Of these latter the best known are shibu-ichi and shakudo, both formed of a basis of copper with varying admixture of silver and gold. Specially noteworthy among these articles, and dear to the heart of countless foreign curio collectors are the tsuba, or guard, and the menuki—small ornaments fixed to one side of the hilt and held in place by the silk cord which binds together the various parts of the handle. The price of a sword by a famous maker would in feudal days, which means well into the nineteenth century, reach a very high sum. Thus a Japanese noble would be found girding a sword the blade of which unmounted was worth in our currency from 200 to 300 pounds, and the mounting, rich in cunning metal work, would be of proportionate value. Weapons of this sort were handed down as heirlooms from father to son and became almost a part of the wearer's own self.

One blow dealt by an expert swordsman, if the enemy failed to ward it off, was usually sufficient to dispose of the business at hand. More than one foreigner has fallen a victim to the terrible "upper cut" of the Japanese assassin. The Anglo-Saxon understanding of the term "upper cut," as applied to the "noble art," is a blow the starting point of which is the striker's hip and the objective of which is generally the point of his opponent's jaw. Should he succeed in the laudable ambition of getting it in, his adversary, nine times out of ten, is so struck by the force of the argument that he quietly subsides. The Japanese upper cut was based upon similar dynamic principles, and was even more effective in its results. The sword was drawn from the scabbard with a long, sweeping motion, but instead of losing valuable time by raising the weapon above the head for a downward stroke—a nashi-ware, or "pear splitter"—the assailant continued the movement from left to right in an upward diagonal direction, his object being to slash his victim open from the right hip to the left shoulder. Of course the force of the blow might be insufficient to carry out this playful little intention, but unless parried early in the day it generally deprived the victim of all interest in the subsequent proceedings. Major Baldwin and Lieutenant Bird, both of H.M. 20th Regiment, were thus slain near Kamakura on 21st November 1864, by two Japanese samurai; in the former case the blow was delivered with such tremendous force as to sever the spinal cord. These murderous attacks upon the intruding alien were dictated by what is known in Japanese as jo-i ("the barbarian expelling spirit"), and it is many years since the last crime of this nature was perpetrated.

But although the sword is no longer worn save by military, naval, and police officials, it would be incorrect to say that the taste for cold steel has entirely disappeared. Even today, when deeds of violence are committed, the murderer usually employs a sword or dagger where an American or a European would in all probability prefer a firearm. Nor is the more disinterested and fanatical recourse to bloodshed a thing of the past. There have been so far during the Meiji era, which commenced in 1868, no fewer than six political assassinations by Japanese. The first to fall was a noted scholar named Yokoi Shonan, who was slain on 5th January, 1868; the second was Omura Masajiro, Vice-Minister of War, who perished in September of the same year; the third was Hirosawa Saneomi, a Privy Councillor, who met his fate on 9th January, 1871; the fourth was the celebrated Okubo Toshimitsu, Prime Minister, who was attacked in his palanquin and foreshortened, so to speak, on 14th May, 1878; the fifth was Mori Arimori, struck down in his own residence on 11th February, 1889; and the sixth was Hoshi Toru, whose sensational taking off on 21st June, 1901, profoundly shocked the capital at the time. The details of this tragedy are so remarkable and characteristic as to justify their reconstruction from the local newspaper files of the day.

Hoshi Toru, one of the most powerful and corrupt politicians of Japan, was sitting in a room of the Tokyo City Hall on Friday afternoon, 21st June, 1901, after having attended a meeting of the council of which he was a member, when the door suddenly opened, and a man, entering quickly, approached him and said, as afterwards appeared, "Do you repent?"

To this Hoshi replied briefly, "Stand back!" when with a movement so rapid and unexpected that none of the other persons present could possibly intervene, the newcomer drew a short sword from under his Japanese garments and stabbed Hoshi no fewer than six times in almost as many seconds. The *Japan Mail* of that day records that the first thrust pierced the victim's right side and reached the lung; the second entered the left side; the third was on the back of the head and laid bare the brain; the fourth was through the back of the lungs; and the fifth in the stomach. After delivering the fifth blow the assassin held Hoshi up to in order to inflict the remaining wounds, the sixth of which was a less serious cut to the shoulder. Immediately on being released the unfortunate Hoshi sank to the floor and expired within five minutes. The assassin offered no serious resistance and was quickly seized by the horrified witnesses of this desperate deed. He proved to be one Iba Sotaro, a man of about fifty, who had until then borne an unblemished character. His family had for generations acted as fencing masters to the Tokugawa Court, and his father, Iba Gumbei, was looked upon as one of the best swordsmen of his day. The assassin himself had been noted as a fencer, but with the dawn of the new era he had turned his attention to more profitable pursuits and had studied English and various branches of science to such good purpose that he was appointed tutor to Viscount Ogasawara. He later founded a school and threw himself enthusiastically into the work of teaching. Agriculture and finance were also among the subjects of which he made a speciality. He was honored with several important offices in business and educational circles. It was, in fact, his connection with the latter which had led to the growth of the strange conviction that upon him devolved the sacred duty of removing one whose influence he regarded as highly pernicious to political and public morality. This resolution was strengthened by the knowledge that his skill in fence was such as to ensure the successful accomplishment of his plan; and, indeed, none but a perfect master of his weapon could have inflicted upon Hoshi in the same brief space of time six wounds of the terrible nature already described.

On searching him the police found a zankanjo, or written statement of reasons for slaying a traitor and vindication of the assassin's deed, in which he set forth the motives of his crime. In this the writer explained that the elevation of a man so depraved as Hoshi to a position of such responsibility as President of the Tokyo Educational Society could not be contemplated with equanimity, and he—Iba Sotaro—had therefore determined to effect his removal.

> "Nothing," he declared, "could be more serious than the fact that this felon should be in a position to demoralize and corrupt the administration of Tokyo and destroy the morality of the citizens... that he should bring misfortune and shame to all, from sovereign to subject, and that, while his accomplices in bribery and corruption were exposed and punished, he alone should show a brazen face and should continue with increased vigor his course of insatiate

plunder, spreading the poison of evil to all classes and destroying the morals of youth. For many generations my family has acted as instructors of swordsmanship in Tokyo. I myself, indifferent as my accomplishments are, have devoted myself to the cause of education and have sought to promote the spirit of learning and of military science. I have also felt it my duty to spare no effort for the improvement of agriculture and the manufacturing industry, though I am well aware that my abilities are an indifferent qualification for such a task."

The writer added evidence to prove that he had had no personal dealings with his victim and bore him no personal grudge whatever. He concluded:

If I now brave the pain of parting from my wife and children—pain as cruel as that of being torn asunder—if I face the voice of public opinion, if I ruin myself for the sake of killing this finished villain, it is because I cannot endure to see such an arch rascal as Hoshi Toru pursuing with fresh vigor his evil courses, as President of the Tokyo Educational Society, teaching the youth to be corrupt and crooked, introducing demoralization and disorder into the administration of Tokyo, and bringing misfortune upon all from the Emperor downwards. Thinking men, I ask you to appreciate and sympathize with the sincerity of my sentiments.

A copy of the foregoing document had been posted to the *Nippon*—a leading native organ—before Iba proceeded to the fatal rendezvous, and he had also taken the added precaution of divorcing his wife. The short sword with which the deed was committed had long been a precious heirloom in the assassin's family, and so great was the strength employed in driving it home that the point was actually broken.

I make no apology for quoting at some length a document of such extraordinary psychological and racial interest. Iba Sotaro was clearly a man of otherwise irreproachable moral character, the superior of his victim, and in full possession of his senses. The crime was inspired by purely disinterested motives and carried out with a perfect appreciation of the consequences. But let us try to imagine an analogous incident in London or New York. If, say, a man of comparable standing were to drop into the County Hall and in broad daylight cut down the Chairman of the County Council with a cavalry saber subsequently explaining that he had felt compelled to act in order to make a terrible example of a man whose personal reputation left a good deal to be desired, we should be furnished with a case not by any means unlike that which I have attempted to describe. And when I add that public sympathy was freely extended to the assassin and that he was sentenced to penal servitude for life, it would seem that there is still some little difference between the ethical standards of Occident and Orient.

No account of this sanguinary incident would be complete without a few words devoted to the character and career of the victim. Hoshi Toru was born in 1850 and was therefore fifty-one years of age at the time of his death. He early applied himself to literary pursuits and in 1872 was appointed superintendent of customs at Kanagawa. He earned an unenviable notoriety among foreigners by his action in issuing orders to the police to prevent them from making use of private landing-places. The affair was ventilated in the courts and the superintendent exposed to even more unfriendly criticism because in one of his dispatches he spoke of Queen Victoria as *Nyo-o* instead of *Nyo-tei*. The former simply means queen whereas the latter term is the proper designation of an empress. Sir Harry Parkes, the "little tiger" of British Far East diplomacy, exalted this discourtesy into a diplomatic question and the offender was forced to seek fresh occupation. In 1874 he went to London where he studied three years and obtained his diploma as a barrister of the Middle Temple. On returning to Japan in 1877 he went in for politics and in 1879 helped to establish the Liberal party. He also made one or two excursions into journalism of a somewhat advanced type until the government discouraged further efforts by suspending his publication. Then a speech of his landed him in jail for a session on the quaint charge—very common in Japan—of bringing officials into contempt, although it often appears to an impartial onlooker that a good many bloated Barnacles of the Circumlocution Offices of East and West need no extraneous aid in arriving at that delectable condition.

After his release he still persisted in his career of agitation and in 1887 was expelled from Tokyo under the provisions of the Peace Preservation Law. Two years later he benefited by the declaration of amnesty which accompanied the promulgation of the Constitution and so returned and was elected Member of the House of Representatives for Tokyo prefecture and chosen President of the House, an office which he filled in the most able manner. His next appointment was that of Minister to Washington, and it was while thus engaged, if tradition does not lie, that he made a special study of the American political "boss" with a view to introducing his methods as a private monopoly into Japan. He returned in 1898 and amassed wealth with such unprecedented rapidity as to encourage the belief that "boodle" was in no small measure responsible. He helped Marquis Ito to organize the Seiyukai and it was at a garden party given at the Imperial Hotel, Tokyo, during 1900, to celebrate the occasion, that I first made the personal acquaintance of this extraordinary man. He was of large physique for a Japanese and credited with the possession of herculean strength, but his face was not by any manner of means prepossessing. Many of his more candid countrymen, indeed, were in the habit of instituting comparisons between Hoshi and the common toad, not at all complimentary to Hoshi. He seemed destined to arouse in the breasts of his contemporaries the extremes of two emotions—hatred and admiration—the former being exemplified by the *Mainichi* newspaper in a campaign of scurrilous abuse to which even the "yellowest" of "yellow" journals in the United States rarely descends in the heat of a party campaign. He was freely accused of every kind of bribery and corruption as a member of the municipal administration of the capital, but the courts exonerated him and he continued to wield despotic authority over the then Marquis Ito, as the *de facto* leader of the latter's new party until the sword of Iba Sotaro cut him off in the heyday of his triumph.

By a grim coincidence the two most striking figures on this memorable occasion fell at the hands of the assassins, but as statesmen and patriots it would be an insult to the glorious memory of Prince Ito to search for points of resemblance. Prince Ito had his enemies and many of them, but while those enemies during his lifetime never scrupled to calumniate him whenever opportunity offered, it is a noteworthy fact that never once was he seriously accused of pecuniary improbity. In a position to have piled up millions had he wished, it is no secret that he died a comparatively poor man, and that more than once during his life his friend and master the emperor paid his debts. It was at this same garden party that I was introduced to the then Marquis Ito and Marquis Yamagata, but strangely enough both these famous Genro, or Elder Statesmen, showed themselves absurdly reticent and neglected to make me the recipient of any State secrets. Some newspapermen who subsequently met the former, then a prince, appear to have been more fortunate in this respect. In one case at least it is recorded that the Prince, at some public function, drew the favored foreign scribe into a convenient alcove and there, in obedience to that instinct which at times irresistibly compels confession, imparted to his flattered *vis-à-vis* his hopes and fears and ambitions for the future. His confidant showed the right spirit by declining to be equally communicative for benefit of the general public, for he felt he had been made the repository of weighty confidences the premature disclosure of which might shake the empire to its foundations. Thus we shall never know why a statesman notoriously prone to keep his own counsel should suddenly have taken it into his head to unburden his soul in a *tête-à-tête* with a foreigner. Perhaps if I were a trifle more imaginative I could recall one or two momentous utterances for my special benefit on the occasion of my meeting with the Marquis, but somehow they seem to have slipped my memory.

Returning to Hoshi Toru. At the time of his assassination a correspondent writing to the *Japan Mail* described him as "a type of Tammany Hall with a cynicism which even the New York bosses would not dare to show publicly. And yet there was another side of his singularly complex character. He had many intellectual tastes. His private library contained no fewer than 100,000 volumes, and he read not only English but Latin, Italian, French and Spanish, and had begun to study German shortly before his death."

An anecdote which well illustrates his unscrupulousness in an amusing and less vicious light than usual was one told me by the late editor and proprietor of the now defunct *Japan Herald* of Yokohama, Mr. H. Brooke, who died very many years ago. Mr. Brooke, before he came to Japan, had had considerable political experience in the colony of Victoria, where he had held for some time the portfolio of Lands and Works, and having made the acquaintance of Hoshi in the early days of the Japanese Liberal Party was invited by that gentleman to attend a convivial gathering of that body and to honor the assemblage with a speech. Mr. Brooke, nothing loath, consented, and after the sake had been permitted to circulate freely rose to his feet amid acclamation. As he could not speak Japanese he had brought an interpreter with him, but Mr. Hoshi undertook to act in his stead and since Mr. Brooke was well aware that Mr. Hoshi spoke English fluently he unsuspectingly acquiesced in that arrangement. The *modus operandi* was for Mr. Brooke to reel off a few hundred words or so in a batch and then to pause while Mr. Hoshi turned them into the vernacular. Mr. Brooke knew full well that these newly fledged Liberals were not in good odor with the Government and that there were police spies in the vicinity eagerly awaiting a pretext for interference, and he therefore purposely refrained from giving utterance to any save the most conventional sentiments. Imagine, then, his surprise when, as Mr. Hoshi proceeded with his interpretation, the audience burst forth into thunders of applause. He remarked to Mr. Hoshi at the close of his oration that the enthusiasm displayed seemed out of all proportion to the merits of the speech, but Mr. Hoshi smiled deprecatingly and assured Mr. Brooke that they had esteemed it an honor and a privilege to listen to the views of so experienced a politician. They parted, and Mr. Brooke returned to the hotel with his interpreter who, on arrival, addressed him as follows:

"I beg your pardon, sir, but Mr. Hoshi made a false interpretation of your speech. He did not say what you said."

"What on earth for?" inquired Mr. Brooke, who had had his suspicions.

"He probably feared," rejoined the Japanese, "that if he made a radical anti-government speech himself he would be arrested, but as the police spies do not understand English they thought he was translating what you said, and so they would not interfere. Mr. Hoshi is a very cunning man!"

Mr. Brooke was of a choleric temperamant, and when he realized how he had been used to serve Mr. Hoshi's turn he referred to the founder of the political party in periods not strictly Pickwickian. But his troubles were not yet over. His supposed speech, reproduced by the newspaper reporters from Mr. Hoshi's Japanese version, appeared the next morning in cold, ideographic type, and evoked from the editor of the *Japan Mail* of strong Japanese official sympathies a scathing criticism in which Mr. Brooke was roundly condemned for having thus taken advantage of his immunity from the laws applicable in these cases in order to deliver a political harangue of an inflammatory character! Mr. Brooke's only witness being his interpreter he chose to grin and bear the soft impeachment rather than make a fuss and confess how neatly he had been exploited by the ingenious Hoshi. Nor, so far as I can recollect, did he wear crape when he heard of Mr. Hoshi's tragic finale.

Perhaps I may be forgiven for including in this chapter a short account of quite an exciting personal experience which brought me far too close for my liking to the "sword of Old Japan." This experience befell me shortly after the treaty of peace between Japan and Russia, signed at Portsmouth, U.S.A. on 23rd August, 1905 and ratified on 5th November, 1905, brought to a close the state of war between these two belligerents. The terms of this treaty proved so unpopular in Japan that widespread rioting broke out by way of protest, more especially in Tokyo where huge mobs fairly ran amok and carried their depredations so far as to burn down many police stations in the capital. These happenings were naturally grist to the mill of an enterprising newspaper correspondent, as I then was, ever avid for a good "story" and so I kept a sharp lookout for further developments of this dangerous situation.

Then one day I spotted a gang of young bloods evidently heading in the direction of the offices of the leading Government organ called the *Kokumin Shimbun* (People's Newspaper), and so in bound duty attached myself to it. Far from resenting my presence the crowd welcomed it vociferously and so more or less in step and at the double we finally reached our objective. Meanwhile other groups of rioters had arrived from other directions and an angry howling mob had gathered outside the *Kokumin* building bent on setting fire to the premises for which purpose petrol-soaked masses of straw and other inflammable material were hurled through the ground-floor windows. It was evidently hoped in this way to destroy or damage the printing presses on the ground floor.

Then suddenly I heard the cry go up, "Batto shita!" meaning "Swords are drawn!" and almost simultaneously from an open doorway four thick-set Japanese in foreign garb and each brandishing a naked katana dashed out to repel the attackers. Even today I can recall the truly sinister swish made by these icy blades as they cut through the air. The swordsmen were apparently members of the soshi (literally "strong man") strong-arm physical force fraternity, more crudely swashbucklers, doubtless hired by the newspaper administration to defend the premises in case of mob attack. The crowd stampeded back in panic at sight of these deadly weapons wielded savagely by the powerful arms of the defenders but not before their keen edges had inflicted some nasty wounds upon several in the front ranks. I noticed one man with blood streaming from a gash in the neck; another had a hand severed at the wrist as he raised his arm with an almost reflex action to ward off a blow; and a third seemed to have lost his nose! the four soshi were slashing recklessly right and left and only the swift retreat of the crowd averted more serious casualties. As for myself, I don't mind admitting that the sight and sound of these swords caused a distinct subsidence in the region of my inadequately developed seika tanden. I realized only too well that my grasp of aiki was imperfect and so deeming discretion to be the better part of valor I bolted for dear life. Then in my hurried retreat I slipped on the curb and fell on one knee expecting any second to become the recipient of the unwelcome attentions of one or more of the soshi swordsmen. However, I got up and took refuge in a convenient alleyway from which point of vantage I surveyed the field of battle now in the undisputed possession of the four soshi who swaggered to and fro still flourishing their blood-stained blades.

But worse was to follow. From an upper window an elderly Japanese looked out, took aim with a revolver and fired. The bullet pierced the brain of a young man in the front rank and he fell dead on the spot. Then soon afterwards a strong force of police arrived on the scene. Using their unsheathed swords they quickly got the situation in hand, drove back the crowd and cordoned off the *Kokumin* building, but not before the ground floor had been partially wrecked. Thereafter martial law was declared and the troops were called out to reinforce the police. Before order could be completely restored throughout the capital many fatalities took place, but with these this record is not concerned. Incidentally, however, in due course the Japanese who had shot and killed the young man was indicted for his act, but thanks to the quaint workings of Japanese jurisprudence and although formally found guilty, the nominal sentence of a year's imprisonment passed upon him was postponed indefinitely!

In closing this incomplete chapter on political assassination I should like to say that in addition to the crimes usually consummated there have been numerous unsuccessful attempts, notably the attack on Count Okuma in 1888, when in consequence of popular excitement evoked by his treaty revision proposals a fanatic hurled a bomb at his coach and inflicted injuries upon his leg which necessitated its amputation, and the attempted murder of the late Tsar, the Crown Prince of Russia, by a mad policeman at Otsu.

# JIUJUTSU

Man at his birth is supple and weak; at his death, firm and strong. So it is with all things. . . . Firmness and strength are the concomitants of death; softness and weakness, the concomitants of life. Hence he who relies on his own strength shall not conquer.—*Tao-Te-King*

I

There is one building in the grounds of the Government College quite different in structure from the other edifices. Except that it is furnished with horizontally sliding glass windows instead of paper ones, it might be called a purely Japanese building. It is long, broad, and of one story; and it contains but a single huge room, of which the elevated floor is thickly cushioned with one hundred mats. It has a Japanese name, too—Zuihokwan—signifying "The Hall of Our Holy Country"; and the Chinese characters which form that name were painted upon the small tablet above its entrance by the hand of a Prince of the Imperial blood. Within there is no furniture; nothing but another tablet

*Translator, journalist, professor, author, and exotic, Lafcadio Hearn (1850–1904) sailed for Japan in 1890 hoping to interest* Harper's *magazine in his dispatches. He so successfully adapted to Oriental life that he married a Japanese woman in 1891, held the chair of English literature first at the government college at Kumato and later at the Imperial University of Tokyo itself, and died under his Japanese name of Koizumi Yakumo.*

and two pictures hanging upon the wall. One of the pictures represents the famous "White Tiger Band" of seventeen brave boys who voluntarily sought death for loyalty's sake in the civil war. The other is a portrait in oil of the aged and much beloved Professor of Chinese, Akizuki of Aidzu, a noted warrior in his youth, when it required much more to make a soldier and a gentleman than it does today. And the tablet bears Chinese characters written by the hand of Count Katsu, which signify: "Profound knowledge is the best of possessions."

But what is the knowledge taught in this huge unfurnished apartment? It is something called jiujutsu. And what is jiujutsu?

Here I must premise that I know practically nothing of jiujutsu. One must begin to study it in early youth, and must continue the study a very long time in order to learn it even tolerably well. To become an expert requires seven years of constant practice, even presupposing natural aptitudes of an uncommon order. I can give no detailed account of jiujutsu, but merely venture some general remarks about its principle.

Jiujutsu is the old samurai art of fighting without weapons. To the uninitiated it looks like wrestling. Should you happen to enter the Zuihokwan while jiujutsu is being practiced, you would see a crowd of students watching ten or twelve lithe young comrades, barefooted and barelimbed, throwing each other about on the matting. The dead silence might seem to you very strange. No word is spoken, so sign of approbation or of amusement is given, no face even smiles. Absolute impassiveness is rigidly exacted by the rules of the school of jiujutsu. But probably only this impassibility of all, this hush of numbers, would impress you as remarkable.

A professional wrestler would observe more. He would see that those young men are very cautious about putting forth their strength, and that the grips, holds, and flings are both peculiar and risky. In spite of the care exercised, he would judge the whole performance to be dangerous play, and would be tempted, perhaps, to advise the adoption of Western "scientific" rules.

The real thing, however—not the play—is much more dangerous than a Western wrestler could guess at sight. The teacher there, slender and light as he seems, could probably disable an ordinary wrestler in two minutes. Jiujutsu is not an art of display at all. It is not a training for that sort of skill exhibited to public audiences: it is an art of self-defense in the most exact sense of the term; it is an art of war. The master of that art is able, in one moment, to put an untrained antagonist completely *hors de combat*. By some terrible legerdemain he suddenly dislocates a shoulder, unhinges a joint, bursts a tendon, or snaps a bone—without any apparent effort. He is much more than an athlete: he is an anatomist. And he knows also touches that kill—as by lightning. But this fatal knowledge he is under oath never to communicate except under such conditions as would render its abuse almost impossible. Tradition exacts that it be given only to men of perfect self-command and of unimpeachable moral character.

The fact, however, to which I want to call attention is that the master of jiujutsu never relies upon his own strength. He scarcely uses his own strength in the greatest emergency. Then what does he use? Simply the strength of his antagonist. The force of the enemy is the only means by which that enemy is overcome. The art of jiujutsu teaches you to rely for victory solely upon the strength of your opponent; and the greater his strength, the worse for him and the better for you. I remember that I was not a little astonished when one of the greatest teachers of jiujutsu told me that he found it extremely difficult to teach a certain very strong pupil, whom I had innocently imagined to be the best in the class. On asking why, I was answered: "Because he relies upon his enormous muscular strength, and uses it." The very name "jiujutsu" means *to conquer by yielding.*

I fear I cannot explain at all; I can only suggest. Everyone knows what a "counter" in boxing means. I cannot use it for an exact simile, because the boxer who counters opposes his whole force to the impetus of the other; while a jiujutsu expert does precisely the contrary. Still there remains this resemblance between a counter in boxing and a yielding in jiujutsu,—that the suffering is in both cases due to the uncontrollable forward impetus of the man who receives it. I may venture then to say, loosely, that in jiujutsu there is a sort of counter for every twist, wrench, pull, push, or bend: only, the jiujutsu expert does not oppose such movements at all. No: he yields to them. But he does much more than yield to them. He aids them with a wicked slight that causes the assailant to pull out his own shoulder, to fracture his own arm, or, in a desperate case, even to break his own neck or back.

## II

With even this vaguest of explanations, you will have already been able to perceive that the real wonder of jiujutsu is not in the highest possible skill of its best professor, but in the uniquely Oriental idea which the whole art expresses. What Western brain could have elaborated this strange teaching—never to oppose force to force, but only to direct and utilize the power of attack; to overthrow the enemy solely by his own strength—to vanquish him solely by his own effort? Surely none! The Occidental mind appears to work in straight lines; the Oriental, in wonderful curves and circles. Yet how fine a symbolism of Intelligence as a means to foil brute force! Much more than a science of defense is this jiujutsu: it is a philosophical system; it is an economical system; it is an ethical system (indeed, I had forgotten to say that a very large part of jiujutsu training is purely moral); and it is, above all, the expression of a racial genius as yet but faintly perceived by those Powers who dream of further aggrandizement in the East.

Twenty-five years ago—and even more recently—foreigners might have predicted, with every appearance of reason, that Japan would adopt not only the dress, but the manners of the Occident; not only our means of rapid transit and communication, but also our principles of architecture; not only our industries and our applied science, but likewise our metaphysics and our dogmas. Some really believed that the country would soon be thrown open to foreign settlement; that Western capital would be tempted by extraordinary privileges to aid in the development of the various resources; and even that the nation would eventually proclaim, through Imperial Edict, its sudden conversion to what we call Christianity. But such beliefs were due to an unavoidable but absolute ignorance of the character of the race—of its deeper capacities, of its foresight, of its immemorial spirit of independence. That Japan might only be practicing jiujutsu, nobody supposed for a moment: indeed at that time nobody in the West had ever even heard of jiujutsu.

And, nevertheless, jiujutsu it all was. Japan adopted a military system founded upon the best experience of France and Germany, with the result that she can call into the field a disciplined force of 250,000 men, supported by a formidable artillery. She created a strong navy, comprising some of the finest cruisers in the world—modeling her naval system upon the best English and French teaching. She made herself dockyards under Franch direction, and built or bought steamers to carry her products to Korea, China, Manila, Mexico, India, and the tropics of the Pacific. She constructed, both for military and commercial purposes, nearly two thousand miles of railroad. With American and English help she established the cheapest and perhaps the most efficient telegraph and postal service in existence. She built lighthouses to such excellent purpose that her coast is said to be the best lighted in either hemisphere; and she put into operation a signal service not inferior to that of the United States. From America she obtained also a telephone system, and the best methods of electric lighting. She modeled her public school system upon a thorough study of the best results obtained in Germany, France, and America, but regulated it so as to harmonize perfectly with her own institutions. She founded a police system upon a French model, but shaped it to absolute conformity with her own particular social requirements. At first she imported machinery for her mines, her mills, her gun factories, her railways, and hired numbers of foreign experts: she is now dismissing all her teachers. But what she has done and is doing would require volumes even to mention. Suffice to say, in conclusion, that she has selected and adopted the best of everything represented by our industries, by our applied sciences, by our economical, financial, and legal experience; availing herself in every case of the highest results only, and invariably shaping her acquisitions to meet her own needs.

Now in all this she has adopted nothing for a merely imitative reason. On the contrary, she has approved and taken only what can help her to increase her strength. She has made herself able to dispense with nearly all foreign technical instruction; and she has kept in her own hands, by the shrewdest legislation, all of her own resources. But she has *not* adopted Western dress, Western habits of life, Western architecture, or Western religion; since the introduction of any of these, especially the last, would have diminished rather than augmented her force. Despite her railroad and steamship lines, her telegraphs, her postal service and her express companies, her steel artillery and magazine rifles, her universities and technical schools, she remains just as Oriental today as she was two thousand years ago. She has been able to remain herself, and to profit to the utmost possible limit by the strength of the enemy. She has been, and still is, defending herself by the most admirable system of intellectual self-defense ever heard of—by a marvelous national jiujutsu.

JOHN STEVENS

# THE FOUNDER, UESHIBA MORIHEI

Useshiba Morihei, the founder of Aikido, was born on December 14, 1883, to a farm family in an area of Wakayama Prefecture now known as Tanabe. He was the fourth born, and only son, among five children. From his solidly built father Yoroku, Morihei inherited a samurai's determination and interest in public affairs, and from his mother Yuki, he inherited an intense interest in religion, poetry, and art.

The boy at first was rather weak and sickly, preferring to read books indoors than play outside. Around the age of eight, Morihei began learning the Chinese classics under the direction of a Shingon priest, but was more fascinated by esoteric Buddhist rites, especially the homa fire service. He loved to listen to the miraculous legends associated with the wonder-working saints En no Gyoja and Kobo Daishi, who spent part of their lives in the sacred Kumano district not far from Morihei's home. Morihei even thought of becoming a Buddhist priest himself someday.

As an antidote to his son's daydreaming and high-strung behavior, Yoroku recounted the exploits of Morihei's famous great-grandfather Kichiemon, said to be one of the strongest samurai of the day, and encouraged the boy to take up sumo wrestling and swimming. Morihei

*John Stevens (b. 1947) has lived in Japan for more than a decade studying and teaching. He is accomplished in several martial arts and has taken his aikido instruction under Hanzawa Yoshimi, director of the Tohoku Aikido Association.*

gradually became stronger, and realized the necessity of possessing adequate power after his father was attacked one night by a gang of thugs hired by a rival politician.

Morihei left middle school after a year—the classes bored him and his nervous energy demanded a more practical outlet. Always good in mathematics, Morihei enrolled in a soroban (abacus) academy; less than twelve months later he was acting as an assistant instructor. Still in his teens, Morihei took a job as an assessor in the local tax office. He was an excellent worker, but during the course of his duties he was obliged to administer a new tax law directed at farmers and fishermen. Convinced that the regulations were grossly unfair, he resigned in righteous indignation and became a leader of the protest movement, much to the chagrin of his councilman father. Yoroko gave him a substantial sum of money, saying, "Take this and try to find something you would really like to do."

Hoping to become a great merchant, Morihei went to Tokyo in 1901. He managed to open a small stationery supply store, but commerce suited him no better than tax accounting, and he closed down the business in a few months. During his brief stay in Tokyo, Morihei did discover that he had a definite affinity for martial arts, greatly enjoying his study of jiujutsu at the Kito-ryu dojo and swordsmanship at the Shinkage-ryu training center. A severe case of beri-beri caused him to return home. Shortly thereafter, at the age of nineteen, he married Itogawa Hatsu.

Morihei quickly regained his health, but was at a loss what to do next. Storm clouds were brewing between Russia and Japan so the impetuous young man decided to enlist in the army and seek some adventure. Unfortunately, Morihei, who stood just over five feet tall, was slightly under the minimum height requirement. Extremely upset, he spent the next several months training alone in the mountains, hanging from branches with weights on his legs to extend his spine the necessary half-inch.

Morihei passed the physical on his next attempt and in 1903 joined the infantry. The tireless energy of the fastidious soldier caught the attention of his superiors and he was rapidly promoted. Morihei earned a reputation for his zeal for hard training and his unusual skill at bayonet fighting. He served with distinction in Manchuria during the Russo-Japanese War of 1904–05, displaying for the first time his uncanny ability to anticipate an attack—he said that he could sense when a bullet was coming his way even before it was fired—and his commanding officer wanted to recommend him for admission to the National

Military Academy. For various reasons, Morihei declined the position and resigned from active duty. During his four years in the military, Morihei greatly improved his physical condition, building himself up to a rock-hard one hundred eighty pounds, and earned his first menkyo, teaching license, for a martial art from Nakai Masakatsu of the Yagyu-ryu. (The dojo was located in Sakai, a suburb of Osaka where Morihei was stationed.)

Morihei returned to the farm and married life, but remained restless. Hot-tempered and irritable, almost manic-depressive, he began to act strangely—locking himself in his room for hours to pray, jumping up in the middle of the night to douse himself with cold water, fasting in the mountains for days on end. Concerned with his son's erratic behavior, Yoroku built a dojo on the property and invited the well-known jiujutsu teacher Takaki Kiyoichi to teach there. Morihei threw himself into the training and his disposition improved considerably.

During this period, Morihei came under the influence of the noted scholar Minakata Kumagusu (who, incidentally, had spent many years studying in the United States and England). Kumagusu vigorously opposed the government's plan to consolidate smaller Shinto shrines under the jurisdiction of larger ones, primarily because he felt the sentiments of the local residents would be ignored. Morihei supported Kumagusu's position, actively petitioning officials, writing protest letters to newspapers, organizing demonstrations, and so on. Morihei's involvement in this affair increased his interest in national politics; when the government called for volunteers to settle in the underdeveloped land of Hokkaido, Kumagusu encouraged him to consider the possibility, especially in light of Japan's future food needs. The pioneer spirit of "creating something out of nothing" appealed to Morihei; in addition, the village now had many unemployed farmers and fishermen. A town meeting was held and more than eighty people agreed to emigrate *en masse*. In the spring of 1912, the twenty-nine-year-old Morihei, with his wife and their two-year-old daughter, led the group to the wilderness of Hokkaido.

The group settled in the frigid northeast section of the island around the village of Shirataki. Things began inauspiciously—no one knew how to grow potatoes, and early frosts, cool summers, and harsh winters wiped out the other crops three years in a row. Having to subsist on wild vegetables and fish, not a few of the pioneers regretted their move, and did not hesitate to blame Morihei for their plight. Luckily, circumstances improved as the demand for lumber soared and the village prospered. A fire that destroyed the central district was a severe blow, but due largely to Morihei's ceaseless efforts, everything was rebuilt within a year. He was elected to the village council and was respectfully known as the "King of Shirataki."

The tremendous muscular strength of Morihei's arms was said to be a result of the years of heavy logging in Shirataki; every day he wrestled with huge 100 to 200 pound pieces of lumber. A number of anecdotes survive from the Shirataki period: once he singlehandedly lifted a horse and wagon from a deep ditch; he subdued three bandits who tried to rob him; he calmed a marauding bear and shared his lunch with it. The most significant event of his stay in Hokkaido was his meeting with Takeda Sokaku, grandmaster of Daito-ryu Aiku-jutsu.

By tradition, the Daito-ryu was founded *ca.* A.D. 1100 by Minamoto (Gebji) Yoshimitsu, sixth generation descendant of the Emperor Seiwa. Yoshimitsu's son Yoshikiyo moved to Koga (present-day Yamanashi Prefecture) and established the Takeda clan; the art was secretly transmitted among family members from generation to generation. In 1574, Takeda Kunitsugu moved to Aizu (Fukushima Prefecture) where the special oshiki-uchi (also known as o-dome) techniques were taught exclusively to high ranking samurai of the Aizu-han for the next three hundred years.

Actually, the origin of the Daito-ryu seems less ancient and more prosaic. Takeda Soemon (1758–1853) taught a system known as aiki-in-yo-ho, "the aiki system of yin and yang," which he passed on to Saigo Tanomo, chief retainer of the Aizu lord. Saigo also had training in Misoguchi-ryu swordsmanship and Koshu-ryu military science. The Aizu samurai were die-hard supporters of the old military regime and fiercely resisted the new Meiji government, being among the last to capitualte in 1868. Certain that Tanomo had been killed in the final battle with the Imperial forces and determined to preserve the honor of the Saigo name, his mother, his wife, his five daughters, and fourteen other members of his family committed ritual suicide. Tanomo's life had been spared, however; following this tragedy, he served as a Shinto priest in various districts and adopted Shida Shiro as his son. The extremely talented Shiro mastered the oshiki-uchi techniques, later applying them with great effect as the star of Kano Jigoro's newly founded Kokodan school of Judo. At an open tournament in 1889, assistant instructor Shiro defeated all comers with his yama-arashi ("mountain-storm") oshiki-uchi technique, thus securing the reputation of the Kokodan. (Shiro's story has been fictionalized in the popular Sugata Sanshiro series of novels and movies.) Not much later, however, Shiro—probably torn between his debt to his adoptive father Tanomo and his respect for Jigoro—abandoned the practice of both systems, moved to Nagasaki, and devoted himself to classical archery (kyudo) the rest of his life.

Fortunately, the aging Tanomo had another worthy heir: Takeda Sokaku (1860–1943), Soemon's grandson. (Since Sokaku's father Sokichi concentrated on sumo wrestling rather than aiki-in-yo-ho, the family tradition temporarily passed to an "outsider.")

Sokaku was no beginner; at an early age he had obtained teaching licenses in ono-ha itto-ryu swordsmanship and Hozoin spear-fighting as well as studying with the "swordsman-saint" Sakakibara Kenkichi of the Jikishin-kage-ryu. A demon swordsman, Sokaku "stormed" dojos all over the country, engaging in thousands of contests. He almost never lost. He reportedly had more than one battle with a live sword; once he got involved in a fight with a group of construction workers and killed seven or eight of them.

When Tanomo transmitted the last of his knowledge to Sokaku in 1898, he told him, "The way of the sword is over; from now on make these marvelous techniques known everywhere." Sokaku modified the oshiki-uchi experience; he designated his composite system "daito-ryu aiki-jutsu," and should rightly be considered its founder.

Now an invincible master of aiki, Sokaku traveled widely, attracting a large number of disciples; he was reputed to have had around thirty thousand disciples and nearly every budoka of note in that era was his student in one way or the other. One of them was a Westerner, an American named Charles Perry.

In 1903, Perry, an English instructor at a secondary school in Sendai, was riding a train and asked the conductor to check the first-class ticket of the shabbily dressed Japanese man down the aisle. When Sokaku demanded to know why only he was requested to show his ticket, the conductor told him the American gentleman didn't think he belonged in this car. The short-tempered Sokaku jumped to his feet and went over to Perry for an explanation. Perry stood up, brandishing both fists, sure that his six-foot height would intimidate the diminutive Sokaku. Sokaku grabbed both of Perry's wrists and applied what modern Aikido students know as yonkyo; the pain brought Perry to his knees and then Sokaku threw him toward the end of the car. After making a humble apology, Perry asked permission to learn something of the art himself. The story goes that Perry later reported this encounter and details of his studies with Sokaku to the State Department in Washington; Teddy Roosevelt heard about it and asked that someone be sent to teach in the United States. Harada Shinzo of Sendai was dispatched to the U.S. for some months and it may well be that an American president was himself introduced to the mysteries of aiki before Ueshiba Morihei.

Sokaku never had a permanent dojo of his own, preferring to attract disciples by Perry-like chance encounters, challenges to local kendo and judo instructors—the loser became the victor's pupil—and formal demonstrations. Sokaku would hold a twisted piece of paper and ask a volunteer to take one end; suddenly the person at the other end would start to rise off the floor. Then Sokaku would have his hands firmly tied behind his back and invite the participants to try and throw or pin him; regardless of what they attempted or from what direction they came, they could not get him down; on the contrary, each one hit the floor himself. For a finale, he would ask all those present to grab him at once; in a flash everyone would be sent flying. Another favorite trick of his was to be lifted on the shoulders of the five or six biggest onlookers; Sokaku somehow made them collapse in a heap with him on top and they would remain there immovable until he let them up. Needless to say, many eagerly became students after such an impressive performance.

Morihei was first introduced to Sokaku in 1915 at an inn in Engaru. Although Morihei was a pretty tough fellow himself—on occasion he was mistaken for Sokaku because they were about the same size—he was no match for the Daito-ryu master. Immediately forgetting about everything else, Morihei stayed at the inn studying with Sokaku for a month (the folks back in Shirataki thought he had perished in a blizzard), the minimum requirement for the shoden mokuroku certificate of 118 basic techniques. Upon his return home, Morihei built a dojo on his property and invited Sokaku to live there. In 1917, Morihei began accompanying Sokaku on teaching tours, having sent his family back to Tanabe in Wakayama because of the intense cold.

In 1919, word came from Tanabe that seventy-six-year-old Yoroku was gravely ill; Morihei sold off some of his property in Shirataki, turned the remainder over to Sokaku, and left Hokkaido for good. On the way back to his hometown—a good ten-day trip in those days— Morihei impulsively stopped at Ayabe, headquarters of the new Omoto-kyo religion he had recently heard so much about, to request a prayer service for the recovery of his father's health. There he met Deguchi Onisaburo, the "Master" of the religion, who told him, "Your father is better off where he is going."

The otherworldly atmosphere of the Ayabe compound enthralled Morihei and he lingered there for three days before resuming his journey. When he arrived home, he found that his father had indeed departed for a "a better place" as Onisaburo had predicted. Sorely distressed and terribly confused, Morihei hardly ate or slept for the next three months; every night he would take to the mountains and swing his sword madly until daybreak. Finally, he announced his intention to sell the ancestral land, move to Ayabe, and study Omoto-kyo.

Like many of Japan's new religions, Omoto-kyo, "The Teaching of the Great Origin," was a mixture of Shinto mythology, shamanism, faith healing, and personality cult. Then at the height of its popularity, with over two million adherents, it was founded by Deguchi Nao, a semiliterate farm woman whose early life was nothing but unrelieved misery. Poverty-stricken from birth, she was forced to work as a housemaid at age ten; her marriage to the poorest farmer in a poor village was tragic—of her eight children, three died in infancy, two ran way from home, and two went insane. After her husband died when she was thirty years old, Nao was reduced to selling rags for a living. In 1892 she had a "revelation" from Tenchi-kane-no-kame, the Great God of the Universe, that a messiah was coming to establish a Kingdom of God on earth and that she must be his prophetess.

In 1898, Nao met clever young Ueda Kisaburo, who claimed he had once left his body, toured every region of the spiritual world, and learned all the secrets of the cosmos. Nao recognized Kisaburo (who later changed his name to Onisaburo) as the promised savior, and after Onisaburo married Nao's daughter Sumiko, they started a religious sect together.

When Moreihei announced his decision to move to Ayabe and study Omoto-kyo, all of his friends and family, including his wife, thought he was crazy. Nonetheless, he would not be deterred, and in the spring of 1920 he and his family rented a house near the Omoto-kyo head shrine. (This year was undoubtedly the most trying of Morihei's life. In addition to his father's death and the painful decision to abandon his home in Tanabe, both of his sons, three-year-old Takamori and one-year-old Kuniji, caught a virus and died within three weeks of each other. His sole surviving son, Kisshomaru, was born in 1921.)

For the next eight years Morihei served as Onisaburo's assistant, taught budo at the "Ueshiba Juku," headed the local fire brigade, farmed, and studied the doctrines of Omoto-kyo, especially chinkon-kishin, "calming the spirit and returning to the divine."

A pacifist, Onisaburo was an advocate of nonviolent resistance and universal disarmament who once said, "Armament and war are the means by which landlords and capitalists make their profit, while the poor must suffer; there is nothing in the world more harmful than war and more foolish than armament." Why did he welcome the martial artist Morihei, building a dojo for him and telling young Omoto followers to study there? Onisaburo realized that Morihei's purpose on earth was "to teach the real meaning of budo: an end to all fighting and contention."

Onisaburo was in constant trouble with the authorities because of his pacifist stance and his serious belief that since he was savior of the world, he should be declared emperor and allowed to run the government. In 1921, he was arrested on the charge of lèse-majesté, but released a few months later during the general amnesty issued at the death of Emperor Taisho.

In 1924, Onisaburo hatched a bizarre scheme to set up a "Heavenly Kingdom on Earth" in Mongolia, site of the "New Jerusalem," with the aid of several Chinese and Korean syncretic religious groups. Once the great spiritual traditions of Asia were united, he believed, the rest of the world could be organized into an association of love and brotherhood under his own direction. Since Onisaburo was under continual police surveillance, the five-man party, including Morihei acting as bodyguard, set out in utmost secrecy. Arriving in China in February, Onisaburo announced himself as the Dalai Lama incarnation of Maitreya Buddha for whom everyone was waiting. His Chinese hosts were not impressed, and only after great difficulty and many adventures (in which Morihei's ability to dodge bullets came in most handy), did they near their destination. However, the group had somehow alarmed the local warlords, who had them promptly arrested, placed in leg irons, and taken to an execution ground to be shot. Fortunately, the Japanese consul intervened and the savior and his party were saved at the last second. The members of the fanciful expedition returned to a hero's welcome in July of the same year.

(Onisaburo, his wife, and fifty of his closest followers were arrested in 1935 and sentenced to life imprisonment; all the Omoto buildings were dynamited and the entire movement suppressed. Onisaburo was released on bail in 1942, and spent the remaining six years of his life studying, composing poetry, and making pottery. Omoto-kyo was revived following the war, but has never recovered from the death of the charismatic Onisaburo; present membership is perhaps two hundred thousand.)

The study of Omoto-kyo and his association with Onisaburo profoundly affected Morihei's life. Even his relationship with Sokaku was influenced. In 1922, Morihei invited Sokaku to Ayabe for a six-month stay, and Sokaku gave him permission to act as an instructor (*shihan-dai*) of daito-ryu aiki-jutsu. (The relationship between daito-ryu aiki-justu and aikido is difficult to clearly assess. There were at least twenty others who were given teaching licenses by Sokaku and Morihei never formally received the "complete transmission" [soden] of Daito-ryu techniques.) Morihei stated that while Sokaku opened his eyes to the essence of budo, his enlightenment came through his Omoto-kyu experiences. Reportedly, Onisaburo advised Morihei to start his own tradition since daito-ryu methods were too combat-oriented and could not serve as a means to unite man with god and promote harmony among all people. Right from the start, the two systems differed greatly in both their approach and execution. Nonetheless, Sokaku continued to visit Morihei almost every year until his death in 1943 even after Morihei had his own training center in Tokyo. Morihei always footed the bill, treating Sokaku with all the respect due one's master, albeit without enthusiasm.

His close calls in China with Onisaburo also had a great effect on Morihei. Upon his return to Ayabe, he trained more intently than ever, arming his disciples with live swords and commanding them to try to cut him in half. Something was up in the spiritual world, too; every morning at eleven o'clock, the living room of Morihei's house would shake violently as an unearthly sound emitted from the household shrine, and every evening at nine o'clock a tremendous "whoosh" was heard as if some huge object was passing by.

One spring day in 1925, a kendo instructor wishing to test Morihei's reputation paid a visit to the Ayabe dojo. Relying on his sixth sense—"a flash of light indicated the direction of the attack"—Morihei easily avoided the cuts and thrusts of the instructor's wooden sword. After he left, Morihei went out into his garden to rest. Suddenly he felt bathed in a heavenly light; the ground quaked as a golden cloud welled up from the earth and entered his body. Morihei imagined that he was transformed into a golden being that filled space; the barrier between the spiritual and material worlds had crumbled—"I am the universe." He realized that the true purpose of budo was love, love that cherishes and nourishes all beings. Morihei was then forty-two years old.

The Ueshiba Juku in Ayabe was originally intended for Omoto-kyo devotees, but as Morihei's fame spread many nonbelievers, mostly military men, applied for admission. The case of Tomiki Kenji, judoka and later founder of the Tomiki system of aikido, was typical. When a couple of his friends, students of Morihei, urged him to meet their master, Tomiki scoffed and said, "I've heard about Ueshiba and his fake demonstrations; if I take on an over-the-hill forty-year-old all my colleagues will laugh at me." They promised not to reveal the meeting to anyone so Tomiki agreed. Tomiki was introduced and moved confidently toward Morihei, but instantly found himself pinned to the floor. He requested another chance, this time vowing to give it his all. He ended up on the other side of the *dojo*, sprang up and rushed again; after hitting the deck for a second time, he bowed and said, "I hope to become your disciple."

Morihei spent much of 1925–26 in Tokyo teaching at the request of Admiral Takeshita and other influential people. The strain of so much travel and training took its toll; Morihei passed out after a practice session and the doctor prescribed complete rest. (Even though Morihei was occasionally physically ill, he still was able to freely perform his aiki techniques. Aiki is perhaps the ultimate example of mind over matter. Ki-power is never diminished, and does not depend on one's physical condition. For example, near the end of his life, Sokaku insisted on conducting his regular training sessions despite the fact that his right side was paralyzed from a stroke, and it is said that while on his deathbed he threw a sixth-degree judoka.)

After a six-month stay in Ayabe, Morihei's health returned. Onisaburo encouraged Morihei to separate himself from the Omoto-kyo organization, move to Tokyo, and found his own unique "Way." In 1927, Morihei and his family rented a house in Sarumachi in Tokyo's Shibe Shirogane district, and Morihei held classes in the remodeled billiard room of Prince Shimazu, one of his early supporters. In 1928, Morihei moved to larger quarters in Mita, and then in the following year to a still larger place in Kuruma-machi. Because the number of applicants continued to increase, land was acquired for a formal dojo and residence in Ushigome (present site of the headquarters dojo).

While the new dojo was being constructed, Kano Jigoro paid a visit to Morihei's temporary training hall in Mejiro. After witnessing Morihei's aiki techniques Jigoro declared, "This is my ideal budo—true judo." He dispatched several of his top Kodokan pupils to study with Morihei; one of them, Mochizuki Minoru, later developed his own aikido-style system.

In 1931, the dojo in Ushigome, called the Kobukan, was finished. (Shirata Sensei became an uchi-deshi later this year.) A "Budo Enhancement Society" was founded in 1932 with Morihei as chief instructor. Shioda Gozo, present head of Yoshikan Aikido, became a disciple around the same time. There has always been a close relationship between aikido and swordsmanship—Sokaku and Morihei were likely the two best swordsmen of the day—and for a time there was a kendo division at the Kobukan. Morihei, evidently concerned that his bookworm son Kisshomaru would not be up to succeeding him, adopted a young swordsman named Tanaka Kiyoshi into the Ueshiba family, but he left a few years later for unspecific reasons.

Up to the outbreak of World War II, Morihei was extremely busy teaching at the Kobukan as well as holding special classes at the major military and police academies (he also gave lessons to actors, dancers, and sumo wrestlers). Here are a few of the many interesting stories handed down from that period:

The famous general Miura, a hero of the Russo-Japanese War, used to be a student of daito-ryu and heard about Morihei from Sokaku. One day he noticed the "Ueshiba Dojo" signboard and went in to see what his "fellow-disciple" had to offer. Although Miura was cynical at first, he was impresed by the different emphasis in Ueshiba aiki-jutsu and decided to study with Morihei. However, still not completely convinced of Morihei's ability, Miura arranged a training session at Toyama Military Academy. The students of jukendo (bayonet fighting) there were noted for their ferocity, size, and strength. They urged Morihei to wear protective armor because things might get a lttle rough; Morihei declined, saying, "Yor are using wooden bayonets, so don't worry. Will you attack one-by-one?"

"Of course," was the reply.

"In my budo, we always expect attacks from all sides. Please come in a group." Disbelieving, only one student stepped forward. When the others saw him land on his rear end, they lost their reserve and moved in together. No one came close to touching Morihei.

A similar incident occurred at the Military Police Academy. The trainees there were particularly ruthless, and one day thought of surprising their instructor. Usually, twenty to thirty students attended the sessions, but this time only one person showed up. Morihei gave a short lesson, and walked out into the open courtyard to return home. All at once, the members of the class, armed with wooden swords, sticks, and bayonets swarmed out to "greet" Morihei. In his customary unruffled manner, he deftly avoided their attacks and passed through the gate as if nothing had happened.

At the central police headquarters in Osaka, Morihei was giving a class, and asked five of the biggest officers to pin him on the floor—one on top with a choke hold, and one on each limb. Although Morihei's entire body was under the weight of the policemen, in an instant they were thrown off. Observers noticed hardly any movement, and when they questioned the men holding Morihei down, they were told, "His body was as soft as silk when we first held it; as he emitted a short *kiai* he became like a piece of iron and we flew off." The man with the choke hold mentioned that he felt his hands being wrenched off Morihei's neck. Morihei laughed as he chided them, "You'd better learn more effective arrest techniques if you are going to deal with dangerous criminals."

Morihei told his uchi-deshi that if they ever caught him off guard even for a moment, he would treat them all to a grand feast. Day and night, the disciples tried to sneak up on him to no avail; even when he was sleeping, as soon as they got near Morihei he stirred. Actually, they thought he was not sleeping at all and was perhaps suffering from some neurotic disorder so they summoned a doctor to examine him. "I feel fine," said Morihei. "Why did you call a doctor?" They related the details of their nightly missions; since he did not seem to be resting well they presumed he was ill. "I was sound asleep," Morihei assured them. "Invisible rays emanate from my body and whenever anyone comes within ten or fifteen feet of me I can immediately sense his presence even in my sleep." In a similar vein, Shirata Sensei recalls that he and the other young uchi-deshi occasionally slipped out to enjoy a modest "night on the town." Even though Morihei's room was quite far from the dojo gate and the disciples took every precaution not to make any noise, invariably the next morning the Founder would ask, "Where did you fellows go last night?"

One day Morihei was riding on a crowded train with several of his disciples. The man next to him suddenly froze with a strange expression on his face; Morihei apparently knew the man, his disciples thought, since he was smiling. At the next stop, Morihei said, "Scram!" and the man ran off the train. "Who was that?" his students asked. "A pickpocket," Morihei told them.

Speaking of trains, Morihei was probably the most demanding traveler in the country. He insisted on being at the station at least an hour before the train was scheduled to depart, which was not so bad; much worse was his disconcerting habit of boarding the train with his luggage and several attendants only to leap up just before the train left the station and declare, "Get off this train! I'm not going anywhere!" The disciples had no choice but to obey his orders. A few minutes after the last train pulled away, he would say, "I feel better now. Let's go." Hypersensitive to the slightest change in mood, Morihei frequently, and capriciously, altered his plans. His disciples never knew what to expect—Morihei's method of keeping them alert?—and he would not stand for inattentive or halfhearted behavior on their part.

One of Morihei's earliest disciples was Niki Kenzo, "Doctor Brown Rice," an advocate of health food. Although Morihei did not care much for brown rice—he had trouble digesting it—he did prefer plain and simple food: vegetables and fish. His secret weapon was chicken soup; whenever he felt out-of-sorts he drank a bowl. Unlike the majority of budoka, Morihei almost never drank sake.

His disciples once asked Morihei if the feats attributed the ninja-e.g., becoming invisible, walking on water—were actually done. "You have been watching too many movies," Morihei said. Grab your swords and sticks and I'll give you a real demonstration of nin-jutsu." Ten or so of them surrounded Morihei in the center of the dojo, and as soon as they attacked, they felt a stream of air and Morihei disappeared. "Over here, over here!" they heard Morihei calling from half way up the second story stairs twenty feet away. Later, however, Morihei got quite upset when they asked him to do some more ninja "tricks." "Are you trying to kill me just to entertain yourselves? Each time one performs such techniques, his life span is reduced five to ten years."

Yet even Morihei lost his footing. Kisshomaru remembers well an incident that occurred when he was a primary school student. He got into a fight with an American boy who lived nearby; the boy started throwing stones, and Morihei, who sensed something wrong, ran out into the street, but slipped in a puddle, allowing the boy to escape. To this day, Kisshomaru is unsure whether Morihei was furious at the American boy for hurling rocks or at his son—then a rather weak and spiritless child—for shrinking from the challenge.

If Morihei's budo stood for love and peace, what was his attitude toward the "Great East Asian War"? Unlike Onisaburo, who never abandoned his pacifist principles and went to prison for his beliefs, Morihei appeared to be an ardent supporter of the Imperial cause. He taught at the major military academies, many of his disciples were among those directing the war, he went to Manchuria as a guest of the puppet government there, and so on. Yet Kisshomaru has written that both prior to and during the war, he heard his father complain bitterly, "The military is dominated by reckless fools ignorant of statesmanship and religious ideals who slaughter innocent citizens indiscriminately and destroy everything in their path. They act in total contradiction to God's will, and will surely come to a sorry end. True budo is to nourish life and foster peace, love, and respect, not to blast the world to pieces with weapons." Morihei hinted that his move to the Iwama outdoor dojo in 1942 was prompted by a "divine command"; he foresaw that the war would not end well for Japan and hoped that aikido would become the creed of a new era.

The war had emptied the Kobukan dojo and Morihei, tired of city life and the burdens of administering a large center, longed to return to the land where he could ideally combine budo and farming, two things that created life and purified the heart. He often said that "Budo and farming are one." Morihei placed the city dojo in the hands of his son, resigned his official positions, and left Tokyo with his wife to settle on their property, purchased some years previously, in the village of Iwama in Ibaragi Prefecture. Morihei lived there quietly for the remainder of the war, practicing, studying, farming, and supervising the construction of the Aiki Shrine and Shuren Dojo. Iwama may be considered the birthplace of aiki-do, "The Way of Harmony." Prior to Morihei's move there, his system was called aiki-jutsu, then aiki-budo, still primarily arts rather than spiritual paths. During the years from 1942—when the name aikido was first formally used—to 1952, Morihei consolidated the techniques and perfected the religious philosophy of aikido.

In the aftermath of Japan's surrender in 1945, his disciples believed that aikido would cease to exist, but Morihei was confident that, on the contrary, aikido would flourish and its true value become known all over the world. In 1948, the Aikikai (Aiki Association) was formed to promote aikido in Japan and abroad. Morihei left the organizing to his son and top disciples, preferring to pursue further training in Iwama. He rose every morning at 5 o'clock (3 o'clock on feast days), prayed and meditated for several hours, and then either farmed or studied, depending on the weather. Every evening he led the training sessions. Saito Morihiro, present head of the Iwama Dojo, recalls: "When the Founder meditated the air was permeated by an intense, grave spirituality, but when he finished we felt the warmth of his love and compassion." Farming and aikido were his life and the entire world his dojo.

This rapid spread of aikido after the war under the direction of the Hombu Dojo, now headquartered in a three-story building in Tokyo, is a well-known story. Morihei became world famous as "O-Sensei," the master of aikido, and received a number of decorations from the Japanese government.

Right to the end of his life, Morihei refined and improved his techniques, never losing his dedication to hard training. In the early spring of 1969, Morihei fell ill, and told Kisshomaru that "God is calling me. . . ." Hospitalized, Morihei's condition was diagnosed as cancer of the liver. (All through his life Morihei had had frequent liver and stomach trouble. He blamed it on a salt-water drinking contest he had with a Japanese yoga practitioner who was pestering Onisaburo or one of the Omoto-kyo believers to take the challenge. A more likely cause was excessively hard training.) He was returned home at his request to be near his dojo. Even though he was no longer able to physically conduct the practices, he could tell exactly what was going on by listening to the sounds in the dojo. Those with him said he was never stronger—his body had wasted away to almost nothing, but he was so heavy ten of his most powerful disciples were unable to lift him.

On April 15, Morihei's condition became critical; as his many disciples and friends made their final calls, he gave his last instructions: "Aikido is for the entire world. Train not for selfish reasons, but for all people everywhere." Early on the morning of April 26, the eighty-six-year-old Morihei took his son's hand, smiled, said "Take care of things," and died. Two months later to the day, Hatsu, his wife of sixty-seven years, followed him.

Morihei's ashes were buried in the family temple in Tanabe, and parts of his hair were enshrined in Ayabe, in the Aiki Shrine, and in the Kumano Juku Dojo (headed by Hikitsuchi Michio). Every year a memorial service is held on April 29 at the Aiki Shrine in Iwama.

## PART II

# MASTERS AND STUDENTS:
# THE PHILOSOPHY

**HERMAN KAUZ**

# THE AIM OF INDIVIDUAL
# FORM PRACTICE

### DEVELOPING SKILL

In most of the martial arts, students are taught to move in ways that sometimes appear difficult and even unnatural at first. As they observe the movements of a skilled practitioner, they are impressed with the grace, power, and flow of each technique. Their own efforts seem awkward by comparison. Learning to move in the manner suggested by their teacher may call for placing the feet and legs in positions that feel uncomfortable, using the hands in unaccustomed or unusual ways and maintaining a perpendicular body despite its desire to incline in various directions. These initial difficulties are often caused by the beginner's lack of previous physical training. His body may be tense, with stiff muscles and shortened tendons and ligaments. These need to be stretched if he is to achieve the necessary range in his movements. Sometimes his arms and legs are too weak to allow him to pull or push as much as is necessary. He may have trouble bending his knees to the correct degree and for the amount of time required. This lack of basic physical ability hampers the beginner in his attempt to learn to use his body in the prescribed way. Nevertheless, as he persists in his efforts

---

*A t'ai chi ch'uan instructor of many years' experience, Herman Kauz has authored instructional handbooks and philosophical texts treating principles of both "hard" and "soft" martial arts. He was a student of Cheng Man-ch'ing (1902–75), grandmaster of Yang style t'ai chi and noted poet, painter, and philosopher.*

he will gradually overcome his deficiencies, and his body will begin to respond to his direction as it should.

In most schools, students practice the various techniques they would use against an opponent without the participation of a partner. The degree to which such solo practice is done varies from art to art. Those martial arts that require a partner for practicing such movements as throwing, grappling, or joint locks make only limited use of individual practice. In judo, for example, a beginner will first learn to fall in various directions. He does this from sitting, squatting, and standing positions, without a partner. As he improves, he may jump into the air, turn a somersault and land on his back without ill effect, breaking his fall in the recommended manner. After he has learned to fall from a respectable height without injury, his teacher or a more experienced student will begin to throw him into the air to allow him to become accustomed to falling when someone is throwing him.

When he can fall correctly, he is taught the mechanics of one or more throwing techniques. In this procedure, the beginner usually performs the technique he is learning with only the imaginary presence of a partner. The footwork combined with the pull and the turn of the body can profitably be done thousands of times without a partner until the movement becomes almost a reflex that occurs in the split second in which an opening occurs. At first, of course, the technique is performed slowly with emphasis on the correct positioning of all parts of the body. This kind of individual practice is useful for the duration of a person's judo training. To simulate an opponent's resistance, the student might also tie his judo uniform belt around a tree or a post and pull on the belt as he practices the throw.

Individual training of this nature enables the student to grow accustomed to the body mechanics involved in the performance of his techniques. He is not distracted by an opponent's shifting about evasively or attempting to counterattack. He has time in which to work on problems concerned with correct foot placement, body position, or pulling direction. In an actual match, the opportunity to perform a throw appears only briefly, allowing insufficient time to give attention to the many factors involved. Certain optimum patterns of movement must be established, and these can only become set if they are repeated almost endlessly. Nevertheless, because judo techniques are performed while maintaining contact with an opponent, as students progress they tend to forego individual practice for practice with a partner. In a sense, however, this practice can still be considered individual because the partner may be asked to cooperate, thereby enabling the student to strengthen and polish his movements.

Because karate training does not involve as much physical contact with an opponent—throwing and grappling are minimal in most styles—it makes more use of individual form practice than judo does. Countless hours are spent in moving forward and backward over the floor while delivering punches, blocks, and kicks. At the outset, the fundamentals of each technique are carefully taught. Foot position of the stance, knee placement, and hip and body rotation in a punching or striking technique are all described in detail. The route of the foot in the delivery of the various kicks and that of the hand in strikes, punches and blocks is demonstrated until the student knows what is required. Once these rudiments of positioning and movement have been learned, it is up to each student to correctly perform each technique with maximum speed and power. Every training session has a period of time devoted to drilling in the basic techniques used in karate. It is thought that success in more advanced karate training, such as the delivery of techniques in combination with the almost simultaneous application of block and counter characteristic of freestyle sparring, depends upon the correct performance of basic movements.

## KATA PRACTICE

These basic movements are also combined in sequential form called kata in Japanese. Students must memorize a number of these sequences over the months and years of their training. In such kata, the performer blocks and counters various attacks delivered by a number of imaginary assailants located at different spots around him. Often the kata as a whole has a certain overriding theme or idea which the student attempts to express as he does the required moves. At the periodic promotional contests, an examining board of teachers grades each student on his performance of one or more of these forms. As his skill increases, a student learns more and more complicated kata. But more importantly, he must perform even the relatively simple ones with better focus and concentration.

Practice of kata constitutes another important segment of each training session. Repetition of a technique, as explained above, provides one kind of training, but the movements are usually done while first advancing a number of steps in one direction and then retreating in the opposite. In kata, on the other hand, the student learns to relate to all directions. From the standpoint of proficiency in karate, kata comes closer than any other training to actual sparring with an opponent; the practice of kata enables each student to sharpen his skill.

Students of t`ai chi ch´uan attach great importance to the correct performance of a sequential form that requires anywhere from five to twenty minutes to complete. The variation in the length of time necessary to complete this form depends upon the particular style in question. Some teachers teach a "short" and a "long" form, others only a "long," and still others only a "short." The short Yang form, which is rapidly gaining popularity in this country, is not as brief as it may sound. It contains fewer movements overall and fewer repetitions than the long form and, depending upon speed of execution, takes seven to ten minutes to complete. Students must spend about six months just learning the pattern of movements it contains, let alone doing them correctly. The form consists of various self-defense movements arranged in sequence and done throughout at the same rate of speed. The movements are often stylized and sometimes only faintly resemble the original fighting technique. The form is done slowly, and the position and the movement of every part of the body receive careful attention. Karate techniques, in contrast, are usually performed with much greater speed and less emphasis on exact placement of various parts of the body. In the t`ai chi form, knees remain bent throughout and the back is held perpendicular to the ground. Again, in contrast to karate kata where at the moment of focus the performer simultaneously tenses a large number of muscles, the body remains as relaxed as possible and only the very minimum of strength is used. Naturally, if the arm and shoulder muscles are employed in a movement, they become operative and would feel hard to the touch, as would be true of the leg that supports the body's weight. But if a hand must be raised to solar plexus height, it is unnecessary to tighten all the muscles of the arm or the torso to accomplish this.

Students of t`ai chi ch´uan who want to learn to deal successfully with an opponent must move while fighting in the way they move in the form. Thus, in doing the form, there is great emphasis on a relaxed body with minimum use of strength, bent knees with consequent low center of gravity and attention to detail which contributes to a growth of concentration and sensitivity. Students are expected to spend at least twenty or thirty minutes daily doing the form. Teachers explain that only through daily practice will the student internalize the correct way of moving. The goal is to practice long enough and hard enough until all the student's movements throughout the day are done in a manner characteristic of the t`ai chi form.

The use of individual form practice in the three martial arts briefly described above is not limited to them but is characteristic of all martial arts I have knowledge of. Practitioners use this method of training to help develop the skill necessary for performing the many complicated techniques that comprise the body of their art. Moreover, their ability to attain maximum power in each movement is thought to stem from individual practice. However, more than the development of the skillful and powerful performance of various techniques can result from this kind of training. Those teachers who view their art as a mental as well as a physical discipline think of individual form practice as a means of bringing about those changes in students that are characteristic of some form of meditation.

## MEDITATIVE ASPECTS
## OF INDIVIDUAL FORM PRACTICE

One may ask what is involved in such mental training and why is it pursued? Investigation reveals that over the centuries, both Eastern and Western religions and secular groups have engaged in meditational practices which they variously claimed achieved union with God, enabled them to see life in its wholeness and instilled tranquility. Meditation was seldom the province of the mainstream of religious observance in the West but was and is usually pursued by groups inclined toward mysticism. In the Middle East the Sufis and in the Far East the Buddhists, Taoists, Shintoists, and Indian Yogis all depend upon meditation to achieve their particular ends. Members of primitive tribes throughout the world engage in one or another form of meditation for spiritual development. The meditation practiced by all of these groups has certain mental and physical methods in common. Chief among them are muscular relaxation and freeing the mind of everyday thoughts. The intention is to learn to focus the conscious mind on something other than our everyday concerns, which usually receive its exclusive attention. Moreover, students attempt to maintain their focus for longer and longer periods of time, undistracted by intruding thoughts or sensations. This concentration of the mind can be accomplished by repeating a word or a sound, by counting the inhalation or exhalation of the breath or in numerous other ways.

The individual practice of form in martial arts, when it is used as mental training, also relies upon some of the forgoing methods to bring about in its students various changes in the way they view the world.

Of course, the light in which a student considers the form, the manner in which he does it and the ultimate outcome of his practice depend in large measure upon the views of his teacher. If his class sees nothing more in it than skill-producing practice, progress in this other direction will still occur but will be slow. Despite the occasional failure of their teacher to point the way, students will notice a change in themselves nonetheless. But usually they will be unaware of the potential for development and unable, therefore, to consciously help the process along.

At any rate, a teacher who believes his student should learn concentration through form practice will proceed by asking him to give the form his complete attention. Intrusive thoughts of past or present problems or of intentions concerning the future might rise in his mind, but the student must not entertain them. Ideas unconcerned with the form may appear, but he should ignore them as they come into his awareness and immediately return his attention to the form. He must endeavor to keep his mind on his every movement and try to do it as well as he can. Moreover, he should try to become fully aware of the position of his body and the changing location of its various parts. As he becomes conscious of errors of positions or execution in his performance, he must try to determine the reason for his mistakes and try to make the necessary adjustments. This general procedure is more characteristic of forms which are performed slowly, but even movements which are ordinarily done with speed can promote such awareness. If speed is too much of a handicap, the form can be slowed down. The drawback in training students to concentrate by the use of forms ordinarily done at a fast pace is that they find it difficult to be fully conscious of what they are doing.

Another facet of individual form training is its emphasis on executing techniques from a low center of gravity. Knees are usually bent in doing a form, but the need for a low center of gravity encompasses more than a superficial lowering of the body. In terms of developing skill, techniques capable of generating maximum power must be done with the whole body. Because the muscles of the legs and hips constitute a large proportion of the body's bulk and form its foundation, or stance, these muscles must be brought fully into play with each movement. Added stability is lent to each technique as the center of gravity is lowered. In addition, even though a punch or a block appears to be done with the arms and shoulders, in reality the main emphasis is on the correct movement of the legs and hips.

### TAN TIEN OR TANDEN

Beyond the apparent lowering of the body and the presence of power in these fighting movements, form practice is designed to effect a more subtle change in the student. This change concerns a gradual sinking or settling of the center of his body, or his conception of his center, to a lower position. This center eventually comes to rest at a point a few inches below the navel. This point is known as the tan tien in Chinese or tanden in Japanese.

Traditionally, the tan tien is a center or reservoir of a form of internal energy which, as discussed earlier, is called chi in Chinese. It is considered a point for the nourishment of life. Attempts by adherents of Western scientific medicine to experimentally discover the physiological presence and location of such a center have met with failure. Yet, from ancient times, teachers of mental and spiritual development in Indian, Chinese, and Japanese cultures have posited its existence and spoken of the benefits resulting from its cultivation. Teachers of this kind, whose writings are extant or who are presently teaching, base their instruction on the findings resulting from thousands of years of close and careful observation of human beings by their predecessors. Moreover, a teacher of this sort has always been a man with an outstanding grasp of practical psychology and skilled in assessing the extent of human awareness. If such men in different cultures speak of the center of the human body, place it in the same location and cite its importance as a place from which one "acts" and "thinks," then we must attach enough credence to the theory to entertain the possibility that something, in fact, goes on there. All our problems of belief and acceptance clear up, however, when we begin to practice and notice the gradual change in ourselves over the years.

### HARA

The Japanese term hara seems to include the qualities connected with the kind of centering involved. Hara can be translated as stomach, but in the sense being used here it indicates the lower abdominal area. In describing a way of functioning that is down to earth, big-hearted, and reflective of a broad and deep understanding of human life, the Japanese speak approvingly of a person acting from his hara or of having a big hara. Beyond the mature way of dealing with life that it immediately signifies, this kind of statement expresses a more fundamental point of view about human relationships and man's place in the world.

It implies an acceptance of the idea that we are connected with the world and with one another. We are not separated from the rest of life. The role of the intellect, or the head, in our activities is not ignored or depreciated, but it is understood that intellect must be rooted in those depths of life from which spring all that we do. Without such a base, intellect can become too extreme. Purely intellectual solutions to problems are probably not possible, because other parts of our mind are certain to exert their influence. However, when we attempt to be as rational as possible in our approach, we often become too narrow or restrictive in our assessment of the "relevant" factors that constitute a problem or its solution. We forget that the world is actually an interrelated and intermeshed whole.

It is thought that a person who acts in a way indicative of a developed hara walks and moves differently from others. He gives a physically settled and solid appearance, which is not the same thing as possessing a corpulent or stocky body. For those who are able to judge such things, there is a clear difference in the way people walk and use their bodies. This difference is evident when we compare a person raised in one country, or culture, with a person from another. For example, Japanese would say of most Westerners that they bounce along as they walk, reflecting the high location of the body's center. In contrast, they feel that Japanese generally walk more heavily and somehow are lower in terms of the body's center, expressing a different approach to life from that held in the West. The student of martial arts also begins to look physically more stable and composed as he continues practicing. At first there is no noticeable evidence of any alteration in his usual way of doing things. But it will be helpful for him to believe that the change he seeks is slowly coming about. When it does occur, he may not even be sure anything has happened because it has come so gradually. The clearest indicator he has that something has changed comes when an acquaintance he has not seen for a time remarks on some difference in him. The student may, in his friends' eyes, hold himself and do things in a more composed manner, partly the result of the center of his body gradually dropping. In those persons studying correctly for some years in a martial art or in some form of meditation, be they Western or Eastern, a settled, composed and tranquil way of doing things is evident.

## ANALYTICAL AND INTUITIVE ASPECTS OF THE MIND

As we learn to concentrate, to physically settle the body and to relax those muscles that are unnecessary for doing a technique, we gradually quiet the analytical, reasoning portion of the mind. Why would this be useful or necessary? In our Western culture, we generally react to the world in a rational manner, often distrusting or thinking of little value a more intuitive approach to our problems. Our Western way of viewing the world lends itself to separating out components of a whole in order to examine them more closely, sometimes forgetting that it is the working of the whole that is important. To try to see things in their totality, as they really are, seems essential to our welfare. Tampering with one or another element of our environment without enough consideration for the effect of such tampering on the whole could lead to calamity in some form or other. In a more personal sense, sometimes a too rational approach to life results in failure to see any connection between our well-being and interests and that of other human beings and other forms of life. Our relations with other life might then become exploitive, causing unhappiness and discontent and perhaps bringing some form of retribution in its wake as the exploited attempt to right the balance.

If we recognize the value of approaching life from an intuitive as well as a rational standpoint, how can we effect such a change in our thinking? To begin with, we must first give ourselves a rest from our usual way of viewing the world. Those of us who live in our fast-paced, crowded, and noisy cities receive a constant bombardment of impressions from our environment. There is usually so much going on that we are in a perpetual state of distraction, unable to concentrate and often unclear about who and what we are. To preserve our sanity we sometimes shut out or ignore many of the impressions clamoring for our attention. We certainly cannot consciously register every impression made upon us by the world around us. Unfortunately, it is probable that this kind of selectivity also results in our failure to see things as they really are. We usually construct some kind of mental image that represents the people or things most familiar to us or that we deal with all the time. We no longer see a person as clearly or as vividly after meeting him two or three times. For example, the first time we meet a person or witness an event we bring all our faculties to bear in an effort to assess this new experience. In succeeding meetings, we actually see less or lose the freshness of the first meeting because we have usually cataloged the impressions we received at the beginning. Thus, if an acquaintance has shaved a mustache or beard, we may not even notice this difference in his appearance because we have mentally classified him in a certain way.

The phenomenon of failing to see the uniqueness of each person is also related to this tendency. We usually categorize the people we meet or see around us. If a person says he is a student, the attributes of that occupation spring to mind and he is pigeonholed. A man engaged in some form of manual labor concerned with the erection of buildings is labeled "construction worker" and takes on the various characteristics we associate with that term. However, the people we meet may not fit the mold we have prepared for them in our minds. The ability to generalize in this way has its uses in our culture, but we often forget that the term "teacher" or "student" or "city dweller" includes a vast array of people, many of whom act in ways that might not fit our mental image of them.

To react to life in this way removes much of the freshness that could be a part of everyday experience. It contributes to boredom. Our awareness becomes limited to dealing with abstractions and we miss what is going on around us. Concentrating on the movements of a form in our training gives us a kind of rest from our accustomed way of dealing with life. We have to focus fully for a time on something real and concrete, something we are not allowing ourselves to form a mental image of. The result, over time, of this change in our way of relating to what we are doing is that when we return our attention to outside concerns, we see things more vividly, as if they were fresh experiences. Moreover, a new perspective results from this focus of our attention. Often, too, a different sense of proportion emerges with reduced use of abstract thinking. Personal problems that seemed overwhelming become easier to solve. Seen in relation to the larger issues of life, our problems are reduced to more easily manageable dimensions.

We seem to be concerned here with the way we apprehend the world which we help form and with which we interact. Some of us seem to try to relate to life logically and analytically, while others favor an approach based on emotion, feeling, and intuition, and perhaps a denial of the primary importance of logic in many areas. Obviously, it is not a question of the exclusive use of one mode of relating or the other, because everyone constantly combines the two in differing proportions. However, observers of human behavior have remarked on a general tendency on the part of most of us to favor either one or the other.

In the West, it seems clear that the logical and analytical has been considered superior to the intuitive, especially over the last two hundred years. For the past generation or two, literature and movies have often contrasted a dominant male way of reasoning with the weaker female, more sensitive method to the solution of a problem. If a point is at issue, the woman is generally portrayed as having a certain "feeling" about it and lacking the ability to present a cogently reasoned argument in favor of her feeling. As a result of this inability to support the product of her intuition with acceptable reasons, the "feeling" is rejected by the male decision-maker. In this same fictionalized treatment, the woman's apprehensions prove to have been well founded and failing to heed them results in some form of disaster. This presentation by writers and our acceptance of it in that form is a recognition that the dominant logical, analytical approach to the problems of life is fallible, especially when it is employed exclusively, and that there is something to be said for using the mind in other ways. Nevertheless, it is usual for the intuitive manner of relating to get short shrift from decision-makers, unless the insightful flash can be translated into a logical, sequential presentation. Women who cannot reason or refuse to are usually considered scatterbrained. An intuitive means of dealing with life is also thought common to artists, poets, and members of some esoteric groups. Although the work done by many people of this kind is considered useful and even valuable to society, they have often been viewed as eccentric and sometimes even dangerous to social stability. This attitude is probably held because the work of these persons usually reflects ideas which are different from currently accepted ones. These ideas are considered irrelevant and perhaps threatening by the great majority during the lifetime of many artists and others with the ability to bring the world into clear focus. In societies that exercise considerable control over the individual, such persons are subject to censorship lest their work present a point of view that runs counter to the official dogma.

Those who subscribe to the theory that the mind has both a logical and an intuitive side, a theory formulated over the millenia through observations of people's behavior, feel on safer ground when this theory is supported by the results of modern scientific studies. This is especially true in the West, given our predilection for evidence which is verifiable under controlled laboratory conditions. In recent years, psychological and physiological research concerned with the brain has given additional support to the earlier thesis. Robert Ornstein in his book *The Psychology of Consciousness* (W.H. Freeman & Co., San Francisco, 1972, 247 pp.) describes the research that has been done on the way the brain works in right-handed human beings. He writes:

On the physiological level, it has recently been shown that the two cerebral hemispheres of the cortex are specialized for different modes of information-processing. The left hemisphere operates primarily in a verbal-intellectual and sequential mode, the right hemisphere primarily in a spatial and sequential mode. The "right hemisphere" mode is often devalued by the dominant, verbal intellect. . . . This second mode often appears inelegant, lacking the formal reasoning, linearity, and polish of the intellect. It is more involved in space than in time, more involved in intuition than in logic and language. . . . Since it is nonlinear, this second mode is not involved in the "ordinary" realm of cause and effect which underlies so much of our personal and intellectual life. . . . (p. 225)

Ornstein makes the point that the two ways of dealing with our environment are complementary. But he seems to feel that the balance in our Western society has tipped on the side of functions handled by the left hemisphere of the brain. We are primarily intellectual and need additional attention to an intuitional, holistic approach to our problems. He argues for using both hemispheres in the kind of synthesis that will promote the well-being and perhaps the survival of our world.

The desirability of this synthesis stems from the conception that the logical, analytical portion of the brain can get valuable information from the intuitive portion. Also, the intuitive portion can benefit by having its total apprehension of a situation translated by the logical into language or symbols that can be communicated to other minds. The flash of intuition concerning the solution of a problem must be worked through in step-by-step fashion by the analytical portion of the mind if the solution or its results are to be made available in the physical world.

From another standpoint, we ought to be able to bring into our conscious minds information about ourselves and the world around us gathered by the intuitive portion of the mind. Some think that the intuitive portion contains suppressed ideas and wishes best left alone or unexamined. But to think this way bars from conscious examination a rich field of our own experience which, like it or not, affects us even if we try to ignore it.

Form training can move the student in this direction. It furthers a quieting of the rational, analytical portion of the mind and allows the right hemisphere of the brain more scope. This process can bring about an opening up of the student's perceptions, heighten his awareness and help him to become conscious of more of the world around him than previously. In his relations with other persons, he might find that he is developing the kind of insight that allows him to sense what is really being thought or felt. Often, verbal statements made by another do not square with the particular feeling he transmits. This does not mean that the verbal expression need be rejected in favor of the intuitive feeling. However, a prudent course would dictate a combination of equal proportions of the two methods of relating to others.

## EXTENSIONS OF
## A MORE INTUITIVE APPROACH TO LIFE

As this sort of practice exerts its influence, the student may alter his method of viewing and solving the problems of daily life. For example, he might begin to admit the possibility of psychic or clairvoyant ability. He might even visit a psychic when he seeks the solution to an important problem. The outcome of such a consultation need not be a total and unquestioning acceptance of the psychic's words. However, what is said could cause the student to encounter and recognize aspects of the problem and possible solutions that he may have missed in taking a generally logical and rational approach.

Increased recognition of the existence and usefulness of mind processes that were earlier thought fantasy or of limited use might turn the student toward such methods of divination as the *I Ching*. The *I Ching*, or *Book of Changes*, is a three-thousand-year-old book of Chinese wisdom. It is often used as a book of oracles, but can be seen to go far beyond this usage when we learn that it provided a source for both Taoist and Confucian philosophy. At any rate, consulting the *I Ching* when faced with the need for a decision on some difficult subject can help the student toward greater insight. Jung, in his foreward to the *I Ching*, states that the mode of divination to which the *I Ching* is put aims at self-knowledge (p. xxxiv, Wilhelm/Baynes, *The I Ching*, Bollingen Series XIX, Princeton University Press, 1950, 740 pp.). It seems to do this by allowing the student to become conscious of his previously unconscious thoughts concerning the question he asked. The questioning process causes the student to meditate on this problem. The particular answer he gets is not always clear, especially since it is couched in somewhat quaint and poetical language. However, in his attempt to make "sense" of the answer, the student finds that ideas and thoughts that were buried in the deeper levels of his mind begin to come to the surface. He thereby gains new insight into his problem and, usually, into himself as well.

Other members of the occult fraternity, such as astrologers, graphologists, and hand analysts, also can help the serious seeker after self-knowledge to see aspects of his character that wishful thinking or inattention might have obscured. Correctly used, such information can be valuable. It can help provide direction and point up those areas in his life to which the student can profitably devote his energies.

Another method the student might begin to employ to gain greater self-knowledge is the analysis of his dreams. Some maintain that they never dream, but such a statement has been disproved by psychologists who study dreaming. Their findings are that we all dream, but that we often fail to remember what we dreamed. They think that this forgetfulness is caused by the conscious mind's censorship of unacceptable desires and thoughts. We do not welcome the appearance of material that fails to support the particular point of view we consciously hold about ourselves or about our relations with others, especially when the new information places us in what we think is an unfavorable light. When we sleep, the activity and strength of the conscious mind is reduced, and these dormant ideas come to the surface. If we try to recall our dreams as soon as we awake we can usually remember their contents. Again, as with the *I Ching*, the material may, to our conscious mind, be distorted. Yet important truths concerning our feelings, attitudes and thoughts reveal themselves in our dreams and can be brought into the conscious mind if we make the effort. Once these feelings surface, we can examine them and see ourselves as we really are rather than as we think we would like to be. The direction is once more toward knowing ourselves a little better.

A word of caution should be voiced against the rise of a kind of self-indulgence in our use of various means toward self-understanding. All of us enjoy hearing about ourselves, especially when we receive hope and direction for the future, in the positive terms in which psychics, hand analysts, or astrologers are wont to express themselves to clients. (This is not to say that persons practicing such arts are not themselves making serious attempts at self-understanding and gaining a clearer perception of the workings of the world. However, they would readily admit that a person who receives a reading is often taking only a faltering first step on his path and that changing the direction of one's life is the work of many years. Moreover, to emphasize negative elements in a client's character or his method of interacting with others might produce in him an unwarranted feeling of the hopelessness of his situation.) Thus, we might run from one occultist to the next in an attempt to get additional favorable information about ourselves, auspicious auguries of the future, or just to have someone devote his attention to our general make-up and our usually unrealized potential. Some of us search avidly for someone who will make an assessment of our character we can accept. We might like to think of ourselves in a particular way and then go from one seer to another, hoping for more information that will support our view. This is unrealistic and hinders the growth of self-understanding. Once we begin to know ourselves a little better, some degree of hoping and wishing for some needed or beneficial change is helpful, but it must be supported by disciplined work.

Boredom with our present state of development or our particular life style may also result in a search for titillation possibly provided by an occultist. However, if we can but recognize that each state of development is complete and whole and where we are at the moment, we will be content with it. When changes come, as they must, we should be content with them too, viewing them as way stations along the road we are traveling. Projecting ourselves into the future or into a hoped for personality is to fail to live in the present and again goes contrary to the result aimed at by our martial arts training.

## DISCIPLINE

Finally, doing the form daily helps the student to bring discipline into his life. By "discipline" I mean developing the ability to do something each day which is not always pleasant and about which one is not always enthusiastic. It is easy to engage in some activity which excites us and which we like. However, even though we have made up our minds to live in a certain way, we will encounter many days or perhaps weeks when we are less than eager to do the work connected with our choice. If we practice only the days we really want to, our progress will be extremely slow. In addition, we are apt to stop our training altogether, because the particular form we are doing becomes easier with daily practice and more difficult when it is done infrequently.

Spending a certain portion of each day in practice, the results of which are not quickly evident, is difficult. Those students who enroll in a school of martial arts which holds daily classes are fortunate, because once the class begins they are swept along in the general procedure. The energy generated by fellow students and the teacher serves to carry each individual along. Those who attend class only once or twice a week, and who must practice alone for a period of time each day have a more difficult time of it. At any rate, the general pattern for students is for discipline to be initially imposed from outside themselves. It is true that beginners usually throw themselves into training with enthusiasm. But when this initial flush of enthusiasm begins to fade, they need help in establishing a steady pattern of training. The class situation provides this pattern. Gradually, however, students fall into the habit of training at certain times of the day. If for some reason they are unable to train, they feel that something has been left undone. Once a certain momentum of practice has been established, it becomes easier to do one's prescribed period of training than to avoid it.

The idea of discipline is not a matter of having our mind on the achievement of some future goal. Nor it it tied to the Protestant work ethic. Instead, it stems from our decision to live our lives in a particular way, to follow a certain road. Once we have made such a decision, we must turn our energy as much as possible toward fully doing the things that are a part of our chosen way. When we practice, we must not think we are sacrificing something or suffering in order to attain some reward. The thing we are doing should have beeen chosen because of its inherent value for us and thus is worth doing for its own sake. Taking the view that we are only practicing in order to get some imagined goal tends to devalue what is being done. The goal we are striving to reach may not exist or, if we feel we have reached it, may not be at all the way we imagined it. All we really have is our daily practice and living our daily life. The method or manner in which we live from day to day affects us in a certain way and results in development of one kind or another. We must go on the assumption that undertaking a certain kind of training will put us in a different place five years from now than if this training had not been done. Beyond carefully making our initial selection of a particular road to follow, it is of little worth to speculate constantly about the kind of human being we might become at some future date. The likelihood is that we will not differ very much from the way we are now. Yet even small changes in self-realization and self-understanding are valuable for us.

Attempting to bring discipline into our lives does not call for the avoidance of joy and pleasure. Students will discover that practicing alone or with a partner is often very enjoyable. The relaxed feeling that comes with doing individual form practice is almost always pleasurable. In working with a partner, depending on the martial art, smiles and even laughter are not uncommon. At the conclusion of a free practice period, participants who have put aside their accustomed social facade to reveal more of themselves, as is common in the heat of the encounter, enjoy a warm feeling for one another. Thus, some kind of disciplined training does not negate feelings of pleasure, but may instead even give rise to them.

Still another facet of discipline concerns the necessity of doing something long enough and in concentrated enough fashion to discover what is beneath the surface. Without almost daily and fairly intensive practice in any of the martial arts, we will only experience what is superficial. Of course, any degree of training, even if very mild, brings some benefit. However, if our practice is not intensive over a period of years, we will fail to come upon those elements which only appear at this particular depth. This idea is clearly illustrated in the development of skill. Those persons who train daily for a number of years reach levels of skill that seem impossible to achieve to those unable or unwilling to devote themselves as fully to training. Similarly, in the area of self-realization and self-development, levels are reached with intensive and continuous training that the dilettante can only guess at.

CARL B. BECKER

# PHILOSOPHICAL PERSPECTIVES ON THE MARTIAL ARTS IN AMERICA

The 1970s have witnessed a surge of interest in applying Asian philosophies, particularly Zen Buddhism, to sports. *Prima facie*, this might indicate that the philosophy of sport, while relatively new on the American scene, may have a longer tradition in the Orient. At the same time, a number of Oriental sports have gained increasing attention in the West—especially the martial arts of judo and karate. Several aspects of these martial arts indeed merit the attention of philosophers, particularly because they illustrate aspects of sports which have generally been undervalued or overlooked in Western sports. Among the potentially important philosophical claims made for the martial arts, we shall focus on three: (A) the idea that there is an intrinsic connection between practicing the martial arts and developing *morality*; (B) the central role of discipline and ritual to the martial arts; (C) the martial arts as giving insight or wisdom through their imaging of the universe.

We shall limit our discussion to those martial arts most widely practiced *as sport* in both East and West: judo, karate, and aikido, excluding Oriental fencing, archery, and armed combat. Like many Western sports, judo, karate, and aikido have existed *as sports* for only about a century, although they were derived and adapted from earlier secret fighting techniques (te, jiujutsu) of feudal Japan, when carrying of arms was restricted. *As sports*, therefore, judo, karate, and aikido

---

*The author of this article (b. 1951) is a professor of philosophy at Southern Illinois University at Carbondale. A specialist in Asian philosophy and ethics, he has taught also at Bukkyo University in Kyoto.*

have taken on new features and dropped old ones; it is no longer appropriate to connect them with the Zen code of the samurai warrior (bushido) any more than the knight's code of chivalry is connected with the rules of modern tennis or golf. The connection with Zen philosophy, if any, is one which must be carefully examined, logically explained and defended, and not simply assumed as an inherent inherited characteristic [Gleeson, p.93]. The focus of this study, then, is not to tie some cute Zen-like phrases into descriptions of karate-chops or football passes, which has already been done *ad nauseum* [Wertz]. Rather, it is to scrutinize the claims that the martial arts have a direct bearing on morality, disciplined ritual, and knowledge of man in the universe.

## MORALITY:
### THE MARTIAL ARTS AND VIOLENCE

It has often been suggested, as by philosopher Paul Ziff, that all too many sports are evidently manifestations of aggression. When one looks at sports in general, aggressive, not aesthetic, aspects are what loom large. Archery, boxing, bull fighting, fencing, football, judo, karate, lacrosse, shooting, wrestling: all offer unmistakable examples of aggressive behavior. As anthropologists and sociologists are beginning to tell us, aggressive behavior is most likely the result of cultural indoctrination. Our society would be better off without such sports. [Ziff, p. 99]

This claim runs directly counter to the common statement of martial artists that their study of the martial arts has led them to become more moral, more nonviolent, more peaceful, and less aggressive. Since Ziff fails to document his highly disputable claims about what "anthropologists and sociologists are beginning to tell us," we cannot directly refute those claims. But we can agree with Ziff that empirical studies are indeed relevant to the truth of such propositions as that "sports lead to violent behavior"—and the evidence shows that, at least in the cases of martial arts, the converse is true.

First, however, some clarification of the meaning of "violence" and "aggression" is in order. Although common parlance may blur fine distinctions, philosophers must pause to preserve them. In common language, any rapid, unexpected striking motion might be labeled "violent," and any psychological or physical attempt to take territory from another or to catch a rival off guard might be considered "aggressive." If we retain these extremely broad terms, then surely there are some forms of "violence" and "aggression" which are to be condemned as immoral, and others which are not (as in the case of violently or aggressively saving a child from danger). We must either subdivide violent and aggressive actions into subsets of morally defensible "violence" and "aggression" and indefensible "violence" and "aggression," or else we must restrict our use of these terms to areas in which the actions are indeed morally questionable, and agree to use other adjectives to refer to moral, swift, initiative-taking, forward-moving acts. I propose that we take the latter tack as more simple and easier to follow, in accord with other philosophers who have written at length on violence. They have suggested, for example, that "violence" as a philosophical term includes the notion of "violation of basic human rights" [Riga, p. 145]. While this may entail the superficially counterintuitive consequence that psychological warfare or the preservation of a class system are in some senses "violent" [Garver], it also enables us to distinguish between physically rapid sports and aggressive sports, a distinction which Ziff would ignore.

From this viewpoint, it would be mistaken to call every sudden move or moment of body contact in sports "violent and aggressive." For the participants have both agreed upon the ground rules under which such movements and body contacts may and may not take place, and they have steeled their bodies and minds against the expectation of precisely such eventualities. In football, karate, and even in prize boxing, the intention of the athletes is less to maim or maul their opponents than to score points leading to a victory. If they stoop to foul play, deliberately violating the rules of the game with the intention of injuring another, then indeed we might condemn the players as violent, just as we would if they attacked a referee. Although we can make ordinary language sense of the fan's remark that "the football linemen crashed violently into a heap," we would also want to agree that nothing of morally reprehensible "violence" had "violated" anyone else there, once we were able to determine that all players had been playing in the best of good will and rules-abiding sportsmanship.

On the foregoing analysis, in order to determine whether a sport breeds violence, it is fruitless to observe merely the speed of motions or proximity of bodies during the rounds of a match. (This would inform us only of "violence" in the overgeneralized sense of the term, and not in any philosophically significant way.) Rather, we must ask about the behavior of such athletes committing violence against other people— either by deliberate and intentional fouls within the ring, or against people who never intended to encounter their sudden martial moves, outside of the sports arena altogether.

As early as 1955, a number of studies were conducted testing the effects on personality of "combative" sports. They concluded, among other things, that sports of direct bodily conflict produced the athletes *least* aggressive outside of their tournament matches [Husman, p.421]. Other studies examined "before and after" characteristics of boxers' personalities, and were able to document that the energy expended and the catharsis achieved in the boxing ring reduced the aggression levels of professional pugilists to substantially below the level of the average citizen outside of the ring [Hutton, p.49]. More intricate, very recent studies by Rothpearl at Fordham documented that suspicion and aggression levels may be slightly increased for martial artists in their intermediate ranks, but that this quality changed to one of nonviolence in the more advanced students. Rothpearl suggested that it is their specific training to restrain themselves from violence which may be responsible for this shift. In any case, the evidence is fairly clear that these Eastern "combat sports" do *not* have the negative effects feared by Ziff, but on the contrary tend to reduce violent tendencies and curb them.

Not content with just knowing these facts, however, philosophers want to know *why* this should be the case. One hypothesis, already alluded to above by physical education researchers, is the "catharsis theory": that in the process of hitting and fighting with other people, athletes "get their aggressions out of their systems," so they no longer feel as energetic and aggressive afterwards. While this might account for the immediate feelings of peacefulness and wanting to take a rest for awhile after a match is over, it does not adequately explain why martial arts practitioners tend to be substantially more peace-loving than handball or basketball players [Pyecha, p.425], who presumably become equally exhausted and may equally "get their aggressions out" in a tough game. Nor are the injuries—inflicted in judo graver or more common than those in handball and basketball. This may be a more real indication of how immorally violent each of these sports is, since the rules and purposes of all of these sports attempt to forestall physical injury. Of nearly a quarter million judo practitioners in this country, only about 70 individuals per year report serious injuries—a figure far lower than for most popular sports [Corcoran, p.132]. If injuring one's opponent "takes out" one's aggressions, then football is a more aggressive sport and football players should have many more cathartic experiences than judo players.

Another theory suggests that it is the association in the dojo (martial arts practice hall) with others who are nonviolent which leads the newcomer to perfect his own tendencies in that direction. This "morality by association theory" would hold that morality is learned by witnessing and copying the models of moral men, and that moral men who abound in the dojos are then copied by their juniors, who become moral men in turn [Back, p.22]. But good sportsmanship is taught and presumably imitated in almost every sport, and this would not explain the preeminence of martial arts in nonviolence. Moreover, this theory still fails to explain why judo attracts and makes moral a group of practitioners in the first place, so that they might be copied by their younger students. To say that the younger students become nonviolent because their elders are nonviolent still leaves open the question of how the elders got that way, and leads only to an infinite regress.

Other studies have also shown that as little as 8 weeks of judo training in a situation where no senior students were available as role models were still productive of a more warm and easygoing personality type [Pyecha, p.430]. Although the presence of senior students is undoubtedly an additional reinforcement and socializing factor, it cannot alone account for the superior cultivation of nonviolence and warm personalities found in martial arts and absent in other sports.

A third theory—which I take to be most correct—is that the martial arts inculcate self-control as a fundamental principle. This self-control is not simply the control which a tennis player seeks in his serve or a golfer in his putt, but a control of the "will to violence" itself, which appears to Western observers as a moral virtue. The very hieroglyphic character of the *ju* of *judo* is the character for gentleness, and the *do* means the way, the path, the Tao. Thus, the principle of judo, from the very beginning, is not one of aggression, but of flowing with things.

This demand for self-control is equally evident in karate tournaments, where all blows must be stopped within a centimeter or two of the opponent's face or body, but *without actually touching him*! [Johnston, p.91]. Such matches may seem less than exciting to American crowds intent on gladiatorial blood, as in "professional wrestling." In fact, some unscrupulous karate promoters have allowed actual contact in their tournaments. Nevertheless, in principle and in practice sessions, the knowledge of the deadlines of the techniques being learned is coupled with a weighty responsibility *not* to employ them in daily life, except to demonstrate their form and speed in the ring. When this requirement that all punches be stopped just short of target is applied to high-speed tournament situations, it imposes tremendous demands on the judgment and skill of the martial artist, who will lose the match more surely if he really hits his opponent than if he is hit [Back].

This points to a profound difference in the philosophy of combat sports in the East and West. Whereas Americans are more likely to think that the physical body contact of the sport adds to our sense of the merit of the victor [Pole, p.72], the Oriental philosophy is to avoid contacts as skillfully as possible. Jigoro Kano, the founder of Japanese judo, was famous for his motto: "Seiryoku zenyo jita kyoei," meaning "produce the best effect with the least effort, self and other cooperating for mutual benefit." The grand masters of aikido are so proficient at avoiding violence that their martial art has been dubbed "the honorable art of getting the hell out of the way." But it is truly amazing to watch an old man subtly sidestep the blows of half a dozen attackers simultaneously, never touching them at all, but allowing them to tire and injure themselves. Even karate, thought to be the most violent of martial arts, stops its punches before contact. While Western emphasis is on youth, strength, and brute force, the Eastern is on gentleness, minimal effort, and skill.

### DISCIPLINE AND RITUAL

Skill in the martial arts does not come naturally to some people, the way some people are natural swimmers or equestrians. It is developed through a long and painful process of discipline and ritual, from a perspective which regards a decade as just a beginning. Mental as well as physical discipline is at the heart of the martial arts, but tends to be relatively downplayed by Americans who take their sports for play and recreation [Kuntz, p.27]. Todd's view is representative of that of many Americans: that the purpose of sports is health and self-improvement, the nonproductive joy of movement itself, and that concern with "making progress" or "moving upward" conflicts with this joy [Todd, p.14]. Although many Americans work fairly seriously for better scores in tennis, golf, or the marathon, few would dispute that they enjoy it, nor that their primary motivations were health and fun. Japanese athletes, by contrast, when asked why they study martial arts generally respond with, "Ii kunren dakara"—because it's valuable discipline. Nor is this discipline restricted to the training of the body to move in certain ways. It begins and ends with rituals.

The student is constantly reminded to remember his place (ba) not only in terms of spatial relationships, such as where he is standing on the mat, but also in terms of where he stands in the hierarchy, in relationship to his master, seniors, competitors, and family. Fox [p.88] has turned the "The Honorific Meaning of Sport" into a largely linguistic analysis of the characteristics of sport as nonproductive activity. In martial arts, however, honor, or face, is everything, and the arts are surrounded with ritual to reinforce the respect of the athlete's relationships. Practice sessions begin and end with rituals of bowing to one's master and competitors, and with silent meditations. The drills may be as repetitive and meaningless (even painful) as repeating one's mathematical tables [Back, p.27]. Ultimately the promotion to higher ranks is based less on one's skill in games and more on one's discipline in the katas, or forms, of each move. This constant ranking and evaluation by teams of elderly judges also reinforces the sense of one's belonging to a structured, disciplined society [Todd, p.19].

In contrast to the flights of soaring abandon described by American authors as typifying the Zen athlete, the serious practitioner of judo or karate spends most of his practice time either bowing and meditating more or less uncomfortably on his knees, or literally mindlessly repeating forms (katas) and motions against a wall or in the air, over and over again. The tendency of the American is to wonder, "When am I going to get to do the real stuff? (i.e., sparring against opponents)." The view of the martial arts master is that the discipline of form (kata) and the practice of ritual *is* the "real stuff," and sparring is only a small tangent to the discipline.

It is this context of discipline and ritual which best enables martial arts to make their case of being appropriate to esthetic criteria. Ziff [pp.100,104] has argued that aesthetic criteria are not appropriately applied to sports, whose aesthetic aspects are purely coincidental and "epiphenomenal," whereas Todd [p.19] has contended that martial arts were impossible except between two athletes with a conflict of wills. These statements show how totally these Western philosophers fail to understand the martial arts. In martial arts the form of the movement is more fundamental than any other results.

When Jigoro Kano wanted to prove to the Japanese ministry of education that judo was a worthwhile sport for Japanese physical education classes, he gave a demonstration of silent, slow-motion dancing movements, exhibiting the grace and power of his system [Corcoran, p.132]. His similar demonstrations in America met with meager and uninterested audiences; it was not until entrepreneuring artists began breaking bricks that Americans began to take interest. Kano also developed aesthetic theories which applied to live wrestling situations, in which he considered tsukuri (the build-up of plot), kake (the making of a decisive move), and kuzushi (the denouement) to be the three components of judo [Gleeson, p.27]. It would take more of an expert martial artist than myself to unpack the implications and delimit the applicability of this metaphor. The important point is that even in the minds of the creators and masters of these sports, artistic rather than aggressive or victory-oriented criteria are predominant.

It is significant that the climax or moment of victory itself is not focused upon at all in this analysis. Rather it is the flow and pattern of movement, the building of tensions requiring resolution, the commitment to one out of a huge variety of possible actions and outcomes, and the resolution, as all things fall to rest in the forms almost inevitably dictated by the dramatic action and characters of the actors [Thomas]. Western philosophers have already argued for the application of aesthetic criteria to athletic activities [Kuntz]. I suggest that their case could be strengthened even further through reference to the martial arts, which are artistic not only in name, but are practiced and judged on aesthetic criteria, and in many cases (e.g., Tai chi chuan) are virtually indistinguishable from the arts of dance and ballet. Here too, there is ample room for philosophical investigation in the future.

## IMAGING THE UNIVERSE

There is yet a third respect in which the martial arts provide a unique link with philosophical concerns: they are held to confer on the part of the practitioner a sort of wisdom or knowledge of the processes, nature, and flow of the universe, with which the martial arts are said to harmonize the practitioner's own actions.

This unique state of mind is not to be confused with simple self-forgetfulness. There is a certain state of mind, perhaps analogous to the very lowest states achieved in Zen meditation, in which self-consciousness is overcome because the mind is directed toward some other object or activity. It is this sort of selflessness which is most often discussed in Western accounts of the spiritual or philosophical value of sports to the individual. We all know what it is like to "lose ourselves" in some activity, particularly when we are intensely attending to it or enjoying it. The misconception that this sort of state is the goal of the Zen practitioner goes back to Suzuki, who was a master of neither Zen nor English. Surely there may be some analogies between the two states, but it is seriously questionable whether enlightenment implies no more than the reduction of discursive thought to enable better performance of any given activity.

Surely "enlightenment" must refer to an experience whose consequences continue to transform one's life and world view from that moment onward. It is precisely for this reason that Zen masters repeatedly examine their students, and hold that one who pronounces his own enlightenment does not really have it. Similarly, claims of temporal distortion or wide-field vision may be common to sports and Zen, but both of these are no more than the effects of particular states of body and brain [Wertz, pp.71–73]. They are without lasting effects on ethics, personality, or knowledge. The knowledge claims made by the martial arts teach that it is only through being acutely aware of oneself and one's body that we gain knowledge [Wertz, p.74]. As the practitioner learns the forms (kata) of his martial art, and pays strict attention to the disciplined ritual therein, he becomes aware of the structure of the universe and man's part within it. This is possible because each of the forms in the martial arts is said to reflect or model some act or aspect of the universe. This claim may be true on several different levels.

On the most primitive level, this is certainly true of those poses and moves in the martial arts which imitate animal movements. It is said that Master Hua To invented many of the martial arts movements (in the third century) after carefully observing the movements of wild animals, and many of the moves in tai chi, kung fu, and karate still preserve the names of animals or parts of their bodies [Gleeson, pp. 87–93]. Thus, an imitation of a snake may indeed make us more aware of our world if it helps us to feel the way a snake might feel its world, or to think about various aspects of animal nature within us. But this imitation of animals is the most primitive of sports [Osterhoudt, p.96], and certainly the knowledge claims of the martial arts go beyond the knowledge of what it might feel like to be a snake.

On a somewhat more sophisticated level, it might be argued that the discipline and ritual discussed at length in the previous section are themselves aspects of "world-making." In this sense, the martial artist comes to know his world not only as its imitator, but in his creation of it. Nor is this "world-making" simply a creation of a stronger or more sensitive body, which might be claimed for a wide range of sports or physical activities. Rather, it is in the establishment of relationships with teachers, seniors, fellows, and juniors, with competitors, judges, and unseen forces (of which more later), which relationships he creates through his repetition of ritual. In this sense, the martial artist comes to know his world not because he learns about what is already there, but because he participates in manufacturing a part of his world in its becoming. As he bows and reveres his master each day, for example, he creates, participates in, and comes to understand a relationship which is very real and important for Asian artists, and which rarely if ever pertains between Western athletes and coaches. Similarly, the acts of meditation prior to action, the swearing of loyalty to one's own martial tradition, and the bowing and honoring of one's opponents creates a world of concern with invisible relations, deeply connected to man's inner spirit and values, and which man can come to know only through his own involvement and commitment to them. To use a Kierkegaardian analogy, one cannot really know faith until he takes an irrational leap from normal, critical consciousness to the realm of faith—at which point he finds his world enriched and transformed by the leap, and things fit together, if not in a totally rational way, at least in a way which "makes sense" to the faithful, while remaining inaccessible to those who insist on strictly logical and critical criteria. In a somewhat similar sense, the martial arts practitioner is creating a new, invisible world, if not of faith, at least of commitments and relationships in the dojo, which only become fully comprehensible and meaningful to him once he has placed himself fully within their hermeneutic framework. Thus, the martial artist comes to understand his world, not only because some of his thoughts and movements mimic it, but also because he shapes part of his experienced world for himself, based on the models of the martial arts community. Having shaped, experienced, and ultimately understood this part of his own new world, he then possesses new knowledge of the way the world is and can be, which he lacked prior to submersion in and submission to the apparently rigid rules and rituals of discipline.

On still a more elevated level, the claim is made that we gain knowledge of the ebb and flow of the universe itself by forming the forms and dancing the dances of the martial arts. To some Westerners, this claim may sound absurd or abstract, for it is certainly founded upon a different, more wholistic, and more *living* view of the universe than our physics and chemistry will consider. In fact, it rests on at least two major philosophical presuppositions, both ontological and epistmological.

First, it holds that the universe is itself an organic, living entity manifesting the interplay of opposing (yin and yang) forces. The basic component of the universe is ch'i (Jap: ki) or life-force. Man himself is a microcosmic subunit of ch'i, explicable in terms of the interplay of yin and yang, as are all processes in the universe. The Chinese analogize man's body and movements to those of the universe, not only by making the universe anthropomorphic, but by seeing the cosmic drama and properties embodied in man, when man moves or flows in certain ways. Times of day, months, and years are named after and analogized to animals whose properties they are seen to possess—and these same properties are seen in the movements of the martial arts. So there is a parallel not only between certain moves and certain animal qualities, but by transitivity, between those moves and times of day, seasons of the year, and/or stages of life. Man's character is also defined in terms of various sensed qualities, which in turn enables the selection of moves particularly suited either to enhance his talents or remedy his deficiencies. While Westerners might tend to dismiss the notion of a universe describable in terms of categories of animal characteristics and sense-perception qualities as too primitive or anthropocentric, the Chinese would respond in turn that a purely mechanistic materialism is equally incapable of capturing and understanding the universe—much less of comprehending the strengths and weaknesses, moods and moves of athletes at certain times of day, faced with human opponents of varying characters. In short, the Chinese may see the universe in terms of analogies which we do not generally perceive or accept in the West. But we should not be too hasty with the labels of "true" or "false" before exploring the advantages or knowledge which such a view point really may possess. It may prove to be the case that the Chinese world-view in this sense is even more capable of explaining the dynamics of human energy and competition than are the mechanisms of chemistry, physics, and biology, to the primitive extent we have developed them in the West to date. But we need not resolve this argument here in order to understand that this might be a basis upon which knowledge claims are made.

Second, as a consequence of this first theory, the martial arts would claim that a knowledge of the nature and structure of the whole is possible through investigation and experience of the parts of it which we contact. Cheng succinctly summarizes this Neo-Confucian principle:

It is assumed that, by engaging in this sort of investigation of things in this large sense, mind will suddenly become clear about the total and final principles of things and itself. This might be described as a step of induction and/or intuitive induction. This intuitive induction is possible because it is assumed that nature, from which the mind receives its rational ability, has contained all the ultimate truth of the world.... This ontological unification of all principles into oneness and one ultimate principle (called tao—the do of judo, aikido, and karatedo) is what makes it metaphysically possible for the mind to make the intuitive inductive jump into total understanding, which can be characterized as seeing different principles in different things and yet seeing them as belonging to one simple truth. [Cheng, pp.22–23]

Of course, many philosophers long ago rejected the knowability of the universe, or that anything in man's paltry experience could be known to parallel the nature of noumenon or reality. The Chinese and Japanese did not. As Shao Yung says, "Man is the model of the universe (or heaven), but when he moves in accord with principle, he becomes equal to the universe (or heaven)" [Chan, p.490,7B]. Although this may sound too mystical or metaphysical for contemporary positivistic tastes, we must try to understand these martial arts masters on their own terms, before we brush the terms away as unintelligible or nonsense. At least one Western writer, watching the unbelievable feats of an old aikido master, concluded that it was indeed the attunement with invisible universal forces which enables such men to resist great forces or move great obstacles [Sekida].

The debate about the nature of the universe, and how man can know about that nature, will surely not stop with "modern" science, but will no doubt proliferate as we study more and more Oriental philosophies— at least if we restrain ourselves from disregarding them at the outset. No less a claim than this—that man gains knowledge of the universe—is being made by the masters of the martial arts. Still other claims are occasionally heard about transcendent knowledge or transcendent states, or paranormal powers, which this essay is in no position to discuss, much less evaluate. But our incredulity at the more extravagant of their philosophical claims should not lead us to an over-hasty rejection of their more defensible pronouncements. We have at least reviewed some of the assumptions which underlie the proposition that knowledge is gained through martial arts practice, and we have attempted to explicate some nontrivial senses in which it might be defended.

# BIBLIOGRAPHY

Back, Allan, and Daeshak Kim. "Towards a Western Philosophy of the Martial Arts." *Journal of the Philosophy of Sport*, VI (1979), pp. 19–28.

Blackburn, Daniel, and Maryann Jorgenson. *Zen and the Cross-Country Skier*. Pasadena, Calif.: Ward Ritchie, 1976.

Chan, Wing-Tsit. *A Sourcebook in Chinese Philosophy*. Princeton, N.J.: Princeton University Press, 1963.

Cheng, Chung-Ying. "Conscience, Mind and Individual in Chinese Philosophy." *Journal of Chinese Philosophy*, II (1974), pp. 22–23.

Corcoran, John, and Emil Farkas. *The Complete Martial Arts Catalogue*. New York: Simon and Schuster, 1977.

DiPorta, Leo. *Zen Running*. New York: Everest House, 1978.

Fox, Richard M. "The Honorific Meaning of Sport," *Philosophy in Context*, IX (1979), pp. 84–94.

Gallwey, W. Timothy. *Inner Tennis*. New York: Random House, 1976.

Garver, Newton. "What Violence Is." *The Nation*. Vol. 24, (June 1968).

Gleeson, Geoff. *The Complete Book of Judo*. Toronto: Coles, 1976.

Gluck, Jay. *Zen Combat*. New York: Ballantine, 1976.

Herrigel, Eugen. *Zen in the Art of Archery*. New York: Random House, 1971.

Husman, Burris F. "Aggression in Boxers and Wrestlers." *Research Quarterly*. XXVI (1955), p. 421.

Hutton, Daniel C., and Warren R. Johnson. "Effects of a Combative Sport upon Personality Dynamics." *Research Quarterly*, XXVI (1955).

Johnston, Richard W. "Dangerous Delusion." *Sports Illustrated*, October 18, 1976, pp. 91–92.

Kuntz, Paul. "From Ziff to Zenn: A Defense in the Aesthetics of Sport." *Philosophy in Context*, IX (1979), pp. 95–101.

Osterhoudt, R. G. "Prolegomenon to a Philosophical Anthropology of Sport." *Philosophy in Context*, IX (1979), pp. 95–101.

Pole, Nelson. "Living by Sports." *Philosophy in Context*, IX (1979), pp. 64–75.

Pyecha, John. "Comparative Effects of Judo and Selected Physical Education Activities on Male University Freshman Personality Traits." *Research Quarterly*, XL (1970), p. 425.

Riga, Peter D. "Violence: A Christian Perspective." *Philosophy East and West*. XIX (1969), p. 145.

Rohe, Frederick. *The Zen of Running*. New York: Random House, 1975.

Rothpearl, Allen. "Personality Traits in Martial Artists." *Perceptual and Motor Skills*, L (1980), pp. 395–401.

Sekida, Katsuki. *Zen Training: Methods and Philosophy*. New York: John Weatherhill, 1975.

Thomas, Carolyn E. "The Tragic Dimension of Sport." *Philosophy in Context*, IX (1979), pp. 35–42.

Todd, William. "Some Aesthetic Aspects of Sport." *Philosophy in Context*, IX (1979), pp. 8–21.

Wertz, Spencer K. "Zen, Yoga, and Sports: Eastern Philosophy for Western Athletes." *Journal of the Philosophy of Sport*, IV (1977), pp. 70–80.

Ziff, Paul. "A Fine Forehand." *Journal of the Philosophy of Sport*, I (1974), pp. 92–109.

### T.T. LIANG
# MY EXPERIENCE

I am nearing eighty years old and have been practicing t'ai chi for more than thirty years. I, personally, have had fifteen teachers.

In the beginning I took up t'ai chi to save my life after a grave illness. At first I became involved because I was afraid I might become ill again. As I got better and had further experience with t'ai chi, I gradually became more and more interested in trying to make the art both more scientific and more aesthetic. I introduced rhythm so that the postures can be practiced to music, slowly, effortlessly, and continuously. After sufficient practice, you will master the 150 postures so thoroughly that you will forget the rhythm, the movement, even yourself—although you are proceeding as usual. At this stage, you are in a trance; your five attributes (form, perception, consciousness, action, and knowledge) are all empty—this is meditation in action and action in meditation. When you finish and come to the end of the postures, suddenly you are back. Where have I been? What have I been doing? I don't know and I don't remember. This is complete relaxation of body and mind lasting thirty minutes. For thirty minutes I really was in another world. In an ideal world, peaceful and quiet. After the total relaxation of body and mind for this thirty minutes in the ideal world, I return to this one. This world is so filled with tension, noise, politics, danger. It seems that half

---

*Liang's* T'ai Chi Ch'uan for Health and Self Defense *(1974) was the first book in English to offer both the t'ai chi classics and detailed commentary by a legitimate master of the Yang school. A teacher, translator, and author, Master Liang has resided in this country since the 1960s.*

the population in the big cities has become crazed by it all. Have you ever tried to avoid these things? How?

I have been teaching t'ai chi in this country for more than a decade. The art has become more and more popular and I have many students including some black belt karate instructors who recently have begun to realize that the hard style is not enough and doesn't always work. If the opponent is stronger and faster, one is bound to lose to him. If one can master both hard and soft styles, one's techniques will reach the highest standard.

**TERRY DOBSON**

# A SOFT ANSWER

The train clanked and rattled through the suburbs of Tokyo on a drowsy spring afternoon. Our car was comparatively empty—a few housewives with their kids in tow, some old folks going shopping. I gazed absently at the drab houses and dusty hedgerows.

At one station the doors opened, and suddenly the afternoon quiet was shattered by a man bellowing violent, incomprehensible curses. The man staggered into the car. He wore laborer's clothing, and he was big, drunk, and dirty. Screaming, he swung at a woman holding a baby. The blow sent her spinning into the laps of an elderly couple. It was a miracle that the baby was unharmed.

Terrified, the couple jumped up and scrambled toward the other end of the car. The laborer aimed a kick at the retreating back of the old woman but missed as she scuttled to safety. This so enraged the drunk that he grabbed the metal pole in the center of the car and tried to wrench it out of its stanchion. I could see that one of his hands was cut and bleeding. The train lurched ahead, the passengers frozen with fear. I stood up.

---

*Studying under aikido's founder for eight years, Terry Dobson (b. 1937) learned to value nonviolent resolution to conflict during his stay in Japan. Now the former marine, cowboy, carpenter, bodyguard, and speechwriter is devoted to putting Master Ueshiba's principles into the American consciousness through his own writing and teaching. His book* Giving in to Get Your Way *(1978) uses daily American life to illustrate aikido's nonviolent tactics.*

I was young then, some twenty years ago, and in pretty good shape. I had been putting in a solid eight hours of aikido training every day for the past three years. I liked to throw and grapple. I thought I was tough. Trouble was, my martial skill was untested in actual combat. As students of aikido, we were not allowed to fight.

"Aikido," my teacher had said again and again, "is the art of reconciliation. Whoever has the mind to fight has broken his connection to the universe. If you try to dominate people, you are already defeated. We study how to resolve conflict, not how to start it."

I listened to his words. I tried hard. I even went so far as to cross the street to avoid the chimpira, the pinball punks who lounged around the train stations. My forebearance exalted me. I felt both tough and holy. In my heart, however, I wanted an absolutely legitimate opportunity whereby I might save the innocent by destroying the guilty.

*This is it!* I said to myself as I got to my feet. *People are in danger. If I don't do something fast, somebody will probably get hurt.*

Seeing me stand up, the drunk recognized a chance to focus his rage. "Aha!" he roared. "A foreigner! You need a lesson in Japanese manners!"

I held on lightly to the commuter strap overhead and gave him a slow look of disgust and dismissal. I planned to take this turkey apart, but he had to make the first move. I wanted him mad, so I pursed my lips and blew him an insolent kiss.

"All right!" he hollered. "You're gonna get a lesson." He gathered himself for a rush at me.

A split second before he could move, somebody shouted, "Hey!" It was earsplitting. I remember the strangely joyous, lilting quality of it—as though you and a friend had been searching diligently for something and he had suddenly stumbled upon it. "Hey!"

I wheeled to my left; the drunk spun to his right. We both stared down at a little old Japanese. He must have been well into his seventies, this tiny gentleman, sitting there immaculate in his kimono. He took no notice of me, but beamed delightedly at the laborer, as though he had a most important, most welcome secret to share.

"C'mere," the old man said in an easy vernacular, beckoning to the drunk. "C'mere and talk with me." He waved his hand lightly.

The big man followed, as if on a string. He planted his feet belligerently in front of the old gentleman, and roared above the clacking wheels. "Why the hell should I talk to you?" The drunk now had his back to me. If his elbow moved so much as a millimeter, I'd drop him in his socks.

The old man continued to beam at the laborer. "What'cha been drinkin'?" he asked, his eyes sparkling with interest. "I've been drinking sake," the laborer bellowed back, "and it's none of your business!" Flecks of spittle spattered the old man.

"Oh, that's wonderful," the old man said, "absolutely wonderful! You see, I love sake too. Every night me and my wife (she's 76, you know), we warm up a little bottle of sake and take it out into the garden, and we sit on an old wooden bench. We watch the sun go down, and we look to see how our persimmon tree is doing. My great-grandfather planted that tree, and we worry about whether it will recover from those ice storms we had last winter. Our tree has done better than I expected, though, especially when you consider the poor quality of the soil. It is gratifying to watch when we take our sake and go out to enjoy the evening—even when it rains!" He looked up at the laborer, eyes twinkling.

As he struggled to follow the old man's conversation, the drunk's face began to soften. His fists slowly unclenched. "Yeah," he said. "I love persimmons too. . . ." His voice trailed off.

"Yes," said the old man, smiling, "and I'm sure you have a wonderful wife."

"No," replied the laborer. "My wife died." Very gently, swaying with the motion of the train, the big man began to sob. "I don't got no *wife*, I don't got no *home*, I don't got no *job*. I'm so *ashamed* of myself." Tears rolled down his cheeks; a spasm of despair rippled through his body.

Now it was my turn. Standing there in my well-scrubbed youthful innocence, my make-this-world-safe-for-democracy righteousness, I suddenly felt dirtier than he was.

Then the train arrived at my stop. As the doors opened, I heard the old man cluck sympathetically. "My, my," he said, "that is a difficult predicament, indeed. Sit down here and tell me about it."

I turned my head for one last look. The laborer was sprawled on the seat, his head in the old man's lap. The old man was softly stroking the filthy, matted hair.

As the train pulled away, I sat down on a bench. What I had wanted to do with muscle had been accomplished with kind words. I had just seen aikido tried in combat, and the essence of it was love. I would have to practice the art with an entirely different spirit. It would be a long time before I could speak about the resolution of conflict.

## GICHIN FUNAKOSHI
# WIN BY LOSING

I should like to recount two incidents that may, I think, help my readers to understand the essence of karate-do. Both incidents occurred many years ago in the Okinawan countryside, and both illustrate how a man may win by losing.

The first took place on a road southwest of Shuri Castle that led to a former governor's villa called Ochaya Goten. Within the compound of the villa stood a teahouse built after the ancient Nara fashion, with a commanding view of the Pacific. The governor, after days of hard work, would come here to relax with his wife and children.

The distance from Shuri was a little over a mile, and the road was paved with stone and lined on both sides by tall and stately pine trees. After the villa, no longer the private property of the governor, was opened to the public, I went there one evening with Master Itosu and a half dozen other karateka for a moon-viewing party. Our group being a

---

*The father of modern karate was born into an aristocratic family in the year of the Meiji Restoration (1868). Funakoshi pursued both a classical Chinese education and his native Okinawan martial art, known only as "te" (hand) or occasionally "Naha-te" (from the province in which he was born). In 1917 he brought karate to Japan proper, astounding audiences with his demonstrations and later founding the first karate dojos. In 1936 he popularized the term "empty (kara) hand (te)" in his second book. Although he turned out during his career many students who would themselves become masters, Funakoshi insisted on a life of humility and service for himself and his students. His style was called "Shotokan," after his pen name.*

congenial one, we lost track of the time and stayed until quite late, talking about karate and reciting poetry.

Finally, we decided that it was indeed time to go home and set out along the tree-lined road to Shuri. The moon was now veiled by a thick mist, and the younger men carried lanterns to help light the way for the teacher. Suddenly the man who was leading the party shouted that we should all douse our lanterns. We did so, only to learn that we were about to be attacked. The number of our assailants seemed to be about the same as the number of our party, so from that point of view we were evenly matched, but unless our assailants were also karate adepts they were doomed to ignominious defeat. It was so dark that we could not see anyone's face.

I turned to Itosu for instructions, but all he said was, "Stand with your backs to the moon! Your backs to the moon!" I was quite surprised, for I thought that surely our teacher would now give us a chance to practice our karate and of course all of us were more than ready to take on this gang of thugs. But Itosu told us merely to turn our backs to the moon! It seemed to make no sense.

After a few minutes, he whispered into my ear, "Funakoshi, why don't you go and have a talk with them? They may not be bad men at heart. And if you tell them that I'm a member of the party, that might make all the difference."

I acknowledged the instruction and started walking toward the waiting gang. "One of them is coming!" I heard someone cry. "One of them is coming! Get ready!" The atmosphere now seemed but a moment away from the start of a battle royal.

As I approached them I could see that our would-be assailants had all covered their faces with towels, so that it would be impossible to identify them. As instructed, I told them politely that Master Itosu was one of our group and that we were all his students. "Perhaps," I added quietly, "this is a case of mistaken identity."

"Itosu? Who's he?" muttered one of the gang. "Never heard of him!"

Another, seeing how short I was, cried, "Hey, you're just a kid! What are you doing—sticking your nose into men's affairs? Just get out of the way!" And with that, he started to grab me by the chest.

I lowered my hips into a karate stance. But at that moment I heard Itosu's voice: "No fighting, Funakoshi! Listen to what they have to say. Talk to them."

"Well," I addressed the men, "what is it you've got against us? Let's hear it!"

Before anyone had a chance to reply, we were joined by a group of men who had obviously had quite a bit to drink and who were now singing boisterously as they made their way home, When they got close enough to realize there was a confrontation in progress, they began to shout happily at the prospect of seeing a good bloody fight. But then one of them recognized our leader.

"You're Master Itosu!" he cried. "Aren't you? Of course you are! What on earth's the matter?" Then he turned to the gang that wanted to attack us. "What, are you guys crazy?" he said. "Don't you know who these people are? That's Itosu, the karate master, with his students. Ten or even twenty of you couldn't beat them in a free-for-all. You'd better apologize, and you'd better be quick about it."

There was, in fact, no apology, but the gang of men muttered among themselves for a moment, after which they quietly faded away into the night. Then Itosu issued another instruction that we all found rather mysterious. Instead of continuing on the way we had started, he ordered us to retrace our steps and take a longer road back to Shuri. Until we reached his house, he did not say a word about the encounter; then he made us all promise not to speak about it. "You've done a good job tonight, boys," he said. "I have no doubt that you'll become first-rate karateka. But don't say a word about what happened tonight to anyone! Not to anyone, do you understand?"

Later I learned that the members of the gang had come rather shamefacedly to Itosu's house in order to apologize. It turned out that the men we had thought to be thieves were in fact sanka—that is, men who worked in a village where the very potent Okinawan liquor called awamori is distilled. They were merely rather rowdy, rough-and-tumble citizens, proud of their physical strength, who had chosen us that night as suitable material upon which to test their prowess. It was only then that I realized how clever the master had been to order us to return to Shuri by a different route so as to avoid any further encounters. Therein, I thought, lies the meaning of karate. My cheeks grew hot and red as I realized that but for Itosu I would have used by skill and my strength against untrained men.

The second incident, which is of somewhat similar nature, has a more satisfactory ending. First, however, I must say a word about my wife's family. For many years they had been experimenting with the sweet potato plant, trying to evolve an improved strain. They had been moderately prosperous but with the Meiji Restoration of 1868 had fallen on hard times and moved to a small farming village, called Mawashi, about two and a half miles from Naha. My wife's father, a staunch adherent of the Obstinate Party, had become something of an eccentric. When the weather was fine, he tended his fields; when it rained, he stayed home and read; and that is all he did.

My wife was very fond of him, and one festival day she went early with the children in order to have a nice long visit. Late that afternoon, I myself started out for the village, as I did not like the idea of my wife and children walking home alone in the dark.

The lonely road to Mawashi wandered through thick pine groves, and in the fading afternoon light was quite dark, so I was taken quite by surprise when two men suddenly sprang from the shelter of the trees into the path to bar my way. Like the other would-be attackers, they had covered their faces with towels. It was evident at once that they were not merely bent on provoking a good natured free-for-all.

"Well," cried one of them, in a most insolent tone, "don't just stand there as if you were deaf and dumb. You know what we want. Speak up! Say, 'Good evening, sir' and tell us what a fine day it is. Don't waste our time, small-fry, or you'll be sorry. I can promise you that!"

The angier they grew, the calmer I felt. I could tell from the way the one who had spoken to me clenched his fists that he was not a karate man; and the other, who was carrying a heavy stick, was also clearly an amateur. "Haven't you mistaken me," I asked quietly, "for someone else? Surely there has been some misunderstanding. I think if we talked it over. . . ."

"Ah, shut up, you little shrimp!" snarled the man with the club. "What do you take us for?"

With this, the two moved a little nearer, but I did not feel intimidated in the least. "It seems," I said, "as though I'm going to have to fight you after all, but frankly my advice to you is not to insist. I don't think it's going to do you very much good because..."

The second of the two men now raised the heavy stick he was carrying.

". . . because," I went on quickly, "If I wasn't sure of winning, I wouldn't fight. I know I'm bound to lose. So why fight? Does that make sense?"

At these words, the two seemed to calm down a bit. "Well," said one of them, "you certainly don't put up much of a fight. Let's have your money then."

"I haven't got any," I replied, showing them my empty pockets.

"Some tobacco then!"

"I don't smoke."

All that I did have, in fact, were some manju, cakes that I was taking to offer at the altar in the house of my wife's father. "Here," I said to the men, "take these."

"Only manju!" Their tone was disparaging. "Well, better than nothing." Taking the cakes, one of them said, "Better get going, shrimp. And be careful, this path's kind of dangerous." With that they disappeared into the trees.

A few days later I happened to be with Azato and Itosu, and in the course of our conversation I told them about the incident. The first to praise me was Itosu, who said that I had behaved with the utmost propriety and that he now considered that the hours he had spent teaching me karate had been well spent.

"But," asked Azato, smiling, "as you no longer had any manju, what did you offer at your father-in-law's altar?"

"Since I had nothing else, " I replied, "I offered a heart-felt prayer."

"Ah, good, good!" cried Azato. "Well done, indeed! That's the true spirit of karate. Now you are beginning to understand what it means."

I tried to smother my pride. Although the two masters had never praised a single kata that I executed during our practice sessions, they were praising me now, and mingled with the pride was an abiding sense of joy.

**C.W. NICOL**
*from*
# MOVING ZEN

The Japanese character *sen* means *ahead* or *before*. The character *sei* has the essence of many meanings—*life, birth, pure, genuine, raw*. If the two characters are put together, they form the word *sensei*, which is poorly translated as *teacher*, and yet is the title given to teachers and to those people who demand great respect.

Mr. Takagi, or rather Takagi Sensei, was the director of the Japan Karate Association, which, in the early sixties, was the largest karate organization in Japan. It was recognized by the ministry of education, its goal to improve and create wider interest in karate. At first glance, Takagi Sensei was not an imposing figure. He was shortish, round-faced, with the air of an affable, good-natured businessman. Yet his eyes carried the steel of the karateka, the practitioner of karate, and he held the fifth degree, or dan, grade of black belt.

This was Tokyo, and I had come here in the late fall of 1962 to devote myself to the study of the martial arts, and in particular to the study of karate, one of the deadliest systems of unarmed combat in the world. But there were many paths to take, many styles to follow, and Takagi sensei had said at our first meeting, "There are other schools. Go to them and see, and then come back if you have truly decided to enter our school."

---

*At the age of twenty-two the author left behind a life as an Artic explorer and adventurer to take up the serious study of karate in Japan. After intervals as a game warden in Ethiopia and an environmentalist in Vancouver, he subsequently returned to Japan where he now writes and continues his martial studies.*

And so I went from place to place in Tokyo, visiting the dojo, or practice hall, of each of the main schools or styles of karate. In Japan, karate is followed as a religion is followed. The student can follow only one way, he cannot switch and change, or be fickle with his loyalties. It is not the karate way.

I saw the wado style. Its practitioners had movements that were graceful and flowing, and there I saw karateka pitted against swordsman in a ritual ballet, and marveled at the lines of the body curving and leaping in and out of the range of the slicing steel, like a mongoose feinting at a cobra.

I saw the goju style. It was powerful and menacing, and its followers developed iron-hard bodies through their special breathing exercises, and by dynamic tension and relaxation, moving in the dojo like angered tigers crouching in the bamboo, breath hissing and rasping through nostrils and throats, now moving slowly, slowly, and then with incredible swiftness. The school was dominated by the Master Yamaguchi, whom they call "The Cat." He wore his hair down to his shoulders, and was never seen in Western dress, preferring the somber dignity of kimono and the wide, skirtlike hakama, traditional male dress of Japan.

I went also to the dojo of the shito school, and there saw a karate that was straight and fast, with movements that were long and deep in the stances, closer to the karate of the Japan Karate Association.

Lastly I visited the school of the kyokushinkai. Approaching from Ikebukuro station (Ikebukuro is a part of Tokyo), I could hear the muffled chorus of yells. Vital and savage, the style was dominated by the presence and personality of the Master Oyama, perhaps the most famous and flamboyant karateka now living, a man who had fought and killed bulls with his bare hands, who trained alone in the mountains and then descended to win the championships, who toured the United States, challenging all comers, awing crowds with his displays of rock, brick, and board breaking.

And then I returned to the headquarters of the Japan Karate Association, to the dojo of the style which outsiders call Shotokan. I liked it best.

Karate was brought to Japan from the southern islands of Okinawa in 1922. In introducing it, the Master Gichin Funakoshi, then ranking fifth dan black belt, had to impress the stern, somewhat chauvinistic warriors of mainland Japan. Frightening stories are told of the master's fights and exploits. Funakoshi Sensei was a warrior, a poet and an artist, and his karate indeed impressed an elite group who began to study under him. Some of these students became masters of their own accord, and became independent, setting up new styles and schools.

The Japan Karate Association was formed after World War II, and until his death in 1957, Funakoshi Sensei was the chief instructor. At the JKA the karateka do not give their karate any other name. They say it is simply karate. However, other schools have called us shotokan. Shoto was Funakoshi Sensei's pen name; he was a great calligrapher, or artist of brush writing. *Kan* means building. So that *Shotokan-ryu* meant "the style they practice at Shoto's building."

The prototype of karate was a secret fighting art developed in Okinawa. The people of that island group had been conquered and forbidden to carry arms. To defend themselves they had developed an art which could, in the hands of a master, defeat an armed, armored man. Not only did they use feet and fists, but also mundane articles like the handle of a rice grinder, sickles, chains, sticks, and small weapons easily disguised or hidden from their samurai overlords. It seems that the art as it was developed in Okinawa was brought there from China. It was then an ancient art, with the lines of its ancestry vague and full of legends, connected to Shaolin temples, to Buddhist teachers, to warrior princes.

But it is the Japanese who have most assiduously developed it into a form that can be practiced as a sport, as well as a fighting art. They are a disciplined, idealistic people, and karate as it is generally practiced in Japan is disciplined and idealistic.

Masters and pupils of each style tend to claim that their karate is best, the true karate, and each will boast of the times that they have defeated other schools. Rivalry is fierce. However, I have seen the main styles, and been impressed, even awed, by all of them. I ignored the stories and chose the JKA because I liked it best, liked the good feeling I got from the headquarters dojo in Yotsuya. (Yotsuya is on Tokyo's Chuo line, and the dojo a few minutes' walk from the station.)

The karate there was fast, powerful, with an emphasis on good form. The stances were low and deep, and punches and thrusts were generally straight and long. Movements were very precise and discipline extremely rigid. They were military in their training ways, yet not militant. It was stern, but friendly. Funakoshi Sensei had been dead for five years, and if his photograph, his writings and his spirit presided over the dojo, they did so with a benevolent gentleness, not with a dominance that might have overpowered me, a Westerner. There was no one great teacher to be revered as a deity. There were many teachers, about thirty in all, and all of them were superb.

The chief instructor now was a quiet, assuring gentleman. He too was a poet and a calligrapher. Masatoshi Nakayama, then ranking fifth dan, began studying under Funakoshi Sensei in 1931. In 1937 he went to Peking to study the Chinese language and various styles of Chinese fighting. Besides being chief instructor of the JKA, he is also director of physical education at the toughest martial-arts-conscious university in Japan—Takushoku University. All of the instructors were university graduates, and most, if not all of them, held black belt ranks in other fighting arts, such as judo and kendo (Japanese fencing). It was with confidence that I decided to take my body and my mind under the training of these men, and thus was to begin a two-and-a-half-year apprenticeship as a full-time student of karate.

The Yotsuya dojo was housed in an old, rickety building, and the front door was loose, rattling and shaking as it opened or closed. Just inside the door was a little square of concrete. On entering the dojo, you had to remove your shoes at that little postage stamp of concrete before stepping onto the polished wood of the floor. I had come to the dojo with Klaus, a German friend, and we both balanced awkwardly, bumping each other, blocking the doorway. By the side of the door was a cupboard with shelves for the shoes, but often the cupboard was full, and you had to leave your footwear in an untidy pile in the porchway, to be kicked and trampled by the incoming and outgoing students. Kicked and trampled, but never stolen.

Once shoeless and up onto the wooden floor, Klaus bowed, and I copied awkwardly. The doorway led directly into the office, small, with three desks jammed together, warm and slightly smelly from an old-fashioned kerosene stove, on the top of which bubbled a kettle. A secretary occupied one desk, Takagi Sensei, the director, occupied another, while the third desk was occupied by one of that day's instructors. Despite the superb quality of the instruction, monthly fees amounted to only a few dollars, and the association was very poor financially. The building was owned by a small movie company, and from the office led stairs to the company's upstairs cutting rooms.

Klaus had been practicing for several months, and had gained the sixth kyu grade, entitling him to wear a green belt. He was at ease, but I was not. He led me over to Takagi Sensei's desk, and I bowed again. The sensei smiled. Klaus told him that I wanted to join, and that I was sure. Takagi Sensei told me to sit down in short, clipped English sentences. At that time I could understand no Japanese. He asked what I had been doing before I came to Japan, and when I told him he was impressed, for I had just finished a one-and-a-half-year expedition to the high Arctic, and I boasted a little, for at the age of twenty-two, this had been my third Arctic expedition.

Takagi Sensei always took great interest in the welfare and character of his foreign students. He told me once that these young men were to interpret karate and spread it throughout the world, and he wanted to ensure that they did not learn a mistaken philosophy. We passed by his desk every day, and he knew who practiced, who behaved well, who was sincere. We talked for an hour, and he himself filled out my application for enrollment.

I was now a member of the Japan Karate Association, and my headquarters dojo was Yatsuya. Tuition was two thousand yen a month (about six dollars), and for this I could train every day except Thursday, when the dojo was closed to beginners.

I bought a karategi, a white uniform of cotton material, with loose pants that were held up by a drawstring and a short jacket that was held around the middle by a white belt. For good reason, the karategi is lighter than the uniform used for judo. It doesn't get yanked and pulled around that much, so it doesn't need the extra strength, and moreover, the heaviness of judogi might slow down the karateka, for even in midwinter, the karateka sweats profusely while training, and needs only a light, very loose covering.

Outside, three tapered posts were embedded in the ground, bound at the top with pads of woven straw rope, or with the more modern pads of canvas and rubber. These were called makiwara, and were targets for punching and striking.

Hips low, bodies turning with each punch, three young black belts struck at the boards, in time with each other, following the sharply exhaled count of the leader. Thump, thump, thump . . . the smack of fist on board and the chantlike counting seemed to punctuate the minutes left before my first formal lesson in karate, and I changed for it in the small and clothes-jumbled dressing room. Klaus had left by now, and I knew nobody. The room was filling, and a few of the students nodded toward me. Those with the black, high-collared Prussian student uniforms bowed and greeted each other with ostentatious and vigorous formality. People laughed and joked, but there was no back-slapping horseplay. Clothes were piled on top of clothes on the floor, or on the old-fashioned coat pegs of which there were far too few. Wallets were left in pockets, for there was no pilfering here, and no fear of it.

I tied the white belt around me and stepped into the dojo itself, bowing as I entered, for this much I had learned long ago in Cheltenham, England, while practicing judo at a YMCA.

Once on the dojo floor, the other students did exercises to loosen and stretch muscles and tendons. A senior student, one of the black belts, barked an order, and everybody hurried into kneeling lines. The teacher, a third-degree black belt, entered the dojo and knelt in front of us. At a second order, all fidgeting ceased. Silence. Stillness. At the furthest end of the rear line, I was conscious of the dull dark polish of the wooden floor, and above, the high dusty ceiling, and on the wall to one side, up and down lines of bold black Japanese letters, but these were on the edges of my vision, for I looked straight ahead like the others. To the front was the red circle of the sun flag, and a photograph of Funakoshi Sensei. Silence. I tried to draw myself into it, but it excluded me, and I held my breath lest I should make a noise, and hovered uncertain on the edge of it, for I did not know, and would not know for some time, exactly what we were doing. The senior shouted another order, and we all bowed to the front, and then to the teacher, who in turn bowed to us.

As the class started, a young teacher came to take me and two other beginners, both Japanese, to one side. First he showed us how to form a fist, folding in the fingers tightly, then binding them strong with the thumb. When the fist was opened, the palm of the hand was white, so tightly was the fist formed. Then we began to learn to stand naturally, feet shoulder-width apart. This is called *shizentai*—natural stance—so utterly simple, and yet we beginners could not stand naturally, for nervousness and eagerness made our shoulders tight, and threw weight back against the curve of our spines.

Now the other students were moving across the floor in lines, blocking, kicking, and punching. My eyes strayed, and the young teacher spoke sharply.

From the natural stance, he showed us the *zenkutsu dachi*—the forward stance—accompanied in this instance by a downward sweep of the arm, fist closed. This movement is called *gedan barai*—down-sweeping block. Oh, in the years that have followed, how many times have I practiced this movement, and still not perfected it? Speaking but a few words of English, the young teacher, whose name was Sasaki, and who later would become my friend, directed our limbs and bodies by pushing and nudging.

...Zenkutsu dachi...forward, strong, long, with feet double shoulder-width apart, forward knee over the great toe, great strength in the muscles of thigh and ankle, lower abdomen slightly tensed, shoulders down, eyes facing the direction of the "enemy."

The stance of the karateka roots him to the earth at the moment of impact. For a split second in time he is a statue, like a stone from the earth, and then, after the blow is delivered, he relaxes, and his body ecoils in preparation for the next move, taking more of the water form of which most his body is made up. Stone, earth, water. Movement and nonmovement.

In the first hour of formal karate, I had begun to learn the stances of the karateka, in their ultimate simplicity, were in fact the most difficult thing. They were *kihon*—basic. They were the strength and balance of the fighter, of the man at peace, of the man in readiness. Upon the stance was built all technique. And also, in this first lesson I learned that despite my muscular one hundred and ninety-five-pound body, I was weak because my stance was weak.

The hour flew, and we were kneeling again, and once more the silence enveloped us, and we tried to push out the murmuring of the city. At a command, the senior student led the kneeling lines in a powerfully chanted oath, the oath of the karateka. I did not understand it at that time, for it was in Japanese of course, but I knew that it was of importance. The students were intense, straight-staring, and in the rhythm and power of the chant I felt the strong and poetic language of the Japanese male. Later, when the language began to unfold to me, the oath took on a beauty I cannot express in English.

> *...The senior, at the head of the line...*
> *"Dojo kun!"* (morals of the dojo)
> *"Hitotsu! Jinkaku kansei ni tsutomuru koto!"*
> *"One! To strive for the perfection of character!"*
> *"Hitotsu! Makoto no michi o mamoru koto!"*
> *"One! To defend the paths of truth!"*
> *"Hitotsu! Doryoku no seishin o yashinau koto!"*
> *"One! To foster the spirit of effort!"*
> *"Hitotsu! Reigi o ozmonzuru koto!"*
> *"One! To honor the principles of etiquette!"*
> *"Hitotsu! Kekki no yu o imashimuru koto!"*
> *"One! To guard aganist impetuous courage!"*

The oath was always chanted with strength, never mumbled with insincerity. Just as movements would become automatic and reflexes conditioned, the simple truths of the oath would also penetrate the mind of the participant.

Again, we bowed to the front, where Funakoshi Sensei's stern image looked down on us, and then we bowed again to the teacher, with spoken thanks. The teacher rose and walked out. Conversation erupted with his departure, animated, jovial, enthusiastic. Now the students were beginning to return to the world of self. But this sudden eruption subsided gradually, while students began to practice individually, and some to spar with each other. Others went out to fetch buckets of water and cloths, and within five minutes the entire floor had been washed clean, ready for the next class. I watched the sparring, or free fighting, for a little while before bowing out of the dojo.

## EUGEN HERRIGEL
### *from*
# ZEN IN THE ART OF ARCHERY

Day by day I found myself slipping more easily into the ceremony which sets forth the "Great Doctrine" of archery, carrying it out effortlessly or, to be more precise, feeling myself carried through it as in a dream. Thus far the Master's predictions were confirmed. Yet I could not prevent my concentration from flagging at the very moment when the shot ought to come. Waiting at the point of highest tension not only became so tiring that the tension relaxed, but so agonizing that I was constantly wrenched out of my self-immersion and had to direct my attention to discharging the shot. "Stop thinking about the shot!" the Master called out. "That way it is bound to fail." "I can't help it," I answered, "the tension gets too painful."

"You only feel it because you haven't really let go of yourself. It is all so simple. You can learn from an ordinary bamboo leaf what ought to happen. It bends lower and lower under the weight of snow. Suddenly the snow slips to the ground without the leaf having stirred. Stay like that at the point of highest tension until the shot falls from you. So, indeed it is: when the tension is fulfilled, the shot *must* fall, it must fall from the archer like snow from a bamboo leaf, before he even thinks it."

---

*Herrigel (d. 1955) wrote perhaps the most famous book ever published on one of the martial arts. A German by birth and a professor of philosophy at Tokyo University between the world wars, the author put himself in the hands of a master archer in hopes of penetrating the mysteries of Zen meditation. His* Zen in the Art of Archery *(1953) is the story of his learning this severe discipline.*

■ 131

In spite of everything I could do or did not do, I was unable to wait until the shot "fell." As before, I had no alternative but to loose it on purpose. And this obstinate failure depressed me all the more since I had already passed my third year of instruction. I will not deny that I spent many gloomy hours wondering whether I could justify this waste of time, which seemed to bear no conceivable relationship to anything I had learned and experienced so far. The sarcastic remark of a country-man of mine, that there were more important pickings to be made in Japan besides this beggarly art, came back to me, and though I had dismissed it at the time, his query as to what I intended to do with my art if ever I learned it no longer seemed to me so entirely absurd.

The Master must have felt what was going on in my mind. He had, so Mr. Komachiya told me later, tried to work through a Japanese introduction to philosophy in order to find out how he could help me from a side I already knew. But in the end he had laid the book down with a cross face, remarking that he could now understand that a person who interested himself in such things would naturally find the art of archery uncommonly difficult to learn.

We spent our summer holidays by the sea, in the solitude of a quiet, dreamy landscape distinguished for its delicate beauty. We had taken our bows with us as the most important part of our equipment. Day out and day in I concentrated on loosing the shot. This had become an *idée fixe*, which caused me to forget more and more the Master's warning that we should not practice anything except self-detaching immersion. Turning all the possibilities over in my mind, I came to the conclusion that the fault could not lie where the Master suspected it: in lack of purposelessness and egolessness, but in the fact that the fingers of the right hand gripped the thumb too tight. The longer I had to wait for the shot, the more convulsively I pressed them together without thinking. It was at this point, I told myself, that I must set to work. And ere long I had found a simple and obvious solution to this problem. If, after drawing the bow, I cautiously eased the pressure of the fingers on the thumb, the moment came when the thumb, no longer held fast, was torn out of position as if spontaneously: in this way a lightning loose could be made and the shot would obviously "fall like snow from a bamboo leaf." This discovery recommended itself to me not least on account of its beguiling affinity with the technique of rifle-shooting. There the index finger is slowly crooked until an ever diminishing pressure overcomes the last resistance.

I was able to convince myself very quickly that I must be on the right track. Almost every shot went off smoothly and unexpectedly, to my way of thinking. Naturally, I did not overlook the reverse side of this triumph: the precision work of the right hand demanded my full attention. But I comforted myself with the hope that this technical solution would gradually become so habitual that it would require no further notice from me, and that the day would come when, thanks to it, I would be in a position to loose the shot, self-obliviously and unconsciously, at the moment of highest tension, and that in this case the technical ability would spiritualize itself. Waxing more and more confident in this conviction I silenced the protest that rose up in me, ignored the contrary consels of my wife, and went away with the satisfying feeling of having taken a decisive step forward.

The very first shot I let off after the recommencement of the lessons was, to my mind, a brilliant success. The loose was smooth, unexpected. The Master looked at me for a while and then said hesitantly, like one who can scarcely believe his eyes: "Once again, please!" My second shot seemed to me even better than the first. The Master stepped up to me without a word, took the bow from my hand, and sat down on a cushion, his back towards me. I knew what that meant, and withdrew.

The next day Mr. Komachiya informed me that the Master declined to instruct me any further because I had tried to cheat him. Horrified beyond measure by this interpretation of my behavior, I explained to Mr. Komachiya why, in order to avoid marking time forever, I had hit upon this method of loosing the shot. On his interceding for me, the Master was finally prepared to give in, but made the continuation of the lessons conditional upon my express promise never to offend again against the spirit of the "Great Doctrine."

If profound shame had not cured me, the Master's behavior would certainly have done so. He did not mention the incident by so much as a word, but only said quite quietly: "You see what comes of not being able to wait without purpose in the state of highest tension. You cannot even learn to do this without continually asking yourself: Shall I be able to manage it? Wait patiently, and see what comes—and how it comes!"

I pointed out to the Master that I was already in my fourth year and that my stay in Japan was limited.

"The way to the goal is not to be measured! Of what importance are weeks, months, years?"

"But what if I have to break off halfway?" I asked.

"Once you have grown truly egoless you can break off at any time. Keep on practicing that."

And so we began again from the very beginning, as if everything I had learned hitherto had become useless. But the waiting at the point of highest tension was no more successful than before, as if it were impossible for me to get out of the rut.

One day I asked the Master: "How can the shot be loosed if 'I' do not do it?"

"'It' shoots," he replied.

"I have heard you say that several times before, so let me put it another way: How can I wait self-obliviously for the shot if 'I' am no longer there?"

"'It' waits at the highest tension."

"And who or what is this 'It'?"

"Once you have understood that, you will have no further need of me. And if I tried to give you a clue at the cost of your own experience, I would be the worst of teachers, and would deserve to be sacked! So let's stop talking about it and go on practicing."

Weeks went by without my advancing a step. At the same time I discovered that this did not disturb me in the least. Had I grown tired of the whole business? Whether I learned the art or not, whether I experienced what the Master meant by 'It' or not, whether I found the way to Zen or not—all this suddenly seemed to have become so remote, so indifferent, that it no longer troubled me. Several times I made up my mind to confide in the Master, but when I stood before him I lost courage; I was convinced that I would never hear anything but the monotonous answer: "Don't ask, practice!" So I stopped asking, and would have liked to stop practicing, too, had not the Master held me inexorably in his grip. I lived from one day to the next, did my professional work as best I might, and in the end ceased to bemoan the fact that all my efforts of the past few years had become meaningless.

Then, one day, after a shot, the Master made a deep bow and broke off the lesson. "Just then 'It' shot!" he cried, as I stared at him bewildered. And when I at last understood what he meant I couldn't suppress a sudden whoop of delight.

"What I have said," the Master told me severely, "was not praise, only a statement that ought not to touch you. Nor was my bow meant for you, for you are entirely innocent of this shot. You remained this time absolutely self-oblivious and without purpose in the highest tension, so that the shot fell from you like a ripe fruit. Now go on practicing as if nothing had happened."

Only after a considerable time did more right shots occasionally come off, which the Master signalized by a deep bow. How it happened that they loosed themselves without my doing anything, how it came about that my tightly closed right hand suddenly flew back wide open, I could not explain then and cannot explain today. The fact remains that it did happen, and that alone is important. But at least I got to the point of being able to distinguish, on my own, the right shots from the failures. The qualitative difference is so great that it cannot be overlooked once it has been experienced. Outwardly, for the observer, the right shot is distinguished by the cushioning of the right hand as it is jerked back, so that no tremor runs through the body. Again, after wrong shots the pent-up breath is expelled explosively, and the next breath cannot be drawn quickly enough. After right shots the breath glides effortlessly to its end, whereupon breath is unhurriedly breathed in again. The heart continues to beat even and quietly, and with concentration undisturbed one can go straight on to the next shot. But inwardly, for the archer himself, right shots have the effect of making him feel that the day has just begun. He feels in the mood for all right doing, and, what is perhaps even more important, for all right not-doing. Delectable indeed is this state. But he who has it, said the Master with a subtle smile, would do well to have it as though he did not have it. Only unbroken equanimity can accept it in such a way that it is not afraid to come back.

"Well, at least we've got over the worst," I said to the Master, when he announced one day that we were going on to some new exercises. "He who has a hundred miles to walk should reckon ninety as half the journey," he replied, quoting the proverb. "Our new exercise is shooting at a target."

What had served till now as a target and arrow-catcher was a roll of straw on a wooden stand, which one faced at a distance of two arrows laid end to end. The target, on the other hand, set up at a distance of about sixty feet, stands on a high and broadly based bank of sand which is piled up against three walls, and, like the hall in which the archer stands, is covered by a beautifully curved tile roof. The two halls are connected by high wooden partitions which shut off from the outside the space where such strange things happen.

The Master proceeded to give us a demonstration of target-shooting: both arrows were embedded in the black of the target. Then he bade us perform the ceremony exactly as before, and, without letting ourselves be put off by the target, wait at the highest tension until the shot "fell." The slender bamboo arrows flew off in the right direction, but failed to hit even the sandbank, still less the target, and buried themselves in the sand just in front of it.

"Your arrows do not carry," observed the Master, "because they do not reach far enough spiritually. You must act as if the goal were infinitely far off. For master archers it is a fact of common experience that a good archer can shoot further with a medium-strong bow than an uninspired archer can with the strongest. It does not depend on the bow, but on the presence of mind, on the vitality and awareness with which you shoot. In order to unleash the full force of this spiritual awareness, you must perform the ceremony differently: rather as a good dancer dances. If you do this, your movements will spring from the center, from the seat of right breathing. Instead of reeling off the ceremony like something learned by heart, it will then be as if you were creating it under the inspiration of the moment, so that dance and dancer are one and the same. By performing the ceremony like a religious dance, your spiritual awareness will develop its full force."

I do not know how far I succeeded in "dancing" the ceremony and thereby activating it from the center. I no longer shot too short, but I still failed to hit the target. This prompted me to ask the Master why he had never yet explained to us how to take aim. There must, I supposed, be a relation of sorts between the target and the tip of the arrow, and hence an approved method of sighting which makes hitting possible.

"Of course there is," answered the Master, "and you can easily find the required aim yourself. But if you hit the target with nearly every shot you are nothing more than a trick archer who likes to show off. For the professional who counts his hits, the target is only a miserable piece of paper which he shoots to bits. The "Great Doctrine" holds this to be sheer devilry. It knows nothing of a target which is set up at a definite distance from the archer. It only knows of the goal, which cannot be aimed at technically, and it names this goal, if it names it at all, the Buddha." After these words, which he spoke as if they were self-evident, the Master told us to watch his eyes closely as he shot. As when performing the ceremony, they were almost closed, and we did not have the impression that he was sighting.

Obediently we practiced letting off our shots without taking aim. At first I remained completely unmoved by where my arrows went. Even occasional hits did not excite me, for I knew that so far as I was concerned they were only flukes. But in the end this shooting into the blue was too much for me. I fell back into the temptation to worry. The Master pretended not to notice my disquiet, until one day I confessed to him that I was at the end of my tether.

"You worry yourself unnecessarily," the Master comforted me. "Put the thought of hitting right out of your mind! You can be a master even if every shot does not hit. The hits on the target are only the outward proof and confirmation of your purposelessness at its highest, of your egolessness, your self-abandonment, or whatever you like to call this state. There are different grades of mastery, and only when you have made the last grade will you be sure of not missing the goal."

"That is just what I cannot get into my head," I answered. "I think I understand what you mean by the real, inner goal which ought to be hit. But how it happens that the outer goal, the disk of paper, is hit without the archer's taking aim, and that the hits are only outward confirmations of inner events—that correspondence is beyond me."

"You are under an illusion," said the Master after awhile, "if you imagine that even a rough understanding of these dark connections would help you. There are processes which are beyond the reach of understanding. Do not forget that even in Nature there are correspondences which cannot be understood, and yet are so real that we have grown accustomed to them, just as if they could not be any different. I will give you an example which I have often puzzled over. The spider dances her web without knowing that there are flies who will get caught in it. The fly, dancing nonchalantly on a sunbeam, gets caught in the net without knowing what lies in store. But through both of them 'It' dances, and inside and outside are united in this dance. So, too, the archer hits the target without having aimed—more I cannot say."

Much as this comparison occupied my thoughts—though I could not of course think it to a satisfactory conclusion—something in me refused to be mollified and would not let me go on practicing unworried. An objection, which in the course of weeks had taken on more definite outline, formulated itself in my mind. I therefore asked: "Is it not at least conceivable that after all your years of practice you involuntarily raise the bow and arrow with the certainty of a sleepwalker, so that, although you do not consciously take aim when drawing it, you must hit the target—simply cannot fail to hit it?"

The Master, long accustomed to my tiresome questions, shook his head. "I do not deny," he said after a short silence, "that there may be something in what you say. I do stand facing the goal in such a way that I am bound to see it, even if I do not intentionally turn my gaze in that direction. On the other hand I know that this seeing is not enough, decides nothing, explains nothing, for I see the goal as though I did not see it."

"Then you ought to be able to hit it blindfolded," I jerked out.

The Master turned on me a glance which made me fear that I had insulted him and then said: "Come to see me this evening."

I seated myself opposite him on a cushion. He handed me tea, but did not speak a word. So we sat for a long while. There was no sound but the singing of the kettle on the hot coals. At last the Master rose and made me a sign to follow him. The practice hall was brightly lit. The Master told me to put a taper, long and thin as a knitting needle, in the sand in front of the target, but not to switch on the light in the target-stand. It was so dark that I could not even see its outlines, and if the tiny flame of the taper had not been there, I might perhaps have guessed the position of the target, though I could not have made it out with any precision. The Master "danced" the ceremony. His first arrow shot out of dazzling brightness into deep night. I knew from the sound that it had hit the target. The second arrow was a hit, too. When I switched on the light in the target-stand, I discovered to my amazement that the first arrow was lodged full in the middle of the black, while the second arrow had splintered the butt of the first and plowed through the shaft before embedding itself beside it. I did not dare to pull the arrows out separately, but carried them back together with the target. The Master surveyed them critically. "The first shot," he then said, "was no great feat, you will think, because after all these years I am so familiar with my own target-stand that I must know even in pitch-darkness where the target is. But the second arrow which hit the first—what do you make of that? I at any rate know it is not 'I' who must be given credit for this shot. 'It' shot and 'It' made the hit. Let us now bow to the goal as before the Buddha!"

The Master had evidently hit me, too, with both arrows: as though transformed overnight, I no longer succumbed to the temptation of worrying about my arrows and what happened to them. The Master strengthened me in this attitude still further by never looking at the target, but simply keeping his eye on the archer, as though that gave him the most suitable indication of how the shot had fallen out. On being questioned, he freely admitted that this was so, and I was able to prove for myself again and again that his sureness of judgment in this matter was no whit inferior to the sureness of his arrows. Thus, through deepest concentration, he transferred the spirit of his art to his pupils, and I am not afraid to confirm from my own experience, which I doubted long enough, that the talk of immediate communication is not just a figure of speech but a tangible reality. There was another form of help which the Master communicated to us at that time, which he likewise spoke of as immediate transference of the spirit. If I had been continually shooting badly, the Master gave a few shots with my bow. The improvement was startling: it was as if the bow let itself be drawn differently, more willingly, more understandingly. This did not happen only with me. Even his oldest and most experienced pupils, men from all walks of life, took this as an established fact and were astonished that I should ask questions like one who wished to make quite sure. Similarly, no master of swordsmanship can be moved from his conviction that each of the swords fashioned with so much hard work and infinite care takes on the spirit of the swordsmith, who therefore sets about his work in ritual costumes. Their experiences are far too striking, and they themselves far too skilled, for them not to perceive how a sword reacts in their hands.

One day the Master cried out the moment my shot was loosed: "It is there! Bow down to the goal!" Later, when I glanced towards the target—unfortunately I couldn't help myself—I saw that the arrow had only grazed the edge. "That was a right shot," said the Master decisively, "and so it must begin. But enough for today, otherwise you will take special pains with the next shot and spoil the good beginning." Occasionally several of these right shots came off in close succession and hit the target, besides of course the many that failed. But if ever the least flicker of satisfaction showed in my face the Master turned on me with unwonted fierceness. "What are you thinking of?" he would cry. "You know already that you should not grieve over bad shots; learn now not to rejoice over good ones. You must free yourself from the buffetings of pleasure and pain, and learn to rise above them in easy equanimity, to rejoice as though not you but another had shot well. This, too, you must practice unceasingly—you cannot conceive how important it is."

During these weeks and months I passed through the hardest schooling of my life, and though the discipline was not always easy for me to accept, I gradually came to see how much I was indebted to it. It destroyed the last traces of any preoccupation with myself and the fluctuations of my mood. "Do you now understand," the Master asked me one day after a particularly good shot, "what I mean by 'It shoots,' 'It hits'?"

"I'm afraid I don't understand anything more at all," I answered, "even the simplest things have got in a muddle. Is it 'I' who draw the bow, or is it the bow that draws me into the state of highest tension? Do 'I' hit the goal or does the goal hit me? Is 'It' spiritual when seen by the eyes of the body, and corporeal when seen by the eyes of the spirit—or both or neither? Bow, arrow, goal, and ego, all melt into one another, so that I can no longer separate them. And even the need to separate has gone. For as soon as I take the bow and shoot, everything becomes so clear and straightforward and so ridiculously simple. . . ."

"Now at last," the Master broke in, "the bowstring has cut right through you."

More than five years went by, and then the Master proposed that we pass a test. "It is not just a question of demonstrating your skill," he explained. "An even higher value is set on the spiritual deportment of the archer, down to his minutest gesture. I expect you above all not to let yourself be confused by the presence of spectators, but to go through the ceremony quite unperturbed, as though we were by ourselves."

Nor, during the weeks that followed, did we work with the test in mind; not a word was said about it, and often the lesson was broken off after a few shots. Instead, we were given the task of performing the ceremony at home, executing the steps with particular regard to right breathing and deep concentration.

We practiced in the manner prescribed and discovered that hardly had we accustomed ourselves to dancing the ceremony without bow and arrow when we began to feel uncommonly concentrated after the first steps. This feeling increased the more care we took to facilitate the process of concentration by relaxing our bodies. And when, at lesson time, we again practiced with bow and arrow, these home exercised proved so fruitful that we were able to slip effortlessly into the state of "presence of mind." We felt so secure in ourselves that we looked forward to the day of the test and the presence of spectators with equanimity.

We passed the test so successfully that the Master had no need to crave the indulgence of the spectators with an embarrassed smile, and were awarded diplomas on the spot, each inscribed with the degree of mastery in which we stood. The Master brought the proceedings to an end by giving two masterly shots in robes of surpassing magnificence. A few days later my wife, in an open contest, was awarded the master title in the art of flower arrangement. From then on the lessons assumed a new face. Contenting himself with a few practice shots, the Master then went on to expound the "Great Doctrine" in relation to the art of archery, and to adapt it to the stage we had reached. Although he dealt in mysterious images and dark comparisons, the meagerest hints were sufficient for us to understand what it was about. He dwelt longest on the "artless art" which must be the goal of archery if it is to reach perfection. "He who can shoot with the horn of the hare and the hair of the tortoise, can hit the center without any bow (horn) and arrow (hair), he alone is Master in the highest sense of the word—Master of the artless art. Indeed, he is the artless art itself and thus Master and no-Master in one. At this point archery, considered as the unmoved movement, the undanced dance, passes over into Zen."

When I asked the Master how we could get on without him on our return to Europe, he said: "Your question is already answered by the fact that I made you take a test. You have now reached a stage where teacher and pupil are no longer two persons, but one. You can separate from me any time you wish. Even if broad seas lie between us, I shall always be with you when you practice what you have learned. I need not ask you to keep up your regular practicing, not to discontinue it on any pretext whatsoever, and to let no day go by without your performing the ceremony, even without bow and arrow, or at least without having breathed properly. I need not ask you because I know that you can never give up this spiritual archery. Do not ever write to me about it, but send me photographs from time to time so I can see how you draw the bow. Then I shall know everything I need to know.

"I must warn you of one thing. You have become a different person in the course of these years. For this is what the art of archery means: a profound and far-reaching contest of the archer with himself. Perhaps you have hardly noticed it yet, but you will feel it very strongly when you meet your friends and acquaintances again in your own country: things will no longer harmonize as before. You will see with other eyes and measure with other measures. It has happened to me too, and it happens to all who are touched by the spirit of this art."

In farewell, and yet not in farewell, the Master handed me his best bow. "When you shoot with this bow you will feel the spirit of the Master near you. Give it not into the hands of the curious! And when you have passed beyond it, do not lay it up in remembrance. Destroy it, so that nothing remains but a heap of ashes."

DON ETHAN MILLER

# A STATE OF GRACE: UNDERSTANDING THE MARTIAL ARTS

In the summer of 1967, I was enrolled as an exchange student from Dartmouth at the University of Leningrad, USSR. One evening, at a talent show presented by the foreign students. I gave a karate demonstration to a large audience of Russian students, professors, and invited friends. I had been studying karate in the States for several years and was fairly proficient at it, though some distance from the black belt level I was to attain three years later. After demonstrating the classic kata, or choreographed forms, and delivering a brief dissertation on the art, the climax of my act was to break a brick with my bare hand—a skill I had acquired a year before, and had repeated dozens of times.

My Russian friends proudly produced a construction brick easily twice the size and three times the weight of the baked red bricks I was accustomed to splitting back home. Undaunted, I set it precisely to bridge the space between a pair of similar bricks laid parallel on the stage floor. I knelt, and held one end of the brick slightly off the base with my left hand. Rising slightly from my kneeling position, I inhaled, raised my right hand in a short arc up to shoulder level, and then, yelling sharply, brought my clenched fist down with the full force of my body behind it, tightening all my muscles just at the moment of impact

---

*Don E. Miller was born in 1947 and holds a black belt in tae kwon do. He has been an instructor in t'ai chi ch'uan since 1973 and has written extensively about the martial arts for the* Atlantic *and other magazines. This article decribes, in part, his shift from an "external" to an "internal" discipline.*

to transmit the force into the stone. Nothing happened. I felt a dull pain in the base of my hand, and the shock wave of the blow traveled back up my arm and shoulder. No matter; this sometimes happens if the blow is not exactly right. I immediately reset the oversize brick and struck down again, quickly, absolutely as hard as I could. But, again, it merely smacked into the base brick and stopped.

I struck again and again, ten or fifteen violent, staccato blows with my right hand, until the flesh broke and the blood spurted out into the audience. Then I switched to my uninjured left hand, hammering down with every particle of strength I possessed: the brick remained indestructible. I was angry, charged, determined; my adrenaline was flowing; I was hitting the thing hard enough, it seemed, to go through steel. But the Russian brick could not be broken.

After a long time, and only after both my hands were smashed and bloody, and my friends in the wings urged me to let the rest of the show continue, did I finally give up. I said something by way of apology to the audience, walked off the stage, changed out of my karate uniform into my street clothes, and walked alone and sullen into the Leningrad night air.

Across the street from the university hall was a construction site, and there, barely visible in the halflight from a distant street lamp, lay a large pile of the very same bricks. I crossed the street and picked one up. Slowly I turned it over in my battered hands and then angrily hurled it to the ground—where it broke on the edge of another brick! I knelt down, grabbed another brick, and half hit, half threw it against two others from close range; this one broke as well. I gathered up an armful of fresh bricks and hurried back inside the auditorium. Over the objections of several performers, I strode onstage and briskly set up the bricks. "Watch this," I said to the audience, in English. I inhaled, raised my fist, and struck downward with a confident yell. The brick didn't break!

I immediately hit it again: Nothing. Two or three more shots in as many seconds, and I realized that to break the brick in this manner was truly impossible. Bewildered and humiliated after this new defeat, I sat back on my heels and closed my eyes—more to avoid looking out at the audience than anything else. I took a deep breath and relaxed my muscles. I forgot about the brick. I forgot about the pain in my hands. White clouds drifted across a purple sky within my mental field of vision. I was aware of the wind of my own breathing. In a few seconds I had almost completely forgotten where I was and what I was "supposed" to be doing.

Just at that moment I opened my eyes, gently cradled the brick in my left hand, and—without tension, without haste, without any real effort—came down smoothly with my right hand, which *passed right through the brick*, without any sensation of impact.

I had, in fact, broken the brick with my hand, but the feeling was much more that it had "parted" in response to the completely new kind of action I had generated. I held up the two halves of the severed brick for the audience to see, but they had already seen and were on their feet, clapping and cheering wildly. The Russians are a people who know a lot about suffering and transcendence, and though I'm sure they had no idea of the particulars of my breakthrough, they recognized a victory of the spirit over insensate matter. I felt sure that it was this victory, rather than the feat itself, that they were applauding.

I began studying the Oriental martial arts twenty years ago, a short, overweight smart kid with glasses on the Upper West Side of Manhattan. I hated being unable to defend myself from the gangs of tough kids around whom I had to thread the most circuitous of routes to reach Junior High School 44 unscathed. Though I was motivated originally by self-defense, something else grabbed hold of me from the very first time I walked into the Downtown Dojo, a school of judo, in 1960. I was taken by the aesthetic of the place: the huge, open, mat-covered practice hall, the shoes lined up outside the door, the neatly displayed wooden membership plaques on the stark white walls. I didn't understand it then, but in the architecture of the place there was a single-mindedness, a focusing of the attention, an austere, negative beauty that moved me strangely, like *déjà vu*. There was a mystery there beyond the mere exoticisms of a foreign culture. After two decades, I can at least name the mystery: the martial arts have been for me a doorway into terrains of experience beyond the normal "limits," into other realms where the common assumptions about conflict and fear, effort and energy, and even the nature of physical reality may be overturned and completely reordered.

I studied kodokan judo for three years, becoming the most avid and devoted junior member of the school. In 1963 I discovered karate (more properly tae kwon do, or Korean karate), and plunged into that discipline with equal fevor. I studied tae kwon do for eight years, under three different teachers, receiving my black belt in the summer of 1970. Earlier that same year, I began my study of t'ai chi ch'uan, a Chinese art of meditation-in-motion that is also a remarkable fighting style. Although I did not see the conflict between them at the time, karate and t'ai chi eventually proved to be antagonistic disciplines, and

I chose the latter. I have studied and taught both meditative t'ai chi and practical self-defense for the past ten years. During this period I also studied aikido and ki development, Western boxing, a smattering of kung fu, sword work, wrestling, and so on. I am recounting this list solely to indicate that, if I wax a little philosophical, it is philosophy that I have not dreamed up but have sweated for.

For the most part, the "external" arts, such as judo and karate, emphasize the acquisition of physical skills—speed, balance, accuracy, coordination, power. They are, especially in the first few years of training, basically athletic disciplines that develop the student's facility in punching, kicking, blocking, throwing, grappling, and so forth. Unfortunately, most students never reach the higher levels of these arts, where physical technique assumes less importance than psychological transformation. Fewer than one out of every hundred students of the martial arts persist to the black-belt level—which, it must be understood, confers not mastery but only the beginning of serious study.

One of the most critical psychological issues with which all martial arts must deal eventually is the problem of fear. In the beginning, a kind of bravado is instilled in students through a physically rigorous, harsh, sometimes militaristic training regime: push-ups on knuckles and fingertips, marching up and down the floor performing kicks, blocks, and shouts in unison, and practice fighting called randori (judo) or kumite (karate). These methods are largely superficial, however, and do not effect change at any psychic depth. I know, because my own stock of fears and anxieties, scared and shaky reactions in dangerous and confrontational situations, was not reduced by all those thousands of punches thrown, flips accomplished, or mock sparring sessions logged on the dojo floor. I was not much more able to control my fears than the average untrained person, and had no experience whatsoever of the psychological state in which fear has been eliminated.

It was not until the year after I had received my black belt that I broke through to the other side of fear. I was teaching a small class in Korean karate at a college in New Hampshire near where I lived. A Japanese karate expert, who was at that time fifth or sixth degree (each degree of rank being roughly equivalent to the entire progression from beginner to first degree), was visiting instructor to a large Japanese karate club at the same school. One evening he walked in toward the end of my class and, after my students left, asked if I would like to spar with him.

I regarded the invitation not as a challenge, but rather as an opportunity to test myself against a superior opponent. As we walked to the center of the gym floor, I put aside any idea of trying to beat the man, but determined solely to acquit myself as well as possible. I felt, however, that I was not only acting as an individual, but also representing the style which I had spent quite a few years studying and teaching; and which he, in some way, *had* challenged by coming to my class.

Although we did not discuss it, I assumed the ground rules to be the same as for almost all karate matches: attacks to the dangerous targets such as the head, neck, or eyes would be stopped an inch or several inches short of impact, while contact to the body (kicks to the ribs, punches to the solar plexus) would be allowed. In the first few minutes, this tradition was adhered to rigorously: I experienced the wind of his pistonlike reverse punches stopped just short of my face, felt several of his driving front and roundhouse kicks penetrate my defense to hit my tightened stomach muscles. He was clearly better than I, his lunging, straightforward attacks harder and faster than I could withstand, his blocking of my sidekicks and backfist strikes uniformly accurate, well-timed—and painful.

Gradually, as we sparred, I managed to adapt my movement to his, becoming able to attack harder, with longer combinations before being repulsed, and to distance myself and block more of his assaults. What always defeated me, however, was an attack in the vicinity of my eyes—sometimes with punches, other times with high roundhouse kicks. He had perceived with amazing accuracy that my fear was concentrated around my eyes. I am nearsighted and was sparring with my glasses on; but it was not so much the fear of the glasses being hit as the general fear that all myopics carry because things are a blur until they are close to you, which makes responses to quick motions more hazardous than normal. Beyond that, there was the deep-seated psycho-physical complex of being a bespectacled, intellectual person—which ten years of martial art training had not eradicated. He attacked to my eyes, or feinted to the eyes to evoke a fear response and then attacked elsewhere.

Still, he was beginning to have a little trouble with me: at one point, immediately following an attack which I had distanced and blocked, with perfect timing I leaped into the air, front knee raised to prevent his counter, and slashed downward with a shudo (edge of the hand) chop to his exposed neck. It was a decent shot, which I stopped just short of the target: he had totally failed to block it. Knowing that he had been scored upon, he immediately spun around (in what I can only interpret as anger) and hit me high on the side of the head with an elbow strike. He did not stop the blow, and the impact knocked me to the floor, my head literally ringing. I jumped to my feet, not sure of what the terms of the encounter had become.

We fought on, rougher than before, the attacks stronger and closer, the blocks harsher. I felt genuinely threatened, not knowing how this lethally powerful man was viewing the situation, nor what he intended to do. Being threatened, I was adrenalized with that combination of fear and anger that is characteristic of the imperfect fighter. I don't remember the exact sequence, but somehow I managed to score on him again—a snapping backfist strike, I think it was. This time, he let a few seconds pass, whirled a full 360 degrees, and hit me with a spinning heel kick—an almost uncontrollable move in which the extended leg lashes up from the floor, swung in a high arc, heel first, by the torquing force of the entire body. His heel struck me above the right eye like a mace, shattering my glasses and driving a jagged edge of the plastic tortoise shell frames into my eyebrow, which began to bleed.

Suddenly, having been hit with tremendous force at the center of my greatest fear, the whole bubble of caution and trepidity burst: I stood on the wood gym floor totally transformed. I knew in that moment that I could beat him. His intimidation of me had run out, and my newly revealed spirit was now more than a match for his. I moved back to the center of the floor to continue the contest, but he made a show of concern for my eyebrow, which was trickling a small stream of blood. I wiped it on the white sleeve of my gi and said, It's nothing, let's continue. He would not do so. At that moment I was calm, unexcited, yet fearlessly energized—a state I would later learn to call *centered*. I wanted to fight on because I knew the experience would be different now that I was no longer afraid. But he had gathered his clothes and was making an exit. I invited him to come back the following week at the same time, but he never did.

One of the major differences between the external arts and those that are termed "internal" (t'ai chi, aikido, pa kua, and a few others) is that the internal schools work on one's state of mind—or rather, *with* one's state of mind—from the very beginning. The acquisition of physical skills is but a secondary outgrowth of one's psychological or spiritual development. Fighting is, in fact, not the real subject of these arts; rather, they deal with the quality of one's energy.

I first encountered the magic of the internal schools in the persona of Master T.T. Liang. It was 1970, and I had brought a group of my karate students to a growth center in southern New Hamsphire called Cumbres, where Liang was ensconced as t'ai chi teacher-in-residence. He was an elderly Chinese man, slightly stooped, it seemed, but with a rich, dramatic voice and shining brown eyes. After demonstrating some of the slow, majestically flowing movements of the long form, Liang lectured briefly on the principles of the art. He listed its ancient tenets: "Sink the ch'i (vital energy). Relax. All movements should be directed by the mind, rather than the external muscular force. Meditation in action; action in meditation."

These were words I had been waiting to hear—a deliberate method that unified the mind and body, that dealt with the inner and outer dimensions simultaneously. I was elated. Liang called me to the center of the floor with him, to show the practical application of the t'ai chi philosophy. He raised one arm slightly in front of his body and invited me to push him. At the moment that my hand touched his wrist, he started to laugh, and I started to laugh with him. I wasn't sure why we were laughing; the situation seemed both silly and sublime—here we were, the young karate man and the old t'ai chi master, our arms touching, our spirits meeting—at what felt to be the center of the whole universe.

"Push," he said. I pushed, expecting his resistance; instead, he turned his body easily to the side, in perfect coordination with my movement, but without severing the connection of my hands to his forearm, so that I had the illusion of pushing something solid when in fact his body had "disappeared" from my line of force. I stumbled forward into the vacuum that his turn created, nearly falling. And we laughed again. Liang was showing the t'ai chi principle of "neutralization," or yielding. I didn't mind being made to look clumsy at all; he liked that. It was the beginning of a beautiful friendship.

I have studied with Liang T'ung T'sai on and off for the last decade, learning a dozen different forms: some with hundreds of separate moves, some using swords and Chinese cutlasses, some taking more than twenty minutes to perform in acutely mindful yet relaxed slow motion. Besides his instruction, the most wonderful hours were passed as he regaled us with tales of the great t'ai chi masters of the Yang family, and stories of his younger days as a hard-drinking customs agent in Imperial Shanghai before the Revolution. In these sessions, Liang revealed himself as a man truly living his second life: deathly ill with hepatitis, pneumonia, and several other diseases by the age of forty-five, he was declared terminal by the doctors and given only a few months to live. But he abandonned his dissipated, stressful life, took up t'ai chi, and regained his health. Now, at age eighty, he is vigorous, alert, quick, graceful, and humorous as ever—living testimony to the value of his art as a health-promoting discipline.

A year or two ago, after a hiatus in my study with Master Liang, I brought a group of my own T'ai Chi students to study with him at his studio in Boston. Often we would come into the school on a winter's night and find him sitting around in his long johns, cooking vegetables on a portable hot plate. He seemed old, lacking in energy, entropic. Gradually, stimulated by the interest and enthusiasm of a dozen young people, he would brighten up, seeming to get younger and more energized as the class went on. What was supposed to be a one-hour lesson would stretch to two hours or more; nobody ever left or bothered to check the time.

One evening, after more instruction than we could handle, and a fresh array of stories, someone discreetly asked him to show a bit of the double sword form—a complex sequence using two double-edged swords. Seeming to begin casually, while still talking, Liang was soon immersed in the form—spinning, leaping, twirling the steel blades and the long colored tassels that trailed from their handles. At the climactic section both swords were a blur, whirring around his body in an intricate series of interwoven figure-eights, faster than the eye could follow. He appeared to be surrounded by a field of flashing metal, yet inside, as one looked at his face, there was no trace of strain, or even of effort: he was in a kind of trance, eyes half-closed, moving with the utmost serenity and gentleness. For a timeless, luminous ten or fifteen seconds he was as close to perfection as anyone that I have ever seen.

The class applauded him soundly when he finished the form, and he returned to being our friendly, funny old teacher again; but what we had seen was something beyond applause and beyond skill. The Chinese call it wei wu wei, "to do without doing," the condition of effortless accomplishment that comes from attunement with Tao, the greater order of Nature. In the West we might call it a state of grace.

In 1975, and again in 1976 and 1977, I had the good fortune to study directly with Koichi Tohei, grandmaster of aikido and arguably the world's foremost living martial artist. At sixty, Tohei moves with the power of an NFL lineman combined with the weightless grace of a ballet dancer. He is the embodiment of the most serious traditions of Oriental budo, or martial ways—but is genuinely nonviolent, compassionate, earthy, and human. The majority of his teaching effort is concerned not with the formal art of aikido but with the system he has evolved for ki development—the cultivation and utilization of each person's own life force.

Using the power of ki, Tohei performs astounding feats: at five foot three and 150 pounds, he can make himself so "heavy" that four young men cannot lift him off the ground. He can resist three six-footers lined up to push him backward—using only the little finger on one hand to stop them. He can inhale and exhale loudly enough to be heard across an open gymnasium floor—yet make a single breath cycle last as long as three minutes. When he performs the characteristic whirling throws of traditional aikido, there is no effort involved: his compact, soft-edged body in the black hakama skirts of the samurai spins, twirls, drops, rises like a tornado or a whirlpool, revolving and spiraling around a steady, calm center of power in the lower abdomen, which he calls seika itten, "the One-point."

In one of the first seminars I attended, he invited me to hold his wrists, as forcefully as I could, and keep him from bringing them together. My arms are strong, from decades of calisthenics, weight lifting, karate, wood chopping; he tenses against them, but cannot move. He smiles; "Ve-rry strong," he pronounces, in a lilting Japanese basso. Once again, please." Again I grasp him tightly, but this time he does not tense against my force: he opens his hands, stretching the fingers, his body relaxed. Something fundamental about the nature of the encounter changes; I suddenly feel that I am holding, or trying to hold, two powerful streams of rushing water—not the constellation of skin, muscle, and bone I had gripped a few seconds earlier. Gently, deliberately, he turns his fingers inward and with the utmost ease moves his hands slowly toward each other. The movement, like a river turning, is impossible to resist. His hands come together softly; when I look into his face, the eyes are shining and kind. We are both smiling. "This," he says, "is coordination of mind and body."

But Tohei is adamant about one thing: that his abilities are nothing special, that they are powers accessible to everyone who trains in the coordination of the mental with the physical. "I am at the center of the universe," he declares, "but the universe is infinite. So you can also be at the center of the universe. Anything I can do, everybody can do." Later, I will learn to perform some of the same "tricks" he has demonstrated—which are not really tricks, but manifestations of the greater power one has easily available when the body is relaxed, the attention is directed, the emotions confident and positive, the mind perfectly calm. This is the state called being *centered*, and it is the basis of Tohei's art and power. One of the most fascinating expressions of the qualities developed by Tohei's method is the kiai—literally the "spirit-unifying shout." Unlike the primal grunts of weight lifters and the angry cries of karate practitioners, Tohei's kiai is piercingly musical, with the potency of anger but devoid of negativity. It is unlike anything one has ever heard before yet instantly comprehended, rising from a dark, low pitch to a loud laser-sharp focus point, like a single lightning bolt of pure personal energy.

One July afternoon I traveled with Tohei to Martha's Vineyard, where he was to give a brief demonstration of aikido and ki development. It was a still, oppressively humid day, with a large and somewhat skeptical crowd gathered in an exquisite small church that smelled faintly of unfinished wood and flowers. Near the end of the presentation, the crowd seemed still restless and unconvinced. Suddenly, Tohei issued a single, startling kiai that cut through the audience like a sword-stroke: the air itself seemed to clear in the wake of this incredibly beautiful shout; there was a long moment of utter silence (smelling the wood, the flowers, nobody moving); and then, softly, raindrops began to patter on the leaves and the ground outside the open window of the church. It was probably half a minute or more before anybody moved or spoke. Tohei's message had been heard.

There *are* ways to make the magic work, with some consistency. I have learned, over the course of my twenty year odyssey through the martial arts, that the capacity of the human mind to coordinate and focus physiological energy is infinitely greater than the standard assumptions of biology and physics would lead us to believe. I have become convinced that there is something, a spirit or vital force, which the Japanese call ki and the Chinese ch'i, which is universal in origin yet manifest uniquely in every living creature; which can be cultivated and increased through certain types of practice. And, since that first night in Leningrad, I have acquired a reliable method for entering that particular state of effortless accomplishment.

Thus, when I now approach a stack of three two-inch cinder blocks to attempt a breaking feat, I do not set myself to "try hard," or to summon up all my strength. Instead, I relax, sinking my awareness into my belly and legs, feeling my connection with the ground. I breathe deeply, mentally directing the breath through my torso, legs, and arms. I imagine a line of force coming up from the ground through my legs, down one arm, and out through an acupuncture point at the base of my palm, through the stone slabs, and down again into the ground, penetrating to the center of the earth. I do not focus my attention on the objects to be broken. Although when I am lifting or holding them in a normal state of consciousness the blocks seem tremendously dense, heavy, and hard, in the course of my one- or two-minute preparation their reality seems to change, as indeed the reality of the whole situation changes. I am no longer a thirty-two-year-old American writer in basketball sneakers doing strange breathing exercises in his suburban back yard in front of a pile of red patio bricks: I am a spiritual traveler, making the necessary preparations for a journey to a different world.

I know that I am in the other "zone" by certain signs: my breathing takes on a deep, raspy, unearthly tone; my vision changes, such that tiny pebbles on the ground appear huge, like asteroids; my body feels denser, yet at the same time light and free of tension. I feel that what I am doing is extremely important, that the attention of the entire universe is focused upon me. When I make my final approach to the bricks, if I regard them at all they seem light, airy, friendly; they do not have the insistent inner drive in them that I do.

I do not hit the bricks; I do not break them. Rather I take a deep breath, hold it for half a second, then *release* suddenly but smoothly, focusing on the energy line and allowing my arm to express it. My palm passes right through the place where the blocks were, but they have apparently parted just before I get there, and there is no sensation of impact, no shock wave, no pain. Whoever is watching usually applauds and congratulates me, but in the zone there is nothing to be congratulated for and it seems silly. One is merely surprised to realize how easy such things are if one is in the correct body-mind state. Gradually, one comes out of it, one tries to explain, but the essence of it is beyond the reach of words. Hours later, what remains is not a sense of destructive power but the feeling of attunement with the mysterious but very real power of life itself. Passing through the bricks is only a way of entering another realm.

The real value of martial arts study, in other words, has nothing to do with physical feats such as brick-breaking; in fact, it is not even primarily concerned with fighting. In our modern technologized society, it would be easier to buy a gun, or carry a can of mace. Their real value lies in what the martial arts tell us about ourselves: that we can be much more than we are now; that we have no need of fear; that our capacities for energy, awareness, courage, and compassion are far greater than we have been led to believe. They tell us that all our personal limits—and by extension, our destructive social and historical patterns—can be transcended. Beginning with the next breath, drawn deeply.

## CAROL R. MURPHY

# THE SOUND OF SILENCE: MOVING WITH T'AI CHI

There are two directions of the meditating mind—a focusing down to an intense point of contemplation, or a wide-angle vision which does not so much shut out the world of the senses as mirror it clearly and love it without clinging. This latter is the meditative way that appeals to an alert and noticing mind while promising to reduce the tendency to reverie or anticipation. Of the kinds of practice that follow this way, one—a Chinese method called t'ai chi ch'uan, is a moving meditation that also disciplines the restless body. (*Ch'uan* means "fist," which I take to mean the fistful of postures in sequential form which express the *t'ai chi* or "ultimate.") As an art form in physical movement, it resembles a slow dance, but is more properly a kind of yoga, a healthful exercise, even training for qualities useful in self-defense; a many-sided nature that points to the fact that meditation should be part of life, as life should be mingled with meditation. I hope its quality will be unfolded as I relate my adventure into it, and that readers will share this adventure mentally, even though this particular yoga may not be their own. All explorers can be helpful to each other, even though their ways to the mountain-top be different. I will alternate between particular experience and more general observations, and these will shift in

---

*As a Quaker lay writer, Carol Murphy has published over a dozen pamphlets and articles on the search for faith. A death in her own family prompted her interest in practical meditation, and coincidence brought her into the serious study of t'ai chi ch'uan at the same time. The following is the story of her effort to create an active, everyday meditation.*

emphasis as my own attitudes change and grow. At times I feel physical and disciplined, at times romantic and creative, at times inward and meditative; t'ai chi has room for them all.

And now, in the quiet that always seems to accompany this exercise, let us begin.

## The Preparation

The flowing, coiling grace of the t'ai chi form beguiles me aesthetically while it makes me wonder whether I can ever accomplish such floating movements. But first I am brought down to earth. I must flex my knees and sink lower until I become a pond cypress with roots deep in the fertile muck of a Southern swamp. At first my knees protest, but later I get a velvety, relaxed, almost sensuous feeling. *This* is meditation?

The sensible Chinese maintain that man is between heaven and earth—a little lower than the angels, we would say. His head may be erect to the sky, but his feet must be planted on the earth. At this root level the practice of the t'ai chi form brings relaxation of the muscles and a health-giving increase in the blood circulation with its flow of nutrients and infection fighters. We are mind-body creatures, and why shouldn't a meditative discipline minister to both aspects, even to the solid satisfaction of managing one's physical motions properly? First, for me at least, comes a searching reminder that for most of my life I have mismanaged my bodily actions. I have teetered and stumbled and banged my elbows. Mea culpa, mea maxima culpa. As I learn to lower my center of gravity, and balance from that, I realize that the prescribed movements are shaped to the proper use of the body and endow it with its proper dignity. Charles Williams has written: "We experience, physically, in its proper mode, the Kingdom of God; the imperial structure of the body carries its own high doctrines—of vision, of digestion, of mysteries, of balance, of movement, of operation."

## The Beginning

Having rooted myself in the earth, the next movement is to raise my relaxed arms slowly in front of me, bring my hands toward me then lower them gently by my side. If the preparatory posture plants roots, this action is to lighten the upper body and set it afloat. The arms then rise of themselves, as it were, as if floating in water rather than air. We are told that the insubstantial must become substantial, and the substantial unsubstantial.

For an intellectual accustomed to neat distinctions, the heavy substantiality of the material world is divorced from the airy insubstantiality of the world of meaning and spirit. For years I have wrestled with such philosophies as Santayana's where blind nature is forever independent of the realm of the perfect and the essential, and any possibility of God is lost somewhere in between. This unhappy division runs throughout Western thought, and I, as one of its victims, cannot either spurn nature to adore the Platonic Forms nor rest, like John Muir spending the night in a Savannah cemetery, in the trust that in spite of death all nature is divine harmony. Yet somehow the mystics and the Chinese Taoists have actually experienced the Original One behind the two divided realms of our everyday experience. Their natural piety is not at war with their ideal aspirations, and they can live in the magnetic field of an unobtrusively powerful Ultimate. In the slow circular withdrawals and returns of the movements I practice, I can sense the reconciliation of acting and being. Will this work its way through my limbs to my mind? As I contemplate the inevitable diminishments of the later years, how I need to grasp this mystical unity of the substantial and the insubstantial!

### Grasp the Bird's Tail
In the next figure in the sequence, I turn to hold between the facing palms of my hands an imaginary ball of air. I don't know why the reference to a bird's tail; but as I become at rare times aware of the livingness of my hands as they move, I can imagine a field of force between them—some invisible bird held captive for a moment?

But birds should be uncatchable, as a dream reminded me after a time of impatience for further progress that I was then ready for. In the dream I parted from my teacher and a group of students as they started upstairs (a higher level?) for an advanced class. Turning into my rooms at the foot of the stairs, I discovered a starling had somehow gotten inside. I opened the back door and I stood back, the bird fluttered toward me, pursued by a smaller whitish bird at whose tail I grasped, only to miss. Awakening, I thought at once of my reach exceeding my grasp, and later remembered a verse of Blake's:

> He who bends to himself a joy,
> Does the winged life destroy;
> But he who kisses the joy as it flies
> Lives in eternity's sunrise.

Here is the inevitable paradox of the spiritual quest: that without perseverance you cannot start on the way, but your very striving for a goal gets in your own path. And the instant you think you have attained something—when you exclaim "Look, I'm meditating!"—it vanishes. Add to this paradox the usual ups and downs of feeling—the days of aridity following days of enthusiasm, and you can end up thinking, "Whatever made me get into this?" So, make a fresh beginning: be like a little child learning a new game for its own sake with a sense of open-ended adventure rather than impatience for results. And we discover another paradox: that though you be attracted to the practice of t'ai chi through seeing its beauty in demonstration, or in reading the philosophy behind it, at last you are doing it by yourself, your mind must remember it, your limbs move with it, and to look elsewhere than yourself for it would be like searching the room for one's own head. Is this analogous to what the mystics mean by the Void where otherness seems to disappear? But just as you give up out-there-ness, you realize that you are still shaping yourself to an objective requirement, a classical form like a Bach fugue, with no room for private self-expression. Yet this form derives from the inner meaning of the body's true movement—another paradox. "I live, yet not I," as long as I yield to the movement of the Tao. In so doing, I experience something of the ultimate structure pointed to by both mystics and modern physics of "a harmonious, unified field of dynamically balanced stresses" (in the words of one scientist-mystic, Lawrence LeShan). What to the mystics is the Reality of all things real has only visited me in fragmentary glimpses amid the confused alarms of mortal existence: glimpses of natural beauty, healing love, and now the numinous grace of t'ai chi. I can only achieve that by learning to move to its measure, it may become more real to myself, and perhaps by my own obedience, to make it in small measure a little more real to others.

### The Single Whip

A recurrent figure involves a pivoting of arms and body, then a wide step. It seems simple, but like most of the postures, involves niceties of timing and balance. One student is said to have taken seven years to perfect himself in this. As in any concentrated effort, my errant attention must be brought under control. I know, as a writer, the reluctance with which I face a blank page, and how easy it is to think of the many trivial tasks that can postpone the beginning of work. As I place myself to begin practice, my eyes are riveted by a spot on the woodwork. I tear my eyes away: no, I will not worry about that spot—not now.

These distractions must be treated as *The Cloud of Unknowing* advises: look over their shoulders and proceed. Mental discipline becomes merged with physical discipline as I realize that in the attempt to relax, I have to loosen up all unneeded tensions. There is the story of a t'ai chi master on whose hand a bird perched; his body was so yielding that the bird could not get enough resistance for its take-off push. Moreover, I have to live in my whole, centered body, not just in my head. And as this is a moving meditation, my centering must move with me. I am not a statue on a plinth, but a wheel rolling, rim and hub.

The childlike playfulness and flowing purposelessness has to be balanced, in yin-yang fashion, with the discipline that seeks the perfection of the way itself. The exercise of the t'ai chi form is no self-executing magic that brings physical or spiritual growth without the commitment of time and concentration. It does provide an opportunity for meditative training in that it is nonverbal yet not monotonous. The mind must accompany the motions without becoming lost in thought or oblivious to the surrounding. Simone Weil speaks of *attente à Dieu*—an intent watchfulness for the Presence. It is this sort of *attente* the exercise should develop through the sober and workmanlike task of knowing one's motions. For it is another paradox of this adventure that I can have two levels of apprehension of t'ai chi—as the moving image of Eternity, and as a thoroughgoing reeducation of every part of my body. If I can set down my feet with soft precision—that will be sufficient for the day in this quest for wholeness. And I do this, not by marking a place on the floor, but by marking my inner balance. I find I have become less absent-minded and accident-prone in daily life. I am learning where my feet and my center of gravity are actually placed, not just where I thought they were.

Ideally, there is a carry-over into daily life, and this in turn should work hand-in-glove with practice to reinforce the spirit of exercise so that it becomes a way of life. Do I notice a slowing of movement as I set about my household tasks, a choreographing of the kitchen count-down to dinnertime? Movement becomes a pleasure, not something that has to be done to get from here to there. Trivial, but perhaps the foundation a state of pure clarity beyond the anxiety to win in which their action becomes immediate and appropriate, like the Zen-trained archer. This is a temporary state, limited by its purpose, but it is always present in the spiritually disciplined person. Lest I seem to be expecting too lofty an outcome from a bodily discipline, I can take encouragement from an unusual book, *Golf in the Kingdom*, by Michael Murphy. Burningbush may be an imaginary golf course, but there are real holes in it. While Murphy's view of golf as mediation is more Hindu than Taoist, a serious student of t'ai chi will surely agree that: "Fascination is the true and proper mother of discipline.... 'Tis slow enough to concentrate the mind and complex enough to require our many parts.... The grace that comes from such a discipline, the extra feel in the hands, the extra strength and knowing', all those special powers ye've felt from time to time, begin to enter your lives."

There is a Hasidic story about a rabbi who went to visit a teacher, not to hear him expound the Torah, but to watch him lace and unlace his shoes. So thoroughgoing is the transformation of authentic master that he lives in harmony with the Torah or the Tao and becomes one with it. Herein lies the true authority of the spiritual teacher of guru. As was said of Jesus, "For he taught them as one having authority and not as the scribes." He had authority because he was what he taught. No doubt the good teacher of t'ai chi wears his or her shoelaces with a difference. The carriage of his head, the rootedness of his stance, the patience of his instruction carry authority. But his teaching is limited by the nonverbal nature of the art itself. He can give hints, he can show you an example, but the listening to your own bodily feelings in practice is up to you. As Buddha said to his disciples, you must be lamps unto yourselves. Perhaps the most a teacher can do is to encourage the confidence that following the Way is not too hard for you, neither is it far off, but very near to you, in your mind and limbs, that you may do it.

### The Seventy-Thirty Stance

As I practice, I move into a well-braced position in which about 70 percent of my weight is on the forward foot. I can pull back to the rear foot, or turn to evade a theoretical counter-thrust, or thrust myself forward. When I announce my discovery of the strategic importance of this stance, I am reminded that I can hardly learn the subtleties of this weight distribution until I can shift my weight entirely from leg to leg and know which is the weight-bearing of "full" foot and which the free or "empty" foot. In addition to an exercise for this, we students are told of the flow of an energizing life force which the Chinese call ch'i, running along the "full" leg to the opposite arm. It envelopes the body in magnetic field, and to align oneself with its lines of force is to generate healing.

All this brings one back to the problem of the relationship between real experience and the ideas which we impose upon this experience. The experience of "full" and "empty" is real, and the healing and energizing quality of the t'ai chi form is real to the teacher; possibly we may feel a little of it ourselves. But I maintain my intellectual independence and sit loose to any concept like ch'i which seems to run together electrical, muscular, and blood-circulation phenomena in one semiphilosophical category. However, as I become increasingly aware of the deep nonverbal realities in this adventure, I am more and more disillusioned with the philosophical word-fencing which I used to read either with excitement or disquiet. All this now seems beside the point.

So, in my practicing, I stand between earth and sky, aware of the strategic parts of the body, head toward the sky, center of gravity below the navel—these two extremities of the river of nervous energy in the spinal cord—palms of the hands sensitive to the air, and soles of the feet pressed to the good earth. We are learning that the mind can be trained to control autonomic functions hitherto thought inaccessible; so possibly through this awareness of the channels of energy, t'ai chi can spread a beneficent influence throughout my body. I have already found for myself the peacefulness that can spread from the relaxation of the hands in t'ai chi when, on a night which I expected to be disturbed by what may have been a minor infection, I felt a half-asleep flow of calm (perhaps even of ch'i) flow through me from my relaxed hands as I dreamed I was at practice. Who knows, ch'i may be the best word for that life-energy after all; at least it may provide a useful image of metaphor by which healing pathways may be opened. And this I shall have to know experimentally.

Moreover, as I go further into this adventure, I am not going to be content to talk of a merely conceptual faith which does not unify both flesh and spirit. Nor will I try to justify the ways of God to man unless and until I meet that divine quality in experience which justifies life without need of argument. And I will not throw out such an experience when it does not fit into the usual categories of thought. And when I see, with John Woolman, "some glances of real beauty... in their faces who dwell in true meekness," I shall acknowledge them without arguing about the Way by which they came to this meekness. In the end I must rely upon my own experience in the spiritual search, and grope for my own way, one step at a time. When I am tempted to peruse books on meditation, I become frustrated by their prescriptions. But in learning t'ai chi I will let my newfound abilities and awareness grow naturally into an unanticipated flowering.

## Rollback and Press

Part of the figure of Grasp the Bird's Tail consists in a withdrawal and then a pushing forward with the hands as if pressing someone gently back. There is throughout the t'ai chi form a continual withdrawal and return, like a kind of breathing. No motion goes too far—at culmination it rounds into the reverse direction. As with motion, so with weight, as each side of the body is "full" or "empty" in turn. With continued practice it almost feels as if the "empty" leg becomes light and floating in contrast to the rootedness of the "full" leg.

Here is an enactment of the basic concept of Chinese philosophy, which is often pictured in the familiar yin-yang symbol of two tear-drop shapes curling around each other within a circle. The nature of things, according to this philosophy, flows constantly in cycles of complementary male-and-female, hot-and-cold, fire-and-earth, strong-and-weak. As one aspect reaches its fullness in actuality, the other is gathering its potential energy and will emerge. Something of the sort was intuited by Jacob Boehme when he wrote: "All things consist in Yes or No. In order to have anything definite made manifest there must be a contrary therein—a Yes and a No." This philosophy, like all such metaphysical pictures of the way of things, is not a scientific statement of the "the truth" so much as it is an artist's organizing vision. If you look at enough Cezannes, apples and landscapes will begin to show emergent geometrical forms such as Cezanne saw. We can learn to see Ruisdael skies, Turner sunsets, and Botticelli maidens. It is silly to ask if these things are "true" or "false." Reality bears their potentiality and the artists shape and reveal them to us. So with the yin-yang philosophy; one can learn to see its signature everywhere: the push-pull of the autonomic nervous system, Newton's law of action and reaction, the complementarity of wave and particle in nuclear physics, entropy and information, death and rebirth, sleep and waking, meditation and action, even in a Christian paradox like the "fortunate fall." These opposites are reconciled in action and interaction, and the t'ai chi form is a way of incarnating the spirit of the process. As Rufus Jones has said of mysticism, in *Spiritual Reformers in the 16th and 17th Centuries*, "The mystical experience is . . . one way. . . of entering the Life-process itself and of gaining an interior appreciation of Reality by living in the central stream and flow of it. . . ."

## Deflect Downward, Parry and Punch

There is one beautifully flowing movement in which, in spite of the peaceful quality of the form, the basic self-defense structure of the t'ai chi movements becomes manifest. My fist swings slowly forward toward the solar plexus of an imaginary opponent. Should I be disquieted by this adversary quality in the form? I also know that advanced students progress to a dual form called push hands in which each partner tries to absorb the push of the other and to take advantage of his slightest disequilibrium. There are lessons in rootedness and attente to another's movements which, we are told, can be learned in no other way. Thus, under the form of combat, each helps the other to meditative awareness.

Somehow we have to come to terms with the fact the yin-yang cycles in the nature of things, as in the t'ai chi form, include opposition as well as harmony, dissolution as well as creation. This may arouse a tension in lovers of peace, so let us approach the matter gently.

I have at times imagined that I had to explain the American two-party system to a Chinese official. I would describe it in terms of yin-yang principle as two opposing forces that alternate and cooperate in forming and criticizing a political administration. Roughly speaking, one party is conservative, the other liberal, but within each, as in the Taoist symbol, there is a little dot of opposite quality—conservatives among the Democrats and liberals among the Republicans. This keeps them from flying apart into irreconcilable enmity. Each depends on the other, and on each other's criticism. To simplify history in making a point, the "sin" of Lyndon Johnson lay in trying to force a consensus to blur the essential adversary relationship, while the "sin" of Richard Nixon was to conceive of the opposition as an enemy to be harassed and eliminated. Conflict is not to be eliminated, but kept creative.

Now we can go a little deeper and find an analogy in the ecological balance of nature. As one scientist has said, the usefulness of enemies is a reality in nature. The wolves need the caribou for food, the caribou need the wolves for natural selection. The survival of each is a function of this relationship. Our very strengths are the gifts of our enemies, who have put sinew in our limbs, sharpness in our senses and quickness in our wit. But wait. As Yeats has said:

> A stricken rabbit is crying out
> And its cry distracts my thought

There is tragedy here which we human beings should not accept too easily. The same poet wrote:

> All things fall and are built again,
> And those that build them again are gay

—but we wonder if the "ancient, glittering eyes" of the Chinese sages are not too gay.

At this point we are in the cosmic conflict ourselves. Should we not, like Robert Frost, have a lover's quarrel with the world? We should wrestle with the angel of the Lord as Jacob did, and as Boehme did when he directed himself to piercing through the ocean of darkness of this world: "I raised up my spirit . . . toward God . . . in the resolution to struggle with the love and mercy of God without ceasing until he blessed me. . . ." We will be in good Biblical company: Abraham pleading for Sodom, Jonah arguing with God's forgiveness, Job pleading his innocence; even Jesus at Gethsemane did not yield too quickly. Possibly God does not want us to knuckle under too soon; he blessed the Jews' holy chutzpah, or sublime impudence, and gave them the I-Thou experience. The other side of the experience of the mystical Void is the intimate over-againstness which gives rise to the sense of the Other. We must often wrestle with God to find him, and in the encounter he appears as both Adversary and Comforter. (If I speak sometimes of "God and sometimes of the "Tao," it is because the Ground of Being is variously felt as Other and Not-other. Teilhard de Chardin spoke of the "Other, more me than myself." My apologies to theologians.)

Florida Scott-Maxwell has written: "Perhaps our 'No' to God is our sacred care. If our otherness matters, . . . if we must fill our human role, represent the sacred tension, and say at the utmost point of our endurance and our yearning, 'You are too different, you ask the impossible. . . .' Then God might answer, 'Of course that is your duty. If I had commanded anything less than the impossible, could you have recognized me as God? . . . This is what creation is. The might and marvel of forever creating out of opposition'" (*The Measure of my Days*).

### Apparent Closure

After the long swinging punch comes a withdrawal, a brushing off of the imaginary opponent's grasp, a moment's disengagement to consider the yielding, one could say "nondirective" kind of defense that is the Taoist way. One must go with the opponent, not counter his thrust, and not be where he expects you to be. To read his intentions in his movements requires an intimate sensitivity like that of love, and so the combat becomes a cooperative pas de deux.

One breezy day I tried to keep my hand in contact with the swaying branch of a hemlock tree. I began to see how firm and yet how light my touch should be, what concentration would be needed to follow its motion with wordless immediacy, and how a sense of oneness with the tree could result. The sense of touch, with its nonverbal immediacy, is less likely than sight to let concepts slide in between perceiver and perceived. The fact that some people withdraw from the intimacy of touch shows that its probe of our ego-defensiveness gets closer to the nerve. (Could it be that we overburden our sexuality by making it our only self-transcending contact, then fear the very loss of self-boundary it promises?) When I had an actual opportunity to try the single-handed form of push hands with someone, the slow circling of our touching wrists and the reciprocal sway of our bodies seemed a living enactment of the yin-yang symbol. The experience was brief, but it reminded me of the sensitivity needed in following the lead of a partner on the dance floor, when I had noted (with some astonishment) its likeness to the bare attention of meditation, and how quickly it is lost by thinking about it. I also recalled reading of an old custom in logging country when an engaged couple had to try their compatibility by the use of a two-man saw.

Later, I had come upon the same kind of *attente*, on the mental plane, in my study of nondirective counseling. And in life itself, I had to learn at the bedside of the dying how to fight on the side of life only as long as was meet, and then to know when to yield to the necessity of death. This is hard for us in the Western culture to learn. We are trained to think competitively in terms of imposing our will on someone and winning or losing a contest. We need the Taoist wisdom that opposites must be reconciled without conquest, for the winner loses and the loser wins. Here the Tao may also manifest itself in us as the sense of humor that reconciles incongruities as it reveals them, deflating the victor and putting a victorious gleam in the loser's eye.

In our quarrel with God and the world we tend to scream and flounder like angry children. We kick against the pricks and get nowhere. In my practice of t'ai chi I can begin to learn a kind of holy obedience to the flow and absorb the wisdom of living where I am; the form moves onward like a river, and cannot be hurried, anticipated, or lingered over in retrospect. There is no place to go for every place is here and now.

This is also true in the growth of the meditative life, which can no more be hurried by impatience than the growth of a fetus *in utero* can be hastened by taking thought. Impatience at one's impatience only increases ego-consciousness and muddies the stream. There could be an endless regress of struggling. In the contemplative view of Taoism, the living being is in polar unity with the world. For our conceptual ego to try to change its own awareness is to try to lift an airliner by straining at your seatbelt, as Alan Watts pointed out in *The Art of Contemplation*: "At this point there is nothing to do except what is happening of itself. All that remains is the simple awareness of what is going on.... It comes out of nothing as sounds come out of silence.... You, as ego, cannot change what you are feeling, and you cannot, effectively, try not to change it." Perhaps this sounds too passive a counsel. It is in the spirit of the Taoistic wu wei, or action in nonaction. There is no guaranteed formula, no magic mantram, to enlighten the mind, but there is room for perseverance and alertness—the "effortless effort" of meditation which obeys the laws of the spriitual life: Take what comes, and do not cling. There is the same spirit of wu wie in Mary Baker Eddy's saying, "God rests in action," a saying that frequently comes to mind in my practice.

As I enter the flow of the t'ai chi form, I recall the insight I had in watching an ornamental fountain which made still, yet flowing, shapes out of jets and sheets of water. If the water were to be turned off, the shapes would disappear; yet with the water the shapes seem as solid as glass. The movement makes the solidity. However solid I feel, therefore, I must trust the stream of energy that creates me at every moment, and live more from my vital center of balance, or tan t'ien, and less from my analytical head which divides my self from the stream. Since I cannot clarify my awareness directly, I can change my attitude to the awareness I have now, and not cling to my strivings for progress or distress at the lack of progress in meditation of t'ai chi. Our individuality, says Chuang-Tzu, is the "delegated adaptability" of the Tao, whose center is everywhere and whose circumference is nowhere. By taking my distractions and quarrels with God as part of the movement of the Tao playing push hands within me, I seem to render more permeable the boundaries of my self-conscious ego, and become more relaxed and *degagée* about the flow of my thought and feelings. (Might I become so relaxed that an inspiration perching on my mind will be unable to fly away before I grasp at least a tail feather?)

I used to balk at Pere de Caussade's teaching of the soul abandoned to God, willing everything that happens, but now perhaps I can glimpse a way of living that flows with the energy of God within and without the little ego we vainly try to protect. Life spares us nothing;

but if we trust its flow in ourselves as well as outside, and enter each turn of events correctly, we will be co-creators of its meaning, and be borne onward into the mainstream. A man of prayer has said that when he prays, coincidences begin. Probably the coincidences were there all the time, and hindsight is easy; but when life is lived nondirectively, the antenna of the mind is more tuned to the flow of happenings around us. Subtle intuitions or leadings may guide one more surely than much anxious forethought. Our rational forethought has often to be based on insufficient data, and as computer engineers say of inadequate or insufficient data: "garbage in, garbage out." And the more we try to plan, the more we ignore the flow of the present. Chuang-Tzu tells a parable about Confucius seeing an old man enter a cataract and emerge singing on the other bank. When asked how he did it, the old man replied: "I have no way. . . . Plunging in with the whirl, I come out with the swirl. I accommodate myself to the water, not the water to me." So it will be with life's last figure—death, if we can learn to trust the deeper wisdom within us to decide when we are to become centered in another state of being without haste to die or clinging to life.

Here is a little fable for the more scientifically-minded: an iron bar lay down with a heavy clank amid iron filings arranged in a pattern. The bar asked them why they were so arranged, and they answered: "Because we are subject to an invisible field of energy. So now are you."

"But I see and feel nothing," replied the iron bar, "And I am so heavy and substantial." The filings told him: "You and I are matter and this is a field; but both are forms of Energy. We are all made of Energy. By means of the equation $E = mc^2$ the substantial can become insubstantial, and the insubstantial can become substantial. Lie still and let your substance be aligned with this magnetic field until you will always point North and draw other filings toward you." So the iron bar lay still, and meditated on whether mass has an energy nature and a dog has the Buddha nature.

Even so we can align ourselves with God's energy field; our struggling and questioning are part of this field and can induce his current in our cores. For we are part of the flow of life, we are made in the image of God, who patiently matches his response to ours and is revealed to us as one with ground of our beseeching.

Who, then, is wrestling within us? And is there victor or loser? And does not the victor wear a crown of thorns? Here the mystics' One and the Hebrews' Thou join in the unity of opposites, and the Taoistic vision of nature merges with the Christian vision of the sign of the Cross on all things.

### Cross Hands

At the end of the first third of the t'ai chi form, and also at its conclusion, comes a wide sweep of the arms ending with crossed wrists and hands which always reminds me of the seraphim of Isaiah's vision folding their wings before their faces.

As I do this I remember the impression that first came to me in observing and participating in t'ai chi of the serene silence that accompanies it, a quiet that enfolds mind and body. In the heat and preoccupation of learning to practice correctly this impression tends to recede into the background, but the possibility of it is always there. Physically, the explanation is simple enough: there is no musical accompaniment, no hard breathing, no thud of footfalls since every step is "empty"—without weight—and always this enchanted slowness of motion. Hence all this bodily movement is noiseless, and the mind is surprised into a stillness of its own. The Zen phrase came to my mind: "The sound of one hand clapping."

Why, then, I wonder, does this silent movement always evoke the idea of music in my mind? Can it be that, in yin-yang fashion, the absolute presence of silence generates a reciprocal kind of music? Unheard melodies are sweeter, as Keats said. So perhaps the one hand clapping calls the other hand into being.

Then one day, while strolling in the quiet of an early spring morning by the shore, I realized that a tranquil silence surrounded every small chirp or rustle. It was the background of all things, only perceived so when I listened with *attente* for sounds that never came. The single hand is silent, but listening for it nevertheless clears the channels of the mind to hear the absence of sound. I remembered that meditative *attente* has been likened (by Anthony Bloom in *Beginning to Pray*) to the watchfulness of a birdwatcher awaiting the first stirring of bird life before dawn. As a birdwatcher myself, I had wondered how one applied this to inward listening; now I understood that it was the expectant listening to the sound of any silence that brings, if only momentarily, liberation from restless thoughts and a silence between the ears. This inner silence may also be sought by way of sitting meditation, involving the paradoxical task of taming the mind. But first, I think, it is needful to have been overtaken by a foretaste of this silence. For you it may have come by a wilderness lake, on a mountain peak, or in a cathedral. For me it was first "heard" in t'ai chi ch'uan.

On a later spring day, when the June foliage was stirred by a fresh breeze, I stood in the sunlight of a meadow surrounded by woods, and quietly moved into the form. I was aware of the silence of t'ai chi, for now at least I had disciplined myself until I could feel my sense of balance, so that I could relax and let my awareness spread to the surroundings and their relation to me. I was now a silently flowing member of the company of holly trees standing around waving their branches as if to say, "Now you are one of us." I was between the earth and sky as I should be, and the final sweep of arms and hands seemed to be affirming that the whole wide world was in God's and my hands. I had often admired a landscape without reference to myself, just as I had often tramped through it wrapped in my own self-concerns; now I began to see myself as part of the landscape. It was related to me and I was related to it, not by thought but by being there. In t'ai chi the loss of ego does not mean the loss of a center. As Al Huang, a philosopher of t'ai chi, says: "Keep that alertness all around, without losing your center. This is the t'ai chi meditation. . . . You meditate, you try to give in and receive what is happening within you and around you. . . . When you meditate, you realize you're moving and being quiet at the same time." Reality for the meditator is a network of relationship, and the self is "lost," not by annihilation but by being in harmony.

Though the bird's tail of enlightenment still eludes me, I am immensely grateful to the experience of t'ai chi for its epiphany of divine harmony in motion, the wisdom it is teaching my inward parts, and the first intuition of the sound of silence as a substantial fullness to rest in rather than an insubstantial emptiness to be fled from. When I remarked to my teacher that I had learned at least how little I knew, she commented, "We all feel how little we know"—this from one who to a student's eye is perfect. Later I wondered whether to consider this a discouraging or an encouraging remark; it depends on whether you think of a cup as half-full or half-empty. Then I realized that it is both; here again the Taoistic unity of opposites lures one along the never-ending road to perfection in a possible/impossible endeavor. So it is with meditation, the possible/impossible *attente à Dieu* which we can never quite do nor do without. Just as the practice of the t'ai chi form and the daily use of your body should interact to reinforce each other, so the practice of t'ai chi meditation should be the focus of a life of inward vigilance, when physical silence becomes sacramental of the creative stillness before the Word of creation, a stillness that surrounds the particulars of existence which emerge from it like mountains from the mist in a Chinese landscape.

## In the End is The Beginning

The flow of the Tao is circular and without end. The flow of t'ai chi ch'uan is circular and brings one back to the beginning. And in t'ai chi I am very much novice; now I should stop talking about it. Here I stand, rooted in the earth, head to the sky. My adventure is just beginning.

Here is where you, too, may stand. Try standing easily, feet firm on the ground, shoulder-width apart, knees a little flexed; feel your head and spine suspended from the sky, your shoulders and chest hanging easily. Swing your pelvis a little, for there is your center gravity. When it is over one leg, that leg is "full" and rooted, the other leg is light and "empty." Let your hands be neither stiffened nor clenched but relaxed with a gentle convex curve of wrist through fingers. Let your arms rise slowly in front of you and while breathing in, elbows relaxed, draw your hands toward you and lower them by your side as you exhale. As you stand there, be aware of your surroundings with calm alertness, and of yourself as related to the sky above the ground beneath. Do not think about them, just be with them. Feel your body's centering. As you move slowly about the circular motions, listen to the silence of your movements. Let your touch sensitively follow a living or moving thing. When thoughts come, consider the flow of your mind to be the delegated adaptability of the Tao and be as alertly nonclinging inwardly as without. As the day continues, consider every approaching event as the next figure in the t'ai chi form of life, and move with it neither hurrying nor lingering.

Finally, the purpose of any kind of meditation, whatever your experiences with it may be, is to become a more real and more compassionate person. The goal is not enlarged awareness for its own sake, but a more complete way of being in God's world and relating to it with serene sensitivity. The silence of Eternity must be interpreted by love.

Listen, then, to the sound of silence, and move to its music.

## PART III

# TRAINING AND DISCIPLINE: THE WAY

## GEORGE LEONARD

# AIKIDO AND THE MIND OF THE WEST

Aikido is a Japanese art of self-defense. Those who have watched demonstrations of judo or jiujutsu may note certain similarities upon first visiting an aikido dojo (place of practice). There are the quilted gi uniforms, the colored belts, the resounding slaps of open palms on the mat, the Japanese terms (shomen-uchi irimi-nage!) that roll off the Western tongue with such esoteric yet innocent charm. But the differences—the characteristics that set aikido apart from the other martial arts—soon become apparent.

The defender takes his stand on the mat. He is relaxed yet alert. He offers none of the exotic defensive poses popularized by the movie and television action thrillers. An attacker rushes at him, but he remains calm until the last instant. There follows a split second of unexpected intimacy in which the two figures, attacker and attacked, seem to merge. The attacker is sucked into a whirlpool of motion, then flung through the air with little or no effort on the part of the defender, who ends the maneuver in the same relaxed posture, while the attacker takes a well-practiced roll on the mat. Unlike judo, aikido has no rules, no static opening positions; the throws are more fluid, the movements

*At different times a senior editor of* Look *and a contributing editor to* Esquire, *George Leonard (b. 1923) has written much about the nature of competition and cooperation in modern society. His associations in Japan after World War II led him to the study of aikido, in which art he now holds a third dan black belt. Leonard often uses aikido in his writing, as he does in this excerpt, as a model for solving conflict without strife.*

more like a dance. The nonaggressive nature of this art is reflected in its terminology. The defender is known as the nage (pronounced nah-gay), from a Japanese word meaning "throw." The attacker is called the uke (oo-kay), from a Japanese word associated with the idea of falling. Thus, in aikido, he who attacks takes a fall.

The art of aikido may achieve a transcendent beauty in the randori, or mass attack, when a single nage is set upon by four or more uke. Whirling, dancing, throwing, the nage seems to travel along unfamiliar lines of space-time. Seemingly trapped by converging attackers, he is, suddenly, *not there*. He moves easily in the midst of ferocious blows and flying tackles, not by opposing but by joining. He deals with the strongest attack by embracing it, drawing it into a circle of concord which, he feels, somehow joins him with the essential unity and harmony of the universe. He has no thought for his own safety or for any goal of external dominance. He is always *here*, it is always *now*, and there is only harmony, harmony. Such grace under pressure, it must be said, comes only after many years of practice and devotion. Mastery of aikido, as of any complete sport, stands entirely outside the familiar American doctrine of Ten Easy Lessons.

My own involvement with aikido began in November 1970. Never having heard of the art, I entered training with the utmost naïveté, after an enthusiastic phone call from a friend. The call came at the right moment; I was just beginning an extended period of research and writing and was grateful for anything that might force me into a schedule of regular physical workouts. During the first few weeks I was often impatient with the hours spent on the nonphysical exercises—calming and centering my body, sensing the approach of others, blending with putative "energy flows," meditating.

My first teacher, Robert Nadeau, had studied several of the martial arts. At age sixteen, he had taught judo to policemen. He went on to spend four years as a police officer himself. Turning to the gentler, more spiritual art of aikido, he traveled to Japan to study for two and a half years in the dojo of Master Morihei Uyeshiba, the founder of the art, who was then in his late seventies. I was amazed to hear Nadeau describe himself as "basically a meditation teacher." This man, with his great knowledge of self-defense, with his smooth, flawless physical techniques, a *meditation teacher*? Nadeau explained that competition is forbidden in aikido. Competition is limiting. Furthermore, it is not the way the universe operates. We would learn by cooperating, not competing, with each other. "Aikido's spirit," according to Master Uyeshiba, "is that of loving attack and that of peaceful reconciliation."

My head could understand all this well enough. By that period of my life, however, I had learned to delight in competition and aggressive physical action. Some time was to pass before I began to incorporate Nadeau's teaching into my body and being. As it turned out, aikido has given me as much physical action as I could wish; and it obviously can be an effective mode of self-defense. But I have found—and this is the most important thing—that aikido's basic teachings erase those barriers the Western mind has erected between the physical and the mental, between action and contemplation.

Western thought, unlike that of the East, has by and large rejected direct experience as a path to the highest knowledge. Plato vacillates on this point but finally seems to conclude that experience can only remind us of what we already know. His approach to knowledge remains largely dialectical and cognitive. The Manichaean and Neoplatonic degradation of embodiment, eloquently experessed in Saint Augustine, widened the gap between sensory and "true" knowledge. The inflexible rationality of medieval thought left little room for subjective verification. In reaction, the scientific revolution of the sixteenth and seventeenth centuries became, as Alfred North Whitehead reminds us, "through and through an anti-intellectualist movement. It was the return to the contemplation of brute fact."

But the "fact" of the scientific philosophers was not personal fact. Galileo, Kepler, Descartes, and Newton lived in a dream world of forces and motion and manipulation without touch or taste or color or smell. Later, Locke and Hume and the Positivists might have been expected to bring us back to our senses, but they only reinforced the scientific mentality that has moved us to control the world and lose ourselves.

And now we are taught from earliest childhood to trust instruments more than our own deepest feelings. We are encouraged to view as true that which is most removed from our own persons. This mode of being finds its polar opposite in the richness and intensity of traditional Eastern thought, which is scientific in another way: if only the individual will find and emulate a good teacher, and follow specific steps, then he will certainly know the Divine Ground, the repository of all truth, by a direct intuition superior to discursive reasoning. But this also tends toward imbalance, because the individual becomes too easily passive, careless of the Divine Ground as manifested in the common matter and energy of our daily world.

For me, aikido balances the extremes. It offers contemplation and transcendence. It is also active and effective. In the ordered interplay between the individual and the world, between the nage and the uke, it allows us to check out theory against action, and perhaps to return the human body to realms from which it has long been absent.

IDEAL FORMS. "Perfection exists. You already know these techniques. I'm here only to remind you." In the matter of ideal forms, my teacher, Robert Nadeau, is an unconscious Platonist. The concept of an immaterial reality informs all his teaching. Nadeau assumes, however, that incorporeal being can be approached through bodily consciousness rather than through conceptions alone.

The shiho-nage (four-way throw) is a particularly beautiful and rather difficult aikido technique. One version of it involves grasping the uke's attacking hand with both of your hands, moving to his side, then spinning so that his hand is brought over your head, thus behind his back. From this position, the uke is easily thrown backward to the mat. Performing the necessary turn while remaining upright and centered can be a tricky matter. Rather than teaching this maneuver piecemeal, Nadeau asks us to meditate on the *idea* of the perfect turn. This turn, he tells us, *already exists* at the uke's side. We may think of it as a whirlpool, already spinning there. Once we have this idea firmly in our minds and bodies (and for Nadeau the two are not separate) all we have to do is move to the uke's side, into the whirlpool, into the perfect turn. Everything else—balance, centering, posture, feet, arms, hands—will take care of itself.

We are Americans and pragmatic. Will it *work*? We give it a try and find that Nadeau is right. The shiho-nage flows most smoothly when the reality of the *idea* is fixed firmly in the consciousness, and no analysis is needed.

The same thing is true of every aikido movement. For example, if the nage resorts to physical force in a certain wristlock, he may bring a stronger attacker down, but only with much muscular effort. Nadeau suggests an ideal form: energy pouring out through the arm and hand, streaming over the uke's wrist like a waterfall, then flowing from the nage's fingers down to the center of the earth. The uke goes down like a shot without the use of any perceptible physical effort. The difference is startling.

Nadeau's teaching methods run counter to the prevailing direction of most physical education and coaching. The physical education experts continue their work of breaking down every skill into smaller and smaller fragments, analyzing every movement and submovement with the help of film, computers, advanced mechanics, and math. Nadeau finds this obesssion with analysis rather amusing. It may help well-coached athletes achieve step-by-step improvements, but it can't bring forth the quantum leaps in human functioning that he feels are possible. Nadeau also questions the prevailing view that specific physical skills are nontransferable. The experts feel that years spent perfecting the kick may do little or nothing to improve the pass. For Nadeau, the essence of one physical movement is transferable to every physical movement. "Most of aikido," he says, "can be taught in one simple, blending movement." What is more, the principles learned in aikido should influence the way you play golf, drive, talk to your children, work at your job, make love—the way you live.

CAUSALITY. What makes things happen? Our particular brand of common sense has a ready answer. The cue ball moves because I strike it with the cue. The seven ball moves because the cue hits it. The attacker falls because I throw him down. It is hard for us to escape the concept Aristotle categorized as "efficient causation." We insist on linking our every action to the chain of necessary cause and effect. Unthinking, we conceive ourselves as creatures who go about the world making things happen without ourselves being changed. This assumption, however you look at it, seems rather naïve. Some two centuries ago, Hume showed that what we call causality is only a measure of subjective expectation. Temporal succession means that A regularly precedes B in time, but does not prove the necessity of cause-and-effect linkage. The Positivists tried to explain the succession of events in terms of a purely objective relative frequency.

In aikido, it is much simpler. Just as the perfect movement *already exists*, each perceived event, even one in which we "do" something, is *already happening*. There is a flow in the universe. Our task is to join it.

> The Way abides in nonaction,
> Yet nothing is left undone.

If Lao-tzu's *Tao Te Ching* seems to offer only paradox on this matter, it is perhaps a good measure of our minds' present limitations. Body and being in action resolve the paradox. Sometimes, even as a relative novice, I can perceive the fields, the flow, the rhythm of the universe. I am part of the universe. The uke is part of the universe. When he attacks me, my body, my arms, and hands, follow a motion that already is happening. There is no waiting, no goal, no *doing*.

Yet nothing is left undone. In these delightful moments, the thrower is not separate from the thrown. We blend in a single motion, a small ripple in an endless sea of existence.

HARMONY. UNITY. All sorts of people come to our dojo—tired businessmen, newly divorced men and women, aging actors and actresses, street people, entrepreneurs of the spirit, new converts to Women's Liberation, experts in other martial arts. There is no beginning, no end. We all step on the mat together, the first-time curiosity seeker along with the dedicated third-degree black belt. We bow, then kneel in the Japanese meditation position around the edges of the mat. In a world of organized hostility and random violence, a world that preaches competition and practices paranoia, we seek universal harmony and the unity of all existence.

Many people come only for a few sessions. Some drop out when they realize they will receive from aikido no violent instrument for their anger. Others are looking for something sequential—progress, "graduation." They cannot grasp the notion of a lifelong journey with no fixed destination. We regulars move about with those who come and go, all of us teachers, all students. Feet get tangled up. Attackers veer off course. On our mat we can see every wound inflicted by our present civilization. The angst, alienation, and anomie of our times appear clearly in the motion of an arm, in the quality of the energy field that surrounds a movement.

And yet, crippled and blind, we eventually begin to sense the *harmonia* that burst upon Pythagoras as a revelation of the whole cosmic system. Behind the curtain of our imperfections there lies the geometry of the humming strings. No matter that we are all different. No matter that our art is built on defense against physical attack. "That which opposes fits," Heraclitus tells us. "Different elements make the finest harmony." We are summer and winter, day and night, smooth and rough, attacker and defender. We are, just possibly, harmony.

There is a sort of dance we often use as a warm-up. Two of us stand facing each other. In three turning steps we pass, face to face, almost touching. We end facing each other again; we have merely changed sides. We repeat the movement again and again, a hundred times, a thousand times. Eventually we can feel that we really are one, a single organism. We are yin and yang, restating our interchangeability. We are a magnet shifting polarity; there is a *click* as we pass, a change in the current. The surface differences between us smooth out. Our bodies tingle. We settle into the eternal present, at home in the universe.

It is said that Pythagoras was the first to call the world *cosmos*, a word that is hard for us to translate, since it contains the ideas of both perfect order and intense beauty. By studying *cosmos*, the Pythagoreans believed, we reproduce it in our own souls. Through philosophy, we assimilate some of the divine within our own bodies. In aikido practice, we simply turn this belief around. Through the experience of our bodies, we come to know *cosmos.*

MULTIPLICITY. Bodies that change size and shape. A manipulable ethereal body superimposed on the physical body. A mysterious inner weight or "true gravity" that the adept can shift at will. Such notions of multiple being within ultimate unity offend the mind of the West, which clings rather desperately to what Blake called "single vision." And yet, multiplicity is central to Oriental thought and to the mystical tradition of all cultures. The Hindu Upanishads describe five koshas, or "soul sheaths," of which the physical body is only one. Indian philosophy in general has much to say about the sukshma shariria, the so-called "subtle," or "feeling," body. In the Western tradition, the Neoplatonists conceived a subtle body and a radiant body, though you won't hear about this in your run-of-the-mill philosophy class.

Our training in aikido calls for no theoretical study. From the beginning, we realize the multiplicity of perception and being through direct experience. Robert Nadeau in no way denies the reality of the physical body with its bones, blood, muscles, and the like. But he offers us other resources. By sensing the flow of ki (life energy), we can create a powerful yet relaxed "energy arm" in and around the physical arm, so that the arm, however you wish to conceive it, becomes virtually unbendable. By making parts of the energy body smaller, we can slip out of a grasp. By lowering our center of gravity and sending a flow of ki down into the earth, we can become seemingly much heavier. At one public demonstration, my daughter, at one hundred ten pounds, moved her ki energy downward so effectively that a weight lifter was unable to budge her. The Western mind rushes for a rational explanation. Mutual hypnotism? That's one way of talking about it. But recent studies in hypnotism have shown that the term is a loose one. In any case, as we'll see in the next chapter, even the most reductive explanation cannot entirely reduce experience.

Simply by considering possibilities commonly ignored or covertly forbidden by our culture, we find ourselves in a far more fascinating universe. We discover adventures that do not require the burning of fuel or the rape of the planet: sensing the energy field of a friend or a tree, making connections that defy conventional space and time, traveling across dazzling new vistas of perception and being. We realize, with the sorcerer don Juan, that our world is "awesome, mysterious, and unfathomable" and that our life is filled to the brim and altogether too short.

Like most of us, I retain a measure of skepticism, sometimes denying my own experience in favor of the artificial cognitive structure erected by this faltering civilization. But I know now that there are other voices, other realities. We sometimes practice aikido techniques while wearing blindfolds, and I am learning that there is a kind of seeing for which the eyes must be closed. Perhaps I can remain agnostic but not blind, skeptical but not so arrogant as to rule out everything my instruments can't measure. "The end of the method of the Pythagoreans," wrote the fifth-century Neoplatonic philosopher Hierocles, "was that they should become furnished with wings to soar to the reception of the divine blessings, in order that, when the day of death comes, the Athletes in the Games of Philosophy, leaving the mortal body on earth and stripping off its nature, may be unemcumbered for the heavenly journey."

VIRTUE. In aikido, as in Plato and in the perennial mystical tradition, virtue is not an end in itself, but the indispensable means to the knowledge of the Good or of divine reality. In his memoir, Master Morihei Uyeshiba wrote: "The secret of aikido is to harmonize ourselves with the movement of the universe and bring ourselves into accord with the universe itself. He who has gained the secret of aikido has the universe in himself and can say, 'I am the universe.'" This universal harmony, it seems to me, stands as the ultimate Good in aikido. According to Uyeshiba, "This is not mere theory. You practice it. Then you will accept the great power of oneness with Nature. Virtue is practice, the steady, disciplined practice of loving attack and peaceful reconciliation."

My teacher, in a radical, ultimately Christian application of virtue in practice, asks us not to master but to serve the attacker. It's up to us to be so sensitive to the attacker's intentions and needs (whether the attack be physical or mental) that we know precisely where he wants to go and what he wants to do. Blending with him, and taking ourselves slightly out of harm's way, we can help the attacker do what he intends. Somewhere, at the completion of the act, there is a point at which he rejoins the harmony of nature. Every attacker is destined, in any case, to take a fall.

Of course, if each of us were to be totally sensitive to the needs and intentions of all those around us, there would be no attacks.

HEAVEN AND EARTH. Perhaps the loveliest of aikido techniques is called tenchi-nage (heaven and earth throw). As in all aikido techniques, the tenchi-nage occurs in many variations, but always involves one arm being raised upward, the other reaching down. In this manner, the attacker's strength and intentions are split between heaven and earth, and there is nothing for him to do—until his moment of reconciliation—but fall.

I am practicing one variation of tenchi-nage. My technique is uncertain. Because I am uncertain, I am rough. I throw down my uke with unnecessary force. This is not aikido. On this occasion the uke is Tom Everett. In his early twenties, Everett is an accomplished aikidoist.

"Let's start again," he suggests. "What qualities do you associate with heaven?"

"Heaven? Clouds, lightness, angels."

"And earth?"

"Solidity, weight, massiveness."

"All right. One of your arms is heaven. The other is earth." He laughs. "It's simple."

I spend a moment investing my arms with these qualities.

"Don't think about technique," Everett reminds me. "Just heaven and earth."

And it *is* simple, if only because I have been led to the right questions.

In the end, every historical period appears to us not in terms of the answers it provides but of the questions it asks. In a period that glorifies "combativeness," from the first physical education class to the last television show, our major questions become conflict-ridden. For example, Norman Mailer, speaking for a significant proportion of our literary-intellectual culture, leads us to believe that the most significant question we can ask of the space program, and most other things as well, is whether it is the work of God or the devil. It is a question for which there seems to be no satisfactory answer. In the same way, the old culture clings to this romantic dualism, to Aristotelian categorization, to the "tragic vision," to the "human condition." Is it possible that we are coming to the end of this kind of thinking?

In a remarkable essay, "New Heaven, New Earth," Joyce Carol Oates writes:

We are satiated with the "objective," valueless philosophies that have always worked to preserve a status quo, however archaic. We are tired of the old dichotomies: Sane/Insane, Normal/Sick, Black/White, Man/Nature, Victor/Vanquished, and above all this Cartesian dualism—I/It. Although once absolutely necessary to get us through the exploratory, analytical phase of our development as human beings, they are no longer useful or pragmatic. They are no longer *true*. . . . What appears to be a breaking down of civilization may well be simply the breaking down of old forms by life itself (not an eruption of madness or self-destruction), a process that is entirely natural and inevitable. . . . The death throes of the old values are everywhere around us, but they are not the same thing as the death throes of particular human beings. We can transform ourselves.

If such a change is indeed upon us, we need balance and harmony, sensitivity and the art of reconciliation—not ego, the test of manhood, the clash of force against force, the battle of God versus the devil. The secret of tenchi-nage is that the separation between heaven and earth is only apparent. Ultimately they are one. In Lao-tzu's words:

> The space between heaven and earth is like a bellows.
> The shape changes but not the form;
> The more it moves, the more it yields.

When my practice goes well, I am, if only for a short while, one with the universe. Within the one are heaven and earth and much more—not only friends and lovers but also the convict in solitary confinement, the dread enemy in the jungle—all part of me, all part of us. The time has come to ask about reconciliation, which starts not at some distant place, but here, in my body and being, and in yours.

**IRA S. LERNER**

# YAMAMOTO

The term martial arts refers to an Oriental phenomenon which combines great personal discipline and spiritual awareness with combat skills. The original martial arts involved many systems of bare-handed combat. Certain systems concentrated on using hitting and kicking techniques, while other systems were based on the concept of lifting your opponent off the ground and throwing him onto his back. In addition to these methods of self-defense, many systems employing spears, bow and arrow, swords, and other exotic weaponry were developed as part of these arts.

The word "martial," meaning warlike, is derived from Mars, the god of war in Roman mythology. This designation is at best incomplete, and perhaps has hindered the understanding of many of these arts. Yamamoto explains:

* * *

Budo is Japanese word for what the West calls martial arts. It has occurred to me that the meaning of this word is long time lost. Budo is actually two words: *bu* and *do*. Bu is made from two characters. The

---

*Yukiso Yamamoto, the speaker and subject of the following commentary, left his native Japan at the age of nineteen to join his parents who had emigrated to Hawaii. Years later, at age forty-nine and as a senior instructor of judo, Yamamoto came under the influence of Koichi Tohei and then began the formal study of aikido. Now a grandfather and accomplished aikidoist, he refers to the teaching of his mind-body art as a spiritual vocation.*

■ 183

first character means "to stop," second character is symbol for the spear. So we have "to stop the spear." The word *do* comes from the Chinese word Tao. Tao means "the way"; so budo means "the way to stop the spear," or "the way to keep the peace." These arts were not to fight, no . . . but to keep the peace. You see, Tao means not just the way, like the way to do something, no. The meaning has to do with the way to lead a spiritual life and to true enlightenment. In old times the student would learn the arts not to hurt others, but to develop mind and body unification, and attain a higher level of awareness.

Budo encompassed all original martial arts, one of which is aikido. I think true meaning of aikido is very beautiful. *Ai* means harmonious or being in harmony. Ki [chi in Chinese] is your spirit and life-energy force. So we have "harmonious spirit." Ai-ki-do means "the way of spiritual harmony."

Ki is hard to explain literally. Ki composes all things, both living and nonliving. Modern science may say that ki is energy; that word may be more easy to understand. Energy you cannot see, but you can put it into action. Science calls this energy; we call it ki. Ki is the very essence of the universe. You are composed of ki. By training you can make use of this ki.

To develop your inner ki you must unify mind and body, and become one with the universe. Some people think that mind and body are two separate things. This kind of thinking creates problems. Mind and body are within yourself. There is no line between mind and body. Which is mind? Which is body? Body you can see. Mind you cannot see, cannot smell, cannot touch. But you know mind is within you. Originally both are one. But people think they are two different things. Based on this, they try to coordinate two different things. Very hard to do. If they can unify mind and body, then it is easy to be in harmony with rest of nature.

Mind and body are both born from ki. You are born from the ki of the universe through your parents. Then why we have such hard time to make this mind and body one? Probably it was not as hard to do thousands of years ago. But now, especially for those in the cities, it is understandable to feel separate from the universe. Modern society does not stress oneness with the universe and the universe says nothing to us.

The ki of the universe only acts, never speaks. So, many people have lost touch completely with ki. Although universe does not speak to us directly, we can learn by observing its ways. Then, through certain training and study, we can become one with the ki of the universe. The movements of aikido are designed to put us back in touch with the natural laws of ki.

When first learning aikido movements I thought, "Oh yes, now I must move this way." But gradually I stopped conscious thought. I just moved, my mind and body together. When you ride in elevator to bottom floor, no doubt your body goes down. But sometimes your mind goes up! No, you must go together. How to do it?

Within yourself you have one point which is the center of you. It is your center of gravity. We call this your *one point*. To become one with the universe you must imagine that the universe itself is concentrated inside your one point. To do this, I concentrate. I keep dividing the universe in half until it is infinitely small. I just think, "Smaller, smaller, half, half, half, half, half. . . ." Concentrating, I bring the universe to my one point, to one microscopic point. Now I am one with the universe.

Next I practice expansion. I imagine ki of the universe flowing from out my one point, traveling forever in all directions. I extend into space. Now I am centered. Space is limitless; it has a limitless radius. Because of this, no matter where I stay I am always center of universe. If I move one hundred feet to the left, I am still in the center! No matter where I go—up, down, side, or like this—I am always in center of universe.

● ● ●

The result of Yamamoto's expansion and contraction technique is both aesthetic and practical. Aesthetically he develops a profound sense of oneness with the universe. It is his ability to see himself as united with it in a positive way which reinforces his love for all things. By acknowledging the universe, something many times more vast than himself, Yamamoto does away with the conceit which causes selfishness.

The physical effect of expansion and contraction is an acute awareness of one's center of gravity. "Keeping one point" or being "centered" are aikido terms for a state of consciousness in which one feels united with the entire universe and is at the same time completely aware of one's bodily relationship to the universe. Suppose a master were seated on a bench and that bench suddenly collapsed. The master, being centered, would be so aware of his bodily relationship with the bench, and so aware of his or her center of gravity, that as the bench began to collapse the master would still maintain his balance and would not fall to the ground. Part of the explanation for this seemingly magical feat is that a master of aikido does not make himself wholly dependent for support upon the chair in which he sits. The master would not fall over the

loose railing of a bridge either, for he would not make himself dependent upon it for support. Yamamoto says that we should try to "maintain
one point" or be "centered" at all times. He then adds that this is
impossible to do, but states that being centered for even one minute
out of an entire day will add to your awareness and enrich your
relationship with the universe.

• • •

When my students practice the meditation, I test them. They must
maintain this concept of being one with the universe. First, they must
remain calm and relaxed. Otherwise they will stop the flow of ki. They
concentrate ki into one point; then they let it flow out continuously.
Their ki flows out from one point like the rays of the sun. They are
completely centered in the universe; they are at one with it. Now I
make test. I press against the chin or shoulder and try to move my
student. If she keeps calm and her ki is flowing outward, then it is
difficult to move her; she is very strong. If student moves easily usually
is one of two reasons. Perhaps the student has tensed her muscles,
trying to use physical strength to stop me from shoving her. This
constriction of the muscles stops the flow of ki. She thinks she is strong,
but she is not. Or, perhaps the student has learned that she should not
tense her muscles, so she tries to relax completely. Sometimes a
student may confuse being "relaxed" with just being limp and soft. She
forgets to send out the ki from her one point and can also be easily
moved.

When Yamamoto slowly places his hand on each student, he has the
possibility of creating physical and emotional stress in each one. He is,
after all, the master. As he nears each student, he can sense whether or
not his mere presence and the anticipation of his test has already
caused the student's mind to waver. Executing the test is simply a
formality in these instances. Other students may keep their ki flowing
until Yamamoto applies a light amount of pressure, at which time they
tense up and stop the flow. Advanced students will stay calm. Yamamoto
cannot move them easily. He will try to trick them, and some will fall
prey to his deception. Others will not. A large smile fills his face when
a student has managed to maintain calmness despite his ploys.

As Yamamoto achieves a state in which he is at once both calm and
energetic, so too does he create another paradox, that of strength and
gentleness. Can one be strong and gentle simultaneously? Yamamoto
believes so. Kindness is closely related to Yamamoto's concept of

gentleness. "Kindness," he says, "is to have a tender heart and good will to all persons." Even as he throws an assailant with kote gaeshi, the wrist-twisting throw, Yamamoto's good will is ceaseless. He seems to be helping, almost nursing his opponent. As we look at the opponent, a blur in midair, we have no fear that he will be injured. Something in the master's manner, in his expression, tells us that everything will be all right. One can feel confident that Yamamoto will guide this person to safety. He believes in good will to all persons, including those who would do him harm. This is because of his belief in the law of karma.

• • •

Whatever you do in the world will always come back to you. This is the law of karma. If you do good—always end up good. You do bad—always end up bad. It does not appear immediately; but ultimately it rules your life.

• • •

The relationship of strength and kindness is suggested in Yamamoto's posture. His hands have a most secure grip on his attacker, but there is no indication of any strain. He performs this action so effortlessly that one must conclude that there is something left unexplained, something below the surface which cannot readily be seen. Yamamoto tells us that this "something below the surface" is the flow of ki, the invisible life force.

Another glance at Yamamoto's posture and that of his opponent brings to light the nature of their feelings toward one another. Yamamoto appears to be bowing with humble respect for his attacker, who is, after all, his student. Oddly enough, the student also seems to be bowing to Yamamoto—in midair and upside down, but still in a posture quite respectful of his teacher. This upside-down bowing on the part of the student is no doubt a mere coincidence and certainly involuntary. However, it is an appropriate coincidence, because a mutual respect does exist between Yamamoto and his student. In part, it is this mutual respect that teacher and student have for one another which allows a seemingly violent act to become an expression of spiritual harmony and good will.

• • •

For those not familiar with aikido, this question may come to mind: "If aikido means way of spiritual harmony, then why we throw each other?" Answer to this question is fascinating. Through breathing and meditation we practice keeping one point. This is first step to spiritual harmony, developing mind and body coordination. But is easy to be in spiritual harmony when you are sitting by yourself in quiet places somewhere. Life is not so easy. Always there is possibility of conflict. We do not sit still in a quiet room all our lives. In aikido practice we learn to maintain one point and be calm when we are in motion and when conflict arises.

When we are attacked this represent possible conflict. In aikido we practice avoid the conflict. We never go against the opponent's strength. Rather we lead the strength away from us. This principle of avoiding conflict can be applied to anything, not only self-defense. However, after you understand how we use this principle in self-defense, it becomes more easy to apply it to your daily living.

When someone tries to hurt an individual, this is going against the natural law of harmony in the universe. If person being attacked fights back with physical strength, then this person also goes against natural law of harmony in universe. If someone attacks you, possibly you might overcome this attack by using your physical strength. But this would only be a short-term victory. Sure, maybe you win this time, but there is always some others who are stronger than you. There is no purpose to compete with individuals. Always there is someone stronger than you. In aikido we practice "winning without fighting." This is absolute. Avoid the conflict and you always win. If someone tries to punch you, simply move out of the way. This is the simplest example. We look at everything in the positive way in aikido. When someone attacks you, he gives you a present of his strength. To make use of this gift you must know how to receive it.

When someone hits you, he is extending his ki toward you. His ki starts to flow even before his body moves. It starts when he thinks he will hit you. And before he can hit you he must think he is going to hit you. His actions are directed by his mind. So, we do not need to deal with his body at all if we can redirect his mind and the flow of his ki. This is the secret: lead his mind and ki away from you and his body will naturally follow.

To lead his mind you must not upset the flow of his ki or give him bad feelings. If you touch his body, you do not push or pull or hit. All these give bad feeling. You touch softly and gently in order to lead his mind. His mind thinks, "This feels good," and so his body follows.

To lead his mind you must keep centered, so you will not be thrown off course. Then, try to feel his ki before it reaches you. This is a sensitivity training, to be sensitive to the flow of another's ki. As his ki approaches, you direct your ki to flow in the same direction as his ki intends to go. Now both your ki and his ki are one, flowing in the same direction. Difference is that you are centered and he is not. Since he extended ki with intent to hit you and you let him keep extending his ki, he is overextended. Maybe he is trying to regain his centering. Now you can lead his ki and direct it. One very important point to lead the mind is keeping the proper distance. Ma-ai is the safe distance between you and another person. With proper ma-ai you can lead someone else's mind easily. If you are too close you may be injured. However, if you are too far away you cannot lead his mind.

When an attack comes you must remember to deal with the mind and flow of ki, not with the physical. If you can lead the mind, the body must follow. To do so you must have a strong flow of ki yourself. When your flow of ki is strong, this energy travels out from your center part to your fingers and continues from your fingertips into the universe. We call this extending your ki. One may have such a strong flow of ki that it is not necessary to physically touch your opponent in order to throw him. The ki flowing from your fingertips is sufficient. We call this *kokyu-nage*, "the touchless throw." In this case you lead the opponent only through the flow of your own ki. This is ideal, but not always possible.

Proper falling technique also follows the aikido philosophy. We must learn proper falling technique in order to practice aikido safely. When you are being thrown it is too late to turn back. So you let your body follow the motion of the throw and roll with it. We do a type of shoulder roll in which we roll over a great part of our body and absorb the shock. In doing this we avoid conflict and prevent serious injury to ourselves. There are many fine points of this art, but the principles are always the same. In practicing aikido we learn whether we are the thrower or the person being thrown. When I throw my students I try to give them a good feeling. From my example they learn not to have bad intentions for others. Also they practice falling, which is a way of avoiding conflict.

I do not practice aikido for self-defense reasons. I do not think any serious students practice this art for self-defense. The movements are simply a way to visually demonstrate the aikido principles. These principles of nondissension and avoiding conflicts can be applied to our everyday life. This is the purpose of studying aikido. If you have love in your heart for all creation, the universe itself is your protector. There is no self-defense for those with ill intentions.

Most important thing I learn from aikido is breathing and meditation. Breathing and meditation are like roots of a tree. Without roots tree doesn't survive; it dies. In Japanese we call this training kon, the root. Very, very essential. If you don't have this breathing and meditation practice you cannot develop your ki very well. This training change my life completely.

One type of meditation is the technique I described earlier in which you become centered in the universe. When doing this meditation, or other kinds, you must use proper breathing methods.

When you breathe you must fill your entire lungs with air. Most people use only top portion of their lungs; they do not fill up the bottom part. If you breathe correctly you will fill up bottom of lungs, as well as the top. Opera singers use this type of breathing. It is no secret; it is the natural way. It is how you breathe automatically when you are asleep. But we have learned so many incorrect ways that when we are conscious we interrupt this natural process with an inferior method. The proper breathing method gives us the most energy with the least amount of work. Once mastered it is effortless.

We are constantly breathing, from the time we are born until the time we die. If we learn to breathe efficiently we will have much more energy to devote to our daily tasks. Early in my judo training I understood this proper breathing. My instructor would ask me to have a match with six, maybe seven boys my own age—one after another. I did not have time to rest, yet after one or two minutes with the fifth of sixth boy he would be more tired than me. I don't think that my skill at that time was much advanced from my peers. But proper breathing made the difference. They always "Puff, puff, puff!" I was not expending such great amounts of energy because I did the proper breathing. Physically, in this example, one can see the difference proper breathing makes. Although it would be hard to measure a difference in mental power, I believe it exists there also, maybe more so. I am convinced that the powers of mental concentration are greatly increased with proper breathing.

Now, why do you sleep? During daytime you exhaust your life power. You get tired because this power is exhausted. So evening time you sleep and replace this life power. If you do proper breathing your power becomes stronger and you need less sleep. I always do one half hour of breathing and meditation exercises before I go to bed. This relaxes my mind and body and makes the sleep more beneficial.

Before I took up proper breathing I get tired all the time. Even though I didn't do too much except wake up, I still get tired. Now that feeling is gone. I feel much pep in the morning. My health in general is so much better! My bedtime is anytime I take a nap. I can nap whenever I wish. So, if I feel tired, just close my eyes for fifteen minutes of sleep. I don't use any alarm clock either. I put the thought into my subconscious mind. You have to look in mirror and command yourself: "You get up at six o'clock in the morning." This is telling your subconscious mind. Then you sleep. Six o'clock, wake up! When I travel to other islands I don't carry alarm clock, I just get up when I wish. If I want, I can get up at three A.M. I don't look in mirror any more. I just think: three o'clock. This is a long type of training. You are training the subconscious mind.

Your subconscious mind affects how you react to things in your daily life. Since breathing and meditation are to train the subconscious mind, this has profound effect on your outlook in life. Training your mind to wake up at a certain time is a useful training, but the value of breathing and meditation goes much deeper than that.

Breathing and meditation teach us to be one with the ki of the universe and to respect all God's creation. When inhaling you are drawing in the ki of the universe to your one point. This ki unites with your body to give you strength. When exhaling we must feel our own ki pour forth from our one point and reach toward the heavens. This sharing of life energy unites us with the universe.

The air we breathe is a most important thing. It is a gift of love from the universe. We must always be grateful. As we become appreciative of the air we breathe, so too must we learn to appreciate everything in the universe. Through breathing and meditation I have come to believe that I am a part of an infinite universe in which all things are united. If you believe that all mankind is united, you will be more considerate of others, for every individual is somehow connected to you through the ki of the universe. This is what breathing and meditation have taught me.

My wife and I have never fought in more than forty-two years of marriage. Maybe we had some harsh words once, but I cannot remember when. We are connected through the ki of the universe. Because we are so close our ki is constantly flowing back and forth to one another. To fight with her would be like fighting with part of myself. This attitude must extend to everyone, not only those close to you. If you hate just one person, it makes it hard to love anyone. When we appreciate all that is around us it makes our love for those close to us even stronger.

• • •

Yamamoto uses the meditation bells to strengthen his ki and develop equanimity. He asserts his inner peace amidst the powerful and clangorous ringing he creates. With each tintinnabulation, Yamamoto chants the rhythmic affirmation: "Toho kami emi tame, toho kami emi tame, toho kami emi tame." "May all the gods have grace on me."

The clanging and chanting are unrelenting. To what end does this man sit, clad in black skirt, with voice and bell united in a deafening thunder? One might easily conclude he is insane! The esoteric nature of his discipline makes many of his practices curious, to say the least.

• • •

Purpose of this training is to remain calm while under stress and to purify your mind and body. We call this practice misogi. Originally, the word misogi comes from the Shinto religion and means to go river and cleanse oneself. We use this word in aikido for certain breathing and meditation exercises because we believe they have a cleansing effect on the mind and body.

This vigorous chanting and bell ringing requires much flow of ki. The beginner cannot do for more than one or two minutes continuously. With practice you can do for twenty minutes with much power. This power must come from a strong ki developed from mind and body unification. Physical strength will not do. Your arm will be tired immediately because the bell is heavy. Also your throat will become hoarse from continuous chanting. When done with a positive flow of ki and correct breathing, you do not feel any ill effects. Sometimes we practice with twenty, fifty, or one hundred students in a room. The sound of bells is so loud and the flow of ki so great that we say, "Even the four walls will learn aikido."

• • •

In ancient times the master of martial arts was expected to defend himself at any given moment. This expectation led to the development of several beautiful and unlikely martial art forms. One is that of the bokken, a stylized wooden sword. Many of the bokken movements are based on the supposition that the master will be forced to defend himself from a seated or kneeling posture. Classically, the master would use this art to defend himself if attacked while having tea. He would not have the time to rise before the assailant's sword cut his throat. And so the master learned to defend himself against two and three attackers without once rising to his feet. Today Yamamoto practices these movements for quite a different reason.

When the bokken is used properly it moves through the air so swiftly that one can hear the air being pushed aside. It comes to rest with quiet perfection, devoid of the slightest movement or fluctuation. As Yamamoto uses the bokken he maneuvers about on his knees with the grace of an Olympic figure skater dancing on ice. The prerequisites for performing these arts are formidable. Yamamoto tells us that the mind controls the body and that the body is the "mirror of the mind."

• • •

When using bokken hold it gently, the way a little baby grabs your finger. A baby holds softly but the grip is snug and firm. To learn proper swinging of bokken, stand in front of a leaf hanging five feet above the ground. Swing the bokken down, just touching the leaf, but without causing it to move. Swing slowly and smoothly. Keep practicing with the bokken until you can touch the leaf without moving it. You must come to a complete stop when you touch. Complete stop means mind must stop first. This is just the beginning.

After you know this, swing bokken fast, at full speed. Swing and swing. Each time just touch the leaf—just touch.

To move the bokken quickly, you must move your mind quickly. It's not the idea to just try swinging bokken more quickly. Your mind must move as fast as the bokken or you are not in control of the movement. Bokken is in control of you in that case. This is not good. We must teach the mind to move swiftly, only then can we train the body to follow.

To stop the bokken completely your mind must not be tense. The body is the mirror of the mind. If your mind is tense or wanders, the bokken will waver instead of stopping completely. If your mind is calm, the bokken will stop without even slightest wavering.

• • •

Practicing with the bokken gives Yamamoto a means of observing his own progress in mind-and-body coordination, for, as he points out, the degrees of control the student can exercise over the bokken are graded in difficulty.

• • •

Next, practice running toward the leaf and swinging. Same thing: just touch! Soon you can run from any distance, swing at full speed, and stop on a pin head. Then your control is good. Now you can hang several leaves from silk thread all around you. Practice with all of them, swinging in all directions: one, two, three, four, five! Just touch each leaf—no movement. This is very advanced.

We believe our spirit enters the bokken as we use it. After many years a part of our spirit is actually in it. For this reason we never let just anybody use our bokken. Whoever uses it will affect its spiritual energy. So, usually, we let no one use it except ourselves.

Sometimes a teacher will loan his bokken to a student in the class. Because the teacher's spirit is in that bokken, this is considered an honor. Several years ago my aikido instructor, Tohei Sensei, gave me his bokken. He was visiting Hawaii and just before he left he said, "Yamamoto, you keep this for me." Well, I didn't know what to say to express my feelings. I felt very privileged. This was a very great honor. Of course, he knew how I felt. I have used his bokken ever since that day. Even now, so many years later, I know that his spirit is still in that bokken.

The masters of aikido and other Japanese martial arts are given the title Sensei. Sen means "before," and sei means "born." In Japanese we use this word to mean "teacher." But literal meaning is "one who is born before." The one who is born before you is your teacher. In reality this is not always the case. Some people learn faster than others, some slower. It has been said that a person may have ten years of experience, or one year of experience repeated ten times. By this we mean that time alone is not the true indication of how much one has learned. Even so, we still use the word sensei to mean teacher.

In martial arts the title sensei is Japanese equivalent of master. It is only given to those who are most deserving. By definition, the master is one who teaches. We believe that only those who are exceptional teachers are true masters. After one reaches a certain level in aikido, only way to substantially further the development is by teaching.

For instance, when I first start teaching my students make all kind of mistakes. Soon I realize that they are just copying me. It is easier to see the mistake in them than in myself. "How did you learn the wrong way?" I used to ask. "Oh, well, I learned it from you!" What can I say?

Through teaching others we find out how little we really know. Student asks a question and you cannot answer it. But moment before, you thought you knew it all. Means you need to do some more studying. When you have to teach someone, you find that you must examine your knowledge much closer. Each student has trouble with different points. You must figure a way to show these trouble points to those who do not comprehend. Each time you can do this successfully the point you teach becomes much better understood by you, It would be quite difficult to reach these understandings without the problem to teach others.

If we want to know what type of teacher a person is, we do not have to study him directly. Simply look at his students. The character and personality of the teacher is always reflected in the students. When I look at my students it's like looking in the mirror. If they don't look too good, something wrong with me.

One difference, I think, between my teaching and teaching in the public schools is the desire of students to learn. In my classes the initiative starts with the students, not me, not the instructor. My students all have the intention to learn before they come to me. This is their attitude: learn, learn, learn. I give certain points. Then let them do. Then I find out the difference between some students and others. I pick out the ones who are a little slow and help them. First, I apply the standard test, but sometimes the slow learner does not comprehend. So then I mention that the mind controls the body. This the student usually understands all right, but sometimes still cannot put into practice. Then I use a more physical explanation. I go up to him and touch his head very softly, applying almost no pressure at all. When I take my hand away his head shakes. This is because his mind is wavering. He is not calm. Maybe he anticipates that I will press hard, so he starts to press back against me. This is a fighting mind. If he pushes against me he is not following the principle of avoid conflict. Maybe he is so worried about whether or not I will be able to move his head that his concentration is upset. Either way his mind is not calm. His mind must learn not to waver just because of slight distraction.

The test itself is not to make them fail. I make test so that they can pass the test. If you ask a student to do certain thing and he fails, you must help him until he pass the test. The test is a learning experience. My purpose is to teach, not to measure how much I have taught. So the test must be a positive feeling. Discouraging is not good testing. Testing is to help them feel the right way. I never say, "You no good." You cannot do that. I let the student complete his move because he doesn't know if it was right or wrong way, but he gains a certain amount of confidence from doing. So, if I stop him, tell him, "This is wrong," it hurts him. That is very bad, even though you are the person who teach.

To teach you must respect certain amount of pride of the student. I always respect the student. Instead of saying, "You are doing wrong," I don't say anything about whether he is doing right or wrong, but "I have a suggestion for you." Then I show the correct way. I don't say this is correction; I just suggest. I give him a positive feeling. If you constantly say, "No, do this way, do that way," even though in a positive way, it is always against the student. Correct by saying, "All right, better, better. . . ," always better. And if he does right or wrong I just look and let go. Then maybe later in class I watch him and he still does wrong, I say nothing. Maybe I help him in next class. If I watch over his shoulder I make him self-conscious, then he will never get it.

Respect. . . every teacher must be respectful. Respect the students' efforts and their self-esteem and they will have respect for you. Patience is also very important. Patience and positive attitude. If you don't care, if you have that "I don't care" attitude, students will know right away. So most important, it doesn't make much difference whether you know the actual technique or not. As far as teaching concerned, first thing of all you must have patience, patience. Then you must always be positive, positive, positive. Yes, these are the two major points in teaching.

I remember when I was practicing the calligraphy lesson in the second grade. I was nine. I was sitting in the last row near the wall. By accident I throw the brush back clear to the wall. It touch the wall and make a black line. The teacher called to me, "Yamamoto, how come you did this bad thing." I explain that I didn't do it intentionally; it just happen when I swung my arm. "All right, you no-good boy. You stand in front of class." He slap me and put me in front of the class. After maybe twenty minutes or so he say. "You don't do that any more?" I say, "No." But I didn't like taking punishment when it was just accident. So, when I sat down I dipped my brush full with ink and put it all over the wall! Boy, oh boy! I really get scolded then; hit, too! Just shows even a child doesn't like to be found guilty when really innocent. This second time I had a good spanking and the teacher took me to the principal of the school. He say, "Yamamoto is a no-good boy!" You know, first time I did not do bad intentionally but I get the scolding. So I say, "All right, if that the case I do like this." Just maybe I felt rage, that's all. I was young. I think this story is similar to many.

My grammar-school teacher didn't understand the positive way. He told me, "Yamamoto, you no-good boy," so I listen to him and I am no-good boy. Instead I put scolding into positive. I say, "You are a good boy! Yeah, good boy. And you stay a good boy if you don't do this." But if you say, "You no-good boy because of this"—same thing, but two different things. So put into positive, not only in teaching but in all your daily life. Work always in the positive thinking and positive way.

I think many teachers like to fight with student when they do scolding. I think they are angry. Their speaking tone become angry, too. That's no good at all. Teacher and children angry. How can such a teacher make good students? Shouldn't be like that. Must always be calm and think of what is good for the student. If you punish the student, that's okay if he or she will benefit from it. Punishment must be for good of student, not for revenge of teacher, or because teacher is still angry. The teacher is really angry at himself because of his inability to cope with the child. Sometimes a teacher may be angry with himself because he cannot teach a slow learner, other times because he cannot make the child behave. If you understand this you will not take your anger out on the child. I never say, "You are no good!" You cannot do that. No matter how poor a student may be, I never lose my hope that I may make him a good student. I try with all my effort.

## JIGORO KANO

# THE CONTRIBUTION OF JIUDO TO EDUCATION

The object of this lecture is to explain to you in a general way what jiudo is. In our feudal times there were many military exercises, such as fencing, archery, the use of spears, etc. Among them was one called jiujutsu which was a composite exercise, consisting principally of the ways of fighting without weapons, using occasionally daggers, swords, and other weapons.

The kinds of attack were mostly throwing, hitting, choking, holding the opponents down, and bending or twisting the opponent's arms or legs in such a way as to cause pain or fracture. The use of swords and daggers was also taught. We had also multitudinous ways of defending ourselves against such attacks. Such exercise, in its primitive form, existed even in our mythological age. But systematic instruction, as an art, dates from about three hundred and fifty years ago.

In my young days I studied this art with three eminent masters of the time. The great benefit I derived from the study of it led me to

---

*Born in Kobe to a wealthy family, the author (1860–1938) was sent by his father to study Tenjin-Shinyo jiujutsu at an early age. In 1881 Kano graduated from the Imperial University and became a teacher of literature, opening his first dojo in the same year. By 1884 he had formulated the rules of a new martial system called judo and opened the Kodokan, a school which was to teach judo as a way of life rather than simply as self defense. Traveling widely abroad, Kano represented Japan to the International Olympic Committee and in the year of his death persuaded the Committee to bring the 1940 Olympics to Tokyo. He is called the father of modern sports in Japan.*

make up my mind to go on with the subject more seriously, and in 1882 I started a school of my own and called it Kodokan. Kodokan literally means "a school for studying the way," the real meaning of "way" being the concept of life. I named the subject I teach jiudo instead of jiujutsu. In the first place I will explain the meaning of these words. *Jiu* means gentle or to give way, *jutsu*, an art or practice; and *do*, way or principle, so that jiujutsu means an art or practice of gentleness or of first giving way in order to gain final victory; while jiudo means the way or principle of the same.

Let me now explain what this gentleness or giving way really means. Suppose we assume that we may estimate the strength of a man in units of one. Let us say that the strength of a man standing in front of me is represented by ten units, whereas my strength being less than his, is represented by seven units. Then if he pushes me with all of his force I shall certainly be pushed back or thrown down, even if I use all my strength against him. This would happen because I used all my strength against him, opposing strength with strength. But if, instead of opposing him, I were to give way to his strength by withdrawing my body just as much as he pushed, remembering at the same time to keep my balance, then he would naturally lean forward and thus lose his balance.

In this new position, he may have become so weak (not in actual physical strength but because of his awkward position) as to have his strength represented for the moment by, say only three units, instead of his normal ten units. But meanwhile, I, by keeping my balance, retain my full strength, as originally represented by seven units. Here then, I am momentarily in an advantageous position, and I can defeat my opponent using only half my strength, that is half my seven units, or three and one-half, against his three. This leaves one-half of my strength available for any purpose. In case I had greater strength than my opponent I could of course push him back. But even in this case, that is, if I wished to push him back and had the power to do so, I should first have given way, because by so doing I should have greatly economized my energy.

This is one simple instance of how an opponent may be beaten by giving way. Other instances may be given.

Suppose my opponent tries to twist my body (as demonstrated) intending to cause me to fall down so. If I were to resist him I should merely be thrown down, because my strength to resist him is not sufficient to overcome his. But if, on the other hand, I give way to him, and while doing so I pull my opponent (as demonstrated) throwing my body voluntarily on the ground, I could throw him very easily.

I will give another example. Suppose that we are walking along a mountain road with a precipice on the side (as demonstrated) and that this man had suddenly sprung upon me and tried to push me down the precipice. In this case I could not help being over the precipice if I attempted to resist him, while, on the contrary, if I give way to him at the same time, turning my body round (as demonstrated) and pulling my opponent toward the precipice, I can easily throw my opponent over the edge and at the same time deposit my body on the ground.

I can multiply these examples to any extent, but I think those which I have given will suffice to enable you to understand how I may beat an opponent by giving way, and as there are so many instances in jiujutsu contest where this principle is applied the name jiujutsu (that is gentle, or giving-way art) came to be the name of the whole art.

But, strictly speaking, real jiujutsu is something more. The ways of gaining victory over an opponent by jiujutsu are not confined to gaining victory first by giving way. We sometimes hit, kick, and choke in physical contest, but in contra-distinction to giving way, there are different forms of positive attack. Sometimes an opponent takes hold of one's wrist. How can one release himself without using his strength against the opponent's grip? The same thing can be said when somebody grips him from behind. If, thus, the principle of giving way cannot explain all the tricks in jiujutsu contest, is there any principle which really covers the whole field? Yes, there is, and that is the principle of the maximum use of mind and body, and jiujutsu is nothing but an application of this all-pervading principle of attack and defense.

Can this principle be applied to other fields of human activity? Yes, this same principle can be applied to the improvement of the human body, making it strong, healthy, and useful, and constitutes physical education. It can at the same time also be applied to the improvement of intellectual and moral power, and constitutes mental and moral education. It can at the same time be applied to the improvement of diet, clothing, housing, way of social intercourse, and carrying on of business, and constitutes the study and training in the ways of living. I gave to this all-pervading principle the name of "jiudo." So jiudo, in its broad sense, is a study and a method of training in mind and body as well as the regulation of life and affairs.

Jiudo, therefore, in one of its phases, can be studied and practiced with attack and defense for its main object. Before I started Kodokan, this attack and defense phase of jiudo only was studied and practiced in Japan under the name of jiujutsu, sometimes called taijutsu, meaning the art of managing the body or yawara, the soft management. But I came to think that the study of the all-pervading principle is more important than the mere practice of jiujutsu, because the real understanding of this principle not only enables one to apply it to all phases of life, but is also of great service in the study of jiujutsu itself.

It is not only through the process I took that one can come to grasp this principle. One can arrive at the same conclusion by philosophical interpretation of the daily transactions of business, or through abstract philosophical reasoning. But when I started to teach I thought it advisable to follow the same course I took in the study of the subject, because by so doing I could make the body of my pupil healthy, strong, and useful. At the same time I could assist him gradually to grasp this all-important principle. For this reason I began the intruction of jiudo with training in randori and kata.

Randori, meaning free exercise, is practiced under conditions of actual contest. It included throwing, choking, holding the opponent down, and bending or twisting the arms or legs. The two combatants may use whatever tricks they like provided they do not hurt each other and obey the rules of jiudo concerning etiquette.

Kata, which literally means "form," is a formal system of prearranged exercises, including hitting, cutting, kicking, thrusting, etc., according to rules under which each combatant knows beforehand exactly what his opponent is going to do. The training in hitting, kicking, cutting, and thrusting are taught in kata and not in randori, because if they were used in randori cases of injury might frequently occur, while when taught in kata no such injury is likely to happen because all the attacks and defenses are prearranged.

Randori may be practiced in various ways. If the object is simply the training in the methods of attack and defense, then the attention should be especially directed to the training in the most efficient ways of throwing, bending, or twisting, without special reference to developing the body or to mental and moral culture.

Randori can best be studied with physical education its main object. From what I have already said, anything to be ideal must be performed on the principle of maximum efficiency. We will now see how the existing systems of physical education can stand this test. Taking athletics as a whole, I cannot help thinking that they are not the ideal form of physical education, because every movement is not chosen for all-round development of the body but for attaining some other definite object. And furthermore, as we generally require special equipment and sometimes quite a number of persons to participate in them, athletics are fitted as a training for select groups of persons and not as a means of improving the physical condition of a whole nation. This holds true with boxing, wrestling, and different kinds of military exercises practiced all over the world. Then people may ask, "Are not gymnastics an ideal form of national physical training?"

To this I answer that they are an ideal form of physical education from their being contrived for all-round development of the body, and not necessarily requiring special equipment and participants. But gymnastics are lacking in very important things essential for the physical education of a whole nation. The defects are:

1. Different gymnastic movements have no meaning and naturally are devoid of interest.
2. No secondary benefit is derived from their training.
3. Attainment of skill cannot be sought for in gymnastics as in some other exercises.

From this brief survey over the whole field of physical education, I can say that no ideal form has yet been invented to fill the necessary conditions for it.

This ideal form can only be devised from a study based on maximum efficiency. In order to fulfill all those conditions or requirements, a system of all-round development of the body as a primary consideration must be devised as in the case of gymnastics. Next, the movements should have some meaning so that they could be engaged in with interest. Again, the activities should be such as require no large space, special dress, or equipment. Furthermore, they must be such as could be done individually as well as in groups.

Those are the conditions or requirements for a satisfactory system of education for a whole nation. Any system that can meet successfully those requirements can, for the first time, be considered a program of physical education based on the principle of maximum efficiency.

I have been studying this subject for a long time and have succeeded in devising two forms which may be said to fulfill all those requirements.

One form is what I call "representative form." This is a way of representing ideas, emotions, and different motions of natural objects by the movements of limbs, body, and neck. Dancing is one of the instances of such, but originally dancing was not devised with physical education for its object, and is therefore not to be said to fulfill these requirements. But it is possible to devise special kinds of dancing made to suit persons of different sex and mental and physical conditions and made to express moral ideas and feeling, so that conjointly with the cultivation of the spiritual side of a nation it can also develop the body in a way suited to all.

This representative form is, I believe, one way or another practiced in America and Europe, and you can imagine what I mean; therefore I shall not deal with it any further.

There is one other form which I named "attack and defense form." In this, I have combined different methods of attack and defense, in such a way that the result will conduce to the harmonious development of the whole body. Ordinary methods of attack and defense taught in jiujutsu cannot be said to be ideal for the development of the body; therefore, I have especially combined them so that they fulfill the conditions necessary for the harmonious development of the body. This can be said to meet two purposes: (1) bodily development, and (2) training in the art of contest. As every nation is required to provide for national defense, so every individual must know how to defend himself. In this age of enlightenment, nobody would care to prepare either for national aggression or for doing violence to others. But defense in the cause of justice and humanity must never be neglected by a nation or by an individual.

This method of physical education in attack and defense form, I shall show you by actual practice. This is divided into two kinds of exercise: one is individual exercise and the other exercise with an opponent (as demonstrated).

From what I have explained and shown by practice, you have no doubt understood what I mean by physical education based on the principle of maximum efficiency. Although I strongly advocate that the physical education of a whole nation should be conducted on that principle, at the same time I do not mean to lay little emphasis on athletics and various kinds of martial exercise. Although they cannot be deemed appropriate as a physical education of a whole nation, yet as a culture of a group or groups of persons, they have their special value and I by no means wish to discourage them, especially randori and jiudo.

One great value of randori lies in the abundance of movements fit for physical development. Another value is that every movement has some purpose and is executed with spirit, while in ordinary gymnastic exercises movements lack interest. The object of a systematic training in jiudo is not only to develop the body but to enable a man or a woman to have a perfect control over mind and body and to make him or her ready to meet any emergency whether that be a pure accident or an attack by others.

Although exercise in jiudo is generally conducted between two persons both in kata and in randori and in a room specially prepared for the purpose, yet that is not always necessary. It can be practiced by a group or a single person, on the playground, or in an ordinary room. People imagine that falling in randori is attended with pain and sometimes with danger. But a brief explanation of the way one is taught to fall will enable them to understand that there is no such pain or danger.

I shall now proceed to speak of the *intellectual* phase of jiudo. Mental training in jiudo can be done by kata as well as randori, but more successfully by the latter. As randori is a competition between two persons, using all the resources at their command and obeying the prescribed rules of jiudo, both parties must always be wide awake, and be endeavoring to find weak points of the opponent, ready to attack whenever opportunity allows. Such an attitude of mind in devising means of attack tends to make the pupil earnest and sincere, cautious and deliberative in all his dealings. At the same time one is trained for quick decision and prompt action, because in randori unless one decides quickly and acts promptly he will always lose his opportunity either in attacking or in defending.

Again in randori each contestant cannot tell what his opponent is going to do, so each must always be prepared to meet any sudden attack by the other. Habituated to this kind of mental attitude he develops a high degree of mental composure. Exercise of the power of attention and observation in the training hall naturally develops such power, which is so useful in daily life.

For devising means of beating an opponent, the exercise of the power of imagination, of reasoning, and of judgment is indispensable, and such power is naturally developed in randori. Again, as the study of randori is the study of the relation existing between two competing parties, hundreds of valuable lessons may be derived from this study but I will content myself for the present by giving a few more examples. In randori we teach the pupil always to act on the fundamental principle of jiudo, no matter how physically inferior his opponent may seem to him and even if he can by sheer strength easily overcome the other. If he acts against this principle the opponent will never be convinced of his defeat, whatever brutal strength may have been used on him. It is hardly necessary to call your attention to the fact that the way to convince your opponent in an argument is not to push this or that advantage over him, be it from power, from knowledge, or from wealth, but to persuade him in accordance with inviolable rules of logic. This lesson that suasion, not coercion, is efficacious—which is so valuable in actual life—we may learn from randori.

Again we teach the learner, when he has recourse to any trick in overcoming his opponent, to employ only as much of his force as is absolutely required for the purpose in question, cautioning him against either an over- or an under-exertion of force. There are not a few cases in which people fail in what they undertake simply because they go too far, not knowing where to stop, and vice versa.

To take still another instance, in randori we teach the learner, when he faces an opponent who is madly excited, to score a victory over him, not by directly resisting him with might and main but by playing him till the very fury of the latter expends itself.

The usefulness of this attitude in everyday transactions with others is patent. As is well known, no amount of reasoning could avail us when we are confronted by a person who is so agitated as to seem to have lost his temper. All that we have to do in such a case is to wait until his passion wears itself out. All these teachings we learn from the practice of randori. Their application to the conduct of daily affairs is a very interesting subject of study and is valuable as an intellectual training for young minds.

I will finish my talk about the intellectual phase of jiudo by referring shortly to the rational means of increasing knowledge and intellectual power. If we closely observe the actual state of things in society we notice everywhere the way we are foolishly spending our energy in the acquisition of knowledge. All our surroundings are always giving us opportunities of gaining useful knowledge, but are we not neglecting the best use of such opportunities? Are we always making the best choice of books, magazines, and newspapers that we read? Do we not often find out that the energy which might have been spent for acquiring useful knowledge is often used for amassing knowledge which is prejudicial not only to self but also to society?

Besides the acquisition of useful knowledge, we must endeavor to improve our intellectual powers, such as memory, attention, observation, judgment, reasoning, imagination, etc. But this we should not do in a haphazard manner but in accordance with psychological laws, so that the relation of those powers one with the other shall be well harmonized. It is only by faithfully following the principle of maximum efficiency—that is jiudo—that we can achieve the object of rationally increasing our knowledge and intellectual power.

I shall now speak about the *moral* phase of jiudo. It is not my intention to speak about the moral discipline given to students in the exercise room, such as the observance of rules of etiquette, courage, and perseverance, kindness, and respect to others, impartiality, and fair play so much emphasized in athletic sports throughout the world. The training in jiudo has a special moral import in Japan because jiudo, together with other martial exercises, was practiced by our samurai, who had a high code of honor, the spirit of which has been bequeathed to us through the teaching of the art. In this connection I wish to explain to you how the principle of maximum efficiency helps us in promoting moral conduct. A man is sometimes very excitable and prone to anger for trivial reasons. But when one comes to consider that "to be excited" is an unnecessary expenditure of energy, giving benefit to nobody but often doing harm to himself and others, the student of jiudo must refrain from such conduct.

A man is sometimes despondent from disappointment, is gloomy, and has no courage to work. Such a man jiudo advises to find out what is the best recourse he can have under the then-existing circumstances. Paradoxical as it may seem, such a man is, to my mind, at the same position with one who is at the zenith of success. In either case, there is only one course to follow, that is, what he deems to be the best at the time. Thus the teaching of jiudo may be said to lead a man from the bottom of disappointment to a state of vigorous activity with a bright hope in the future.

The same reasoning applies to those persons who are discontented. Discontented persons are often in a sulky state of mind and blame other people without attending to their own business. The teaching of jiudo will make such persons understand that such conduct is against the principle of maximum efficiency, and will make them realize that by the faithful pursuance of that principle they will become more cheerful. Thus the teaching of jiudo is, in a variety of ways, serviceable to the promotion of moral conduct.

Finally, I wish to add a few words to the *emotional* phase of jiudo. We are all aware of the pleasurable sensation of muscles through exercise, and we also feel pleasure at the attainment of skill, in the use of our muscles, and also through the sense of superiority over others in contest. But besides these pleasures there is one derivable from assuming graceful attitudes and performing graceful movements and also in seeing such in others. The training in these together with the pleasure obtainable from watching various movements symbolical of different ideas constitute what we call the emotional or the aesthetic phase of jiudo.

I believe you have already come to see what kind of thing jiudo really is, in contra-distinction to jiujutsu of feudal times.

If I now state in concise form what I have spoken, it would be summed up as follows:

Jiudo is a study and a training in mind and body [original text unclear—ed.] enroll, in order to learn the technique under the guidance of a teacher[.] [S]o that they may be able to continue defense I became convinced that they all depend on the application of one all-pervading principle, namely: "Whatever be the object, it can best be attained by the highest or maximum use of mind and body for that purpose." Just as this principle applied to the methods of attack and defense constitutes jiujutsu, this same principle applied to physical, mental, and moral culture, as well as to ways of living and carrying on of business, constitutes the study of, and the training in, those things.

Once the real import of this principle be understood, it may be applied to all phases of life and activity and enable one to lead the highest and most rational life.

The real understanding of this principle need not necessarily be arrived at through the training in the methods of attack and defense, but as I come to conceive of this idea through the training in these methods, I made such training in contest and the training for the development of the body the regular means for arriving at the principle.

This principle of maximum efficiency when applied to the keying-up or perfecting of social life, just as when applied to the coordination of mind and body—in the science of attack and defense—demands, first of all, order and harmony among its members, and this can only be attained through mutual aid and concession, leading to mutual welfare and benefit.

The final aim of jiudo, therefore, is to inculcate in the mind of man a spirit of respect for the principle of maximum efficiency and of mutual welfare and benefit, leading him so to practice them that man individually and collectively can attain the highest state of advancement, and, at the same time, develop the body and learn the art of attack and defense.

If we closely observe the actual state of society all over the world, notwithstanding the fact that morality in all its forms (religious, philosophical, and traditional) is meant to improve man's conduct in society and make the world ideal, the fact seems quite the contrary. We notice vices, quarrels, and discontent in every level of society, from the highest to the lowest. While we are taught hygiene and correct ways of living in school from childhood up to mature age, we still are prone to neglect the rules of good clean living and of hygienic and orderly lives.

The actual facts prove that our society is lacking in something which, if brought to light and universally acknowledged, can remodel the present society and bring greater happiness and satisfaction to this world. This is the teaching of maximum efficiency and mutual welfare and benefit. I do not mean to say that our time-honored moral precepts and hygienics may be less observed. However, let those precepts and advices be as much respected even as they used to be, but in addition to these our principle of maximum efficiency and mutual welfare and benefit would ever be paramount. This I emphatically say, because at this age of criticism and new ideas, for every teaching and advice to have force, it must have some indubitable reason for facts in the background. We do not hear the thinking man today say, "Because I believe in such and such a thing, therefore you must believe in it," or "I came to such and such a conclusion through my own reasoning process; therefore you must also come to the same conclusion." Whatever one affirms must be based on facts or reasoning which no sane person could deny or doubt. Certainly none can deny the value of the principle, "whatever be the objective, it can best be attained by the highest or maximum efficient use of mind and body for that purpose." Again, none can deny that it is only by aiming that every member of society can keep from discord and quarreling, and live in peace and prosperity. Is it not because of the universal recognition of these facts that people come to talk so much about efficiency and scientific managements and that everywhere these are being advocated? In addition to this, the principle of give-and-take is more and more coming to be the determining factor in the lives of all humanity. Is it not because this principle of mutual welfare and benefit has been recognized that we come to form the League of Nations and the Great Powers of the world come to meet for the decrease of naval and military armaments? These movements are also automatic acknowledgments of the crying need of efficiency and mutual welfare and benefit. They must be fostered by the educational forces of every country.

## C.W. NICOL
*from*
# MOVING ZEN

Mrs. Atsumi, my mother-in-law, had bought a house in Akitsu, a little village just inside the outer boundaries of greater Tokyo. I was so happy when she invited Sonako and me to live in her house with her and to use the six-tatami room upstairs—a bright, airy little place that overlooked fields and woods and a scattering of other small houses.

Akitsu station was thirty-five minutes by fast train from Ikebukuro, a main suburb from which all parts of the city could be reached by train and subway. Unfortunately, it was going to take me three hours a day to commute to the Yotsuya dojo, but that didn't matter; I could read and think and study Japanese on the trains.

From Akitsu station, with its summer swallows' nests, its pigeons, and the goldfish ponds which the stationmaster cherished, I had to walk home through the main street of the village with its friendly, busy little shops, and then past fields and bamboo groves, and under tall elms and cedars, and then across a little bridge until I reached our house. It was a fifteen-minute walk along a narrow road bordered by carefully cropped tea hedges, past ancient stone Buddha statues—wayside shrines—and big old thatched farm houses with their lines of white oak trees standing guard around them. I could watch the people working in the fields, and see raucous long-tailed jays and shrikes and crows, and even an owl once in a while. Such a relief from downtown Tokyo!

From that summer expedition to Great Bear Lake, I had fallen into a way of life that was truly Japanese, and a hundred-fold more real and

---

*See page 123 for the author's biographical note.*

joyful than my foreign-bachelor isolation. I was part of a family now. I had a wife, a mother-in-law, sisters, cousins. Each day was an object lesson in living, and I had so much to learn.

Apart from a French Catholic priest who spoke no English, we knew no foreigners in Akitsu. To learn to speak and understand Japanese was very important to me now, and apart from being an official student of the karate dojo, with a student visa, I had also enrolled in the Tokyo School of the Japanese Language for afternoon classes. In the evenings, to stretch out my all-too-meager savings, I taught English conversation at a couple of English Conversation Schools (of which there are many in Tokyo).

The Japan that I had read and dreamed about began to unfold to me, and even now as I write about how I felt, or about what it all meant to me, a thousand images flood my mind, each seeming so precious.

My own personal happiness was reflected from my friends, especially my three sempai, Sasaki, Okuda and Seto. They in particular no longer gave me the leeway or patronization reserved for gauche foreign visitors. They undertook my education in earnest.

Soon after I had returned to the dojo after the summer away, I got my right arm very badly bruised from directly blocking a very powerful kick. The arm was purple, black, puce and green from elbow to wrist. I took the kick on a Wednesday, and on Thursday the dojo was closed for teachers' practice, so I trained at home as usual, strengthening my own kicks with iron clogs. On Friday I went to the dojo and attended the morning class, but when it came time for the kumite, or fighting, part of the lesson, I bowed out of the dojo, not wanting to hurt my arm anymore.

Okuda came out of the dojo and berated me for leaving the class. I protested—"But my arm . . ."

"No difference! You have worn your karategi and you have entered the lesson. It is improper and impolite to leave before the end, especially for such a minor affair. Come back in!"

Once back in the dojo I had to fight, and if I had thought that the others would go easy on the injured arm, then I was much mistaken. In favoring the injured arm I showed it to my opponents as a weakness, and as such it was used. The rest of the lesson was a fierce and angered misery of jolting pain and subdued rage. But I surprised myself and fought well, defeating a couple of blue belts.

As we were changing, after the cold shower outside, I asked another black belt why my sempai had disregarded the fact that I had an injury.

"They did not disregard it," he replied. "They did this for your own sake. If you put on your green belt and step onto the dojo floor you signify that you are willing to accept the responsibility of your actions and of your rank. You must therefore be willing to fight, willing to win, willing to lose. I watched you, Nic-san. You fought well. So do not expect us to pander to your weaknesses. We would be very bad sempai if we did that. Your weakness would only be magnified, and soon any excuse could stop you from fighting—or to fight and not accept the results. We are like soldiers. When a soldier puts on his uniform, carries a weapon and goes to war, he is obviously willing to fight and kill his enemies. If he is willing to kill, then he must be prepared to die. It is only right. We must cultivate spirit. You must be grateful to your sempai for showing you so much attention. If Okuda did not care about you, he would have let you leave. Understand?"

I bowed. "Yes! I understand!"

And so I learned that if ever I had an injury serious enough for me to want to protect it, I either fought hard enough to defend the injury, or I just didn't go to the dojo. You couldn't go and just watch. You got ordered out onto the floor. It was reasoned that if you were fit enough to walk around, catch trains, stand on two feet, then you were fit enough to train. By these means we were to learn "spirit." The dojo was a theater of life and death. No favors were granted for weaknesses, and the degree of pressure put upon you was equal to the color of the belt and to the rank which you bore.

But the color of a belt is not everything. A high-ranking student from another dojo might come to train, and out of courtesy, decline to wear his color. Indeed, once I fought with a white belt and was very soundly beaten. His movements were fast and focused, and his round-house kicks whipped at my head too fast for me to block. I felt shame, for a green belt to be beaten by a white belt, I thought, was very poor. The sempai were laughing at me. Later, after much teasing, they told me that the "white belt" had in fact held the rank of first dan black belt.

"Then why does he wear white?" I asked, with some indignation.

"For nearly three years he has not trained at the dojo, and thus he does not feel worthy of the black belt. Later, after he is in good condition, our sensei will tell him to wear his rank again."

The discipline of the dojo was harsh, but conversely, slack or insincere students were not pushed. Another Japanese paradox. Perhaps hard to understand, but for one thing, such a student was always of lower grade. Without sincerity and hard training you could not win through to the colored belts. A white belt could slack off, and bow out of the dojo without shedding a drop of sweat—that was up to him. He would be ignored. However, bad manners and lack of dojo etiquette were dealt with very severely. Foreigners, however, could be a problem. They had so much to learn that to an extent their ignorance was tolerated until they showed sincerity and the desire to learn.

It was because of this very tolerance that unpleasantness developed. There were two Canadians training at the dojo, nice enough fellows, hard working in their way, but ignorant and boorish to extreme. I could never understand why the hell either of them came to Japan, and I felt embarrassed for my adopted country. They resisted every move to correct their behavior. They laughed and joked and acted in an unseemly manner in the dojo. They walked and lounged around like slovenly louts. They refused to learn the kata, saying that they wanted only to fight. And fight they did, fairly well, but already we could see that they were soon reaching their plateau, and after that could not progress without development of mind and spirit.

Our sensei should have leaned hard on them, and forced them, physically if need be, to conform. They had the authority and strength to do so. But the sensei let things slide because the two men were strangers, and as such were expected to behave like badly brought-up children. And like spoiled children, the two Canadians got worse and worse.

The most intolerable thing about them though was the fact that they were not very clean. I don't know how often they bathed, but certainly neither of them ever washed his karategi. Soon everybody complained of the stink. The majority of Japanese believe that foreigners, Westerners in particular, are a stinky bunch, and these two were the epitome, the perfect example, to reinforce an old prejudice. The Japanese are a scrupulously clean people, and for them it was especially distressing. The stench was overpowering. Angered students time and time again tossed the offending uniforms out of a window. Even Donn Draeger got to hear about it and had words with them, to no avail.

It is sadly true that there is a stereotyped image of toughness in North America—it goes with coarse speech and rough manners, with swagger and disregard for traditions and social niceties. It is an unfortunate image, enhanced by American movies of a decade or so past, and quite false, for the truly tough North American is not like that at all.

Anyway, one day I was so nauseated by the stink of the two Canadians that I left the dojo, and when Enoeda sensei told me to go back in, I refused.

He was quite taken aback, because nobody refused him. "What!"

"I am sorry, sensei, I refuse to go back in."

"Why?"

"The dojo is a place to respect, but our dojo stinks. I will not train in there because I will vomit. Forgive me."

In defense of my actions I must state that I am not a finicky or delicate individual. Even at that time I had lived under primitive conditions, performed autopsies on long-dead seals, eaten raw and slightly rotten meat with Eskimos, and gone unwashed for periods of time. But this was worse by far.

Enoeda Sensei glowered and nodded, letting me go. As soon as the two Canadians came out of the dojo he grabbed them both. Neither of them spoke much Japanese.

"You smell bad. Wash. You not go into dojo again and make bad smell. Wash!"

As soon as he turned away the Canadians grinned at each other. See. These Japs just couldn't take it.

Within a few weeks the situation grew very tense. Okuda was in a fury. He had watched it all develop and said that if a teacher didn't fix the Canadians, then he or somebody else would. I later heard other threats, and they increased in violence and vehemence. The Canadians were on the books to get a beating, and I knew they would try to fight, and get so much worse for it.

On thinking of the struggle I had been fighting within myself to control my own temper through the discipline of karate; I felt a disappointment. And so I prepared a little speech, having learned all the right words, and thus prepared I confronted Takagi Sensei. He was at his desk. He looked up at me. The office was muggy with the stream from the tea kettle on the kerosene stove. Two other teachers were standing by, one in his karategi.

"Takagi Sensei, I am thinking about withdrawing from this school." Surprise came into his eyes. It was he who had sponsored me, got me through the first eight months of difficulties with the immigration authorities. The other teachers looked up.

"Two foreigners at this dojo have shown bad manners and have behaved without etiquette. In my thoughts, this is not only their fault, but the fault of the teachers for not being strict with them as they would with a Japanese. I have believed in the principles of equality. Now these foreigners have angered some people to such an extent that I have heard several threats. They are mere white belts, but they are being threatened by second and third dan karateka. This is against the morals of the dojo. If these men are harmed I would not be able to respect the dojo." I bowed as I finished my speech.

Takagi Sensei stood up and bowed to me. "Thank you, Mr. Nicol, for bringing this matter so clearly to my attention. I knew of the trouble but not of the threats. Do not worry. I will handle it."

I bowed again and went in to practice. I could hear short and angry questions being asked.

The next week, for the first time in the history of the Japan Karate Association in Tokyo, two foreign students were handed notice of expulsion. It was done with cold ceremony. They had received one last warning, but it had not worked.

Later, they laughed about it, but I think it shocked them a little. They don't know how lucky they were. As some of the black belts had said, they might have had "their parts scattered."

I write this now ten years later, and I am now in the position of having to stand before a class and teach karate, and well I remember how hard it was to correct bad manners after they have been ignored. If any student in our class steps across the line, he gets hell, and if he objects, he is asked to leave. If he refuses to leave, he is bodily removed. I am a Westerner myself, and recognize that often in the Western nations gentleness and politeness can be misunderstood as weakness. We are polite and gentle—up to a point. Would that I had the strength of a true master, like Mr. Nakayama and a few others, who can be gentle always!

Two weeks later. While free fighting with a brown belt I dropped my arm to stop a powerful side thrust kick (delivered with the edge of the foot in a sideways thrust from the hip). The arm took the force of the kick and I was hurled against the wooden wall. The word was out now, and foreigners no longer got special favors, so we were all going through the mill. I fought hard, and it was not until that night, hanging from a strap ring in the crowded Akitsu train, trying to read between the jostling rushes that punctuated each station stop, that the arm injured before now began to ache. Like a bastard.

The following morning it had stiffened up, but I went to the dojo, where my sempai, especially Okuda-san, were solicitous about it, and helped me bind it up with an elastic bandage. Was I sure that I should practice? Oh yes, I was sure.

The first part of the lesson was very basic, mostly repeated lunge punches and front snapping kicks, but performed with great intensity, and with each move we had to drive forward, hips low and full of power, moving ten or twelve feet across the floor with each lunge, sweat-soaked karategi slapping with the focus, and the dojo filling with the thunder of our shouts, and drops of sweat marking myriad spots on the dark floor.

Then there was a two-minute break before the black belts lined up to face the rest of us. They stood relaxed, feet apart, a few of them with their black belts already fulfilling the circle—returning to whiteness by the fraying of constant use. We lower graders presented ourselves in line for them, and at a command from the teacher, the front man in each line fought a black belt until he was defeated. It was a great test for the black belts, for most of the colored belts attacked furiously, knowing that they would be defeated, but at the same time wishing to make a good fight of it. We had strength, but poor control, so the black belt had to be doubly aware of our blows. For the most part the furious onslaughts were parried almost contemptuously until a final "killing" blow was driven home.

Our line faced Okuda. A tall Japanese student, rather awkward despite his green belt, waited his turn to fight in front of me. He bowed and stepped out, his nervousness clearly visible in his eyes and movements. Perhaps the barrage of sound and the fierce fighting going on around him had awed him. He hung back.

Okuda feinted a lunge, and the fellow jumped back like a scared kitten. "Fight!" Okuda glared and yelled at him, but still the student minced around, tossing out half-hearted kicks, taking care to keep his distance. "Is this karate? Fight!" Now all of those not actually fighting were looking at the two of them. It was inevitable. By not fighting, the student betrayed his rank, his teachers, his dojo. By not fighting he insulted his sempai, from whom he should have had nothing to fear, for his blows were under control. Okuda leaped forward, and with one hand he seized the student by the throat and drove him out of an open window. The window was quite high off the dojo floor, so to do this, the student's body had to leave the ground, his feet clearing the ground two feet or more. The force of the lunge took him through the window and landed him in the muck outside. Tokyo is a smoggy place. In hard training students often brought up muck from their lungs, and they often sneaked over to that particular window to spit outside on a pile of rubble and dirt. He was gone from sight. Nobody dared to look, but we knew that he had to be covered with crap. The teacher sauntered over to the window and peered out.

"Have you received injury?"

"No."

"Then come back in!"

The student started to come through the window, but gently, the teacher pushed him back with one hand on his chest.

"Oh no. It is ill-mannered to leave and enter by a window. We will excuse the exit, but use the front door now. And wash your feet when you come in."

The poor guy had to walk around via a busy street, receiving many stares. After today, I knew that he would either quit the dojo, or would begin to fight like a tiger.

And thus my turn came, and I was facing Okuda, whose eyes were fierce, and whose chest was runneled with sweat. With fury, and with all the strength and speed I could muster, I attacked him. He deflected the attack and hurled me to the floor with a footsweep, following with a thrusting heel to my ribs. I fell onto the bad arm and it hurt, but I rolled over and came immediately to my feet, attacking him again. This time he did not throw me, but let me spar with him, slowing down his movements so that I could see and understand the openings. At the end of it he told me that it was well done, then yelled out "Next!" with a ferocity that might have scared a lion.

I went to the back of the line, as I should have, but the teacher grabbed me and put me in front of another fierce-eyed black belt, and in the eyes of the teacher I thought I saw the suspicion of a grin.

By the end of it all my right arm hung like a limp rag, and after the shower I had to get another student to help me into my jacket.

As I went to leave, Takagi sensei stopped me.

"Nicol, you have hurt your arm. Let me see."

With difficulty, I got the jacket off and rolled up the sleeve. He poked at it.

"Ah, this is just a bruise on the muscle, that is nothing. Move your arm this way."

I tried, and pains knifed through the elbow.

"Hmm. There is no fracture. I don't think that bandage you wore would help much. Give me the arm. Here, sit down."

With his thumbs, he found the sore point and pressed very firmly. The pain was exquisite, and almost pleasurable in its intensity, and gradually, as he pressed, the pain faded away. He found another point and pressed that with both thumbs, and I felt the same sharp pain, fading as he pressed.

"Now move your arm like this."

I did so, and to my astonishment, the pain was all gone, and the joint moved freely. I thanked him and asked him why he had known this.

"Our knowledge of the body does not only give us power to inflict injury and death; it also gives us knowledge to relieve pain and to retrieve from death. Maybe you will one day learn enough to understand. Now, tonight, take a hot, hot bath, take a drink of plum wine, and come back tomorrow to train hard. Soon you must take the examination for blue belt."

I left the dojo, greatly elevated in spirit, and much at peace with myself.

## GICHIN FUNAKOSHI

# ENTERING THE WAY

### LOSING A TOPKNOT

The Meiji Restoration and I were born in the same year, 1868. The former saw the light of day in the shogun's former capital of Edo, which came to be known as Tokyo. I was born in the district of Yamakawa-cho in the royal Okinawan capital of Shuri. If anyone were to take the trouble to consult official records, he would learn that I was born in the third year of Meiji (1870), but the true facts are that my birth occurred in the first year of the reign and that I had to falsify my official record so as to be allowed to sit for entrance examinations to a Tokyo medical school.

At that time, there was a regulation that only those born in the year 1870 or thereafter could be considered qualified to take the examinations, so I had no alternative but to tamper with the official records, which was easier to do then because, strange as it may seem, registration was not so strict as it is today.

Having thus altered the day of my birth, I sat for the examinations and passed them, but still did not enter the Tokyo medical school. The cause, which seemed very reasonable then, would seem rather less so now, I imagine.

Among the many reforms instituted by the young Meiji government during the first twenty years of its life was the abolition of the topknot, a masculine hairstyle that had been a traditional part of

---

*See page 117 for the author's biographical note.*

Japanese life for much longer than anyone could possibly remember. In Okinawa, in particular, the topknot was considered a symbol not simply of maturity and virility but of manhood itself. As the edict banning the revered topknot was nationwide, there was opposition to it throughout the country, but nowhere, I think, were the lines of battle so fiercely drawn as in Okinawa.

Here those who believed that the future destiny of Japan required it to adopt Western ideas and those who believed the opposite were at constant loggerheads on almost every reform instituted by the government. Nothing, however, seemed to stir Okinawans to such heights of frenzy as the question of the abolition of the topknot. In general, men born into the shizoku (or privileged) class were obstinately opposed, while those of the heimin (or common) class as well as a few of the shizoku supported what might be called the abolition bill. The latter group was known as the Kaika-to (the "Enlightenment Party"), the former the Ganko-to (literally, the "Obstinate Party").

My family had for generations been attached to a lower-ranking official, and the whole clan was unanimously and adamantly opposed to the cutting of the topknot. Such an act was utterly abhorrent to every member of my family, although I myself did not feel strongly one way or another. The outcome was that I bowed to family pressure, for the school refused to accept students who persisted in the traditional style, and thus the whole future course of my life was influenced by so slight a matter as a bushy topknot.

Eventually, of course, like everyone else, I was to conform, but before I tell how that came about, I must go back a few years in time. My father Gisu was a minor official, and I was his only son. Born prematurely, I was rather a sickly baby, and since both parents and grandparents agreed that I was not destined to a long life, they all took special care of me. In particular, I was coddled and pampered by both pairs of grandparents. Indeed, not long after my birth I was taken to live with my mother's parents, and there my grandfather taught me the Four Chinese Classics of the Confucian tradition—essential for the sons of the shizoku.

It was during my stay at my grandparents' home that I began attending primary school, and after a time I became close friends with one of my classmates. This too was destined to alter the course of my life (and in a far more fundamental way than the topknot), for my classmate was the son of Yasutsune Azato, a most amazing man who was one of Okinawa's greatest experts in the art of karate.

Master Azato belonged to one of the two upper classes of shizoku families in Okinawa: the Udon were of the highest class and were equivalent to a daimyo among clans outside Okinawa; the Tonochi were hereditary chiefs of towns and villages. It was to the latter group that Azato belonged, his family occupying this exalted position in the village of Azato, located between Shuri and Naha. So great was their prestige that the Azatos were treated not as vassals by the former governor of Okinawa but rather as close friends on an equal footing.

Master Azato not only was unsurpassed in all Okinawa in the art of karate but also excelled in horsemanship, in Japanese fencing (kendo), and in archery. He was, moreover, a brilliant scholar. It was my good fortune to be brought to his attention and eventually to receive my first instruction at his remarkable hands.

At that time the practice of karate was banned by the government, so sessions had to take place in secret, and pupils were strictly forbidden by their teachers to discuss with anyone the fact that they were learning the art. I shall have more to say on this subject later on; for the moment, suffice it to note that karate practice could then be held only at night and only in secret. Azato's house was situated quite a distance from that of my grandparents, where I was still living, but once my enthusiasm for the art began to take hold I never found that nighttime walk too long. It was after a couple years' practice that I realized my health had improved tremendously, and that I was no longer the frail child I had been. I enjoyed karate but—more than that—I felt deeply indebted to the art for my increased well-being, and it was around this time that I began to seriously consider making karate-do a way of life.

However, the thought did not enter my mind that it might also become a profession, and since the thorny topknot controversy had put a medical career beyond my reach, I now began to consider alternatives. As I had been taught the Chinese classics from early childhood by both my grandfather and Azato, I decided to make use of that knowledge by becoming a schoolteacher. Accordingly, I took the qualifying examinations and was granted a position as an assistant instructor at a primary school. My first experience in taking charge of a classroom occurred in 1888, when I was twenty-one years old.

But the topknot still obtruded, for before I could be permitted to enter upon my duties as a teacher I was required to get rid of it. This seemed to me entirely reasonable. Japan was then in a state of great ferment; tremendous changes were occurring everywhere, along every facet of life. I felt that I, as a teacher, had an obligation to help our younger generation, which would one day forge the destiny of our nation, to bridge the wide gaps that yawned between the old Japan and the new. I could hardly object to the official edict that our traditional topknot had now become a relic of the past. Nevertheless, I trembled when I thought about what the older members of my family would say.

At that time, school teachers wore official uniforms (not unlike those worn by students in the Peers' School before the last war), a dark jacket buttoned up to the neck, the brass buttons embossed with a cherry blossom design, and a cap with a badge that also bore a cherry blossom design. It was while wearing this uniform, having been shorn of my topknot, that I paid a visit to my parents to report that I had been employed as an assistant instructor in a primary school.

My father could hardly believe his eyes. "What have you done to yourself?" he cried angrily. "You are the son of a samurai!" My mother, even angrier than he, refused to speak to me. She turned away, left the house through the back door, and fled to her parents' home. I imagine all this hullabaloo must strike the youth of today as almost inconceivably ridiculous.

In any case, the die had been cast. Despite all the strenuous parental objection, I entered the profession that I was to follow for the next thirty years. But I by no means abandoned my first true love. I taught school during the day and then, as the ban against karate was still being enforced, I made my stealthy way in the dead of night, carrying a dim lantern when there was no moon, to the house of Master Azato. When, night after night, I would steal home just before daybreak, the neighbors took to conjecturing among themselves as to where I went and what I was doing. Some decided that the only possible answer to this curious enigma was a brothel.

The truth of the matter was very different indeed. Night after night, often in the backyard of the Azato house as the master looked on, I would practice a kata ("formal exercise") time and again week after week, sometimes month after month, until I had mastered it to my teacher's satisfaction. This constant repetition of a single kata was grueling, often exasperating and on occasion humiliatiing. More than once I had to lick the dust on the floor of the dojo or in the Azato backyard. But practice was strict, and I was never permitted to move on to another kata until Azato was convinced that I had satisfactorily understood the one I had been working on.

Although considerably advanced in years, he always sat ramrod stiff on the balcony when we worked outside, wearing a hakama, with a dim lamp beside him. Quite often, through sheer exhaustion, I found myself unable to make out even the lamp.

After executing a kata, I would await his verbal judgment. It was always terse. If he remained dissatisfied with my technique, he would murmur, "Do it again," or "A little more!" A little more, a little more, so often a little more, until the sweat poured and I was ready to drop: it was his way of telling me there was something to be learned, to be mastered. Then, if he found my progress satisfactory, his verdict would be expressed in one word, "Good!" That one word was his highest praise. Until I had heard it spoken several times, however, I would never dare ask him to begin teaching a new kata.

But after our practice sessions ended, he would become a different kind of teacher. Then he would theorize about the essence of karate or, like a kindly parent, question me about my life as a school teacher. As the night was drawing to a close, I would take my lantern and head for home, conscious as my journey ended of the suspicious eyes of the neighbors.

I must under no circumstances omit mention of a good friend of Azato, a man who was also born to a shizoku family of Okinawa and who was considered to be as proficient in karate as Azato himself. Sometimes I would practice under the tutelage of the two masters, Azato and Itosu, at the same time. On these occasions I would listen most attentively to the discussions between the two, and by doing so I learned a great deal about the art in its spiritual as well as its physical aspects.

Were it not for these two great masters I would be a very different person today. I find it almost impossible to express my gratitude to them for guiding me along the path that has provided my chief source of gratification during eight decades of life.

### RECOGNIZING NONSENSE

I feel that it is essential, right here at the start, to insert a brief comment about what karate is *not*, for there has been so much nonsense written on the subject in recent years. Later on, as the occasion arises, I shall attempt to make clear what karate in fact *is*. But before going any further I think it only right to sweep away some of the misconceptions that continue to obscure the essential nature of the art.

Once, for example, I heard someone who professed to be an authority tell his astonished listeners that "in karate we have a kata called nukite. Using only the five fingers of one hand, a man may penetrate his adversary's rib cage, take hold of the bones, and tear them out of the body. This is, of course," the so-called authority went on, "a very difficult kata to master. One begins to train for it by thrusting one's fingers into a cask full of beans every day for hours and hours, thousands upon thousands of times. At first, one's fingers will become lacerated by the exercise, and one's hand will bleed. Then, as time after time the blood coagulates, the shape of one's fingers will alter grotesquely.

"Eventually the sensation of pain will disappear. Then the beans in the cask must be replaced by sand, for sand of course is much more unyielding and the fingers encounter much greater resistance. Nonetheless, as the training proceeds, the fingers will eventually pierce the sand and reach the bottom of the cask. After training with sand comes training with pebbles, until here too after long practice success is attained. Finally comes training with pellets of lead. At last, with lengthy and strenuous training sessions, the fingers will have become strong enough not only to shatter a thick slab of wood but also to crush with little difficulty a heavy stone or pierce the hide of a horse."

No doubt many who heard this strange exposition came away believing it. Many students of karate still choose, for one reason or another, to foster such myths. For example, a man who is relatively unfamiliar with the art may say to an adept: "I understand that you practice karate. Tell me, can you really shatter a huge rock with your fingers? Can you really make a hole in a man's belly with them?" Should the adept reply that either one of these two feats is quite impossible, he would be telling no more than the naked truth. Yet there are some adepts, or pretended adepts, who will shrug deprecatingly and murmur, "Well, sometimes I . . ." As a result, the layman receives a totally false, and indeed intimidating, impression of the art; he wonders, with both fear and awe, if the adept has acquired superhuman powers.

The fact is that the karate enthusiast who overstates and exaggerates and indeed perverts the nature of the art is a skillful conversationalist, true enough, and he will certainly succeed in fascinating his listeners and convincing them that karate is something frightful. But what he is saying is utterly untrue, and furthermore he knows it. As to why he does it—well, it sounds good.

Perhaps, in the distant past, there were karate experts capable of performing such miraculous feats. To that I cannot testify, but I can assure my readers that, at least to my fairly wide knowledge, there is no man living, who, however much he may have trained and practiced, can exceed the natural bounds of human powers.

Yet there are adepts who continue to claim otherwise. "In karate," they say, "a strong grip is essential. To acquire it one must practice hour after hour. The best way is, using the tips of the fingers of both hands, to pick up two heavy buckets, preferably full of something like sand, and swing them around many, many times. The man who has strengthened his grip to the maximum in this way is easily capable of ripping the flesh of his adversary into strips."

What nonsense! One day such a man came to my dojo and offered to teach me the secret of ripping flesh into strips. I begged him to demonstrate on me but burst into laughter when, at last, he succeeded in pinching my skin a bit without even causing a single black and blue mark.

Now, it goes without saying that a strong grip is of great advantage to the practitioner of karate. I recall hearing of a man who could circle his house in Okinawa by swinging along the eaves—no mean feat, as anyone will realize who knows Okinawan houses. I myself have seen Master Itosu crush a thick bamboo stem in his bare hand. This may seem a prodigious feat, but it is my belief that his remarkably strong grip was a natural gift, not acquired by training alone, although obviously enhanced by it. Any man will be able, after sufficient practice, to accomplish remarkable feats of strength, but he may only go so far and no farther. There is a limit to human physical strength that no one can exceed.

While it is true that a karate expert has the power to break a thick board or several layers of tile with one stroke of his hand, I assure my readers that anyone is capable of doing the same thing after undergoing sufficient training. There is nothing extraordinary about such an accomplishment.

Nor has it anything to do with the true spirit of karate; it is merely a demonstration of the kind of strength that a man may acquire through practice. There is nothing mysterious about it. I am often asked by people unfamiliar with karate whether the ranking of an adept depends upon the number of boards or tiles he is capable of breaking with one slash of his hand. There is, of course, no relation between the two. Inasmuch as karate is one of the most refined of the martial arts, any karate adept who boasts about how many boards or tiles he can break with his bare hand or who claims to be able to rip flesh into strips or tear ribs from their cage is one who has very little conception of what true karate is.

### THE TEACHER

At the time I began my academic career, there were four categories of primary school instructors: those who taught the most elementary classes, those who instructed higher grades, those who had charge of special courses and those who served as assistants. At that time, four years of primary school education were compulsory. Teachers in the first category had classes in the first and second grades, while teachers in the more advanced category were qualified to take the last two compulsory grades, the third and fourth, as well as the upper grades (five through eight), which were not compulsory.

Although I was first hired as an assistant, not long thereafter I passed the examinations that qualified me to act as a lower-grade instructor. I was then transferred to Naha, the seat of the Okinawan prefectural government. This transfer, which was in fact a promotion, I considered to be a most fortunate thing, as it allowed me more time and greater opportunity for karate practice.

Later, I also qualified as an instructor in the higher grades. Since, however, I was not a graduate of a teacher's training college, and an increasing number of such graduates were entering the Okinawan school system, I realized that further promotion was going to be a very slow process.

At length, the principal of my school recommended that I be advanced to a higher post. This particular promotion I turned down, for acceptance would have meant going to outlying districts or remote islands in the archipelago and, consequently, separation from my karate teachers. This I could not possibly accept.

There was, in fact, another reason why I was permitted by my superiors to remain in Naha, which brings us once again to the controversy that raged about the topknot. The families of many of my pupils were staunch supporters of the Obstinate Party, and although we were by now in the twenty-fourth or twenty-fifth year of Meiji (1891 or 1892), the government edict banning the topknot was far from being faithfully observed in Okinawa. Inasmuch as my own family also supported the Obstinate Party, I could well understand the emotion that prompted this defiance of the government's orders. At the same time, aware of the tremendous reforms that were changing virtually every aspect of Japanese life, I could not but regard the matter as of little importance.

The Ministry of Education, however, did not see things in the same light. Appalled by Okinawan resistance to its will, it decreed that every pupil on the island must be shorn of his topknot forthwith. This was not quite so easy a matter as it may sound, for many children, insistent upon retaining their topknots, had delayed their entry into primary school as long as possible. The result was that they were hardly children any longer, and they were more than a match for their scissors-wielding teachers. Moreover, many of them had trained in karate, which was then practiced more openly in Okinawa. Primary school teachers, seeking to impose their will on these "children," sometimes found the shears entirely useless.

It was for this reason that instructors who were familiar with karate were given the task of coping with obstinate topknotted pupils who were also karate adepts. I can still recall the sight of pupils, captured after a lively scuffle, submitting to the odious shears with tears in their eyes and their fists tightly clenched as though they would like nothing better than to annihilate the despoilers of those tokens of manhood. However, it was not long before all our boys had their heads closely shaved. The topknot furor had ended forever.

Meanwhile, I continued assiduously with my karate, training under a number of teachers: Master Kiyuna, who with his bare hands could strip the bark from a living tree in a matter of moments; Master Toonno of Naha, one of the island's best-known Confucian scholars; Master Niigaki, whose great common sense impressed me most deeply; and Master Matsumura, one of the greatest karateka, about whom I will have more to say later. This is not to say that I neglected either of my first two masters. On the contrary, I spent as much time with them as possible, and from them I learned not only karate but a great deal else besides.

Master Azato, for example, was an extremely astute observer of political affairs. I recall his saying to me once, "Funakoshi, after the Trans-Siberian Railroad is completed, war between Japan and Russia will become inevitable." This was many years before the outbreak of hostilities between the two countries in 1904. What once had seemed unlikely became actuality, and I found myself, once war broke out, deeply impressed by Azato's political acumen and foresight. It was he who, at the time of the Meiji Restoration, advised the governor of Okinawa to cooperate to the fullest with the newly formed government, and when the edict against the topknot was promulgated, he was among the first to obey it.

Azato was also a highly skilled fencer of the Jigen school of kendo. Although by no means a braggart, he had utter confidence in his fencing ability, and I once heard him say, "I doubt very much that I would lose to any one in the country if it came to a duel to the death." This quiet confidence was later proved to be well founded when Azato met Yorin Kanna, one of Okinawa's most famous swordsmen.

Kanna was an enormous, muscular man with great bulging arms

and shoulders; indeed, people used to say that his shoulder muscles were two stories high! He was a brave man and utterly without fear, and he well merited his reputation for proficiency in the martial arts. He was also a man of great learning, thoroughly at home in both the Japanese and Chinese classics. Clearly, one would have thought, he was more than a match for Azato.

However when, in the famous encounter, he attacked Azato with an unblunted blade, he was very much surprised to find his attack turned aside by his unarmed adversary, who, with a deft flip of his hand, not only managed to evade the thrust but also brought Kanna to his knees. When I asked Azato to describe for me what had actually occurred, he described Kanna as a highly skilled swordsman who, due to his reputation of being both indomitable and fearless, was able to terrify his opponent at the very start of the encounter and then come in quickly for the kill. However, Azato said, if the opponent refuses to be terrified, if he remains coolheaded, and if he searches for the inevitable gap in Kanna's defense, victory cannot be all that difficult. This counsel, like all the rest of Azato's guidance, was to prove of great value to me.

Another of his maxims was, "When you practice karate, think of your arms and legs as swords." Indeed, Azato's own exhibitions of karate were living examples of this philosophy. Once a man asked him the meaning and application of ippon-ken (single-point fist). "Try to hit me," Azato replied calmly. The man did as he had been told, but in the twinkling of an eye the blow as parried and Azato's own single-point fist flew toward his opponent's stomach, where it stopped, at a distance of perhaps the thickness of a sheet of paper. The celerity of the whole movement was incredible. The man who had asked the question did not even have time to blink his eyes before he realized that that fist, had it actually struck his solar plexus, might have killed him.

Azato had highly detailed information about all karate experts living in Okinawa at the time, which included not only such mundane facts as their names and addresses but also intelligence about their abilities and their special techniques, where they were strong and where they were weak. He used to tell me that knowledge of an opponent's ability and his technical skills was half the battle, quoting the old Chinese adage, "The secret of victory is to know both yourself and your enemy."

Both Azato and his good friend Itosu shared at least one quality of greatness: they suffered from no petty jealousy of other masters. They would present me to the teachers of their acquaintance, urging me to learn from each the technique at which he excelled. Ordinary karate instructors, in my experience, are reluctant to permit their pupils to study under instructors of other schools, but this was far from true of either Azato or Itosu.

If they had taught me nothing else, I would have profited by the example they set of humility and modesty in all dealings with their fellow human beings. And, indeed, they never dwelled upon the "heroic" deeds of karate that were attributed to them, brushing these aside as "wild acts" attributable to their youth.

The two men shared other qualities, including, interestingly enough, a first name, Yasutsune. But philosophically they held quite divergent points of view regarding karate, and physically they were very different indeed. While Master Azato was tall with broad shoulders and had sharp eyes and features reminiscent of the ancient samurai, Master Itosu was of average height, with a great round chest like a beer barrel. Despite his long moustache, he rather had the look of a well-behaved child.

It was a deceptive look, for his arms and hands possessed quite extraordinary power. However many times he was challenged by Azato to a bout of Okinawan hand wrestling, he always emerged victorious. In this particular version of the sport, the two combatants clench their fists and cross their wrists one against the other; they do not clasp hands as they would in a bout of the Tokyo version of hand wrestling. After being inevitably overpowered, Azato would murmur wryly that never would he get the better of Itosu—not even, he would add, if he used both hands.

Indeed, Itosu was so well trained that his entire body seemed to be invulnerable. Once, as he was about to enter a restaurant in Naha's amusement center, a sturdy young man attacked him from the rear, aiming a hearty blow at his side. But the latter, without even turning, hardened the muscles of his stomach so that the blow glanced off his body, and at the very same instant his right hand grasped the right wrist of his assailant. Still without turning his head, he calmly dragged the man inside the restaurant.

There he ordered the frightened waitress to bring him food and wine. Still holding the man's wrist with his right hand, he took a sip of the wine from the cup that he held in his left hand, then pulled his assailant around in front of him and for the first time had a look at him. After a moment, he smiled and said, "I don't know what your grudge against me could be, but let's have a drink together!" The young man's astonishment at this behavior can easily be imagined.

Itosu had another famous encounter with a rash young man, this one the karate instructor of a certain Okinawan school. Belligerent by nature and full of pride at his strength, the youth had the rather unpleasant habit of lurking in dark lanes, and when a lonely walker happened to come strolling by he would lash out at the poor man. So self-confident did he finally become that he decided to take on Itosu himself, believing that, no matter how powerful the master was, he could be beaten if set upon unawares.

One night, he followed Itosu down the street and, after a stealthy approach, aimed his mightiest punch at the master's back. Bewildered at the quite evident fact that he had made no impression whatsoever, the young bully lost his balance and at the same instant felt his right wrist caught in a viselike grip. The youth tried to free himself with his other hand, but of course he did not succeed. The power of Itosu's grip was proverbial in Okinawa; he could, as I recounted earlier, crush a thick bamboo stalk with one hand.

Itosu now walked on, hauling the other behind him without even bothering to look back. Realizing that he had failed completely, the young man begged the master's forgiveness. "But who are you?" Itosu asked softly.

"I'm Goro," replied the youth. Now Itosu looked at him for the first time.

"Ah," he murmured, "you really shouldn't try to play such tricks on an old man like me." With that, he let go and strolled away.

Vivid pictures jostle one another in my mind as I think back about my two teachers and their different philosophies of karate-do. "Regard your arms and legs as swords," Azato used to tell me, while Itosu would advise me to train my body so that it could withstand any blow, no matter how powerful. What he meant, of course, was that I not only must train my body until it became as hard as nails but also must practice daily all the various karate techniques.

I now recall a well-known incident when Itosu was set upon by a group of young toughs, but before long the hoodlums were all lying unconscious in the street. An eyewitness, seeing that Itosu was in no danger, rushed off to tell Azato about the incident. Interrupting his account, Azato said, "And the ruffians, of course, were all lying unconscious, with their faces to the ground, were they not?" Much surprised, the witness admitted that that was true, but he wondered how Azato could have known.

"Very simple," replied the master. "No karate adept would be so cowardly as to attack from the rear. And should someone unfamiliar with karate attack from the front, he would end up flat on his back. But

I know Itosu; his punches would knock his assailants down on their faces. I would be quite astonished if any of them survive."

Another time, Itosu was awakened during the night by some suspicious noises at the gate of his house. As he moved silently toward the sound, he realized that someone was trying to pick the lock of his gate. Without a moment's pause, he shattered the gate's wooden panel with a single blow of his fist. Simultaneously he thrust his hand through the hole and caught hold of the wrist of the would-be robber. Now normally, if the average karateka had punched a hole through a thick wooden panel, the hole would be jagged and the wood would splinter in one direction or another. In this particular case, there was only a round hole, and I know that to be true because I was told so by Azato himself.

I have always been conscious of the compliment paid me by these two masters. In return I performed a rite—not only in their honor but in honor of all masters who have ever taught me—which I recommend to every student of karate today: I burned incense at the Buddhist altar of each instructor and pledged myself never to make use of my trained body for any illicit purpose. I think it was this pledge, which I have most faithfully honored, that resulted in my being treated like a member of the family, long after I myself was married and had children of my own—indeed, until the deaths of the two older men.

I frequently took my children to their homes, where on these occasions they would demonstrate certain kata for the children and then bid them to do the same. As a treat, the two masters would give my children sweets of a kind that I could not myself afford to buy for them. (The best I could do at the time was an occasional sweet potato!) The masters loved the young ones and behaved toward them as to their own grandchildren. Soon the youngsters began to visit the masters by themselves, just as I had done when I was a child. And soon they came to love karate as I did.

Now that I look back, I realize that I and my children, the two generations of us, have all benefited enormously from the teachings of these two masters. Where shall I find words to express my gratitude?

## MAXINE HONG KINGSTON
### *from*
# THE WOMAN WARRIOR

When we Chinese girls listened to the adults talking-story, we learned
that we failed if we grew up to be but wives or slaves. We could be
heroines, swordswomen. Even if she had to rage across all China, a
swordswoman got even with anybody who hurt her family. Perhaps
women were once so dangerous that they had to have their feet bound.
It was a woman who invented white crane boxing only two hundred
years ago. She was already an expert pole fighter, daughter of a teacher
trained at the Shao-lin temple, where there lived an order of fighting
monks. She was combing her hair one morning when a white crane
alighted outside her window. She teased it with her pole, which it
pushed aside with a soft brush of its wing. Amazed, she dashed outside
and tried to knock the crane off its perch. It snapped her pole in two.
Recognizing the presence of great power, she asked the spirit of the
white crane if it would teach her to fight. It answered with a cry that
white crane boxers imitate today. Later the bird returned as an old
man, and he guided her boxing for many years. Thus she gave the
world a new martial art.

    This is one of the tamer, more modern stories, mere introduction.

---

*Born in Stockton, California, on October 27, 1940, the author grew up
listening to her mother's stories of a girlhood in China. These half legends,
half reminiscences challenged Kingston's Chinese-American identity and at
the same time called forth a strong sense of justice. Kingston herself
blended myth, history, and biography in her award-winning book* The
Woman Warrior, *from which the following excerpt is taken.*

My mother told others that followed swordswomen through woods and palaces for years. Night after night my mother would story-talk until we fell asleep. I couldn't tell where the stories left off and the dreams began, her voice the voice of the heroines in my sleep. And on Sundays, from noon to midnight, we went to the movies at the Confucius Church. We saw swordswomen jump over houses from a standstill; they didn't even need a running start.

At last I saw that I too had been in the presence of great power, my mother talking-story. After I grew up, I heard the chant of Fa Mu Lan, the girl who took her father's place in battle. Instantly I remembered that as a child I had followed my mother about the house, the two of us singing about how Fa Mu Lan fought gloriously and returned alive from war to settle in the village. I had forgotten this chant that once was mine, given me by my mother, who may not have known its power to remind. She said I would grow up a wife and a slave, but she taught me the song of the warrior woman, Fa Mu Lan. I would have to grow up a warrior woman.

The call would come from a bird that flew over our roof. In the brush drawings it looks like the ideograph for "human," two black wings. The bird would cross the sun and lift into the mountains (which look like the ideograph "mountain"), there parting the mist briefly that swirled opaque again. I would be a little girl of seven the day I followed the bird away into the mountains. The brambles would tear off my shoes and rocks cut my feet and fingers, but I would keep climbing, eyes upward to follow the bird. We would go around and around the tallest mountain climbing ever upward. I would drink from the river, which I would meet again and again. We would go so high the plants would change, and the river that flows past the village would become a waterfall. At the height where the bird used to disappear, the clouds would gray the world like an ink wash.

Even when I got used to that gray, I would only see peaks as if shaded in pencil, rocks like charcoal rubbings, everything so murky. There would be just two black strokes—the bird. Inside the clouds— inside the dragon's breath—I would not know how many hours or days passed. Suddenly, without noise, I would break clear into a yellow, warm world. New trees would lean toward me at mountain angles, but when I looked for the village, it would have vanished under the clouds.

The bird, now gold so close to the sun, would come to rest on the thatch of a hut, which, until the bird's two feet touched it, was camouflaged as part of the mountainside.

\*    \*    \*

The door opened, and an old man and an old woman came out carrying bowls of rice and soup and a leafy branch of peaches.

"Have you eaten rice today, little girl?" they greeted me.

"Yes, I have," I said out of politeness. "Thank you."

("No I haven't," I would have said in real life, mad at the Chinese for lying so much. "I'm starved. Do you have any cookies? I like chocolate chip cookies.")

"We were about to sit down to another meal," the old woman said. "Why don't you eat with us?"

They just happened to be bringing three rice bowls and three pairs of silver chopsticks out to the plank table under the pines. They gave me an egg, as if it were my birthday, and tea, though they were older than I, but I poured for them. The teapot and the ricepot seemed bottomless, but perhaps not; the old couple ate very little except for the peaches.

When the mountains and the pines turned into blue oxen, blue dogs, and blue people standing, the old couple asked me to spend the night in the hut. I thought about the long way down in the ghostly dark and decided yes. The inside of the hut seemed as large as the outdoors. Pine needles covered the floor in thick patterns; someone had carefully arranged the yellow, green, and brown pine needles according to age. When I stepped carelessly and mussed a line, my feet picked up new blends of earth colors, but the old man and old woman walked so lightly that their feet never stirred the designs by a needle.

A rock grew in the middle of the house, and that was their table. The benches were fallen trees. Ferns and shade flowers grew out of one wall, the mountainside itself. The old couple tucked me into a bed just my width. "Breathe evenly, or you'll lose your balance and fall out," said the old woman, covering me with a silk bag stuffed with feathers and herbs. "Opera singers, who begin their training at age five, sleep in beds like this." Then the two of them went outside, and through the window I could see them pull on a rope looped over a branch. The rope was tied to the roof, and the roof opened up like a basket lid. I would sleep with the moon and the stars. I did not see whether the old people slept so quickly did I drop off, but they would be there waking me with food in the morning.

"Little girl, you have now spent almost a day and a night with us," the old woman said. In the morning light I could see her earlobes pierced with gold. Do you think you can bear to stay with us for fifteen years? We can train you to become a warrior."

"What about my father and mother?" I asked.

The old man untied the drinking gourd slung across his back. He lifted the lid by its stem and looked for something in the water. "Ah, there," he said.

At first I saw only water so clear it magnified the fibers in the walls of the gourd. On the surface, I saw only my own round reflection. The old man encircled the neck of the gourd with his thumb and index finger and gave it a shake. As the water shook, then settled, the colors and lights shimmered into a picture, not reflecting anything I could see around me. There at the bottom of the gourd were my mother and father scanning the sky, which was where I was. "It has happened already, then," I could hear my mother say. "I didn't expect it so soon." "You knew from her birth that she would be taken," my father answered. "We'll have to harvest potatoes without her help this year," my mother said, and they turned away toward the fields, straw baskets in their arms. The water shook and became just water again. "Mama. Papa," I called, but they were in the valley and could not hear me.

"What do you want to do?" the old man asked. "You can go back now if you like. You can go pull sweet potatoes, or you can stay with us and learn how to fight barbarians and bandits."

"You can avenge your village," said the old woman. "You can recapture the harvests the thieves have taken. You can be remembered by the Han people for your dutifulness."

"I'll stay with you," I said.

So the hut became my home, and I found out that the old woman did not arrange the pine needles by hand. She opened the roof; an autumn wind would come up, and the needles fell in braids—brown strands, green strands, yellow strands. The old woman waved her arms in conducting motions; she blew softly with her mouth. I thought nature certainly works differently on mountains than in valleys.

"The first thing you have to learn," the old woman told me, "is how to be quiet." They left me by streams to watch for animals. "If you're noisy, you'll make the deer go without water."

When I could kneel all day without my legs cramping and my breathing became even, the squirrels would bury their hoardings at the hem of my shirt and then bend their tails in a celebration dance. At night, the mice and toads looked at me, their eyes quick stars and slow stars. Not once would I see a three-legged toad, though; you need strings of cash to bait them.

The two old people led me in exercises that began at dawn and ended at sunset so that I could watch our shadows grow and shrink and grow again, rooted to the earth. I learned to move my fingers, hands, feet, head, and entire body in circles. I walked putting heel down first, toes pointing outward thirty to forty degrees, making the ideograph "eight," making the ideograph "human." Knees bent, I would swing into the slow, measured "square step," the powerful walk into battle. After five years my body became so strong that I could control even the dilations of the pupils inside my irises. I could copy owls and bats, the words for "bat" and "blessing" homonyms. After six years the deer let me run beside them. I could jump twenty feet into the air from a standstill, leaping like a monkey over the hut. Every creature has a hiding skill and a fighting skill a warrior can use. When birds alighted on my palm, I could yield my muscles under their feet and give them no base from which to fly away.

But I could not fly like the bird that led me here, except in large, free dreams.

During the seventh year (I would be fourteen), the two old people led me blindfolded to the mountains of the white tigers. They held me by either elbow and shouted into my ears, "Run. Run. Run." I ran and, not stepping off a cliff at the edge of my toes and not hitting my forehead against a wall, ran faster. A wind buoyed me up over the roots, the rocks, the little hills. We reached the tiger place in no time—a mountain peak three feet from the sky. We had to bend over.

The old people waved once, slid down the mountain, and disappeared around a tree. The old woman, good with the bow and arrow, took them with her; the old man took the water gourd. I would have to survive barehanded. Snow lay on the ground, and snow fell in loose gusts—another way the dragon breathes. I walked in the direction from which we had come, and when I reached the timberline, I collected wood broken from the cherry tree, the peony, and the walnut, which is the tree of life. Fire, the old people had taught me, is stored in trees that grow red flowers or red berries in the spring or whose leaves turn red in the fall. I took the wood from the protected spots beneath the trees and wrapped it in my scarf to keep dry. I dug where squirrels might have come, stealing one or two nuts at each place. These I also wrapped in my scarf. It is possible, the old people said, for a human being to live for fifty days on water. I would save the roots and nuts for hard climbs, the places where nothing grew, the emergency should I not find the hut. This time there would be no bird to follow.

The first night I burned half of the wood and slept curled against the mountain. I heard the white tigers prowling on the other side of the fire, but I could not distinguish them from the snow patches. The morning rose perfectly. I hurried along, again collecting wood and edibles. I ate nothing and only drank the snow my fires made run.

The first two days were gifts, the fasting was so easy to do, I so smug in my strength that on the third day, the hardest, I caught myself sitting on the ground and staring at the nuts and dry roots. Instead of walking steadily on or even eating, I faded into dreams about the meat meals my mother used to cook, my monk's food forgotten. That night I burned up most of the wood I had collected, unable to sleep for facing my death—if not death here, then death someday. The moon animals that did not hibernate came out to hunt, but I had given up the habits of a carnivore since living with the old people. I would not trap the mice that danced so close or the owls that plunged just outside the fire.

On the fourth and fifth days, my eyesight sharp with hunger, I saw deer and used their trails when our ways coincided. Where the deer nibbled, I gathered the fungus, the fungus of immortality.

At noon on the tenth day I packed snow, white as rice, into the worn center of a rock pointed out to me by a finger of ice, and around the rock I built a fire. In the warming water I put roots, nuts, and the fungus of immortality. For variety I ate a quarter of the nuts and roots raw. Oh, green joyous rush inside my mouth, my head, my stomach, my toes, my soul—the best meal of my life.

One day I found I was striding long distances without hindrance, my bundle light. Food had become so scarce that I was no longer stopping to collect it. I had walked into dead land. Here even the snow stopped. I did not go back to the richer areas, where I could not stay anyway, but, resolving to fast until I got halfway to the next woods, I started across the dry rocks. Heavily weighted down by the wood on my back, branches poking maddeningly, I had burned almost all of the fuel not to waste strength lugging it. Somewhere in the dead land I had lost count of the days. It seemed as if I had been walking forever; life had never been different from this. An old man and an old woman were help I had only wished for. I was fourteen years old and lost from my village. I was walking in circles. Hadn't I already been found by the old people? Or was that yet to come? I wanted my mother and father. The old man and old woman were only a part of this lostness and this hunger.

One nightfall I ate the last of my food but had enough sticks for a good fire. I stared into the flames, which reminded me about helping my mother with the cooking and made me cry. It was very strange looking through water into fire and seeing my mother again. I nodded, orange and warm.

A white rabbit hopped beside me, and for a moment I thought it was a blob of snow that had fallen out of the sky. The rabbit and I studied each other. Rabbits taste like chickens. My mother and father had taught me how to hit rabbits over the head with wine jugs, then skin them cleanly for fur vests. "It's a cold night to be an animal," I said. "So you want some fire too, do you? Let me put on another branch then." I would not hit it with the branch. I had learned from rabbits to kick backward. Perhaps this one was sick because normally the animals did not like fire. The rabbit seemed alert enough, however, looking at me so acutely, bounding up to the fire. But it did not stop when it got to the edge. It turned its face once toward me, then jumped into the fire. The fire went down for a moment, as if crouching in surprise, then the flames shot up taller than before. When the fire became calm again, I saw the rabbit had turned into meat, browned just right. I ate it, knowing the rabbit had sacrificed itself for me. It had made me a gift of meat.

When you have been walking through trees hour after hour—and I finally reached trees after dead land—branches cross out everything, no relief whichever way your head turns until your eyes start to invent new sights. Hunger also changes the world—when eating can't be a habit, then neither can seeing. I saw two people made of gold dancing the earth's dances. They turned so perfectly that together they were the axis of the earth's turning. They were light; they were molten, changing gold—Chinese lion dancers, African lion dancers in midstep. I heard high Javanese bells deepen in midring to Indian bells, Hindu, Indian, American Indian. Before my eyes gold bells shredded into gold tassels that fanned into two royal capes that softened into lions' fur. Manes grew tall into feathers that shone—became light rays. The dancers danced the future—a machine-future—in clothes I had never seen before. I am watching the centuries pass in moments because suddenly I understand time, which is spinning and fixed like the North Star. And I understand how working and hoeing are dancing; how peasant clothes are golden, as kings' clothes are golden; how one of the dancers is always a man and the other a woman.

The man and the woman grow bigger and bigger, so bright. All light. They are tall angels in two rows. They have high white wings on their backs. Perhaps there are infinite angels; perhaps I see two angels in their consecutive moments. I cannot bear their brightness and cover my eyes, which hurt from being open so wide without a blink. When I put my hands down again to look again, I recognize the old brown man and the old gray woman walking toward me out of the pine forest.

It would seem that this small crack in the mystery was opened, not so much by the old people's magic, as by hunger. Afterward, whenever I did not eat for long, as during famine or battle, I could stare at ordinary people and see their light and gold. I could see their dance. When I get hungry enough, then killing and falling are dancing too.

The old people fed me hot vegetable soup. Then they asked me to talk-story about what happened in the mountains of the white tigers. I told them that the white tigers had stalked me through the snow but that I had fought them off by burning branches, and my great-grandparents had come to lead me safely through the forests. I had met a rabbit who taught me about self-immolation and how to speed up transmigration: one does not have to become worms first but can change directly into a human being—as in our own humanness we had just changed bowls of vegetable soup into people too. That made them laugh. "You tell good stories," they said. "now go to sleep, and tomorrow we will begin your dragon lessons."

"One more thing," I wanted to say. "I saw you and how old you really are." But I was already asleep; it came out only a murmur. I would want to tell them about that last moment of my journey; but it was only one moment out of the weeks that I had been gone, and its telling would keep until morning. Besides, the two people must already know. In the next years, when I suddenly came upon them or when I caught them out of the corners of my eyes, he appeared as a handsome young man, tall with long black hair, and she, as a beautiful young woman who ran bare-legged through the trees. In the spring she dressed like a bride; she wore juniper leaves in her hair and a black embroidered jacket. I learned to shoot accurately because my teachers held the targets. Often when sighting along an arrow, there to the side I would glimpse the young man or young woman, but when I looked directly, he or she would be old again. By this time I had guessed from their sexless manner that the old woman was to the old man a sister or friend rather than a wife.

After I returned from my survival test, the two old people trained me in dragon ways, which took another eight years. Copying the tigers, their stalking kill and their anger, had been a wild, bloodthirsty joy. Tigers are easy to find, but I needed adult wisdom to know dragons. "You have to infer the whole dragon from the parts you can see and touch," the old people would say. Unlike tigers, dragons are so immense, I would never see one in its entirety. But I could explore the mountains, which are the top of its head. These mountains are also *like* the tops of *other* dragons' heads," the old people would tell me. When climbing the slopes, I could understand that I was a bug riding on a dragon's forehead as it roams through space, its speed so different from my speed that I feel the dragon solid and immobile. In quarries I could see its strata, the dragon's veins and muscles; the minerals, its teeth and bones. I could touch the stones the old woman wore—its bone marrow. I had worked the soil, which is its flesh, and harvested the plants and climbed the trees, which are its hairs. I could listen to its voice in the thunder and feel its breathing in the winds, see its breathing in the clouds. Its tongue is the lightning. And the red that the lightning gives to the world is strong and lucky—in blood, poppies, roses, rubies, the red feathers of birds, the red carp, the cherry tree, the peony, the line alongside the turtle's eyes and the mallard's. In the spring when the dragon awakes, I watched its turnings in the rivers.

The closest I came to seeing a dragon whole was when the old people cut away a small strip of bark on a pine that was over three thousand years old. The resin underneath flows in the swirling shapes of dragons. "If you should decide during your old age that you would like to live another five hundred years, come here and drink ten pounds of this sap," they told me. "But don't do it now. You're too young to decide to live forever." The old people sent me out into the thunderstorms to pick the red-cloud herb, which grows only then, a product of dragon's fire and dragon's rain. I brought the leaves to the old man and old woman, and they ate them for immortality.

I learned to make my mind large, as the universe is large, so that there is room for paradoxes. Pearls are bone marrow; pearls come from oysters. The dragon lives in the sky, ocean, marshes, and mountains; and the mountains are also its cranium. Its voice thunders and jingles like copper pans. It breathes fire and water; and sometimes the dragon is one, sometimes many.

I worked every day. When it rained, I exercised in the downpour, grateful not to be pulling sweet potatoes. I moved like the trees in the wind. I was grateful not to be squishing in chicken mud, which I did not have nightmares about so frequently now.

On New Year's mornings, the old man let me look into his water gourd to see my family. They were eating the biggest meal of the year, and I missed them very much. I had felt loved, love pouring from their fingers when the adults tucked red money into our pockets. My two old people did not give me money, but, each year for fifteen years, a bead. After I unwrapped the red paper and rolled the bead about between thumb and fingers, they took it back for safekeeping. We ate monk's food as usual.

By looking into the water gourd I was able to follow the men I would have to execute. Not knowing that I watched, fat men ate meat; fat men drank wine made from the rice; fat men sat on naked little girls. I watched powerful men count their money, and starving men count theirs. When bandits brought their share of raids home, I waited until they took off their masks so I would know the villagers who stole from their neighbors. I studied the generals' faces, their rank-stalks quivering at the backs of their heads. I learned rebels' faces, too, their foreheads tied with wild oaths.

The old man pointed out strengths and weaknesses whenever heroes met in classical battles, but warfare makes a scramble of the beautiful, slow old fights. I saw one young fighter salute his opponent— and five peasants hit him from behind with scythes and hammers. His opponent did not warn him.

"Cheaters!" I yelled. "How am I going to win against cheaters?"

"Don't worry," the old man said. "You'll never be trapped like that poor amateur. You can see behind you like a bat. Hold the peasants back with one hand and kill the warrior with the other."

Menstrual days did not interrupt my training; I was as strong as any other day. "You're now an adult," explained the old woman on the first one, which happened halfway through my stay on the mountain. "You can have children." I thought I had cut myself when jumping over my swords, one made of steel and the other carved out of a single block of jade. "However," she added, "we are asking you to put off children for a few more years."

"Then I can use the control you taught me to stop this bleeding?"

"No. You don't stop shitting and pissing," she said. "It's the same with the blood. Let it run." ("Let it walk" in Chinese.)

To console me for being without family on this day, they let me look inside the gourd. My whole family was visiting friends on the other side of the river. Everybody had on good clothes and was exchanging cakes. It was a wedding. My mother was talking to the hosts: "Thank you for taking our daughter. Wherever she is, she must be happy now. She will certainly come back if she is alive, and if she is a spirit, you have given her a decent line. We are so grateful."

Yes, I would be happy. How full I would be with all their love for me. I would have for a new husband my own playmate, dear since childhood, who loved me so much he was to become a spirit bridegroom for my sake. We will be so happy when I come back to the valley, healthy and strong and not a ghost.

The water gave me a close-up of my husband's wonderful face—

and I was watching it when it went white at the sudden approach of armored men on horseback, thudding and jangling. My people grabbed iron skillets, boiling soup, knives, hammers, scissors, whatever weapons came to hand, but my father said, "There are too many of them," and they put down the weapons and waited quietly at the door, open as if for guests. An army of horsemen stopped at our house; the foot soldiers in the distance coming closer. A horseman with silver scales afire in the sun shouted from the scroll in his hands, his words opening a red gap in his black beard. "Your baron has pledged fifty men from this district, one from each family," he said, and then named the family names.

"No!" I screamed into the gourd.

"I'll go," my new husband and my youngest brother said to their fathers.

"No," my father said, "I myself will go," but the women held him back until the foot soldiers passed by, my husband and brother leaving with them.

As if disturbed by the marching feet, the water churned; and when it stilled again ("Wait!" I yelled. "Wait!"), there were strangers. The baron and his family—all of his family—were knocking their heads on the floor in front of their ancestors and thanking the gods out loud for protecting them from conscription. I watched the baron's piggish face chew open-mouthed on the sacrificial pig. I plunged my hand into the gourd, making a grab for his thick throat, and he broke into pieces, splashing water all over my face and clothes. I turned the gourd upsidedown to empty it, but no little people came tumbling out.

"Why can't I go down there now and help them?" I cried. "I'll run away with the two boys and we'll hide in the caves."

"No," the old man said. "You're not ready. You're only fourteen years old. You'd get hurt for nothing."

"Wait until you are twenty-two," the old woman said. "You'll be big then and more skillful. No army will be able to stop you from doing whatever you want. If you go now, you will be killed, and you'll have wasted seven and a half years of our time. You will deprive your people of a champion."

"I'm good enough now to save the boys."

"We didn't work this hard to save just two boys, but whole families."

Of course.

"Do you really think I'll be able to do that—defeat an army."

"Even when you fight against soldiers trained as you are, most of them will be men, heavy footed and rough. You will have the advantage. Don't be impatient."

"From time to time you may use the water gourd to watch your husband and your brother," the old man said.

But I had ended the panic about them already. I could feel a wooden door inside of me close. I had learned on the farm that I could stop loving animals raised for slaughter. And I could start loving them immediately when someone said, "This one is a pet," freeing me and opening the door. We had lost males before, cousins and uncles who were conscripted into armies or bonded as apprentices, who were almost as lowly as slave girls.

I bled and thought about the people to be killed; I bled and thought about the people to be born.

During all my years on the mountain, I talked to no one except the two old people, but they seemed to be many people. The whole world lived inside the gourd, the earth a green and blue pearl like the one the dragon plays with.

When I could point at the sky and make a sword appear, a silver bolt in the sunlight, and control its slashing with my mind, the old people said I was ready to leave. The old man opened the gourd for the last time. I saw the baron's messenger leave our house, and my father was saying, "This time I must go and fight." I would hurry down the mountain and take his place. The old people gave me the fifteen beads, which I was to use if I got into terrible danger. They gave me men's clothes and armor. We bowed to one another. The bird flew above me down the mountain, and for some miles, whenever I turned to look for them, there would be the two old people waving. I saw them through the mist; I saw them on the clouds; I saw them big on the mountaintop when distance had shrunk the pines. They had probably left images of themselves for me to wave at and gone about their other business.

When I reached my village, my father and mother had grown as old as the two whose shapes I could at last no longer see. I helped my parents carry their tools, and they walked ahead so straight, each carrying a basket or a hoe not to overburden me, their tears falling privately. My family surrounded me with so much love that I almost forgot the ones not there. I praised the new infants.

"Some of the people are saying the Eight Sages took you away to teach you magic," said a little girl cousin. "They say they changed you into a bird, and you flew to them."

"Some say you went to the city and became a prostitute," another cousin giggled.

"You might tell them that I met some teachers who were willing to teach me science," I said.

"I have been drafted," my father said.

"No, Father," I said. "I will take your place."

My parents killed a chicken and steamed it whole, as if they were welcoming home a son, but I had gotten out of the habit of meat. After eating rice and vegetables, I slept for a long time, preparation for the work ahead.

In the morning my parents woke me and asked that I come with them into the family hall. "Stay in your nightclothes," my mother said. "Don't change yet." She was holding a basin, a towel, and a kettle of hot water. My father had a bottle of wine, an ink block and pens, and knives of various sizes. "Come with us," he said. They stopped the tears with which they had greeted me. Forebodingly I caught a smell—metallic, the iron smell of blood, as when a woman gives birth, as at the sacrifice of a large animal, as when I menstruated and dreamed red dreams.

My mother put a pillow on the floor in front of the ancestors. "Kneel here," she said. "Now take off your shirt." I kneeled with my back to my parents so none of us felt embarrassed. My mother washed my back as if I had left for only a day and were her baby yet. "We are going to carve revenge on your back," my father said. "We'll write out oaths and names."

"Wherever you go, whatever happens to you, people will know our sacrifice," my mother said. "And you'll never forget either." She meant that even if I got killed, the people could use my dead body for a weapon, but we do not like to talk out loud about dying.

My father first brushed the words in ink, and they fluttered down my back row after row. Then he began cutting; to make fine lines and points he used thin blades, for the stems, large blades.

My mother caught the blood and wiped the cuts with a cold towel soaked in wine. It hurt terribly—the cuts sharp; the air burning; the alcohol cold, then hot—pain so various. I gripped my knees. I released them. Neither tension nor relaxation helped. I wanted to cry. If not for the fifteen years of training, I would have writhed on the floor; I would have had to be held down. The list of grievances went on and on. If an enemy should flay me, the light would shine through my skin like lace.

At the end of the last word, I fell forward. Together my parents sang what they had written, then let me rest. My mother fanned my back. "We'll have you with us until your back heals," she said.

When I could sit up again, my mother brought two mirrors, and I saw my back covered entirely with words in red and black files, like an army. My parents nursed me just as if I had fallen in battle after many victories. Soon I was strong again.

A white horse stepped into the courtyard where I was polishing my armor. Though the gates were locked tight, through the moon door it came—a kingly white horse. It wore a saddle and bridle with red, gold, and black tassels dancing. The saddle was just my size with tigers and dragons tooled in swirls. The white horse pawed the ground for me to go. On the hooves of its near forefoot and hindfoot was the ideograph "to fly."

My parents and I had waited for such a sign. We took the fine saddlebags off the horse and filled them with salves and herbs, blue grass for washing my hair, extra sweaters, dried peaches. They gave me a choice of ivory or silver chopsticks. I took the silver ones because they were lighter. It was like getting wedding presents. the cousins and the villagers came bearing bright orange jams, silk dresses, silver embroidery scissors. They brought blue and white porcelain bowls filled with water and carp—the bowls painted with carp, fins like orange fire. I accepted all the gifts—the tables, the earthenware jugs—though I could not possibly carry them with me, and culled for travel only a small copper cooking bowl. I could cook in it and eat out of it and would not have to search for bowl-shaped rocks or tortoiseshells.

I put on my men's clothes and armor and tied my hair in a man's fashion. "How beautiful you look," the people said. "How beautiful she looks."

A young man stepped out of the crowd. He looked familiar to me, as if he were the old man's son, or the old man himself when you looked at him from the corners of your eyes.

"I want to go with you," he said.

"You will be the first soldier in my army," I told him.

I leapt onto my horse's back and marveled at the power and height it gave to me. Just then galloping out of nowhere straight at me came a rider on a black horse. The villagers scattered except for my one soldier, who stood calmly in the road. I drew my sword. "Wait!" shouted the rider, raising weaponless hands. "Wait. I have traveled here to join you."

Then the villagers relinquished their real gifts to me—their sons. Families who had hidden their boys during the last conscription volunteered them now. I took the ones their families could spare and the ones with hero-fire in their eyes, not the young fathers and not those who would break hearts with their leaving,

We were better equipped than many founders of dynasties had been when they walked north to dethrone an emperor; they had been peasants like us. Millions of us had laid our hoes down on the dry ground and faced north. We sat in the fields, from which the dragon had withdrawn its moisture, and sharpened those hoes. Then, though it be ten thousand miles away, we walked to the palace. We would report to the emperor. The emperor, who sat facing south, must have been very frightened—peasants everywhere walking day and night toward the capital, toward Peiping. But the last emperors of dynasties must not have been in the right direction, for they would have seen us and not let us get this hungry. We would not have had to shout our grievances. The peasants would crown as emperor a farmer who knew the earth or a beggar who understood hunger.

"Thank you, Mother. Thank you, Father," I said before leaving. They had carved their names and addresses on me, and I would come back.

Often I walked beside my horse to travel abreast of my army. When we had to impress other armies—marauders, columns of refugees filing past one another, boy gangs following their martial arts teachers—I mounted and rode in front. The soldiers who owned horses and weapons would pose fiercely on my left and right. The small bands joined us, but sometimes armies of equal or larger strength would fight us. Then screaming a mighty scream and swinging two swords over my head, I charged the leaders; I released my bloodthirsty army and my straining war horse. I guided the horse with my knees, freeing both hands for sword work, spinning green and silver circles all around me.

I inspired my army, and I fed them. At night I sang to them glorious songs that came out of the sky and into my head. When I opened my mouth, the songs poured out and were loud enough for the whole encampment to hear; my army stretched out for a mile. We sewed red flags and tied red scraps around arms, legs, horses' tails. We wore our red clothes so that when we visited a village, we would look as happy as for New Year's Day. Then people would want to join the ranks. My army did not rape, only taking food where there was abundance. We brought order wherever we went.

When I won over a goodly number of fighters, I built up my army enough to attack fiefdoms and to pursue the enemies I had seen in the water gourd.

My first opponent turned out to be a giant, so much bigger than the toy general I used to peep at. During the charge, I singled out the leader, who grew as he ran toward me. Our eyes locked until his height made me strain my neck looking up so vulnerable to the stroke of a knife that my eyes dropped to the secret death points on the huge body. First I cut off his leg with one sword swipe, as Chen Luan-feng had chopped the leg off the thunder god. When the giant stumbled toward me, I cut off his head. Instantly he reverted to his true self, a snake, and slithered away hissing. The fighting around me stopped as the combatants' eyes and mouths opened wide in amazement. The giant's spells now broken, his soldiers, now seeing that they had been led by a snake, pledged their loyalty to me.

In the stillness after battle I looked up at the mountaintops; perhaps the old man and woman were watching me and would enjoy my knowing it. They'd laugh to see a creature winking at them from the bottom of the water gourd. But on the green ledge above the battlefield I saw the giant's wives crying. They had climbed out of their palanquins to watch their husband fight me, and now they were holding each other weeping. They were two sisters, two tiny fairies against the sky, widows from now on. Their long undersleeves, which they had pulled out to wipe their tears, flew white mourning in the mountain wind. After a time, they got back into their sedan chairs, and their servants carried them away.

I led my army northward, rarely having to sidetrack; the emperor himself sent the enemies I was hunting chasing after me. Sometimes they attacked us on two or three sides; sometimes they ambushed me when I rode ahead. We would always win, Kuan Kung, the god of war and literature riding before me. I would be told of in fairy tales myself. I overheard some soldiers—and now there were many who had not met me—say that whenever we had been in danger of losing, I had made a throwing gesture and the opposing army would fall, hurled across the battlefield. Hailstones as big as heads would shoot out of the sky and the lightning would stab like swords, but never hit those on my side. "On *his* side," they said. I never told them the truth. Chinese executed women who disguised themselves as soldiers or students, no matter how bravely they fought or how high they scored on the examinations.

One spring morning I was at work in my tent repairing equipment, patching my clothes, and studying maps, when a voice said, "General, may I visit you in your tent, please?" As if it were my home, I did not allow strangers in my tent. And since I had no family with me, no one ever visited inside. Riverbanks, hillsides, the cool sloped rooms under the pine trees—China provides her soldiers with meeting places enough. I opened the tent flap. And there in the sunlight stood my own husband, with arms full of wildflowers for me. "You are beautiful," he said, and meant it truly. "I have looked for you everywhere. I've been looking for you since the day the bird flew away with you." We were so pleased with each other, the childhood friend found at last, the childhood friend mysteriously grown up. "I followed you, but you skimmed over the rocks until I lost you."

"I've looked for you too," I said, the tent now snug around us like a secret house when we were kids. "When ever I heard about a good fighter, I went to see if it were you," I said. "I saw you marry me. I'm so glad you married me."

He wept when he took off my shirt and saw the scarwords on my back. He loosened my hair and covered the words with it. I turned around and touched his face, loving the familiar first.

## LINDA ATKINSON

# PATTIE DACANAY

Pattie Dacanay moves slowly, with a calm presence that seems to come from somewhere deep inside her. Her dark eyes are clear, her face serene, and when she speaks, you know you are listening to a woman who is at ease in the world and at peace with herself. You can't imagine that she was ever different. But she was.

"If you had met me ten years ago," Pattie says with a smile, "you certainly would not have said I was serene. A more likely word would have been 'frantic.'"

Ten years ago, Pattie had never heard of t'ai chi ch'uan, the ancient Chinese art of which she is now a master. She was living in Seattle, Washington, working in the sales department of a company that handled tapes and records, and she was married to a rock and roll musician.

"I was a rock and roll musician's wife, and everything you hear about that is true. My husband's band was the number one band in the city, so they were constantly working. And I was at all the gigs, every weekend, handling public relations, taking care of everyone. My head was filled with noise, and I was always exhausted because during the

---

*Herself a student of karate, Linda Atkinson set out in her 1983 book* Women in the Martial Arts *to profile individual women against the background of their chosen martial arts. The result was an eloquent blending of biography and description suggesting that the martial arts continue to evolve even as the practitioners themselves strive for ancient goals.*

week when they slept late and kept their own hours, I was at my 'other' job."

At a friend's urging, Pattie visited a small studio in Seattle's Chinatown where t'ai chi ch'uan was being taught.

"I was entranced," Pattie says, "from the moment I stepped into the room."

The studio was silent and immaculate, as austere as a "monastery cell." Photographs of t'ai chi masters hung on one wall. Classical Chinese weapons were mounted on another. And beside the open window was an altar holding oranges, incense, and autumn leaves. The students moved very slowly, without making a sound.

"It was like poetry. It was like a ballet. The range of motion and the balance they maintained in slow motion were incredible to me. I had never seen anything like it before, or anything like that atmosphere, the silent peaceful energy that just filled the room. I didn't understand what it was, but I knew it was what I needed, and I felt as though I belonged there."

Master John S.S. Leong, the founder and chief instructor of the school, was a quiet man with an "aura of strength and dignity." He had been trained in China, in the traditional, highly disciplined way.

"There was no outside world competing for his attention," Pattie says. "You could see his concentration, his full commitment in every move he made. T'ai chi was the center of life for him. His identification with it was complete, and he expected his students to feel the same way."

Most of the students seemed to be in awe of Master Leong. They could hardly speak to him. But Pattie felt a special bond with him from the beginning, and she quickly became his most devoted student.

"I had no special gift," she says, "except my stubbornness. My family always said that the harder you work, the more you get back, and I believed that. If I hadn't, I would have given up. I've seen hundreds of people come and go over the years, but I was just determined."

Pattie doesn't advise other people to go about it the way she did. "I pushed myself to the limit," she says. "I was told the flexibility and balance would come in time, but I couldn't wait. I forced myself to hold stretches I wasn't ready for, and I was in pain, I was in agony for months. I could barely walk up and down the stairs, but I was willing to go through anything in order to do the postures perfectly. Now I am extremely limber and I have experienced some of the ecstasy of my art—

and I hope I'll have it for many years to come, because I'll never forget the agony."

There are no ranks in t'ai chi. You learn certain forms and then you go on to the next ones. Pattie's growing mastery was acknowledged by her Sifu (Chinese for "respected teacher") when, after one year's training, he invited her to learn an advanced form done with a sword.

"I resisted working with a sword for a while because it seemed so foreign and external," she says. "But my Sifu taught me to think of it as an extension of my body. He said that working with it would strengthen my concentration and my balance. And it did, and I loved it."

Sifu Leong also asked Pattie to teach beginning students in one of his branch schools. She had mixed feelings. "I felt as though I was being kicked out of the nest, and I didn't want to go."

Pattie turned out to be an excellent teacher, and in fact, while growing up, had planned to be one. The oldest child in a family of four children, she had always taken care of her younger brothers and sisters, and she had been something of a "mother hen" to an extended family that included thirty cousins.

"My family was very close and very big," she laughs. "We were everywhere, even though neither of my parents was originally from Seattle. My father was born in the Philippines and my mother was born in South Dakota. But soon after they settled in Seattle, the whole family gravitated there. I was usually put in charge of the kids, and I always thought I would be a teacher."

Pattie had been set to attend the University of Washington and to major in education there before being sidetracked by her job, her marriage, and her husband's career. Now that she was teaching t'ai chi, she felt as though she had come full circle. And the more she taught and studied, the clearer it became that she had found the center of her life in "the t'ai chi spirit."

"The things I had pushed for so hard in the beginning began to come naturally, and I really began to change, especially my breathing, which is so essential in t'ai chi. Each movement is done to an exhale or an inhale, and you work and work to increase the depth of your breathing. It was after about a year that I could feel my breath sink, and I began to breathe abdominally, the way you are supposed to. I could take in more air, I breathed more slowly, and my movements slowed down too. That's when the real fluidity and the real fine tuning of your body begins."

She began to study Chinese herbal medicine, massage, calligraphy, and nutrition. She took on responsibility for classes in Sifu Leong's outlying schools, and was soon the head t'ai chi trainer at the University of Washington branch and the branch in suburban Burien. Many times, after her classes were over, she would return to central Seattle to work out on her own until after midnight. Inevitably, as her priorities changed, the other parts of her life changed too. The differences showed up first in her marriage.

"I had always been my husband's main support. I was with him and for him seven days a week and even in my own mind, what he was doing took first place. Suddenly I wasn't there anymore. He felt neglected—and he was right. I *was* neglecting him, compared with the way I had been before. But I couldn't go back. Something had begun to grow in me and it was important, and I wanted to devote myself to it entirely."

Pattie and her husband parted without rancor. "We didn't have the kinds of personal problems you hear about. But I had to let go of him and be on my own."

The second shift had to do with her job. Pattie had been aware for some time that she was not being treated fairly. She was doing the same work that the men in her company were doing, but she did not have the same title, and she did not get the same salary. Now she spoke up, and when her employer refused to upgrade her, she quit.

In 1978, Pattie made the last shift. She decided to leave Seattle altogether and move to Athens, Ohio. A good friend had decided to go to school there, and Pattie felt it was time she too set out on her own. This move seemed to be what all the other changes had been leading to. Nevertheless, it was difficult.

"I was leaving the city in which I had been born and raised, leaving my friends, my family, my school. But the hardest of all was leaving my teacher, Master Leong," Pattie says. "I thank him every day for what he shared with me."

Athens is a small college town in a part of southeast Ohio that has been honored in Indian legend and history as one of the earth's great gathering places for spiritual energy. Pattie loved the area and had no trouble getting settled there. She proved to be an excellent organizer.

"When I arrived," she says, "I could count on the fingers of one hand how many people knew what t'ai chi was. There certainly was not a ready audience for it. But an audience developed."

Pattie began by holding t'ai chi demonstrations to which she invited people from the press, the university, the media, and the general public. She visited schools, social service centers, hospitals. Newspaper articles were written about her and about t'ai chi. A radio station asked her to do a short weekly broadcast about t'ai chi and other aspects of Chinese culture. The university of Ohio invited her to make a series of programs for its cable television project. In the course of the twelve segments, Pattie explained some of the basic exercises that she thinks are the most important part of early training.

"The exercises were simple—from just bending over and touching your toes to standing on one leg and raising the other out to the side about knee height, holding it, and returning it to the ground. But I would explain that if they did the exercises correctly, with breathing and relaxation, every muscle in the body would have been well stretched, and if they did them daily, they would increase their range of motion and their flexibility almost without limit. I usually did the exercises the way I thought most of the people in the audience would do them, but sometimes I did them to my own capacity to show them what could be achieved. Flexibility and balance come to everyone with enough repetitions. Even with older people who have lost it, it can be regained."

When the television project was finished, Pattie was invited to teach in person at the university's Continuing Education Center. By the spring, she was holding workshops for health educators, professional dancers, and the Athens Senior Citizen's Center. Soon she established her own school.

The next winter, Pattie made a trip to the island of Taiwan, where the most accomplished t'ai chi artists in the world can be found. As in China itself, almost everyone in Taiwan practices one martial art or another. They practice early in the morning, in the fields and squares of every town and village.

"I think of myself as a pretty energetic person," Pattie says, "but in Taiwan, I felt lazy! People of all ages were outside and working out at 4:00 A.M.! On the first morning, they were finished by the time I got there! Training is their first commitment, their top priority, seven days a week, rain or shine."

Pattie was primarily interested in the self-defense and fighting aspects of t'ai chi, since that was the area in which she had the least experience. She watched each of the masters at work in Taipei Park, and then decided to study with Sifu Tsheng, the leading practitioner of tui-sau, "push-hands," the t'ai chi technique that comes closest to sparring.

Push-hands starts out with two people facing each other, feet planted in one spot, wrists and arms up and touching lightly. As one person slowly pushes the arms and wrists of the other in show circular motions, the other yields, then pushes back. Feet do not move, and as you yield and push in turn, great care must be taken to maintain your balance.

"One pushes, one retreats, flowing as one, always connected," Pattie explains. "In Chinese they say the you 'eat the other's mind.' You feel the other person's movement from its inception. You yield to it, bend with it, so it loses its force and does not push you over."

On advanced levels, push-hands can be very fast and aggressive. On the highest level, you may work "free style," moving about the floor, maintaining contact with your partner and keeping your balance while trying to get your partner to lose hers. Expertise comes only with experience.

"As you learn to relax your own muscles," Pattie says, "you can feel the other person's tension and energy. It is transmitted through the hands, arms, shoulders, like an electric shock, mild but constant, and you know when your opponent is going to move, unless she too can relax her muscles. A trained person can fool you, and feel the second your balance is not rooted—and then over you go! The sensitivity involved takes years to develop. My teacher used to say, 'A thousand repetitions is a good beginning.' Anyone can push. Few can feel."

Pattie was introduced to Sifu Tsheng as a t'ai chi teacher from America. He had never instructed an American woman before, and he welcomed her courteously. The next day, she arrived in the park in time to do the stretching exercises she still considers the most important part of daily training. The noises from the bus terminal just outside the main gate didn't affect her concentration at all, and as she soon realized, she was more flexible than anyone there.

"I stretched my foot up to the branch above my head and held it there for several minutes to get a good stretch—and several other students came around to watch. They watched me do the other exercise for balance and flexibility my Sifu had taught me. The next day, a few students came to ask me whether I would be their teacher. I was so honored I hardly knew how to respond. But I had to tell them that I was there to study and learn myself and I just couldn't teach."

Sifu Tsheng thought Pattie's concentration, agility, and timing were extraordinary. Before she had been there a week, he invited her to be his own partner in the push-hands exercise.

"I was deeply grateful to my Sifu for the training he gave me, because everyone recognized it right away. I was treated like a queen. It was incredible."

Pattie's legs and back were already strong, but still she was not prepared for the intensity of the work she did with Sifu Tsheng.

"We started out with basic slow motion exercises, and at first I could only work with him for half an hour at a time. He pushed me so hard I was arched into a back bend. I hurt so bad I could hardly get out of bed in the morning. But after a while I could work for three hours with just a break to shake out a little every hour or so."

When masters from other parts of the island came to Taipei Park to pay their respects to Sifu Tsheng, he introduced them to Pattie and invited them to work with her. "Their strength and experience in the martial arts were to their advantage. My flexibility and sensitivity to movement—all of which I had learned, none of which was natural to me—were to my advantage. I didn't get surprised very often."

Sifu Tsheng invited Pattie to take part in the push-hands competition at the upcoming festival of the World T'ai Chi Association. Although she had only been training for two months, he assured her that she would win in her class. But Pattie could not stay for the festival. Her visa would be up before then, and she would have to return to the United States. Nevertheless, since only masters are allowed to enter, the invitation was a great honor. Pattie left Taiwan feeling encouraged, inspired, and immensely strengthened. But her good feelings disappeared when she returned to Ohio.

"I guess it was a kind of cultural shock," she says. "And maybe I should have expected it. But I didn't. I had felt so much at home in Taiwan, and I had been welcomed so warmly and so completely by the people. In Ohio, I felt as though I was standing alone again, after having been part of a real community. I felt cut off and isolated in a way I never had before."

But as the weeks turned to months, Pattie found new ways to use her t'ai chi energy. When one of her students became pregnant, Pattie realized how helpful t'ai chi exercises would be for women during pregnancy and childbirth. She began working with her student and then agreed to be with her when the time came for the baby to be born.

"It was the first birth I ever attended," Pattie says. "The little boy, Miles, is my godson and I feel now that there is a wonderful bond between us."

Shortly after Miles's birth, Pattie began to work as an apprentice to two local midwives and thought she would like to become a midwife herself. But then she had to miss a t'ai chi class because she was at a birth. It was the only class she had ever missed.

I realized that I couldn't commit myself to an apprenticeship at that time," she says. "It required a person who could attend meetings regularly—be able to run at a moment's notice at the time of labor— and I just couldn't do that. My own t'ai chi training would not have had such an overwhelming effect on my entire life if my Sifu was not at class when he said he would be. He instilled discipline in me because of his dedication. I wanted to do the same for my students."

Later in the year, Pattie began to work with patients at the Athens Mental Health Center. She designed a program of modified t'ai chi exercises as a relaxation-movement class. She volunteered her services and asked the center only for space and permission.

"The director of activities, whom I had met on our local women's volleyball team, said I wouldn't have any trouble getting permission, but she warned me not to be disappointed if no one came to my classes," Pattie remembers, "or if no one came back a second time. But the classes have been an unqualified, 100 percent success."

One class is made up of women who are considered so disturbed they are kept in a locked ward.

"When they first came, they were very skeptical and suspicious," Pattie says. "I would ask them to relax and close their eyes and I would see them peeking at me when they thought I wasn't looking. But slowly, we managed to relax together and then we began to move together. By the time class is over, they are always calmer and stronger."

Pattie also works with aged men and women from the geriatric ward. Some of them have been on medication for years. They suffer from twitches and other involuntary movements, and their coordination is very poor. "Movement of almost any kind is difficult for them. But they work hard, and they improve. In some cases, I can actually see them getting better."

Pattie would gladly continue her work with these people on a volunteer basis. But the center is now committed to the program and has put her on salary. She has also been invited to increase the number and size of her classes.

In addition to running her own school and the work she does at the health center, Pattie also works at an out-patient clinic with people who suffer from arthritis, with a professional dance troupe, and with a university theater group, which contacted her when they were per- forming a play involving a Vietnamese wedding ceremony where tran- quility was the hallmark. After the play's run, she was offered a permanent job with the drama department at the University of Ohio.

"The more I train, the more energy I have," Pattie says. "It seems endless. Master Leong told me years ago that this would happen, but it still feels like a surprise!"

Pattie worked with a group of holistic health educators to organize her most ambitious project so far: an annual retreat to the countryside. This year, close to one hundred people will attend. The retreat, which is held at a farm, is especially important to Pattie because it is a celebration of the cycles of the earth and the balance of nature. As such, it is closely tied to the Taoist idea of the harmony of the universe.

"We need to find ways of relating to nature that are not possessive and destructive," she says. "We need traditions and rituals that celebrate the harmony and beauty of the universe, and the solstice is one of them. If we can experience the harmony of the universe, we will be able to find it in our own lives, too."

The retreat emphasizes the connection between respect for the planet and loving care of the self. It features workshops in various aspects of natural and holistic health care, methods of self-healing, group meditation, and of course t'ai chi exercises. Although it didn't start out that way, the event is now for women only.

"Men were in on the early planning stage," Pattie says, "but after a while, the core group became an all-women's group. I think now that it's very important for women to work together. The bonding that takes place when we do is just incredible. Women have had so little power in the past, but now that we are coming together and finding our voices, I think we will be a great force for balance and joy in the universe. I have more and more respect for our capabilities as time goes by."

Today Pattie lives in a one-room cabin in the woods thirteen miles outside of Athens. The cabin has no running water and no electricity. It is heated only by a wood stove. She is happy there and with the work she is doing in Athens. But she doesn't think she will stay forever. "I feel that there were important reasons for me to be in Athens. But I don't think I'm going to be here for the rest of my life."

Where will she go? She doesn't know.

"One thing will lead to the next," she says, "and things will work out the way they are supposed to. Ten years ago, I could not have predicted the direction my life would take. But I am very happy with the way things have gone, and I have absolutely no regrets. I just try to do the right thing in the present, and I try to be open to the meaning of the present, and to the things it makes possible."

"The world is ruled by letting things take their course," said Lao Tsu. That is the principle Pattie lives by.

### MIYAMOTO MUSASHI

# THE WATER BOOK

The spirit of the ni ten ichi school of strategy is based on water, and this Water Book explains methods of victory as the long-sword form of the ichi school. Language does not extend to explaining the Way in detail, but it can be grasped intuitively. Study this book; read a word then ponder on it. If you interpret the meaning loosely you will mistake the Way.

The principles of strategy are written down here in terms of single combat, but you must think broadly so that you attain an understanding for ten-thousand-a-side battles.

Strategy is different from other things in that if you mistake the Way even a little you will become bewildered and fall into bad ways.

If you merely read this book you will not reach the Way of strategy. Absorb the things written in this book. Do not just read, memorize, or imitate, but so that you realize the principle from within your own heart study hard to absorb these things into your body.

---

*Musashi lived from 1585 to 1645, a folk hero and arguably the greatest swordsman in the history of Japan. His* Book of Five Rings *is considered to be one of the world's great texts on strategy, studied even today by businessmen, politicians, and martial artists alike. Musashi's Nito Ryu teaching is based on two swords, one for each hand; and he himself insisted that the sword was part of the person. "One who masters the sword after long years," said Musashi, "also learns to master the self."*

## SPIRITUAL BEARING IN STRATEGY

In strategy your spiritual bearing must not be any different from normal. Both in fighting and in everyday life you should be determined though calm. Meet the situation without tenseness yet not recklessly, your spirit settled yet unbiased. Even when your spirit is calm do not let your body relax, and when your body is relaxed do not let your spirit slacken. Do not let your spirit be influenced by your body or your body be influenced by your spirit. Be neither insufficiently spirited nor over spirited. An elevated spirit is weak and a low spirit is weak. Do not let the enemy see your spirit.

Small people must be completely familiar with the spirit of large people, and large people must be familiar with the spirit of small people. Whatever your size, do not be misled by the reactions of your own body. With your spirit open and unconstricted, look at things from a high point of view. You must cultivate your wisdom and spirit. Polish your wisdom: learn public justice, distinguish between good and evil, study the Ways of different arts one by one. When you cannot be deceived by men you will have realized the wisdom of strategy.

The wisdom of strategy is different from other things. On the battlefield, even when you are hard-pressed, you should ceaselessly research the principles of strategy so that you can develop a steady spirit.

## STANCE IN STRATEGY

Adopt a stance with the head erect, neither hanging down, nor looking up, nor twisted. Your forehead and the space between your eyes should not be wrinkled. Do not roll your eyes nor allow them to blink, but slightly narrow them. With your features composed, keep the line of your nose straight with a feeling of slightly flaring your nostrils. Hold the line of the rear of the neck straight: instill vigor into your hairline, and in the same way from the shoulders down through your entire body. Lower both shoulders and, without the buttocks jutting out, put strength into your legs from the knees to the tips of your toes. Brace your abdomen so that you do not bend at the hips. Wedge your companion sword in your belt against your abdomen, so that your belt is not slack—this is called "wedging in."

In all forms of strategy, it is necessary to maintain the combat stance in everyday life and to make your everyday stance your combat stance. You must research this well.

### THE GAZE IN STRATEGY

The gaze should be large and broad. This is the twofold gaze "Perception and Sight." Perception is strong and sight weak.

In strategy it is important to see distant things as if they were close and to take a distanced view of close things. It is important in strategy to know the enemy's sword and not to be distracted by insignificant movements of his sword. You must study this. The gaze is the same for single combat and for large-scale strategy.

It is necessary in strategy to be able to look to both sides without moving the eyeballs. You cannot master this ability quickly. Learn what is written here; use this gaze in everyday life and do not vary it whatever happens.

### HOLDING THE LONG SWORD

Grip the long sword with a rather floating feeling in your thumb and forefinger, with the middle finger neither tight nor slack, and with the last two fingers tight. It is bad to have play in your hands.

When you take up a sword, you must feel intent on cutting the enemy. As you cut an enemy you must not change your grip, and your hands must not "cower." When you dash the enemy's sword aside, or ward it off, or force it down, you must slightly change the feeling in your thumb and forefinger. Above all, you must be intent on cutting the enemy in the way you grip the sword.

The grip for combat and for sword-testing is the same. There is no such thing as a "man-cutting grip."

Generally, I dislike fixedness in both long swords and hands. Fixedness means a dead hand. Pliability is a living hand. You must bear this in mind.

### FOOTWORK

With the tips of your toes somewhat floating, treat firmly with your heels. Whether you move fast or slow, with large or small steps, your feet must always move as in normal walking. I dislike the three walking methods known as "jumping-foot," "floating foot," and "fixed-steps."

So called "yin-yang foot" is important in the Way. Yin-yang foot means not moving only one foot. It means moving your feet left-right and right-left when cutting, withdrawing, or warding off a cut. You should not move one foot preferentially.

## THE FIVE ATTITUDES

The five attitudes are: upper, middle, lower, right side, and left side. These are the five. Although attitude has these five divisions, the one purpose of all of them is to cut the enemy. There are none but these five attitudes.

Whatever attitude you are in, do not be conscious of making the attitude; think only of cutting.

Your attitude should be large or small according to the situation. Upper, lower, and middle attitudes are decisive. Left side and right side attitudes are fluid. Left and right attitudes should be used if there is an obstruction overhead or to one side. The decision to use left or right depends on the place.

The essence of the Way is this. To understand attitude you must thoroughly understand the middle attitude. The middle attitude is the heart of the attitudes. If we look at strategy on a broad scale, the middle attitude is the seat of the commander, with the other four attitudes following the commander. You must appreciate this.

## THE WAY OF THE LONG SWORD

Knowing the Way of the long sword means we can wield with two fingers the sword we usually carry. If we know the path of the sword well, we can wield it easily.

If you try to wield the long sword quickly you will mistake the Way. To wield the long sword well you must wield it calmly. If you try to wield it quickly, like a folding fan or a short sword, you will err by using "short sword chopping." You cannot cut a man with a long sword using this method.

When you have cut downwards with the long sword, lift it straight upwards; when you cut sideways, return the sword along a sideways path. Return the sword in a reasonable way, always stretching the elbows broadly. Wield the sword strongly. This is the Way of the long sword.

If you learn to use the five approaches of my strategy, you will be able to wield a sword well. You must train constantly.

## THE FIVE APPROACHES

1. The first approach is the middle attitude. Confront the enemy with the point of your sword against his face. When he attacks, dash his

sword to the right and "ride" it. Or, when the enemy attacks, deflect the point of his sword by hitting downwards, keep your long sword where it is, and as the enemy renews the attack cut his arms from below. This is the first method.

The five approaches are this kind of thing. You must train repeatedly using a long sword in order to learn them. When you master my Way of the long sword, you will be able to control any attack the enemy makes. I assure you, there are no attitudes other than the five attitudes of the long sword of nito.

2. In the second approach with the long sword, from the upper attitude cut the enemy just as he attacks. If the enemy evades the cut, keep your sword where it is and, scooping up from below, cut him as he renews the attack. It is possible to repeat the cut from here.

In this method there are various changes in timing and spirit. You will be able to understand this by training in the ichi school. You will always win with the five long sword methods. You must train repetitively.

3. In the third approach, adopt the lower attitude, anticipating scooping up. When the enemy attacks, hit his hands from below. As you do so, he may try to hit your sword down. If this is the case, cut his upper arm(s) horizontally with a feeling of "crossing." This means that from the lower attitudes you hit the enemy at the instant that he attacks.

You will encounter this method often, both as a beginner and in later strategy. You must train using a long sword.

4. In this fourth approach, adopt the left side attitude. As the enemy attacks, hit his hands from below. If as you hit at his hands he attempts to dash down your sword, with the feeling of hitting his hands, parry the path of his long sword and cut across from above your shoulder.

This is the Way of the long sword. Through this method you win by parrying the line of the enemy's attack. You must research this.

5. In the fifth approach, the sword is in the right side attitude. In accordance with the enemy's attack, cross your long sword from below at the side to the upper attitude. Then cut straight from above.

This method is essential for knowing the Way of the long sword well. If you can use this method, you can freely wield a heavy long sword.

I cannot describe in detail how to use these five approaches. You must become well acquainted with my "in harmony with the long sword" Way, learn large-scale timing, understand the enemy's long sword, and become used to the five approaches from the outset. You will always win by using these five methods, with various timing considerations discerning the enemy's spirit. You must consider all this carefully.

### THE "ATTITUDE NO-ATTITUDE" TEACHING

"Attitude No-Attitude" means that there is no need for what are known as long sword attitudes.

Even so, attitudes exist as the five ways of holding the long sword. However you hold the sword it must be in such a way that it is easy to cut the enemy well, in accordance with the situation, the place, and your relation to the enemy. From the upper attitude as your spirit lessens you can adopt the Middle attitude, and from the middle attitude you can raise the sword a little in your technique and adopt the upper attitude. From the lower attitude you can raise the sword a little and adopt the middle attitude as the occasion demands. According to the situation, if you turn your sword from either the left side or right side attitude towards the center, the middle or the lower attitude results.

The principle of this is called "existing attitude-nonexisting attitude."

The primary thing when you take a sword in your hands is your intention to cut the enemy, whatever the means. Whenever you parry, hit, spring, strike, or touch the enemy's cutting sword, you must cut the enemy in the same movement. It is essential to attain this. If you think only of hitting, springing, striking, or touching the enemy, you will not be able actually to cut him. More than anything, you must be thinking of carrying your movement through to cutting him. You must thoroughly research this.

Attitude in strategy on a larger scale is called "Battle Array." Such attitudes are all for winning battles. Fixed formation is bad. Study this well.

### TO HIT THE ENEMY "IN ONE TIMING"

"In one timing" means, when you have closed with the enemy, to hit him as quickly and directly as possible, without moving your body or settling your spirit, while you see that he is still undecided. The timing of hitting before the enemy decides to withdraw, break or hit, is this "In one timing."

You must train to achieve this timing, to be able to hit in the timing of an instant.

### THE "ABDOMEN TIMING OF TWO"

When you attack and the enemy quickly retreats, as you see him tense you must feint a cut. Then, as he relaxes, follow up and hit him. This is the "abdomen timing of two."

It is very difficult to attain this by merely reading this book, but you will soon understand with a little instruction.

### NO DESIGN, NO CONCEPTION

In this method, when the enemy attacks and you also decide to attack, hit with your body, and hit with your spirit, and hit from the Void with your hands, accelerating strongly. This is the "no design, no conception" cut.

This is the most important method of hitting. It is often used. You must train hard to understand it.

### THE FLOWING WATER CUT

The "flowing water cut" is used when you are struggling blade to blade with the enemy. When he breaks and quickly withdraws trying to spring with his long sword, expand your body and spirit and cut him as slowly as possible with your long sword, following your body like stagnant water. You can cut with certainty if you learn this. You must discern the enemy's grade.

### CONTINUOUS CUT

When you attack and the enemy also attacks, and your swords spring together, in one action cut his head, hands and legs. When you cut several places with one sweep of the long sword, it is the "continuous cut." You must practice this cut; it is often used. With detailed practice you should be able to understand it.

### FIRE AND STONES CUT

The fire and stones cut means that when the enemy's long sword and your long sword clash together you cut as strongly as possible without raising the sword even a little. This means cutting quickly with the hands, body and legs—all three cutting strongly. If you train well enough you will be able to strike strongly.

### THE RED LEAVES CUT

The red leaves cut means knocking down the enemy's long sword. The spirit should be getting control of his sword. When the enemy is in a long sword attitude in front of you and intent on cutting, hitting, and parrying, you strongly hit the enemy's long sword with the Fire and Stones Cut, perhaps in the spirit of the "no design, no conception" cut. If you then beat down the point of his sword with a sticky feeling, he will necessarily drop the sword. If you practice this cut it becomes easy to make the enemy drop his sword. You must train repetitively.

### THE BODY IN PLACE OF THE LONG SWORD

Also "the long sword in place of the body." Usually we move the body and the sword at the same time to cut the enemy. However, according to the enemy's cutting method, you can dash against him with your body first, and afterwards cut with the sword. If his body is immoveable, you can first cut with the long sword, but generally you hit first with the body and then cut with the long sword. You must research this well and practice hitting.

### CUT AND SLASH

To cut and to slash are two different things. Cutting, whatever form of cutting it is, is decisive, with a resolute spirit. Slashing is nothing more than touching the enemy. Even if you slash strongly, and even if the enemy dies instantly, it is slashing. When you cut, your spirit is resolved. You must appreciate this. If you first slash the enemy's hands or legs, you must cut them strongly. Slashing is in spirit the same as touching. When you realize this, they become indistinguishable. Learn this well.

### CHINESE MONKEY'S BODY

The Chinese monkey's body is the spirit of not stretching out your arms. The spirit is to get in quickly, without in the least extending your arms, before the enemy cuts. If you are intent upon not stretching out your arms you are effectively far away, the spirit is to go in with your whole body. When you come to within arm's reach it becomes easy to move your body in. You must research this well.

### GLUE AND LACQUER EMULSION BODY

The spirit of "glue and lacquer emulsion body" is to stick to the enemy and not separate from him. When you approach the enemy, stick firmly with your head, body and legs. People tend to advance their head and legs quickly, but their body lags behind. You should stick firmly so that there is not the slightest gap between the enemy's body and your body. You must consider this carefully.

### TO STRIVE FOR HEIGHT

By "to strive for height" is meant, when you close with the enemy, to strive with him for superior height without cringing. Stretch your legs, stretch your hips, and stretch your neck face to face with him. When you think you have won, and you are the higher, thrust in strongly. You must learn this.

### TO APPLY STICKINESS

When the enemy attacks and you also attack with the long sword, you should go in with a sticky feeling and fix your long sword against the enemy's as you receive his cut. The spirit of stickiness is not hitting very strongly, but hitting so that the long swords do not separate easily. It is best to approach as calmly as possible when hitting the enemy's long sword with stickiness. The difference between stickiness and entanglement is that stickiness is firm and entanglement is weak. You must appreciate this.

### THE BODY STRIKE

The body strike means to approach the enemy through a gap in his guard. The spirit is to strike him with your body. Turn your face a little aside and strike the enemy's breast with your left shoulder thrust out.

Approach with the spirit of bouncing the enemy away, striking as strongly as possible in time with your breathing. If you achieve this method of closing with the enemy, you will be able to knock him ten or twenty feet away. It is possible to strike the enemy until he is dead. Train well.

### THREE WAYS TO PARRY HIS ATTACK

There are three methods to parry a cut:

First, by dashing the enemy's long sword to your right, as if thrusting at his eyes, when he makes an attack.

Or, to parry by thrusting the enemy's long sword toward his right eye with the feeling of snipping his neck.

Or, when you have a short "long sword," without worrying about parrying the enemy's long sword, to close with him quickly, thrusting at his face with your left hand.

These are the three methods of parrying. You must bear in mind that you can always clench your left hand and thrust at the enemy's face with your fist. For this it is necessary to train well.

### TO STAB AT THE FACE

To stab at the face means, when you are in confrontation with the enemy, that your spirit is intent on stabbing at his face, following on the line of the blades with the point of your long sword. If you are intent on stabbing at his face, his face and body will become rideable. When the enemy becomes as if rideable, there are various opportunities for winning. You must concentrate on this. When fighting and the enemy's body becomes as if rideable, you can win quickly, so you ought not to forget to stab at the face. You must pursue the value of this technique through training.

### TO STAB AT THE HEART

To stab at the heart means, when fighting and there are obstructions above or to the sides, and whenever it is difficult to cut, to thrust at the enemy. You must stab the enemy's breast without letting the point of your long sword waver, showing the enemy the ridge of the blade square-on, and with the spirit of deflecting his long sword. The spirit of this principle is often useful when we become tired or for some reason our long sword will not cut. You must understand the application of this method.

## TO SCOLD "TUT-TUT!"

"Scold" means that, when the enemy tries to counter-cut as you attack, you counter-cut again from below as if thrusting at him, trying to hold him down. With very quick timing you cut, scolding the enemy. Thrust up, "Tut!" and cut "TUT!" This timing is encountered time and time again in exchanges of blows. The way to scold Tut-TUT is to time the cut simultaneously with raising your long sword as if to thrust the enemy. You must learn this through repetitive practice.

## THE SMACKING PARRY

By "smacking parry" is meant that when you clash swords with the enemy, you meet his attacking cut on your long sword with a *tee-dum*, *tee-dum* rhythm, smacking his sword and cutting him. The spirit of the smacking parry is not parrying, or smacking strongly, but smacking the enemy's long sword in accordance with his attacking cut, primarily intent on quickly cutting him. If you understand the timing of smacking, however hard your long swords clash together, your swordpoint will not be knocked back even a little. You must research sufficiently to realize this.

## THERE ARE MANY ENEMIES

"There are many enemies" applies when you are fighting one against many. Draw both sword and companion sword and assume a wide-stretched left and right attitude. This spirit is to chase the enemies around from side to side, even though they come from all four directions. Observe their attacking order, and go to meet first those who attack first. Sweep your eyes around broadly, carefully examining the attacking order, and cut left and right alternatively with your swords. Waiting is bad. Always quickly resume your attitudes to both sides, cut the enemies down as they advance, crushing them in the direction from which they attack. Whatever you do, you must drive the enemy together, as if tying a line of fishes, and when they are seen to be piled up, cut them down strongly without giving them room to move.

## THE ADVANTAGE WHEN COMING TO BLOWS

You can know how to win through strategy with the long sword, but it cannot be clearly explained in writing. You must practice diligently in order to understand how to win.

Oral tradition: "The true Way of strategy is revealed in the long sword."

## ONE CUT

You can win with certainty with the spirit of "one cut." It is difficult to attain this if you do not learn strategy well. If you train well in this Way, strategy will come from your heart and you will be able to win at will. You must train diligently.

## DIRECT COMMUNICATION

The spirit of "direct communication" is how the true Way of the nito ichi school is received and handed down.

Oral tradition: "Teach your body strategy."

Recorded in the above book is an outline of ichi school sword-fighting.

To learn how to win with the long sword in strategy, first learn the five appraoches and the five attitudes, and absorb the Way of the long sword naturally in your body. You must understand spirit and timing, handle the long sword naturally, and move body and legs in harmony with your spirit. Whether beating one man or two, you will then know values in strategy.

Study the contents of this book, taking one item at a time, and through fighting with enemies you will gradually come to know the principle of the Way.

Deliberately, with a patient spirit, absorb the virtue of all this, from time to time raising your hand in combat. Maintain this spirit whenever you cross swords with an enemy.

Step by step walk the thousand-mile road.

Study strategy over the years and achieve the spirit of the warrior. Today is victory over yourself of yesterday; tomorrow is your victory over lesser men. Next, in order to beat more skillful men, train according to this book, not allowing your heart to be swayed along a side-track. Even if you kill an enemy, if it is not based on what you have learned it is not the true Way.

If you attain this Way of victory, then you will be able to defeat several tens of men. What remains is sword-fighting ability, which you can attain in battles and duels.

The second year of Shoho, the twelfth day of the fifth month (1645)

**PETER URBAN**

# THE THREE SONS

In the olden days there was a very famous grand master of the sword who was greatly pleased to receive a visit from another old gentleman of his art. As the two senseis, chatting and sipping tea, recalled their youth and valiant deeds, the conversation gradually centered on their respective families and the progress of their children. The host had three sons who had naturally devoted their lives to the task of mastering the sword, as had their father and his father, and his father before him. Greatly desiring to display his sons' skills, and at the same time wishing to teach them a lesson, the father winked mirthfully at his guest. With the stealth of a cat, he took a heavy vase from an alcove in the wall and placed it above the opening corner of the sliding doors that were the entrance to the room. The vase was in such a position that, should the door be opened, the piece of ceramic art would topple onto the head of the person entering.

With twinkling eyes, the two wise patriarchs returned to their tea and talk, for they were patient and had many things to discuss. After quite a while, the grand master called out for his eldest son. As was his nature, the number one son was quick to hear his father's call and came swiftly and gracefully to the door. There was an almost imperceptible

*One of the few outsiders ever to compete in the All Japan Collegiate Championships (in 1957), Urban, who was born in 1935, began his martial arts career at age eighteen by studying under Richard Kim. The author himself became a teacher of many notable students and is credited with bringing goju-ryu karate to the United States for the first time in 1959.*

pause. The son smoothly pulled the door open to his right, at the same time reaching through and up with his left hand. Grasping the heavy vase before it had time to fall, he spun clockwise into the room, holding the vase above his head. With a beautiful gesture, he slid the door shut and replaced the vase in its original position above the door. Then, without a word or glance, he bowed humbly to the two old masters.

The father's face beamed as he performed the introduction, saying, "This is my eldest son." His old friend looked deep into the son's eyes for a long moment. Then with a big smile and a low bow to the father, he replied, "I am very happy for you. He has learned everything well and is mastering the sword. He is worthy of your name." At this, both the father and the son bowed in return, and there were tears in the eyes of the grand master, for he knew that his old friend had just accepted his son as a young master of the sword.

After a short time, the father again called out, this time for his second son, who was also quick to respond. He came to the door and immediately opened it. Out of the corner of his eye, he glimpsed the falling vase, and his action was swift and conclusive: nimbly and smoothly he leaped to one side, catching the vase in his arms. His startled eyes glanced around the room, questioning everyone and everything. Politely suppressing his instinct to cry out or ask about the vase, he turned to the door, shut it, and after a moment of fumbling, managed to replace the vase in its original position. Bows were exchanged, whereupon the father introduced him with the following words: "This is my second son. He doesn't know very much, but he studies hard and is getting better and better every day."

The guest smiled, bowed to them both, and remarked, "He is growing superbly; he will be a source of great pride to you some day."

All were quiet for a few moments, reflecting on what had been said and what had taken place. With what might have been a sigh, the host turned and poured more tea into his friend's cup. They both sipped in silence. Then, placing his cup with a tiny, definitive clip on the lacquered surface of the table, the old sensei clapped his hands and called out for his youngest son.

As youngest sons often are, he was a little slow in responding to his father's call. At the last minute he tried to make up for his tardiness and ran the rest of the way to the door. As he slid it to one side and dashed into the room, the heavy vase toppled down, striking him a tremendous blow on the head. As it did, it bounced slightly, and during that instant the youngest son whipped around like a bolt of lightning, drew his sword and slashed the vase in half before it hit the tatami floor. He was so angry he didn't feel any pain. The vase lay in tiny bits all over the room, shattered by the blow. The boy sheathed his short sword without bothering to clean it properly and gave all those present a happy, but sheepishly embarrassed, grin. "This is my youngest son," said the old sensei with a broad, affectionate smile. "As you can see, he still has a lot to learn."

"Ah so," replied his old friend. "Still, he is very fast and very strong."

During the remainder of the afternoon, their father's honored guest spoke to all three sons, asking them about their school and teachers. He joked and talked seriously in turn, and so fascinated were the three sons by their father's old comrade-in-arms that, before they knew it, daylight was fading and their guest rose to take his leave.

It was his custom to give small gifts to his friends before going home, and he beckoned to the three sons. To the eldest he bowed very low and presented to him a marvelous gold pin with a small diamond in the center. He then looked him long in the eyes but said not a word.

To the second son he bowed very low and presented to him a heavy book, bound in magnificently tooled leather saying, "The pages of this book are blank, as the pages of your life are blank. What you write in it is up to you."

To the third son he also bowed very low, and presented him with a beautifully polished silver pocket watch saying, "If you wish to learn, you must start by being aware of time. Then you cannot use it wrongly, even if you do nothing."

The two old senseis then embraced each other in the martial arts manner, and the honored guest departed, leaving both sorrow and joy behind him.

## MICHEL RANDOM

# THE WAY OF THE BOW AND THE HORSE

### THE SUBCONSCIOUS ACTION OF MASTER ANZAWA

Kneeling in the seiza position, Master Anzawa, the greatest master of bowmanship in Japan, collects his thoughts. The noise from the nearby town can be heard in the dojo at the bottom of his garden, but he hears nothing. He has created a silence within himself. With movements in which breathing and deliberation are in harmony, he kneels down with the bow on his left touching the ground. His feet in tightly fitting white stockings (tabi) slide softly on the shiny wooden floor of the dojo. It's like watching some sort of choreography display by the Noh theater company, in which the slightest action seems to last an eternity; then he gets up, carries out various actions, slides forward, bares his left shoulder, kneels down, and remains still. He then takes hold of his bow, positions the first white-fletched arrow, takes a second arrow which he will hold in his fingers whilst preparing to shoot the first. Slowly the axis of the bow is raised to head level and turns to face the target. The unity of tension in the bow and inward concentration is complete at the moment of true accomplishment, the arrow is loosed, like a flower opening, accompanied by a short sharp cry—the kiai.

---

*In 1968 the author went to Japan in hopes of producing a film based on the martial arts, having been profoundly affected by Eugen Herrigel's* Zen in the Art of Archery *(see pages 131-141). Random in fact made two films and published a book based on his researches. The following excerpt from* The Martial Arts *(English translation, 1978) mentions Master Anzawa, one of Herrigel's own teachers who was still alive in 1970.*

For a moment, the master's eye remains trained on the target, for the arrow continues spiritually; it is the symbol of energy itself; nothing can stand it its way. "One arrow, one life," says Master Anzawa; he is 83. Then comes a gradual unwinding, the point of concentration that released the arrow is relaxed, the master is himself again. After shooting a second arrow, he will slide to the back of the dojo as before, place his bow before him, bow to it, almost touching the floor with his forehead. A perfect action will have taken place,

Between the moment when he picked up his bow and when he shot his first arrow, a long time elapsed, during which the master eliminated from his mind all that was not connected with the thought of the action; inward concentration reflected the alchemy of the unity: man, bow, target were as one. At the peak of concentration, the arrow flies spontaneously, like a child who inadvertently drops something in all innocence: it is the perfect involuntary action that accomplishes the loose; in addition, the goal is attained.

### THE WAY OF THE BOW AND THE HORSE

The Way of the bow and the horse did not originate in Japan. Chinese bowmen have taught it since the 11th century, using different bows for different occasions (fighting, hunting, shooting on foot, shooting from horseback, etc.).

But it was at the time of the Taira and Minamoto clans in the second half of the 12th century that the "Way of the bow and the horse" took on its full meaning. The bow became the principal weapon, to the extent that a warrior was designated "he who carries the bow and arrow."

### ORIGIN OF THE JAPANESE BOW

The oldest known evidence of bows goes back to drawings found on the walls of prehistoric caves or caverns.

The earliest asymmetrical bow found in Japan dates from the time of Kofun-bunka-jidai (third or fourth century A.D.). It was found near Lake Tokos, in the province of Nara, in the very heart of Yamato, the cradle of Japan. After examining it, the experts deduced that it was powerful, was strung in the opposite way to the resting position of the curve and, judging from a few traces of bands, must have been laminated. This discovery is important as it destroys the simplistic tendency to regard ancient bows as being of primitive conception, both in shape and substance.

Two main factors have affected the development of the Japanese bow: density of material—with the introduction of *take* (a type of very hard bamboo exclusive to Japan)—and application.

Originally, the basic material used was a shrub, which would explain the bow's asymmetry: the upper part of the shrub being weaker in effect than the very much stronger lower part. So, the Japanese would have decentered the grip in order to concentrate most of the power on the strongest part.

The length of the bow is determined by its use: target practice (from varying distances), hunting, use in battle, or on ceremonial occasions. Later on, the combination of laminating materials and the choice of base material permitted variations in power. It is interesting to note that the take found in Kanto (Tokyo) and in Yamato (Kyoto-Nara) possesses intrinsic qualities appropriate for the ceremonial bows, whilst the take from Kagoshima (Kyushu) is particularly suited to fighting bows.

During the Mongol invasion in the thirteenth century, the Japanese discovered the Mongol bows, made of a fairly slender core of pliable wood, reinforced with horn plating on both the belly and the back. After that two or three layers of ox tendons were added and the whole thing glued and left in a mold so that the bow would take its final shape. The Japanese exploited this method of manufacture by reinforcing the take with different types of wood: mulberry, cherry, and wild cherry, these woods being glued on both sides and held by bands made of cane or plaited bamboo bark.

So, by way of a number of metamorphoses, Japanese bows took on the definite shape which they were to keep right up to the present day.

The bow in effect measures 8 feet, 10 inches (2.20 m) long and is bent in the shape of a double curve. The grip from where the bow is drawn is positioned 28 inches (73 cm) from the base, such that the tension occurs, as it were, a third of the way up the bow. The bow's great length, making it relatively difficult to handle in battle, is exclusive to the Japanese people. All other nations have adopted shorter and therefore more easily transportable varieties. These are usually drawn at the center of the curve, whilst the Japanese bow is the only one which is held below the center. The Japanese have always shown a particular form of reverence toward the bow, quite beyond its use in battle. One has to go back as far as the Assyrians to find this same veneration for the bow, for they considered it to be the most noble of all weapons. As for the Japanese, the Way of the sword and the Way of the bow rule supreme. There is a Japanese expression: "the house of bow and arrows" which denotes a person's quality as a result of noble birth. The arrow which draws the bow is like the strength in man which can draw in the subtle power of the universe.

Finally, the bow and arrow were considered to be sacred by the Assyrians when they belonged to kings or generals.

In Shinto, the arrow is often an aid to purification. In fact, many temples have taken to selling arrows, which are carried home and which, during the course of the year, absorb all things evil and impure. These arrows are then burnt during the end of year ceremonies. The manufacture of arrows itself has to follow a set of rules, which means the work always carries with it a deep significance.

### MANUFACTURE OF THE BOW AND ARROW

The arrows are cut around the time of the winter solstice and left to dry for two to three months. It is very difficult to make a good arrow. In effect, one must know how to find the perfect bamboo cane and only one in two hundred can be used. It is necessary to choose a very straight bamboo cane and, as they all have knots, these must not be too prominent. So, three-year-old canes are selected, the younger ones being too soft and older ones too hard. Nor must the arrows be too light or too heavy. If the bow is very powerful, the arrows must be tough and hard. If the bow is light, the arrows must of course be selected accordingly. The most difficult thing is to find arrows of the same quality at one time.

There once existed a type of arrow (kabura-ya) with a sort of ball on the tip, which gave off sounds intended to get rid of evil spirits when the arrow flew through the air. The size of the arrow is in itself beneficent or maleficent: if it is 2 feet, 8 inches (81 cm) long, the arrow is beneficent. In fact, the figure itself is considered to be beneficent. According to Shinto interpretation, the figure 8 represents the circle. It is the sign of infinity, in other words the indeterminate number of things: 8,888,888, etc.

The feathers (eagle or falcon) attached to the arrows also have a meaning. If white feathers are chosen, it is because evil spirits are concealed in dark places and are frightened by white feathers; similarly, the bowstrings made from hemp and pine resin have particular qualities and make very special sounds.

The bow's draw-weight is considerable and measures from 33 to 88 lb (15 to 40 kg). It is generally the thickness of the bamboo surfaces and the different types of wood used which, in part, determine the draw-weight.

The arrow with the white eagle feathers is always used first. It measures from 38 inches (97.5 cm) to 42 inches (1.1 m) long, that is 1.2 inches (3 cm) longer than all the other arrows. It is shot first as much to get rid of evil forces as to serve as a guide mark on the target. The other traditional arrows, four in all, are slightly shorter. They are also made of bamboo but scored with fine grooves. The four arrows, all alike, are grouped in pairs and must also be used in a certain order.

In traditional ceremonial archery, the five arrows are contained in a quiver made of cherry wood. The Japanese know that only the bamboo arrow can provide the sensory pleasure caused by the clearness of the noise made by the string when a shot occurs. Another characteristic of the bow: it is made in such a way that it is twice as light above the grip as below.

When in use, its asymmetrical length allows great beauty of movement; furthermore, the Japanese bow is the only long bow that can be used on horseback. Because it held at the shortest end, it can easily be passed over the horse's neck from one side to the other.

There are three different types of bowmanship: standing, sitting, and on horseback (yabusame).

The standing form includes two aspects (as in all the martial arts): kyu-jitsu, or physical training in bowmanship, the object of which is to hit the target, and shado, which is the spiritual training, the object of which is truth, goodness, and beauty. The latter is primarily what Master Anzawa used to teach.

### HERRIGEL AND MASTER AWA'S TEACHING

In 1923, a German professor of philosophy named Herrigel arrived in Tokyo. After three years spent in learning about Japanese thought, Zen in particular, he met the great master of kyudo: Awa. Under his guidance, Herrigel spent five years learning what he later called *Zen in the Chivalrous Art of Bowmanship,* the title of a small indispensable book describing this experience.

The instruction begins by shooting at the makiwara, a sort of straw bundle on which the novice practices shooting arrows. He learns how to position his feet, draw the bow, control his breathing and his stomach muscles.

The master would take hold of Herrigel's bow and guide his arm in practice, then step back. Herrigel would now be standing with the bow drawn, awaiting the order to shoot. "Not yet," the master would say and Herrigel would begin to tremble with the effort required of him. "Not yet," the master would say again, slapping Herrigel's stomach with the palm of his hand. "Try harder! Stretch your stomach muscles!" he would cry and when the bow was fully drawn: "Breathe out fully but do not breathe in and do not shoot yet." From time to time the master would come up and put his ear against the pupil's nose to check he was not breathing in, and would then slap his stomach and repeat "Not yet, not yet! Patience! Hold on!"

Herrigel would finish the exercise completely exhausted. "As long as you insist on using your strength, you can do nothing," the master would say. "To shoot well, you must forget your physical strength and shoot only with your strength of mind."

It took more than a year's training before Herrigel had mastered the tanden (control over the abdomen and breathing) and could shoot without calling on his physical strength.

Every time the pupil made some progress, the master would let him shoot at the proper target. "Never think of the target when you shoot the arrow," the master would say. "It is a banal action to shoot at the target a hundred times, but if you do shoot a hundred times, it is a sacred action to complete a hundred perfect shots." And again: "To shoot at the target is no different from shooting at one's self."

Herrigel left Sendai Imperial University in August 1929 to return to Germany. He was a new man. Apart from the bow, Master Awa had made him discover the unity of teaching which was also a unity of life: not the skillful execution of the shot but the opposite, a self-control over both mind and techniques, like deep, natural breathing.

### THE THOUGHTS OF MASTER ANZAWA

The shot must enhance a form that is wise and profound, great and supreme. The natural expression of oneself in kyudo must be an accomplishment of the unity of the three principles: Truth, Goodness, and Beauty.

Basic principle: one life, one shot. Spend your whole lifetime shooting one arrow.

The skill is learnt without speech.

If you want to live in harmony with heaven and earth, which is the way of kyudo, do not try to attain the goal. Do not seek the pleasure of reaching the goal; take the path that unites body and soul.

The true form of the shot lies in the identification of the conscience and the act of shooting.

All training lacking in the spirit of the Way can include violence. The shot with no Way is always a mediocre and degenerate shot.

The "true self," that is to say the authentic self, is divinity, Buddheity, or the profound ego (according to which term you prefer) but it is above all the immortal soul that has its place in the stomach (tanden). This pure soul which exists in the tanden works effectively and is the very thing that must be called the "true self."

The disciples of shado who want to live in this supreme and noble Way must never for a moment forget the great spirit of spontaneity, of self-abandon, which enables one to enter the sacred world of the Absolute, of the non-ego, and there to achieve supreme beauty.

So, it is necessary to define the fundamental difference between the Way of bowmanship: kyudo or shado, and the technique: kyujutsu. Kyudo or shado is a means of putting oneself to the test by the relationship that exists between oneself and the target, whilst kyujutsu, from feudal times, principally means the handling of the weapon with a view to murdering the enemy.

DAVE LOWRY

# MATTERS OF CONCENTRATION

"Osu!" Kotaro Sensei murmured a greeting as he strode through the door.

The mystery lady who had refused so many of my requests for instruction, and who was Kaoru, I discovered, Kotaro Sensei's wife, had a voice that intrigued. Sensei's voice, on the other hand, possessed a quality of controlled power that, more than anything else, intimidated. He spoke softly, deliberately punctuating his words.

The polo shirt and slacks he had worn at our previous meeting were gone, replaced by a quilted kimono jacket tucked into the black hakama that rustled with his step. A bokken was in his hand. (The wide-legged hakama are the same kind of trousers once worn by the samurai; a bokken is a sword made of hard oak, shaped and balanced like a real one. This sword is used in kenjutsu practice to avoid the injuries that would soon result from wielding a sharp steel blade.)

Following Mrs. Kotaro's instructions, I was waiting for my first lesson in what I guessed was originally the house's living room; it had been converted into a dojo, a "place for learning the Way." It was expansively empty, bare except for a rack of wooden poles and bokken

---

*In 1968 Dave Lowry, then a teenager living in St. Louis, put himself into the hands of a Japanese swordmaster and thus began an education that set him apart from his adolescent friends. Years later Lowry published his reminiscence of those days mingled with a historical account of the Yagyu Shinkage school of swordsmanship; the book was called* Autumn Lightning: The Education of an American Samurai.

on one wall. On the other side, the space of a second doorway was walled up with planks and remodelled into a small alcove of the kind the Japanese call a tokonoma. Above the tokonoma sat a shelf with a miniature, steep-roofed house perched upon it.

Sensei paused in front of the shelf to bow slowly from the waist. He straightened, stood silently, then turned to me.

"Seiza," he said, gesturing to the floor in front of where I stood.

"Sir?"

"Seiza," he repeated briefly. "You understand? Seiza is sitting down bow."

I understood. The seiza, or formal, seated bow is done by kneeling down, first on the left knee, then on both and sitting back to rest the buttocks on one's heels. In judo and karate dojo, classes are customarily started and concluded this way.

Sensei waited for me to begin. When I did, dropping onto my left knee, I caught the smallest movement in the corner of my eye, a twitch, I thought, of Sensei's shoulders. *Wham!* The bokken smashed into my side with such force that I was pitched over, sprawling onto the floor.

"What the hell is going on?" I wondered while I stumbled to my feet. One of my elbows took the impact of the fall, and I worked it back and forth gingerly, trying also to suck air back into lungs that were emptied by the force of the sword's strike. The throbbing in my side reached from hip to armpit. Sensei's command allowed no more than a couple of seconds for me to wonder what manner of sin I had committed to deserve the assault.

"Try again." A lot more stiffly, still hurting, I tried again, getting no further than before when the bokken came at me in the same unseen way, whacking against my arm, knocking me down again. And again and again. That first afternoon as a bugeisha, I learned that pain concentrated on a specific spot can only be centralized for so long before it will become more general and so, more bearable. In fact, Kotaro Sensei wasn't really hitting me all that hard. It was the terrifying speed of the bokken and the helplessness I felt against it that made me flinch with anticipation. On the fourth or fifth try, I finally glimpsed from where Sensei's sword was coming and, jumping to the side, I succeeded in ducking out of its path. After I managed to bob out of the way when he swung at me a few more times, he nodded, indicating for me to go on. Hands at my sides, I knelt on both knees and, as I expected, Sensei struck hard with the bokken, thrusting it this time so the end of the weapon punched into my chest like a sharp fist. Once more it took repeated tries and several jolting shocks before I could twist away from the blunt point of the sword when it stabbed out at me. Sensei's gaze remained obdurate, expressionless. Still there was no explanation from him and I didn't have a chance to wonder much about it now that my senses were taking over, tuning themselves for self-preservation.

On both knees, I went ahead with the final posture of seiza, easing back to sit on my heels. Since I was facing Sensei fully and wary for the slightest movement, I figured I would be able to dodge any thrust or swing of the bokken, yet just as I pressed my bottom to my heels, my teacher reversed his grip on the sword, striking with it upward at my chin. I jerked my head aside spastically. Even though the bokken wasn't sharp, it was as dangerous as any club and with the speed and force he used, I was certain my jaw would be crushed if hit. The other blows I had begun to anticipate, but the angle of the last attack was completely unexpected. The blood in my temples pumped. Panting, every muscle strained, I waited for Sensei to bring the oak blade down. Instead, he stepped back.

"Good. Now try again."

I stood shakily to begin the whole process again. Kneeling, I pivoted away from the sword's lateral strokes. On my knees, I twisted to let the thrust go past. Sitting back, my head cocked away in time for the upper cuts to whistle by.

"Now, not so much movement," Sensei commanded. "No need to jump a foot," he mimed my wide, frantic dodges, "When sword is only an inch wide." I tried to follow his advice, shifting myself as little as possible to avoid the strikes, and by the end of an hour I could often escape from the bokken without losing my balance or posture. Finally, when I made it all the way to the floor and bowed without being hit once, Sensei returned the bow and slipped into the position of seiza beside and at right angle to me. It is customary for a Japanese of higher status to be seated at such an angle to an inferior, allowing the former to observe the latter without being watched too closely himself. In a culture where attitudes are measured by discerning the slightest of reactions, that arrangement gives the more respected individual a considerable advantage in conversation.

Sensei sighed. "For the bugeisha," he said, "it is not enough to be alert just when holding a weapon. He must be ready for the unexpected every moment, always ready. Sitting down, getting up, eating, sleeping— all the time. The bugeisha has to be aware all the time. We call this, say in Japanese, 'zanshin.'"

• • •

Along with the tremendous social and political turbulence of the Sixties there came a plague of crime. Riots erupted in most cities and with the climate of lawlessness they produced came increasing incidents of rapes and muggings and random violence. More and more Americans began looking for, if not a solution to the problems, at least a personal measure of protection from them. Many turned to the martial arts in the fanciful hope that those disciplines could mold them into invincible masters of self-defense. (Amidst their number, no doubt, were countless males partially motivated by the film exploits of the spy/playboy James Bond, who was the best-known martial artist of that era.)

In community sponsored classes or privately run studios as well as in a variety of books published on the subject, teachers of self-protection advocated a consistently similar approach. If such and such an attack was made, they taught, such and such a response was appropriate. It was a clever assortment of joint locks, strikes, and throws that were practiced until they could be recalled at a moment's notice by the student who then went on his way, secure in the knowledge that he was safe from any threats short of a full-scale Soviet invasion.

As some of these students later discovered to their dismay, the flaw in their instruction was that the muggers and rapists have always had the disconcerting habit of assaulting victims in ways that might not have been covered in self-defense courses. Then too, while adroit kicks and acrobatic throws might be impressive enough in the gym where they were taught, trainees found that their tactics could be a lot more difficult to execute with an armful of groceries in tow, or while bent over, loosening the nuts on a flat tire. When I started my own martial arts training, newspaper stories appeared almost daily recounting incidents of men and women attacked while they were preoccupied with those ordinary tasks, dredging purses and pockets for car keys or waiting absentmindedly for a streetlight to change.

A principal reason why so many of those criminal assaults were successful was not because victims were unable to defend themselves physically—in many incidents they were, or would have been—but because they were unprepared mentally. Under Sensei's tutelage, I learned that the bugeisha of old faced exactly the same problem. He could be superbly skilled with a score of different weapons, but if he was caught off guard, his skills wouldn't have done him any good at all. That is why, in addition to his regular training, the bugeisha made it a constant practice to cultivate zanshin, literally, "continuing mind."

• • •

Zanshin can take many different forms. One afternoon, a couple of months after I had started the study of the bugei, I was upstairs at Sensei's home in the bathroom. Among the first tasks Sensei and his wife had undertaken upon moving into the house on the quiet street was to disconnect and haul out the claw-footed, cast iron tub in the second floor bathroom, to replace it with a Japanese furo. The wooden tub, made of slats bound together with metal bands, was compact, barely wide enough to hold two bathers. A traditional Japanese bath is filled with water heated by a fire built underneath it (a piece of sheet metal forms the tub's bottom, with a wooden rack set over it to prevent the soakers from being burned), and Mrs. Kotaro told me that her husband took considerable convincing before he decided that an open fire was not the most advisable addition to a second story bathroom in a Western home.

The toilet was on the opposite side of the room from the tub and partially screened off by a waist-high panel, but if I leaned over in the squatting, feet-on-the-floor posture nearly all Americans take when emptying their bowels, I could admire the soft, umber-stained finish of the furo's sides and wonder what it would be like to sit and soak in it. Lost in reverie, that's what I was doing when Sensei walked in unannounced to rummage for something in the bathroom closet. He ignored me, as he often did in those days when he wasn't actually teaching me. He found the towel he was looking for and left, leaving me red-faced to finish my business hurriedly.

The next day I found Sensei sitting at the living room table, drinking tea. We talked for a bit and then he pushed back his chair.

"When you use toilet, is like this?" He bent over and propped his elbows on his knees, an Oriental version of Rodin's *Thinker*.

I nodded, "Yes, Sensei."

"What would have happened yesterday," he asked, straightening up, "if I had been bad guy, come breaking in to kill you? Pants down, no way to make strong stance or defend. No zanshin. Too bad, you would have died."

Kotaro Sensei went on to show me how a bugeisha sat properly on the toilet so that even at an awkward moment he retained zanshin. I learned to pull the right leg of my pants completely off and then to sit upright, spine stretched, with my right leg folded over and that foot resting on my left thigh. In that posture he showed me how it was possible to stand quickly. Without the hobble of my pants leg flopping about my ankles, I could move freely to defend myself. Sitting straight, one leg bent in what yoga practitioners might've described as a half-lotus position was also a healthy way for the body to be emptying its wastes, Sensei pointed out, allowing abdominal muscles to be strengthened and taking strain off the lower back.

"Martial arts in the toilet!" I groaned inwardly as he lectured on. When Kotaro Sensei had told me the bugei would change my life, I hadn't guessed it would include instructions for potty training, but he calmly insisted that every action of a bugeisha reflected his quality of zanshin, so I listened carefully.

Though Sensei's lesson was animated and comical—"This is the way old men in Japan sit at benjo, squatting so not to hurt bad knees. . . . Fat men bend over this way, too lazy to do right"—his intent was perfectly serious, for in the days of the samurai, bathrooms and toilets seemed to have been awfully hazardous places. At his castle in Kai Province, Takeda Shingen kept a bokken in a corner of the Japanese version of an outhouse, to ensure against surprise attacks there. His precaution wasn't all that paranoid in light of the circumstances surrounding the death of Uyesugi Kenshin, his lifelong enemy. An assassin secreted himself in the open space underneath the toilet of Uyesugi's private chamber one night and while the general was sitting there the following morning he met what must have been a painful demise when he was stabbed with a short spear. To guard against similar kinds of ambushes in their baths, many samurai customarily soaked with a dirk or short sword in the steaming water beside them—a measure of security, according to annals of the time, that saved more than one life.

Actually, in the bath or anywhere else, my efforts at maintaining zanshin in those early days of my training were not spectacularly successful. An entertaining program on television, an injury at judo practice, or the passing of a young and braless lady would instantly divert my mind from thoughts of self-defense. But I kept on practicing, imagining myself to be the modern counterpart to Matajuro, the hero of a tale told by generations of Yagyu swordsmen.

I first heard of Matajuro from Mrs. Kotaro after I absentmindedly walked through the corner of one of her iris beds and she clipped me on the back of the head with the handle of her hoe. (Between Sensei and his wife, I was beginning to take a lot of whacks with various objects around the house, and while none of them caused any real injury, the bruises they produced were difficult at times to explain to my parents and friends, who couldn't imagine what I kept bumping into.)

• • •

Matajuro was born into the Yagyu family after their clan had already gained a reputation as talented bugeisha. As a boy, his interest in the art of the blade was encouraged. He proved to be a promising but lazy pupil, in danger of never realizing the limits of his potential. In an attempt to shake him from his lethargy, his father banished him from the dojo.

Matajuro was stung by the harshness of the punishment. He was determined to dedicate himself to mastering kenjutsu—even if only to show his family how wrong they had been—so he set off to find a worthy master. The young fencer's travels took him to the province of Kii, to a region of mountains there threaded with forty-eight magnificent waterfalls, some of them cascading over four hundred feet into a rock-bordered pool where mists swirl constantly. In a thick forest at the foot of the Nachi Falls, the tallest and most beautiful of the cataracts, sits the Kumano Nachi Shrine, the site of ancient and mysterious rituals since time began in Japan.

More importantly, as far as Yagyu Matajuro was concerned, was that, according to rumors he'd heard in sake shops and inns along the highway, a swordmaster of incomparable skill was living near the shrine. After a long journey, the young Yagyu reached the Kumano Shrine, where he was told by the priests to follow a barely visible path even further back into the forest. At the end, the priests said, was a senile hermit named Banzo who was reputed to have once been a swordsman. The track led Matajuro to a ramshackle hut.

"I've come to learn swordsmanship," Matajuro announced confidently, although to no one in particular since there wasn't a sign of another person about. Nervously, he softly added, "How long will it take?"

In the doorway of the hut Banzo appeared. "Ten years," he said.

"That's too long." The young Yagyu shook his head. "How about if I work extra hard and practice twice as much?"

"Twenty years," answered Banzo.

Matajuro could guess in what direction the conversation was leading, so wisely he argued no further but simply requested that he be taken as a student, to which the master fully agreed.

It was a peculiar apprenticeship. Matajuro was forbidden to handle a sword or even to speak of fencing. Instead he was put to work cutting firewood, cooking for Banzo, and cleaning the hut, chores that lasted every day from before dawn until after he lit the lanterns that chased away the forest's darkness. Rarely did his master speak and never did he mention anything about teaching the boy swordsmanship.

Finally, after a year of ceaseless work, Matajuro grew frustrated, suspecting at last that he had been tricked into becoming nothing more than a servant for the surely demented Banzo. Angrily chopping at a log one day, he nearly convinced himself to find instruction somewhere else. There were plenty of teachers around who would be honored to have a member of the famous Yagyu family as a student—and plenty of conniving old swordslingers who made slaves of eager, would-be disciples, he concluded bitterly as he eyed the stack of wood still left to be cut. He sank the blade of his axe into a log, as if the cutting could remedy the problems absorbing him. He failed to notice that he was no longer alone until he was sent reeling into the woodpile by a vicious blow. (It was pleasing to me, as Sensei told me the tale of Yagyu Matajuro, to know that we had both had an initial experience in kenjutsu that included being knocked senseless.) Dazed, he looked up from the ground to find the master brandishing a length of hard green bamboo above him. Wordlessly, Banzo left as silently as he had come, leading Matajuro to conclude that his beating was for inattention to his chores.

The offspring of samurai blood was ashamed of slighting his responsibilities, even if he was plotting to leave the crazy old man. He decided to make the next chore of the day, that of washing Banzo's clothes, his last, but he would do such a good job of it that his master could find no fault with his work. It was a couple of hours later, while the boy was scrubbing clothes near the falls, that Banzo struck again, harder this time, driving Matajuro splashing into the water. Behind him, Banzo roared over the dashing of the falls.

"You expect to learn of swordsmanship, but you cannot even dodge a stick!"

Yagyu Matajuro's aristocratic pride was once more inflamed. Just as he had left his home to show his father that he could become a great fencer, he resolved to stay at the Nachi Shrine to prove the old master wrong. He began to concentrate, no matter what else he was doing, on keeping himself ready for an attack. Banzo struck five times a day, then ten, then twenty, always when his student was busy at his chores. He was so stealthy that Matajuro's only warning would be a rustle of hakama or the whoosh of the bamboo stick cutting down. Weeding in the garden, washing at the falls, mending the hut's leaky roof, Matajuro would be occupied with one task or another, to find himself suddenly jumping at the slightest unusual noises and missing more and more of the swipes aimed at him.

When Banzo failed to connect his stick to Matajuro's head or shoulders or even to touch him with it a single time for a period of many months, he switched his strategy. In addition to the daytime assaults, he started slashing at Matajuro while the boy slept. Matajuro was forced to redouble his efforts, teaching himself to sleep lightly with his unconsciousness remaining alert. Grimly he realized that the more successful he became at avoiding the bamboo stick, the more frequently it was lashed at him. Seventy, eighty, a hundred times a day and night his master would appear like a ghost, swinging at him. It was growing increasingly harder for Banzo to catch him unaware, though, for his instincts were sharpened to a level almost supernatural.

On an evening four years after he had first come looking for the sword master at the Nachi Shrine, Matajuro was preparing a meal of chirashizushi, a steamed mixture of rice and vegetables. He was carefully peeling a burdock root for the dish when Banzo struck from behind. Matajuro didn't move from his crouching position by the fire. With one hand, he snatched up a pot lid and fended off the blow, then returned to his cooking without a pause.

That night, Banzo presented his student with a certificate of full proficiency in the art of fencing and a fine old sword, Matajuro needed neither. Without ever taking a formal lesson or even handling a weapon, he had reached the highest peak of the bugei—the master of zanshin.

The walk between Sensei's house and my own home took me through a couple of acres of neatly manicured grass and trees that were preserved as a park on the homesite of the city's first resident. Even in the heat of the September evening, when I began my training in the bugei, the park's air was pleasantly fresh. Squirrels scampered about, hiding walnuts for the coming winter. Toddlers explored with faltering steps only to be called back by parents who lounged on blankets spread under the trees, listening to the impromptu concerts of university music students. Along the border of the park ran a stream contained by WPA workers during the Depression into a channel made of natural stone and mortar. Bridges of the same construction spanned the stream.

I made it to one of the bridges before fatigue dragged me down and I slid down the face of the channel and stretched myself out with my back to the coolness of the bridge's concrete base. Above me hummed the tires of cars. Beyond my feet the dark ribbon of the stream trickled softly. Inside, I ached. My arms were still numbed with the battering they had taken from Sensei's bokken, and my calves and thighs throbbed from the unaccustomed exertion of crouching in seiza. In addition to the physical pain, Sensei had overwhelmed me by delivering all his instructions in a pidgin mixture of Japanese and English that continued to reel in my mind long after I had bowed a final time and left the dojo. Since his English wasn't normally that poor, I imagined that it was a plan to confuse me and cause me to quit in discouragement. Kotaro Sensei's final words to me that evening, though, were a lift.

"Next time you try make zanshin again," he said. "More practice, more practice, get better. So, hakkeyoi."

From judo I knew "hakkeyoi" was a colloquial expression that meant "Keep at it." Alone under the bridge massaging my bruised legs until they felt good enough to carry me home, I hoped that I would.

## PART IV
# OTHER ASPECTS

## DONALD N. LEVINE

# THE LIBERAL ARTS AND THE MARTIAL ARTS

A compleat rhetoric for liberal education must address the following six questions:

1. What is "liberal" about liberal education?
2. What kinds of cultural forms are most suitable for the constitution of a liberal program?
3. What kinds of individual capacities should liberal training foster?
4. What are the characteristics of training programs designed to cultivate those capacities?
5. What is the relationship between liberal and utilitarian learning?
6. What is the ethical justification of liberal learning?

In what follows I propose to clarify these questions by asking what we might gain by comparing the liberal arts with the martial arts—those forms of physical training and expression epitomized in the cultures of East Asia by kung fu, t'ai chi ch'uan, judo, karate-do, kendo, and aikido. My point is not to argue that some form of athletic training ought to be an integral part of the liberal curriculum, though on that question I find myself in accord with the views expressed by William Rainey Harper, who said, "The athletic work of the students is a vital part of student life. . . . The athletic field, like the gymnasium, is one of the University laboratories and by no means the least important one."

---

*Since 1980 Levine (b. 1931) has been Dean of the College at the University of Chicago. A Guggenheim fellow and author of many books and articles, he has concerned himself in his writings with the interplay of sociology, philosophy, and culture.*

My argument, rather, is that courses of training in the martial arts often constitute exemplary educational programs, and that we might learn something of value for the liberal arts by examining them closely. Just to propose this will perhaps seem to some an act of buffoonery. To suggest that the martial arts are worthy of consideration on the same plane at that usually reserved for the liberal arts—surely that is nothing more than a bad pun. So I must begin by justifying my brazenness in coupling the arts, liberal and martial.

Before proceeding to justify my topic, however, I must confess that one thing about it is indeed gauche. Its two contrasting terms, "liberal" and "martial," are not logically comparable. For "martial" refers to a kind of content—physical training for self-defense—while "liberal" refers to a quality of approach in training. A logical contrast to the martial arts would be either some other kind of physical training, or else some kind of nonphysical training—which, of course, is what we have in mind, what might be called mental of intellectual arts. The logical contrast to liberal would be ... illiberal. If we provisionally define liberal arts as signifying pursuits undertaken for the sake of personal growth and self-development, then it is clearly the case that both the martial arts and the intellectual arts have both liberal and illiberal forms. So the comparison I want to make here is between the liberal (intellectual) arts and the (liberal) martial arts.

So rephrased, my topic will be justified by arguing that the very culture that originated and legitimated the basic conception of liberal arts we follow in the West supported, at the same time, a conception of martial training as an integral part of the ideal educational program; and that, moreover, the tradition that provided the matrix for the martial arts in the East saw them as a part of what can be called an Oriental program of liberal education as well. Once I have defended those propositions, I shall turn to the comparison that is the heart of this exercise.

I

To talk about liberal training is to talk about a form of education that emerged historically only in two very special cultures, those of classical Greece and China. In ancient Greece, this kind of educational aspiration was linked to the ideal of paedeia, the notion of using culture as a means to create a higher type of human being. According to Werner Jaeger, who wrote a celebrated book on the subject, the Greeks believed that education in this sense "embodied the purpose of all human effort. It was, they held, the ultimate justification for the existence of both the individual and the community." That ennobling education took two major forms that were equally praised by the writers of ancient Greece, albeit with different emphases at different times—the cultivation of combative skills, on the one hand, and the contemplative intellect, on the other.

To see the affinity between the martial arts and the arts of contemplation in ancient Greece, let us look at two notions central to Greek thought: the concept of arete and the understanding of the divine.

Arete, often translated by the word "virtue," was the Greek term that conveyed the notion of qualitative excellence. Arete signified a special power, an ability to do something; its possession was the hallmark of the man of nobility. The same term arete was used to designate both the special powers of the body, such as strength and vigor, and the powers of the mind, such as sharpness and insight. In the Homeric epics, martial prowess was the kind of arete that was preeminently extolled, but with Xenophanes and other writers of the sixth century B.C., the attainment of sophia, or intellectual culture, was hailed as the path to arete. Although Xenophanes wrote in a rather polemical vein against the older ideals of martial arete, most classical Greek writers embraced them both. Thus, the poet Simonides could write, "How hard it is to become a man of true arete, four-square and faultless in hand and foot and mind." For Plato and Aristotle, the list of preeminent virtues begins with courage, and ends with philosophic wisdom (with prudence and justice in the middle).

Although the Greeks are best known to us as the progenitors of secular science and philosophy, they are known to classical scholars as a God-intoxicated people as well. And, so far as I can tell, there are preeminently two human activities that are repeatedly described as divine in Greek thought—the achievements of victors in athletic contests, and the activities of philosophic speculation. Since earliest known history Greek gymnastic activity was connected with the festivals of the gods. The four great pan-Hellenic games, of which the Olympics was the most famous, were cloaked in religious symbolism; thus, both the Olympian and the Nemean games were held in honor of Zeus. As Norman Gardiner has written of the former, the games were "much more than a mere athletic meeting. It was the national religious festival of the whole Greek race." The poetry of Pindar celebrated this linkage with . . . Pindaric rapture. In his triumphal hymns for victors of the athletic contests, Pindar expressed the religious significance of the spectacle of men struggling to bring their humanity to perfection in victorious combat.

One finds the pursuit of metaphysical speculation described with tones no less transcendent. Greek natural philosophers of the sixth century created a conception of a cosmos under the rule of law that offered a focus for their religious ideals; and Pindar's contemporary, Heraclitus, developed a doctrine that located man in that cosmos, one that held that "through its kinship with the 'everlasting fire' of the cosmos the philosophical soul is capable of knowing divine wisdom and harbouring it in itself." A century later, Plato and Aristotle in different ways depicted the activity of philosophic contemplation of pure Being as the most godlike of human activities.

In the classic Greek synthesis, then, the arts of combat and the arts of intellect were conjointly eulogized. They were the vehicles of that supreme educational effort, the cultivation of the virtues, and of the journey to transcendence. In both, the Greeks found a supreme expression of their aesthetic quest, the beauty of the bodily form perfected, and the beauty of the universe refracted in the contemplation of pure cosmic forms.

By the end of the fifth century, however, the unity of body and spirit that Simonides and others idealized became fractured. Due to heightened importance of prizes and spectators, the athletic games became much more competitive. Athletics became professionalized; physical training no longer sought all-round development but aimed to produce strength at the expense of vitality, health, and beauty. More-over, once the Greeks began to feel that the spirit was separate from or even hostile to the body, Jaeger tells us, "the old athletic ideal was degraded beyond hope of salvation, and at once lost its important position in Greek life."

During the Hellenistic period, the liberal program underwent changes that were fateful for the subsequent evolution of education in the West. Although athletic sports continued as a popular public spectacle, their formative role as part of liberal training declined markedly, and disappeared altogether by the time of the Christian period. There was a similarly progressive decline and eventual disappearance of artistic, especially musical, education, which had also been a major component of education in the classical period. What emerged as the sole respectable form of liberal education was literary studies.

During the Roman period the literary curriculum was further elaborated, particularly the study of grammar and rhetoric. Although early Christian fathers were suspicious of these pagan subjects, by the fourth century A.D. Christian leaders like Augustine embraced major elements of the classical curriculum. Consequently, when the barbarian invasions had swept aside the traditional Roman schools, the Christian church, needing a literary culture for the education of its clergy, kept alive many of the educational traditions that Rome had adapted from the Hellenistic world.

By the sixth century A.D. the clergy had rationalized the literary curriculum into the trivium—the art of logic, grammar, and rhetoric—and a few centuries later institutionalized the quadrivium—the ancient Pythagorean program of mathematics consisting of arithmetic, geometry, astronomy, and music.

In the ninth century, Charlemagne restored some semblance of higher studies, drawing on traditions that had been maintained in Italian and Irish monasteries. The Carolingian Renaissance, reinforced by the rise of scholasticism, the beginnings of law and medicine as professions, and the recovery of classical knowledge nourished the liberal arts curriculum until it was securely established in the medieval university. During the Renaissance this curriculum was enriched by an emphasis on the humanistic significance of the classic texts. The Reformation brought a renewed effort to subordinate the trivium and quadrivium to religious materials and purposes.

The liberal arts tradition (in its English manifestation) came to America with the Puritan divines in Massachusetts. Liberal education came to be instituted in the American college in a framework that combined Protestant piety and mental discipline. The mental discipline approach, justified in English and Scottish moral philosophy, held that mental faculties were best developed through their exercise. In the course of recitations in the areas of Latin, Greek, and mathematics, the student disciplined mental and moral faculties such as will, emotion, and intellect. As William F. Allen wrote: "The student who has acquired the habit of never letting go a puzzling problem—say a rare Greek verb—until he has analyzed its every element, and understands every point in its etymology, has the habit of mind which will enable him to follow out a legal subtlety with the same accuracy."

The rapid modernization of American society after the Civil War gave rise to new perspectives on the role of higher education. Laurence Veysey has identified three rationales of academic reform, which came to compete with that of "mental discipline" in the late nineteenth century. He calls these the programs of utility, research, and liberal culture. The advocates of utility argued that the American university should prepare students to serve the needs of American society for skilled leadership in modern industry, business, and government. Inspired by the model of the German university, the advocates of research insisted that the sole mission of the American university should be the furthering of the frontiers of knowledge. The advocates of liberal culture, however, condemned utility for its crass philistinism, and research for its encouragement of what they considered sterile specialization. In their emphasis on a refined sense of value, through the study of language and literature, the advocates of liberal culture in late nineteenth century America harkened back to the humanists of the Renaissance. The discovery of an essential and irreducible humanity, which they called "character," was made possible by breadth of learning. This, together with the aim of self-realization, was the appropriate rationale for higher education according to such advocates of liberal culture as Barrett Wendell, Charles Eliot Norton, Andrew F. West, and Woodrow Wilson. Such was the intellectual background behind those well-known experiments in the liberal curriculum following World War I associated with the general education program at Columbia, with Alexander Meiklejohn at Amherst and Wisconsin, and with the Hutchins College at the University of Chicago.

## II

Contemporary with the archaic and classical periods of ancient Greece, in China during the Chou dynasty we find an educational program that bears significant resemblance to that of the Greeks. The goal of education was to produce a broadly cultivated person, and this included training both in literary and martial subjects. The curriculum codified during the Chou period consisted of six subjects, often referred to as the liberal arts of classical Chinese education: rituals, music, archery, charioteering, writing, and mathematics. According to the historian Ping Wen Kuo, "A liberal education included five kinds of ritual, five kinds of music, five ways of archery, five ways of directing a chariot, six kinds of writing, and nine operations of mathematics. . . . The training was moral, physical, and intellectual in character. . . . The ideal of education of the time of the Chou seems to have been the harmonious and symmetrical development of the body and mind, and may be said to represent a combination of Spartan and Athenian ideals of education, which called for a training at once intellectual and moral, as well as physical and military."

During the latter sixth century B.C., Confucius articulated the conception of the ideal person to be produced by this Chinese version of paedeia. He defined that ideal as one who possesses wisdom and courage, who is also magnanimous and accomplished in courtesy, ceremonial, and music. He heavily stressed the virtue of sincerity and held that education was a means to gain an enlightened mind, enlightened in the sense of coming to grasp the remarkable harmonies of nature.

In later centuries this ideal of liberal learning was eroded as the study of Confucian texts became viewed in a more utilitarian vein, simply as preparation for the requirements of bureaucratic office. The martial subjects were dropped from the standard curriculum. However, new forms of martial training were incorporated in disciplines followed in Chinese monasteries. To understand that development, we must digress for a moment to ancient India.

When the Hindus rationalized a program of muscular and breathing training in the discipline of yoga, they created a system directed toward the perfection of the body with the intent of making it a fit instrument for spiritual perfection—a perfection consisting of beauty, grace, strength, and adamantine hardness. At an early stage in the development of Buddhism, systematic physical training became a central component of religious discipline. It is said that Gautama was so impressed with Indian fist-fighting as an effective method of unifying mind and body that fist art was incorporated into the framework of Buddhism. This can be seen in the images of certain gods of the Buddhist pantheon—the two Guardian deities, the Devas, and the twelve Divine Generals—who appear in ancient fist-fighting stances.

The movement of Buddhism to China was not only a fateful episode to the history of Buddhism but in the evolution of the martial arts as well. The agent of that migration was the Buddhist monk Boddhidharma, considered the twenty-eighth patriarch in a direct line from Gautama Buddha. In the sixth century A.D., Boddhidharma journeyed from India to China, where he introduced the form of Buddhism known as Dhyana (in Sanskrit), Ch'an (in Chinese), and Zen (in Japanese). While in China, Boddhidharma lived at the Shaolin Monastery in Honan Province. He found the monks there solely concerned with achieving spiritual enlightenment and negligent of their physical health. In fact, they were sickly and fell asleep during zazen (seated meditation). As a member of the kshatriya (warrior class) as well as a monk, Boddhidharma was very well versed in the fighting arts and understood the interdependence of mental, physical, and spiritual health. He introduced a series of eighteen exercises (the "eighteen hands of the Lo-han") to the monks for the improvement of their health and for their protection against dangerous forces. These exercises became the basis of Shaolin Temple boxing, which, along with other varieties of Chinese boxing, later influenced the development of the fighting arts in Japan, Korea, and Okinawa.

A second line of development in the liberal martial arts of Asia derives from another Chinese religious tradition, that of Taoism. T'ai chi ch'uan (grand ultimate boxing) was evolved to combine certain forms of Shaolin boxing with an emphasis on breathing and inner control based on Taoist breathing practices and medical lore. According to the most prevalent account of the origins of t'ai chi, a Taoist monk of the late Sung Dynasty (twelfth or thirteenth century A.D.), Chang San-feng, created the thirteen basic postures of t'ai chi as bodily expressions of the eight trigrams of the ancient text *I Ching*, and the five basic elements of ancient Chinese cosmology. Somewhat later, a school teacher named Wang Chang-yueh is believed to have linked those postures in a continuous sequence of movement that formed the disciplinary core of the t'ai chi training program.

Yet another set of innovations in the martial arts took place in Japan following the rise of the samurai class after the tenth century and the introduction of Zen Buddhism there in the twelfth century. From this time the culture of bushido, the "way of the warrior," developed gradually from ideas drawn from Buddhism, Confucianism, and Shintoism. Samurai training included unarmed combat, the use of weapons, literary subjects, and training in Zen Buddhism, which provided the courage to face possible death every day. Following the unification and pacification of Japan during the Tokugawa Shogunate, many samurai adapted that Buddhist strain to transform the martial arts from illiberal to liberal uses, vehicles for training that emphasized the spiritual development of participants.

After the suppression of the samurai under the Meiji regime in the latter part of the nineteenth century, new martial arts were specifically created as forms of liberal training. This was the same period, incidentally, when Yang Lu-Chan for the first time taught t'ai chi publicly, in Beijing; until then it had been a secret heritage carefully guarded by certain elite Chinese families. In Japan a number of masters sought to revive the old bushido-Zen ethic by creating new forms that were nonlethal in intent and designed to provide personal growth and spiritual uplift. In 1882, Jigoro Kano, an educator proficient in jiujutsu, founded the first Judo Institute in Tokyo. The change from jiujutsu to judo exemplifies, in terminology and practice, the self-conscious transformation of the martial arts from lethal weapons to means of self-development. The suffix "jitsu" means technique; jiujutsu was, thus, a technique for inflicting serious damage on an opponent. The suffix "do" means "way." It derives from the Chinese Tao, and in Japanese has connotations related to the outlook of Taoism. More fully, "do" means the way to enlightenment, self-realization, and understanding. As conceived by Jigoro Kano, judo—literally, the gentle way—adapted the best techniques from jiujutsu, eliminated the harmful ones, and modified others so they could be practiced safely. As practiced by Kano and his followers, the aim of judo is to perfect oneself by systematic training of the mind and body so that each person works in harmony with others.

Comparable developments took place a little later with other arts. Around 1905, when karate was introduced from Okinawa into mainland Japan, the symbol kara (signifying "Tang," or "Chinese,") was reinterpreted by invoking another meaning of the word kara: "empty." This was to allude not only to the idea of fighting with empty hands—without weapons—but also to the notion of "emptiness" in Zen, that is to say, emptiness of mind, mind like a mirror or water that reflects without distortion, and thus to connote the ideals of selflessness, austerity, and humbleness. Later, this philosophic component was stressed by adding the suffix "do," and some of the preeminent schools now refer to themselves as teaching karate-do; that is, the way of life centering on the empty hand.

In the early 1920s, when experiments to revive liberal learning began to flourish in the United States, a gifted master experienced in all the traditional Japanese martial arts, Morihei Ueshiba, evolved a new system which he called aikido. In this art, he created a program for the cultivation of ki, the cosmic energy that flows through one's body and is thought to produce health and spiritual uplift, and the capacity for ai, harmonious blending, a blending of the forces within oneself, with other people, and with the natural universe.

A major institutional locus of the martial arts in the Far East today is the educational system. They have come out of the secrecy of monasteries and esoteric cults into the curricula of school systems and the clubs of universities. Although divided into hundreds of specialized forms, which vary considerably in style, techniques, attitudes, and objectives, what can arguably be called their most rationalized forms—those that involve a coherent approach to dealing with aggressive attacks, a systematic approach to training, and a nontrivial grounding in philosophic beliefs—all pursue the goals of developing a harmonious blending of mental and physical powers, a sensitivity to the responses of others, the virtues of calmness and courage under stress, and some form of an experience of transcendence.

This survey of the paedetic curriculum in two great traditions suggests, then, that the coupling of the intellectual and the martial arts is no mere trick of the tongue. Indeed, my sketch suggests that developments within the two traditions where each was perfected exhibit some instructive evolutionary parallels. 1) By the sixth century B.C., both in Greece and China, an ideal and a program of liberal training had evolved, which included both intellectual and martial components. 2) In both cases, this ideal became corrupted in later centuries, as combative arts became commercialized in the Hellenistic period, and as Confucian training became bureaucratized. 3) During the sixth century A.D., a liberal component of the older curriculum became codified and institutionalized in those havens of ideal pursuits, the monasteries. 4) In the medieval period, these paedetic curricula became enriched and extended, with the firm establishment of the trivium and quadrivium in medieval universities, and of the arts of kung fu and t'ai chi ch'uan in Chinese monasteries. 5) In the late nineteenth century, mainly in the United States and Japan, the ideals of those curricula were revived and propagated in the form of new secular programs of liberal training.

III

Let us proceed now to draw on these suggestive parallels between the intellectual arts and the martial arts to address the set of questions I posed at the outset. To begin with, what is liberal about liberal education?

The terms in which Westerners are inclined to think about the distinction between education that is liberal and education that is not—or illiberal, or banausic—were classically formulated by Aristotle. Aristotle's emphasis was not so much on different kinds of subjects as on the spirit in which a subject out of utility, as reading, is useful because it enables one to find numbers in a telephone directory. Or one may pursue a subject because, as we would say, of peer pressure: It is the fashionable "thing to do." But by definition, to act from necessity is not the mark of being free; to seek for utility everywhere is not suited for men who are great-souled and free; and to follow some pursuit because of the opinion of other people, says Aristotle, would appear to be acting in a menial and servile manner. In contrast to these kinds of motives,

Aristotle describes motives for the sort of learning that befits a free person: learning that is undertaken for its own sake, learning that is appropriate for promoting happiness and a good life. And, although Aristotle certainly does not deny the need to study the useful arts, he insists that they should not constitute the whole point of learning: People should study drawing, he urges, not merely to avoid being cheated in buying and selling furniture, but for the liberal reason that this study makes one observant of bodily beauty.

Now one does not need to turn to the martial arts to catch the import of Aristotle's distinction, although it may be useful to see how readily it can be exemplified in that domain. Illiberal training in the martial arts, then, would be undertaken out of necessity—learning to fight to prevent your community from being enslaved or slaughtered by an invader; or, for utility—to know how to defend yourself in case you happen to get mugged on the street. And there are other kinds of reasons for studying the martial arts that would render the pursuit illiberal—as when one trains because it is the glamorous thing to do, or to impress one's friends. By contrast, when the martial arts are taught and practiced in a liberal manner, it is for the sake of perfecting oneself as a human being and for acquiring a kind of culture that is intrinsically valuable.

At this juncture, I'd like to share an observation from my own experience with the martial arts that suggests an instructive elaboration on the Aristotelian notion of liberality in education. When I ask persons who have progressed rather deeply into the study of the martial arts why they are doing it, I get an answer that is typically different from what brings people to training in the first place. The reasons why people begin martial arts training are frequently illiberal: for self-defense, or to cure an ailment, or as an outlet for aggression, or because of social inducements. Once they have been training for a while, their motivations usually undergo some subtle change. By the time one has been actively training for a year or two, the reasons tend to converge on a single rationale: I'm training to perfect my mastery of the art. What emerges is the sense of a lifelong quest for perfection, wherein each moment is intrinsically satisfying, but the experience is framed as a part of an unlimited pursuit of growth and improved expression. One is reminded of what John Dewey wrote concerning the fine arts: that "the works of the fine arts are not merely ends in themselves which give satisfaction, but their creation and contemplation whet the appetite for new effort and achievement and thus bring a continuously expanding satisfaction." What this suggests is a criterion for liberal learning that amends the familiar classical definitions: that education is free and liberating insofar as it involves the quest for mastery of some domain of autonomous forms, forms that are in themselves the free creation of human spirit. And because that world of form is in principle limitless, this entails a connection with transcendence that is part of the attraction toward liberal learning.

So I would add, as another component of the generic definition of liberal education, martial and intellectual, that it is an enterprise devoted to the acquisition of cultural forms for their own sake. Having said this, my next question is then: what types of cultural forms are most suitable for a liberal program?

Once we have distinguished liberal education from the various illiberal forms of training—training for occupations, for solving particular social problems, for transmitting a certain tradition, and the like— there remains the more complicated problem of defining the best content for a liberal curriculum. Different philosophies of liberal education tend to take one of three positions. One position holds that the liberal curriculum should consist of a set of fundamental questions and plausible answers, e.g., those contained in a list of Great Books, or those simply having to do with the nature of the world and man's place in it. A second position holds that the liberal curriculum should consist of the most important structures of organized knowledge, e.g., basic acquaintance with the principal disciplines of the humanities, social sciences, and natural sciences. A third position holds that the liberal curriculum should represent primarily those basic modes of inquiry and expression exemplified in the disciplines, e.g. how a scientist conducts experiments, or how a poet constructs a sonnet.

A strong case could be made for viewing each of these as the central principle for a liberal curriculum, and perhaps an even stronger case for a perspective that attempted to represent them all in some balanced way. But what all of them have in common is a stress on what Georg Simmel called objective culture: the external representations of reality and the externalized expressions of meaning that have been created in human history. The true cultivation of individuals, by contrast, takes place in what Simmel called subjective culture: the personal growth that comes about through the internal appropriation of cultural forms.

The advantage of looking at the martial arts in this context is that such training is almost exclusively concerned with the development of subjective culture—in this case, the competences of bodily movement that enable one to defend oneself in certain stylized ways. There is simply no way to think about the martial arts curriculum without dealing with the ways in which personal capacities of various sorts—perceiving, moving, responding—are nurtured and shaped and perfected. Thus, the martial arts curriculum provides a model for a kind of liberal training in which the principle of the learner's capacities is unmistakably and unavoidably at the center of attention. Although this principle was prominent in early nineteenth-century American notions of liberal intellectual learning, which focused on the goal of mental discipline, it has fallen by the way in contemporary discussions. The principle deserves, I believe, to be revived and viewed afresh as an important basis for organizing the modern liberal curriculum.

Once we have set the cultivation of subjective capacities as a primary goal of liberal education, however, we must deal with what is perhaps the most complicated of all the questions in the theory and practice of liberal education: What competences should be cultivated? And the obvious answer to that question is another question: What competences are there? Open ten books about competences, and you will find seventeen lists. How does one compose an inventory of competences that can be ordered and ranked so as to provide a set of priorities for liberal education?

Because I do not think this is a matter that can be resolved definitively for all time, or even that there is a single best way to resolve it at any given moment, I would not look to the martial arts for a model of how to solve it. The problem of identifying a basic list of competences is nearly as intractable in the martial as in the intellectual arts. But the martial arts can be helpful on the question, because they illustrate so transparently what the issues are and how one might grapple with them.

The complications here stem from the fact that disciplines emerge historically as concrete traditions, while technical competences can be generalized and used across a variety of disciplines. For example, aikido is a tradition that uses diffused energy, circular body movements, and wrist and elbow throws, while karate relies on concentrated energy, direct body movements, and punches, blocks, and kicks. Yet in both of them a basic movement is the straightforward punch. Moreover, both have a variety of defenses against said punch. So one could imagine a type of competence called punching and responding to punching, the first learnable within either of the two arts but usable beyond, the other requiring some new curricular effort to bring together a wide variety of defenses against punches into a single training program. Just in the last few years, in fact, some martial arts programs have come out with eclectic training approaches not unlike this.

There is, moreover, a set of generalized competences involved in various ways in all the martial arts that may be formulated as follows: Know oneself; know the other; and observe the right timing in one's response to the other. The idea of self-knowledge in the martial arts is tied to a concern for being centered. One must be in touch with the true center of one's being. One must be unified, the hands with the arms, the limbs with the torso, the body with the feelings and the mind. One must be poised in a state between relaxation and readiness to move—at all times. In the words of the seventeenth-century martial artist, Miyamoto Musashi, "Do not become tense and do not let yourself go. Keep your mind on the center and do not waver. Calm your mind, and do not cease the firmness for even a second. Always maintain a fluid and flexible, free and open mind."

And yet preoccupation with oneself and one's readiness to act, by itself, would be foolhardy. One must be alert to the dispositions and responses of others no less. One must be aware of the other's balance points, the "four corners" of his position in which he is vulnerable. One must sense the precise direction and intensity of an attack from the other. In aikido, the term ai, or harmony, refers in an important sense to the idea of blending effectively with the energy of one's attacker.

Finally, the relational field between self and other must be viewed in dynamic terms, such that the timing of one's response to the other is all important. It does no good to be centered in oneself, and aware of the flow of the other's energy, if one responds too soon, or too late, to the other's attack. So a great deal of emphasis in training focuses on these three areas: how to maintain one's own center; how to perceive and blend in with the energy of the other; and how to time one's responses with pinpoint precision.

What this suggests for the intellectual arts is that we might well start looking for basic forms of intellectual competence that are not tied to concrete traditions. In my judgment, this constitutes one of the most exciting challenges facing the academic profession today. Those who are honest about the matter acknowledge that a concrete tradition—sociology, say, or biochemistry—is rarely coterminous with a particular set of competences. I know, for example, that the distinctive skills needed to analyze social phenomena in the economistic terms of rational exchange, or the culturological terms of symbolic codes, are practiced across all of the social science disciplines, including cultural anthropology and economics. The challenge today is to take stock of the enormous changes in all the intellectual disciplines over the last few decades and, for purposes of liberal training, attempt to translate them into competence fields that can be truly defensible components of a future liberal curriculum.

Closely connected to the question of what subjective capacities are to be cultivated in the liberal curriculum is that of the kind of training program best suited to develop those capacities. On this question, I believe, training programs in the martial arts offer much that might be relevant to the design of training programs in the intellectual arts. Of many possible suggestions, let me mention two:

The first is the stress on practice—regular, systematic, unremitting practice. The components of each art must be identified and laid out in such a way as to admit increasing mastery through incessant practice. As Miyamoto Musashi has written: "Practicing a thousand days is said to be a discipline, and practicing ten thousand days is said to be refining." One must practice continuously, and make a lot of mistakes, so that one can be corrected, and be ever on the lookout for ways to refine one's art.

Second, there is a sequence of phases in developing the practice of one's art. Gradations of rank, marked by a succession of tests that examine clearly defined levels of competence, form a crucial part of the training. Beyond that, there is a kind of progression, common to all arts, that I would call the road to the transcendence of mere technique. One begins by self-consciously practicing a certain technique. One proceeds slowly, deliberately, reflectively, but one keeps on practicing until the technique becomes internalized and one is no longer self-conscious when executing it. After a set of techniques has been thoroughly internalized, one begins to grasp the principles behind them. And finally, when one has understood and internalized the basic principles, one no longer responds mechanically to a given attack, but begins to use the art creatively and in a manner whereby one's individual style and insights can find expression.

Notions like these seem to me enormously suggestive for training programs in the intellectual arts. As one of their possible implications, I would stress the importance of some specialization as an essential component of a truly liberal education. There is simply no way to acquire any art to the point where it becomes truly effective as a means of advanced personal growth without the intensity of involvement that requires years of work and progressive mastery. Whether the capacity in question is knowing how to interpret an ancient text, or how to perform chemical experiments in the lab, or to formulate and analyze a problem of public policy, an enormous amount of practice is required in order to be able to progress in some field from techniques to principles to expression (and, indeed, if you will, to develop a sense of personal groundedness and sensitivity to the objects and knowledge of how and when to time interventions). That is the rationale, I believe, for including concentration programs as an integral component of a full curriculum in liberal education.


IV


I want now to discuss the question of the relationship between liberal and utilitarian learning. The rhetoric of liberal educators vacillates between two apparently contradictory positions. On the one hand, we say that liberal training is a good in itself, superior in worth to those illiberal pursuits that are merely practical. On the other hand, we often say that liberal education is really the most practical of all. Is this just double-talk, somewhat like saying: I never borrowed your book, and besides, I returned it to you last week?

Perhaps, but let us look at the martial arts once more to see if some clarification of this matter can be found. In the martial arts, the question of practical utility is always right at hand. In training dojos one often hears an instructor make some offhand reference to what might happen in real situations—"on the street," as they say. Yet nothing could be more clearcut than the difference between an applied training program in self-defense and a liberal curriculum in the martial arts. If you want to acquire some immediate skills for the street, I would say: don't take up one of the martial arts, but take a crash eight-week course in self-defense; just as I would say, if all you want is a job as a lab technician or an interviewer in a survey research organization, take a crash vocational course in those areas. Yet there is, I believe, a higher practical value in the liberal form of self-defense training. By proceeding to the point where one has mastered the basic principles of the art of self-defense, one has acquired resources for responding to a much wider range of threatening situations and a readiness to respond that flows from basic qualities of self-control, calmness, and courage that one has internalized as a result of years of dedicated training. It certainly would be advantageous to combine some techniques of practical self-defense with a liberal martial training—remember that Aristotle, after all, advocated that training in useful arts can be combined with liberal training—but then the former are enhanced by being grounded in a broader conception of the principles of direct combat. The argument may proceed similarly in regard to the liberal intellectual arts: by learning not merely the specific facts and techniques of a particular subject matter but its most basic principles and methods and by understanding these as exemplified in a range of fields, one has gained capacities that enable one to respond intelligently and independently, critically, and creatively, to the conditions of a complex and rapidly changing environment, the kind of environment in which all of us are now fated to spend our lives. This is like the ideal that Pericles attributed to the free citizens of Athens, "To be able to meet every variety of circumstance with the greatest versatility—and with grace."

The last question I want to raise in this comparative exercise may be put as follows: Isn't there something basically immoral in this program for liberal training? Doesn't it focus too much on the individual at the expense of the community? What's worse, couldn't it simply set people up—by training them in the arts—to carry out amoral or even vicious purposes? No matter how much the arts are glamorized, do they not only amount to sets of technical skills that can be put to evil purposes? And if my argument that liberal training produces a higher form of utilitarian competence is sound, then does it not follow that the person with an advanced liberal education has the capacity to be more evil than others?

Certainly this is a question that can never be far from the mind of those training in the martial arts. Indeed, the old masters in Asia were often very selective about whom they allowed to train with them, for they feared the consequences of putting their lore into the hands of those who might use these very potent powers for destructive purposes. In Japanese culture there is in fact a social type associated with that negative possibility—the ninja. The ninja is precisely one who has mastered martial techniques but puts them to selfish or destructive purposes. And I must say, before we liberal educators take too much pride in offering a wholly blameless product, that we must come to terms with the possibility of creating intellectual ninjas—people who are very adept indeed in the manipulation of linguistic and mathematical symbols, and other intellectual capacities, and use them in the service of the basest opportunistic motives and even for destructive purposes.

To say this is to raise the most fundamental issue of all about the liberal arts: the need for an ideological framework in which they find some ethical grounding. Precisely because the immoral potentialities of martial arts are so transparent, this question is harder to dodge. It is answered forthrightly by ethical formulations associated with the educational programs of all those martial arts I would call liberal today. In a manual of t'ai chi ch'uan, for example, one reads:

> The technique of self-defense... implies a coherent vision of life that includes self-protection. The world is viewed as an ever-changing interplay of forces. Each creature seeks to realize its own nature; to find its place in the universe. Not to conquer, but to endure. The assumption is that there are hostile forces. One can be attacked by animals, by angry or arrogant people, or just by the forces of Nature, within and without. In the human world, attack is verbal and emotional as often as it is physical. The most subtle and manipulative struggles are the ones of which we are the least conscious. But the prescription for survival is always the same— integrity. [In the martial arts] this is more than a moral adage, it is a physical actuality.

The practice of aikido is suffused by the kind of ethical vision embodied in these words by its founder, Morihei Ueshiba:

> Understand Aikido first as budo and then as a way of service to construct the World Family.
>
> True budo is the loving protection of all beings with a spirit of reconciliation. Reconciliation means to allow the completion of everyone's mission.
>
> True budo is a work of love. It is a work of giving life to all beings, and not killing or struggling with each other. . . . Aikido is the realization of love.

V

As college educators face the need to develop a fresh rhetoric for liberal education, a rhetoric responsive to the enormous changes undergone in recent decades by the academic world and the global environment, we may do well to seek the insights and suggestions that can come from stepping outside our customary universe of discourse on the subject. This is a process we are familiar with from the numerous instances of cross-fertilization among the intellectual arts and disciplines. The foregoing essay at comparison has explored one such channel of cross-fertilization, with the following results:

1. We have raised the question of the difference between liberal and illiberal learning. The experience of the martial arts suggests that

one principle of the liberal program might be formulated as the cultivation of free cultural forms for their own sake.

2. We have asked about the kinds of cultural forms appropriate to a liberal program. The martial arts exemplify for us a neglected type of culture, that which concerns the perfection of the capacities of human subjects.

3. We have asked about the types of subjective cultivation that constitute a plausible inventory. The martial arts clarify for us the problem of distinguishing between concrete traditions and general technical capacities.

4. We have asked about the character of training programs appropriate to develop such capacities. The martial arts exemplify for us the significance of practice; of a phased program of development, from techniques to principles to expression; and of the need for specialized work to develop any capacity through that curriculum.

5. We have asked about the relation of liberality to utility. The martial arts exemplify the way in which liberally acquired powers are of especial utilitarian value in a complex and changing environment.

6. We have asked about the moral justification of liberal training. The martial arts provide models in which those questions are resolved through being linked to an ethical worldview.

## E.J. HARRISON

# STRANGULATION EXTRAORDINARY

Under the general heading of kubigatame, or necklocks, the Kano School of Judo has a very extensive repertoire of effective methods of choking an obstreperous adversary into submission, and unless surrender comes in the nick of time the victim will infallibly lose consciousness. Although the recital in the absence of a photographic commentary must be little better than a Chinese alphabet for the majority, as the Russian saw has it, I may mention the namijujijime (literally "normal cross," the Japanese equivalent for the word "cross" being "sign of ten"), gyakujujijime (reverse cross), katajujijime (half-cross), hadakajime (naked stranglehold), okurierijime (sliding collar lock) and sodeguruma (sleeve wheel). Many more could be cited but as this is not a textbook the foregoing will suffice.

It must be well within the recollection of any ordinary reader of the newspapers and of fiction that the would-be descriptive, picturesque writer not infrequently indulges in heroics when it comes to dealing with the sensations of an individual undergoing strangulation, while the question whether or not our common form of capital punishment is the most humane one possible in the circumstances also occasionally furnishes food for lengthy polemics. It also happens that I am in a position to write intelligently on the subject of strangulation for the simple reason that I personally have been choked into insensibility, and have scores of friends and acquaintances who have undergone a similar experience. I will say, and they will say that being choked by a competent hand is,

*See page 43 for a brief note on the author.*

per se, a bagatelle not worth making a fuss over. Indeed, beyond the preliminary sensations, as in the case of being chloroformed—another of my personal experiences—the sensation is rather pleasant than otherwise and if the victim is intelligently revived by means of katsu—a method of resuscitation afforded by the overall system termed kappo—he feels fit as ever five minutes afterward. So lightly do the Japanese practitioners of judo and jiujutsu regard strangling that apart from the accidental cases which are bound to occur quite frequently during judo contests, it is the time-honoured custom to choke deliberately all newly appointed shodan, or students of the art who hold the lowest teaching grade, the outward symbol of which is the black obi or belt. The idea at the bottom of this seemingly cold-blooded procedure is both to steel the victim's nerves and round off his experience, as it were, and to afford the newly promoted members an opportunity of putting into practice certain forms of kappo, which are demonstrated by an expert teacher before the strangulation takes place.

My particular friend of those early days, D.T. Weed...first underwent the above experience and then afterwards furnished me with an account thereof which, I think, makes interesting reading.

Weed first practiced the art at the dojo of Keio University, Tokyo, the instructor of which was the famous Iizuka, then holder of the sixth-grade (rokudan) but years later promoted to the highest grade of judan (tenth-grade). Of stature somewhat below the average even for a Japanese, he was built on the lines of a miniature Hercules, and although in those days some thirty-seven or thirty-eight years of age, was still more than a match for the strongest and most expert of his pupils ten and fifteen years younger. Shortly after his promotion together with some ten others Weed attended the customary lecture and strangulation ceremony—if it may be so called—at the private residence of Mr. Fukuzawa, the son of the revered founder of Keio University, Yukichi Fukuzawa. Mr. Iizuka delivered the lecture, which dealt generally with the ethical aspects of judo and this was followed by a demonstration of specific methods of kappo, the art of resuscitation, and finally by the choking of all eleven shodan and their speedy restoration to consciousness by the application of the appropriate katsu the details of which every initiate was under the most solemn pledge never to reveal to outsiders. It should perhaps be added that since those days the veil of mystery wherein kappo was then shrouded has been largely lifted and anybody interested can now buy for himself in several European languages quite reliable printed descriptions of these methods. The proceedings were so arranged that every new shodan alternately choked a colleague, was choked by another, and revived a third by the application of the special katsu, which had shortly before been illustrated either by Mr. Iizuka or some other high-class yudansha present. The room in which the ceremony was performed was of course in Japanese style and matted, and the shodan participating in these experiments wore the usual keikogi or practice garments, also called judogi, as most suitable for such an occasion.

Weed was asked by Mr. Iizuka whether he had ever been deliberately choked outside an actual judo contest. On receiving a negative reply Mr. Iizuka cheerfuly rejoined, "Well, in that case you had better go through with it; otherwise you cannot regard yourself as a full-fledged judoka."

Affecting the air of easy nonchalance, which he cheerfully confessed, was very far from being a faithful reflection of his true state of mind, Weed lay down on his back, and the famous expert, having secured a good hold in the katajujijime style, in which the loose collar of the upper garment is tightly constricted against the depression below the Adam's apple by the dual motion of pressing against it with the right hand and pulling the left lapel of the jacket downward with the left hand, deftly dispatched Weed into the land of nod in forty seconds by actual watch count. Weed informed me however that he lost consciousness after the timekeeper had counted eleven, this being the last sound he heard, but his legs and arms continued to move convulsively for twenty-nine seconds more, so that the full count of forty seconds must be accepted as the interval required to "put him to sleep." As a matter of fact, with the exception of one student who took forty-five seconds to go off, Weed displayed the greatest resisting power of anybody present. It should be added that under these conditions the victim does not try to resist but rather to cooperate with the operator in consummating this congenial task. To that end he is required to empty his lungs as far as possible and to relax the muscles of the throat which are at other times brought into play when the subject has no overmastering desire to take a nap merely to oblige another. As already stated generally, so in Weed's case the first sensations were the usual ones of suffocation, the symptoms of which are a singing in the ears and a black void before the eyes. Complete oblivion speedily ensued. While in this state all perception of time and space is lost. Weed's earliest realization of his own identity took the form of a dim, confused attempt to balance a series of conflicting figures which presented themselves to his mind, but to no purpose. Next he heard the dull murmur of voices, and then suddenly regained complete consciousness with a start, and opened his eyes to find himself sitting on the mats surrounded by a circle of grinning comrades.

The older or more advanced yudansha, who had on previous occasions undergone this ordeal, did not scruple to indulge in uncomfortable jests at the expense of their juniors whose turn had yet to come on this memorable evening. These juniors, looking decidedly green about the gills, vainly sought to conceal their nervousness and anxiety beneath an assumption of coolness and indifference that succeeded in deceiving nobody, and laughed artificially in response to the grimly jocular comments of their seniors. "Sayonara!" ("Good-bye!"), "Mata chikai uchi ni!" ("See you again shortly!"), "Have you any last words or messages for your friends?" etc., were among the commonest forms of wit employed as one of the members of the gallant eleven passed temporarily into the Ewigkeit. It is a notable fact that these experiments have no bad effect that can be traced, and seeing that even the Kano School of Judo has been in existence for more than seventy years the data under this head are by this time sufficiently voluminous to enable those responsible to estimate the danger, if any, of adherence to this practice. Weed showed no other sign of wear and tear the next day than a pair of slightly bloodshot eyes, but these symptoms rapidly disappeared and the experience remained thereafter in his memory as something which he was glad to have endured but had no overwhelming wish to undergo again!

In my own case the effect was unrehearsed. It was during the Russo-Japanese War and I had gone to the Kodokan in Koishikawa for my customary afternoon practice, at the end of which I was wont to while away an extra hour or so "yarning" with the rest and occasionally participating in trials of skill and strength not always strictly confined to judo. On one of these occasions a certain genius bethought him of an effective method of testing the resisting power of the human neck. The scheme was for one man to pass a sash around the neck of another from behind, the loop being carefully adjusted so as to press exactly upon the slight depression an inch or so beneath the Adam's apple—i.e., the most sensitive part of the throat and the one which, in conjunction with the jugular vein and the carotid arteries, yields most speedily to attentions of this description. The loop having been thus adjusted, the first man seized the two free ends of the sash, turned his back upon the other man, and passing the two ends of the sash over his shoulders raised the second man in such a manner that virtually the entire weight of the second man hung from his neck and exerted corresponding pressure upon the impromptu noose by which he as being carried pickaback. The object of the second man was, of course, to resist gradual strangulation by hardening the muscles of his throat. The carrier would then move forward at a rapid pace, but the moment the second man gave notice by clapping his hands that he had reached the limit of endurance, the carrier would drop him. The winner of this novel competition was the man who could hold out while his mount carried him over the largest area of mats.

I was an amused and interested spectator of these proceedings until a dozen or so fellows had with varying fortune coquetted with strangulation, but so far not one had failed to give the signal in time. Then suddenly certain members of the group turned to me and invited me to have a try. I may say without undue vanity that I then possessed a neck and throat of more than average strength and thickness, especially for my height which is only about 5 feet, 6 inches. After years devoted off and on to catch-as-catch-can before I went to Japan, and jiujutsu and judo almost from the day of my arrival in the country, I had developed special muscles to such purpose that it was no easy task for an ordinary man to choke me even when I made no use of my hands to ward off the attack but relied solely upon those muscles in doing so. I therefore consented with something like alacrity to have a go for the record and was soon under way. I can at this moment recall quite clearly how I took count of the mats as my bearer stepped over them and how the thought passed through my mind that I must be ready to give the signal as soon as I had improved on the distance of my most successful predecessor, if I could possibly hold out so long. The old familiar symptoms were soon declaring themselves. My temples were throbbing, my ears singing, and things began to dance before my eyes. I saw that I had gone one better than the previous winner, and I was just thinking to myself, "Now, now I'll clap my hands!" and my arms were raised in the very act when I knew no more. As the Japanese vernacular has it, I fell (ochiita). The transition from consciousness to unconsciousness appeared in this case to be exceptionally abrupt. My first awakening thought was one of locality. I felt puzzled to know where I was—whether in England, America, Japan, or where? "Where the blazes am I?" was the problem that never ceased to worry me. Following this stage I became aware that I was sitting on the floor, but where, I could not yet be sure. Then, with a suddenness rivaling that with which I had succumbed to strangulation, I regained my full senses and opened my eyes. But immediately before I did this I heard the dull confused murmur of human voices which entered into Weed's experience, though I had been unable to distinguish words or associate the sound with individuals whom I knew. On opening my eyes I found myself surrounded by a small crowd of laughing fellows, but I did not know until some time afterward that I had been brought round by the application of kappo and that the yudansha who had performed the operation was one named Karino, holder of the third-grade at that time and a recognized expert in "groundwork." My first words before rising to my feet were "What a pleasant sensation!" ("Domo ii kokoromochi da!") whereat everybody roared more loudly than ever. Thus the incident terminated and I felt absolutely no ill effects from the ordeal.

Ever since that time I have been less ready to sympathize with the actual physical sensations of the victims of capital punishment or of hanging generally, since, on the score of physical pain alone, a tooth-ache or a severe kick on the shins is infinitely worse. Still, if it is all the same to the reader, like Weed, I am not hankering after additional experience of a like nature.

INAZO NITOBE

# THE TRAINING AND POSITION OF WOMAN

The female half of our species has sometimes been called the paragon of paradoxes, because the intuitive working of its mind is beyond the comprehension of men's "arithmetical understanding." The Chinese ideogram denoting "the mysterious," "the unknowable," consists of two parts, one meaning "young" and the other "woman," because the physical charms and delicate thoughts of the fair sex are above the coarse mental calibre of our sex to explain.

In the Bushido ideal of woman, however, there is little mystery and only a seeming paradox. I have said that it was Amazonian, but that is only half the truth. Ideographically the Chinese represent wife by a woman holding a broom—certainly not to brandish it offensively or defensively against her conjugal ally, neither for witchcraft, but for the more harmless uses for which the besom was first invented—the idea involved being thus less homely than the etymological derivation of the English wife (weaver) and daughter (*duhitar*, milkmaid). Without confining the sphere of woman's activity to *Küche, Kirche, Kinder*, as the present German Kaiser is said to do, the Bushido ideal of womanhood

---

*Educator, diplomat, and author, Nitobe (1862–1933) made great efforts throughout his career to interpret Japanese culture for Westerners. He was at different times an exchange professor at a number of American universities, an Under-Secretary General of the League of Nations, and a member of the Japanese House of Peers. Ironically his 1899 book* Bushido: The Soul of Japan, *from which the following excerpt is taken, was misinterpreted as being violently nationalistic.*

was pre-eminently domestic. These seeming contradictions—domesticity and Amazonian traits—are not inconsistent with the Precepts of Knighthood, as we shall see.

Bushido being a teaching primarily intended for the masculine sex, the virtues it prized in woman were naturally far from being distinctly feminine. Winckelmann remarks that "the supreme beauty of Greek art is rather male than female," and Lecky adds that it was true in the moral conception of their art. Bushido similarly praised those women most "who emancipated themselves from the frailty of their sex and displayed an heroic fortitude worthy of the strongest and bravest of men." Young girls, therefore, were trained to repress their feelings, to indurate their nerves, to manipulate weapons,—especially the long-handled sword called *nagi-nata*, so as to be able to hold their own against unexpected odds. Yet the primary motive for exercise of this martial character was not for use in the field; it was twofold—personal and domestic. Woman owning no suzerain of her own, formed her own bodyguard. With her weapon she guarded her personal sanctity with as much zeal as her husband did his master's. The domestic utility of her warlike training was in the education of her sons, as we shall see later.

Fencing and similar exercises, if rarely of practical use, were a wholesome counterbalance to the otherwise sedentary habits of women. But these exercises were not followed only for hygienic purposes. They could be turned into use in times of need. Girls, when they reached womanhood, were presented with dirks (*kai-ken*, pocket poniard), which might be directed to the bosom of their assailants, or, if advisable, to their own. The latter was very often the case; and yet I will not judge them severely. Even the Christian conscience with its horror of self-immolation, will not be harsh with them, seeing Pelagia and Dominina, two suicides, were canonized for their purity and piety. When a Japanese Virginia saw her chastity menaced, she did not wait for her father's dagger. Her own weapon lay always in her bosom. It was a disgrace to her not to know the proper way in which she had to perpetrate self-destruction. For example, little as she was taught in anatomy, she must know the exact spot to cut in her throat; she must know how to tie her lower limbs together with a belt so that, whatever the agonies of her death might be, her corpse be found in utmost modesty with the limbs properly composed. Is not a caution like this worthy of the Christian Perpetua or the Vestal Cornelia? I would not put such an abrupt interrogation were it not for a misconception, based on our bathing customs and other trifles, that chastity is unknown among us. On the contrary, chastity was a pre-eminent virtue of the samurai woman, who taken prisoner, seeing herself in danger of violence at the hands of the rough soldiery, says she will obey their pleasure, provided she be first allowed to write a line to her sisters, whom war has dispersed in every direction. When the epistle is finished, off she runs to the nearest well and saves her honour by drowning. The letter she leaves behind ends with these verses:

> For fear lest clouds may dim her light,
> Should she but graze this nether sphere,
> The young moon poised above the height
> Doth hastily betake to flight.

It would be unfair to give my readers an idea that masculinity alone was our highest ideal for woman. Far from it! Accomplishments and the gentler graces of life were required of them. Music, dancing, and literature were not neglected. Some of the finest verses in our literature were expressions of feminine sentiments; in fact, woman played an important role in the history of Japanese *belles-lettres*. Dancing was taught (I am speaking of samurai girls and not of *geisha*) only to smooth the angularity of their movements. Music was to regale the weary hours of their fathers and husbands; hence it was not for the technique, the art as such, that music was learned; for the ultimate object was purification of heart, since it was said that no harmony of sound is attainable without the player's heart being in harmony with itself. Here again we see the same idea prevailing which we notice in the training of youths—that accomplishments were ever kept subservient to moral worth. Just enough of music and dancing to add grace and brightness to life, but never to foster vanity and extravagance. I sympathise with the Persian Prince, who, when taken into a ballroom in London and asked to take part in the merriment, bluntly remarked that in his country they provided a particular set of girls to do that kind of business for them.

The accomplishments of our women were not acquired for show or social ascendancy. They were a home diversion; and if they shone in social parties, it was the attributes of a hostess—in other words, as part of the household contrivance for hospitality. Domesticity guided their education. It may be said that the accomplishments of the women of Old Japan, be they martial or pacific in character, were mainly intended for the home; and, however far they might roam, they never lost sight of the hearth as the centre. It was to maintain its honour and integrity that they slaved, drudged, and gave up their lives. Night and day, in tones at once firm and tender, brave and plaintive, they sang to their little nests. As daughter, woman sacrificed herself for her father, as wife for her husband, and as mother for her son. Thus from earliest youth she was taught to deny herself. Her life was not one of independence, but of dependent service. Man's helpmeet, if her presence is helpful she stays on the stage with him: if it hinders his work, she retires behind the curtain. Not infrequently does it happen that a youth becomes enamoured of a maiden who returns his love with equal ardour, but, when she realizes his interest in her makes him forgetful of his duties, disfigures her person that her attractions may cease. Adzuma, the ideal wife in the minds of samurai girls, finds herself loved by a man who is conspiring against her husband. Upon pretence of joining in the guilty plot, she manages in the dark to take her husband's place, and the sword of the lover-assassin descends upon her own devoted head. The following epistle written by the wife of a young daimio, before taking her own life, needs no comment:

> I have heard that no accident or chance ever mars the march of events here below, and that all is in accordance with a plan. To take shelter under a common bough or a drink of the same river, is alike ordained from ages prior to our birth. Since we were joined in ties of eternal wedlock, now two short years ago, my heart hath followed thee, even as its shadow followeth an object, inseparably bound heart to heart, loving and being loved. Learning but recently, however, that the coming battle is to be the last of my labour and life, take the farewell greeting of thy loving partner. I have heard that Kowu, the mighty warrior of ancient China, lost a battle, loth to part with his favorite Gu. Yoshinaka, too, brave as he was, brought disaster to his cause, too weak to bid prompt farewell to his wife. Why should I, to whom earth no longer offers hope or joy—Why should I detain thee or thy thoughts by living? Why should I not, rather, await thee on the road which all mortal kind must sometime tread? Never, prithee, never, forget the many benefits which our good master Hideyori hath heaped upon thee. The gratitude we owe him is as deep as the sea and as high as the hills.

Woman's surrender of herself to the good of her husband, home, and family, was as willing and honourable as the man's self-surrender to the good of his lord and country. Self-renunciation, without which no life-enigma can be solved, was the keynote of the loyalty of the man as well as of the domesticity of woman. She was no more the slave of man than was her husband of his liege-lord, and the part she played was recognized as *naijo*, "the inner help." In the ascending scale of service stood woman, who annihilated herself for man, that he might annihilate himself for the master, that he in turn might obey Heaven. I know the weakness of this teaching and that the superiority of Christianity is nowhere more manifested than here, in that it requires of each and every living soul direct responsibility to its Creator. Nevertheless, as far as the doctrine of service—the serving of a higher cause than one's own self, even at the sacrifice of one's individuality; I say the doctrine of service, which is the greatest that Christ preached and was the sacred key-note of His mission—so far as that is concerned, Bushido was based on eternal truth.

My readers will not accuse me of undue prejudice in favor of lavish surrender of volition. I accept in large measure the view advanced and defended with breadth of learning and profundity of thought by Hegel that history is the unfolding and realization of freedom. The point I wish to make is that the whole teaching of Bushido was so thoroughly with the spirit of self-sacrifice, that it was required not only of woman but of man. Hence, until the influence of its precepts is entirely done away with, our society will not realise the view rashly expressed by an American exponent of woman's rights who exclaimed, "May all the daughters of Japan rise in revolt against ancient customs!" Can such a revolt succeed? Will it improve the female status? Will the rights they gain by such a summary process repay the loss of that sweetness of disposition, that gentleness of manner, which are their present heritage? Was not the loss of domesticity on the part of the Roman matrons followed by moral corruption too gross to mention? Can the American reformer assure us that a revolt of our daughters is the true course for their historical development to take? These are grave questions. Changes must and will come without revolts! In the meantime let us see whether the status of the fair sex under the Bushido regimen was really so bad as to justify a revolt.

We hear much of the outward respect European knights paid to "God and the ladies,"—the incongruity of the two terms making Gibbon blush; we are also told by Hallam that the morality of chivalry was coarse, that gallantry implied illicit love. The effect of chivalry on the weaker vessel was food for reflection on the part of philosophers, M. Guizot contending that feudalism and chivalry wrought wholesome influences, while Mr. Spencer tells us that in a military society (and what is feudal society if not militant?) the position of woman is necessarily low, improving only as society becomes more industrial. Now is M. Guizot's theory true of Japan, or is Mr. Spencer's? In reply I might aver that both are right. The military class in Japan was restricted to the samurai, comprising nearly two million souls. Above them were the military nobles, the *daimio*, and the court nobles, the *kuge*—these higher sybaritical nobles being fighters only in name. Below them were masses of common people—mechanics, tradesmen, and peasants—whose life was devoted to arts of peace. Thus what Mr. Spencer gives as the characteristics of a militant type of society may be said to have been exclusively confined to the samurai class, while those of the industrial type were applicable to the classes above and below it. This is well illustrated by the position of woman; for in no class did she experience less freedom than among the samurai. Strange to say, the lower the social class—as, for instance, among small artisans—the more equal was the position of husband and wife. Among the higher nobility, too, the difference in the relations of the sexes was less marked, chiefly because there were few occasions to bring the differences of sex into prominence, the leisurely nobleman having become literally effeminate. Thus Spencer's dictum was fully exemplified in Old Japan. As to Guizot's, those who read his presentation of a feudal community will remember that he had the higher nobility especially under consideration, so that his generalisation applies to the *daimio* and the *kuge*.

I shall be guilty of gross injustice to historical truth if my words give one a very low opinion of the status of woman under Bushido. I do not hesitate to state that she was not treated as man's equal; but, until we learn to discriminate between differences and inequalities, there will always be misunderstanding upon this subject.

When we think in how few respects men are equal among themselves, e.g., before law courts or voting polls, it seems idle to trouble ourselves with a discussion on the equality of sexes. When the American Declaration of Independence said that all men were created equal, it had no reference to their mental or physical gifts; it simply repeated what Ulpian long ago announced, that before the law all men were equal. Legal rights were in this case the measure of their equality. Were the law the only scale by which to measure the position of woman in a community, it would be as easy to tell where she stands as to give her avoirdupois in pounds and ounces. But the question is: Is there a correct standard in comparing the relative social position of the sexes? Is it right, is it enough to compare woman's status to man's, as the value of silver is compared to that of gold, and give the ratio numerically? Such a method of calculation excludes from consideration the most important kind of value which a human being possesses, namely, the intrinsic. In view of the manifold variety of requisites for making each sex fulfill its earthly mission, the standard to be adopted in measuring its relative position must be a composite character; or to borrow from economic language, it must be a multiple standard. Bushido had a standard of its own and it was binomial. It tried to gauge the value of woman on the battlefield and by the hearth. There she counted for very little; here for all. The treatment accorded her corresponded to this double measurement—as a social-political unit not much, while as wife and mother she received highest respect and deepest affection. Why, among so military a nation as the Romans, were their matrons so highly venerated? Was it not because they were *matrona*, mothers? Not as fighters or lawgivers, but as their mothers did men bow before them. So with us. While fathers and husbands were absent in field or camp, the government of the household was left entirely in the hands of mothers and wives. The education of the young, even their defence, was entrusted to them. The warlike exercises of women, of which I have spoken, were primarily to enable them intelligently to direct and follow the education of their children.

I have noticed a rather superficial notion prevailing among half-informed foreigners, that because the common Japanese expression for one's wife is "my rustic wife" and the like, she is despised and held in little esteem. When it is told that such phrases as "my foolish father," "my swinish son," "my awkward self," were in current use, is not the answer clear enough?

To me it seems that our idea of marital union goes in some ways farther than the so-called Christian. "Man and woman shall be one flesh." The individualism of the Anglo-Saxon cannot let go of the idea that husband and wife are two persons—hence when they disagree, their separate *rights* are recognised, and when they agree, they exhaust their vocabulary in all sorts of silly pet-names and nonsensical blandishments. It sounds highly irrational to our ears, when a husband or wife speaks to a third party of his or her other half—better or worse—as being lovely, bright, kind, and what not. Is it good taste to speak of one's own self, and self-praise is regarded, to say the least, as bad taste among us—and I hope, among Christian nations too! I have diverged at some length because the polite debasement of one's consort was a usage most in vogue among the samurai.

The Teutonic races beginning their tribal life with a superstitious awe of the fair sex (though this is really wearing off in Germany!), and the Americans beginning their social life under the painful consciousness of the numerical insufficiency of women (who, now increasing, are, I am afraid, fast losing the prestige their colonial mothers enjoyed), the respect man pays to woman has in Western civilization become the chief standard of morality. But in the martial ethics of Bushido, the main water-shed dividing the good and the bad was sought elsewhere. It was located along the line of duty which bound man to his own divine soul and then to other souls in the five relations I have mentioned in the early part of this paper. Of these, we have brought to our reader's notice loyalty, the relation between one man as vassal and another as lord. Upon the rest I have only dwelt incidentally as occasion presented itself; because they were not peculiar to Bushido. Being founded on natural affections, they could but be common to all mankind, though in some particulars they may have been accentuated by conditions which its teachings induced. In this connection there comes before me the peculiar strength and tenderness of friendship between man and man, which often added to the bond of brotherhood a romantic attachment doubtless intensified by the separation of the sexes in youth,—a separation which denied to affection the natural channel open to it in Western chivalry or in the free intercourse of Anglo-Saxon lands. I might fill pages with Japanese versions of the story of Damon and Pythias or Achilles and Patrocolos, or tell in Bushido parlance of ties as sympathetic as those which bound David and Jonathan.

It is not surprising, however, that the virtues and teachings unique in the Precepts of Knighthood did not remain circumscribed to the military class. This makes us hasten to the consideration of Bushido on the nation at large.

# BIBLIOGRAPHY

## GENERAL

Atkinson, Linda. *Women in the Martial Arts: A New Spirit Rising*. New York: Dodd, Mead, 1984.

Draeger, Donn F. *Classical Budo*. New York: Weatherhill, 1973.

———. *Classical Bujutsu*. New York: Weatherhill, 1973.

———. *Modern Bujutsu and Budo*. New York: Weatherhill, 1974.

Draeger, Donn F., and Robert W. Smith. *Asian Fighting Arts*. New York: Kodansha, 1969.

Elkin, Jim. "Why Learn Violent Art?" *Sport and Recreation* (January 1980): pp. 36–37.

Farkas, Emil, and John Corcoran. *Martial Arts: Traditions, History, People*. New York: Smith Publications, 1983.

———. *The Overlook Martial Arts Dictionary*. Woodstock, N.Y.: Overlook Press, 1985.

Gibson, Michael. *The Samurai of Japan*. London: Wayland, 1973.

Gluck, Jay. *Zen Combat*. New York: Ballantine, 1962.

Harrison, E.J. *The Fighting Spirit of Japan*. Woodstock, N. Y.: Overlook Press, 1982.

Kauz, Herman. *The Martial Spirit: An Introduction to the Origin, Philosophy, and Psychology of the Martial Arts*. Woodstock, N.Y.: Overlook Press, 1977.

Keane, Christopher, and Herman Petras. *Handbook of the Martial Arts*. New York: Barnes and Noble, 1983.

Leggett, Trevor. *The Warrior Koans: Early Zen in Japan*. London: Arkana, 1985.

Singer, Kurt. *Mirror, Sword, and Jewel: The Geometry of Japanese Life*. New York: Kodansha, 1973.

Wong, James I. *A Source Book in the Chinese Martial Arts: Medicine, Meditation, Military History*. 2 vols. Stockton, Calif.: Koinonia, 1982.


## AIKIDO

Clapton, M.J. *Aikido: An Introduction to Tomiki-Style*. London: P.H. Crompton, 1975.

Heckler, Richard S., ed. *Aikido and the New Warrior*. Berkeley, Calif.: North Atlantic, 1985.

Klickstein, Bruce. *Living Aikido: Form, Training, Essence*. Berkeley, Calif.: North Atlantic, 1986.

Leonard, George. "Aikido: The Nonviolent Martial Art." *Esquire* (July 1983): pp. 132ff.

———. "The Art of Loving Combat: The Power of Aikido Flows from a Paradox. . . ." *Esquire* (May 1985): p. 181.

Makiyama, Thomas. *The Power of Aikido*. New York: Lancer Books, 1960.

Saito, Morihiro. *Aikido: Its Heart and Appearance*. Boston: Cheng and Tsui, 1984.

Tohei, Koichi. *Aikido: The Arts of Self Defense*. New York: Japan Publications, 1963.

Ueshiba, Kisshomaru. *Aikido*. New York: Japan Publications, 1963.


## JUDO

Dominy, E.N. *The Art of Judo*. Hertsfordshire, England: Stellar Press, 1954.

Gleeson, Geoffrey Robert. *Anatomy of Judo*. New York: A.S. Barnes, 1969.

Hancock. H.I., and Higashi Katsukuma. *Complete Kano Jiu-Jitsu, Jiudo, the Official Jiu-Jitsu of the Japanese Government. . . .* New York: G.P. Putnam's, 1925.

Harrison, E. J. *The Art of Jiu Jitsu*. Philadelphia: David McKay, 1932.

Kano, Jigoro. *Judo*. Tokyo: Tourist Library, 1937.

———. *Kodokan Judo*. New York: Kodansha, n.d.

Kobayashi, Kiyoshi, and Harold E. Sharp. *The Sport of Judo as Practiced in Japan*. Tokyo: Pacific Stars and Stripes, 1955.

Kodokan, The. *What Is Judo?* Tokyo: privately printed, 1947.

Smith, Robert W., ed. *Complete Guide to Judo: Its Story and Practice.* Rutland, VT.: Tuttle, 1958.

Tomiki, Kenji. *Judo.* Tokyo: Japan Travel Bureau, 1956.

## KARATE

Feld, M.S., et al. "Physics of Karate." *Scientific American* (April 1979): pp. 150–158.

Funakoshi, Gichin. *Karate-do: My Way of Life.* New York: Kodansha, 1975.

Haines, Bruce A. *Karate's History and Traditions.* Rutland, VT.: Tuttle, 1968.

Hamada, Hiroshi. *Spirit of Karate-Doh.* Dubuque, Iowa: Kendall-Hunt, 1982.

Hassell, Randall. *Shotokan Karate: Its History and Evolution.* Farmington, Mich.: Focus Publications, 1984.

Kim, Richard. *The Weaponless Warriors: An Informal History of Okinawan Karate.* John Scurra, ed. Burbank, Calif.: Ohara, 1974.

Reilly, Robin L. *Karate Training: The Samurai Legacy and Modern Practice.* Rutland, VT.: Tuttle, 1984.

So, Doshin. *Shorinji Kempo: Philosophy and Techniques.* New York: Japan Publications, 1970.

Urban, Peter. *The Karate Dojo: Traditions and Tales of Martial Art.* Rutland, VT.: Tuttle, 1967.

## KUNG FU

Chow, David, and Richard Spangler. *Kung Fu: History, Philosophy, and Technique.* Garden City, N.Y.: Doubleday, 1977.

Kenn, Charles W. *A Brief History of Gung-Fu.* privately printed, 1963.

Medeiros, E.C. *The Complete History and Philosophy of Kung Fu.* Rutland, VT.: Tuttle, 1975.

Salzman, Mark. *Iron and Silk: In Which a Young American Encounters Swordsmen, Bureaucrats & Other Citizens of Contemporary China.* New York: Random House, 1987.

Smith, Robert W. *Chinese Boxing: Masters and Methods.* New York: Kodansha, 1974.

———. *Secrets of Chinese Temple Boxing.* Rutland, VT.: Tuttle, 1964.

Wong, James I. *The Northern Kung-Fu System: History & Form.* Stockton, Calif.: Koinonia, 1981.

————. *The T'ang-Lang Praying Mantis Martial System: History and Introductory Forms.* Stockton, Calif.: Koinonia, 1980.


### SUMO

Cuyler, Patricia. *Sumo: History, Rites, Traditions.* New York: Weatherhill, 1979.

Sackett, Joel. *Rikishi: The Men of Sumo.* New York: Weatherhill, 1986.

Sergeant, J.A. *Sumo: The Sport and the Tradition.* Rutland, VT.: Tuttle, 1959.

Trumbull, R. "Way of Sumo." *New York Times Magazine* (3 March 1957): pp. 44ff.

Uenoda, S. "Traditions of Sumo: Ancient Customs of the Wrestling Ring." *Trans-Pacific* (2 February 1929): p. 6.


### TAE KWON DO

Cho, Sihak H. *Korean Karate.* Rutland, VT.: Tuttle, 1968.

Chun, Richard, and P.H. Wilson. *Tae Kwon Do: The Korean Martial Art & National Sport.* New York: Harper and Row, 1976.

Read, Stanton E. *Taekwondo: A Way of Life in Korea.* Taiwan: L.C. Publishing Company, n.d.

Son, Duk Sung, and Robert J. Clark. *Korean Karate: The Art of Tae Kwon Do.* Englewood Cliffs, N. J.: Prentice-Hall, 1968.


### T'AI CHI CH'UAN

Cheng, Man-Ching, and Robert W. Smith. *T'ai Chi: the Supreme Ultimate Exercise for Health, Sport and Self-Defense.* Rutland, VT.: Tuttle, 1965.

Delza, Sophia. *Mind and Body in Harmony.* Philadelphia: McKay, 1961.

Deng, Ming-Dao. *The Wandering Taoist.* New York: Harper and Row, 1983.

Horwitz, Tom, and Susan Kimmelman, eds. *Tai Chi Chuan.* Chicago: Chicago Review Press, 1977.

Kauz, Herman. *Tai Chi Handbook: Exercise, Meditation, Self-Defense.* Garden City, N.Y.: Doubleday, 1974.

Liu, Da. *T'ai Chi Ch'uan and I Ching: A Choreography of Body and Mind.* New York: Harper and Row, 1972.

Lo, Benjamin P., et al. *The Essence of T'ai Chi Ch'uan: The Literary Tradition*. Richmond, Calif.: North Atlantic, 1979.

White, Douglas, ed. *Tai Chi Touchstones: Yang Family Secret Transmissions*. Brooklyn, N.Y.: Sweet Ch'i Press, n.d.

## WEAPONS

All Japan Kendo Federation. *Fundamental Kendo*. Tokyo: Japan Publications, 1973.

Demura, Fumio. *Bo: Karate Weapon of Self-Defense*. Burbank, Calif.: Ohara, 1976.

———. *Kama: Karate Weapon of Self-Defense*. Burbank, Calif.: Ohara, 1973.

———. *Nunchaku: Karate Weapon of Self-Defense*. Burbank, Calif.: Ohara, 1971.

———. *Sai: Karate Weapon of Self-Defense*. Burbank, Calif.: Ohara, 1974.

———. *Tonfa: Karate Weapon of Self-Defense*. Burbank, Calif.: Ohara, 1982.

Finn, Michael. *Iaido: The Way of the Sword*. London: P.H. Crompton, 1984.

Gambordella, Theodore. *The Complete Book of Karate Weapons*. Boulder, Colo.: Paladin Press, 1981.

Herrigel, Eugen. *Zen in the Art of Archery*. New York: Pantheon, 1953.

Lowry, Dave. *Autumn Lightning: The Education of an American Samurai*. Boston: Shambhala, 1985.

Marks, Tom, ed. *Chinese Kung Fu: Tai Chi Sabre for Self-Defense*. Taiwan: Martial Arts Research Institute, 1975.

Musashi Miyamoto. *A Book of Five Rings*. Woodstock, N.Y.: Overlook Press, 1974.

Parulski, George R., Jr. *The Art of Karate Weapons: A Complete Manual of Traditional and Modern Applications*. Chicago: Contemporary Books, 1984.

Random, Michel. *The Martial Arts*. London: Octopus Books, 1977.

Robinson, Basil W. *The Art of the Japanese Sword*. Rutland, VT.: Tuttle, 1961.

Sasamori, Junzo, and Gordon Warner. *This Is Kendo*. Rutland, VT.: Tuttle, 1964.

Suh, In H. *Korean Weaponry*. Hollywood, Calif.: Unique Publications, 1976.

# PERMISSIONS

From *Aikido: The Way of Harmony* by John Stevens, copyright 1984.
Reprinted by arrangement with Shambhala Publications, Inc.

From *Autumn Lightning: The Education of an American Samurai* by
Dave Lowry, copyright 1984. Reprinted by arrangement with
Shambhala Publications, Inc.

From *A Book of Five Rings* by Miyamoto Musashi, copyright 1974.
Reprinted by permission of Overlook Press.

From *Bushido: The Soul of Japan* by Inazo Nitobe. Reprinted by
permission of Overlook Press.

From *The Fighting Spirit of Japan* by E.J. Harrison. Reprinted by
kind permission of the publishers, W. Foulsham & Co., Ltd.,
England. Copyright E.J. Harrison, 1904.

From *Giving Up the Gun* by Noel Perrin, copyright 1979 by Noel
Perrin. Reprinted by permission of David R. Godine, Publisher,
Inc.

From *The Karate Dojo* by Peter Urban, copyright 1967. Reprinted
by kind permission of the Charles E. Tuttle Co., Inc. of Tokyo,
Japan.

From *Karate-Do: My Way of Life* by Gichin Funakoshi, published by
Kodansha International, Ltd., copyright 1975. Reprinted by permission. All rights reserved.

From *Karate's History and Traditions* by Bruce Haines, copyright
1968. Reprinted by kind permission of the Charles E. Tuttle Co.,
Inc. of Tokyo, Japan.

"The Liberal Arts and the Martial Arts" by Donald L. Levine, copy-